Islam and Literalism

People often say “Be Quiet!”, but they don’t tell you how long to be quiet for. Or you see a sign which says, KEEP OFF THE GRASS but it should say KEEP OFF THE GRASS AROUND THIS SIGN or KEEP OFF ALL THE GRASS IN THIS PARK because there is lots of grass you are allowed to walk on.

(Christopher John Francis Boone)

Islam and Literalism

Literal Meaning and Interpretation in Islamic Legal Theory

Robert Gleave

EDINBURGH
University Press

For Joshua

Our live-in literalist

First published in hardback in 2012 by
Edinburgh University Press Ltd
22 George Square, Edinburgh EH8 9LF
www.euppublishing.com

This paperback edition 2013

Typeset in Times Beyrut Roman by
3btype.com, and
printed and bound in Great Britain by
CPI Group (UK) Ltd, Croydon CR0 4YY

A CIP record for this book is available from the British Library

ISBN 978 0 7486 2570 3 (hardback)
ISBN 978 0 7486 8986 6 (paperback)
ISBN 978 0 7486 3113 1 (webready PDF)
ISBN 978 0 7486 5554 0 (epub)

Epigraph taken from: Mark Haddon, *The Curious Incident of the Dog in the Night* (London, 2003), p. 39.

Contents

Prologue

The aim of this book is to trace the emergence and development of the simple but compelling idea of literal meaning in Islamic legal hermeneutics. The concept of literal meaning I am using here is derived from the distinction found in modern linguistic philosophy between "what is said" and "what is meant", which is a vernacular and approximate distinction between the subject matter of semantics and pragmatics. The literal meaning is the meaning a text or statement has irrespective of what the author intends to convey or an audience (including professional exegetes) understands to be its message. Of course, the idea that a text "has" a meaning is an anthropomorphism, and it has been seriously undermined in recent hermeneutic thinking. In medieval Islamic legal hermeneutics, this idea of a meaning "owned" by a text is often explicitly addressed; it is also sometimes assumed within hermeneutic discussions. The idea of literal meaning in modern linguistic philosophy does not, then, have a perfect analogue within the works of *uṣūl al-fiqh* (or *uṣūl*, Muslim legal theory) which form the main sources for the discussions in this book; instead the idea of a meaning inherent within the text underpins many *uṣūl* discussions. The most regular contenders for a direct analogue of literal meaning are the concepts of *ḥaqīqa* and *ẓāhir*, and both of these have been translated as "literal meaning" by commentators in the past. *Ẓāhir* relates to the notion of what is manifest, obvious or apparent; *ḥaqīqa* relates to what is true, real or proper; literal, as we know, relates to the construction of words through individual letters. The linkage between these terms developed in this book is, then, conceptual rather than etymological. Accordingly, there is much discussion in the following pages of how these two terms, the meanings of which change over time within works of *uṣūl*, relate to the "literal meaning" as the term is being used here. There is also a regular use of the term "literalism", which is used in two senses: the belief that there is such a thing as the literal meaning of a text (and in this sense the mainstream tradition of *uṣūl* is literalist), and the belief that this meaning is the only one that matters in the exegetical process. The two senses are linked. There may be extensive and complex mechanisms whereby an utterance's literal meaning is bypassed in the search for the speaker's intended meaning, but this does not mean either that it does remain as a possible meaning, or that it has a sort of primacy. As we shall see, the difference between the first type of literalists and the second is, in fact, one of degree. Those who believe the literal meaning to be the only valid meaning (literalists of the second type) usually end up either holding a variant of the first view (in which the occasions on which the literal meaning is bypassed are not non-existent but rather extremely limited) or redefining the literal to include meanings which would, under a different schema, be considered outside of its remit. This pattern is not restricted to Muslim writings, and can also be identified in other textual religious traditions.

There is, I admit, a certain artificiality in using a modern technical concept (literal meaning) in an analysis of a medieval Muslim intellectual system. It might be thought anachronistic or, even worse, an almost colonial imposition of a foreign idea on a complex pre-existent system of thought. If required, my defence is that "literal meaning" is used here as an analytic tool which, though imperfect, does capture one of the elements of that tradition nicely. It has enabled me to inform my reading of Islamic legal hermeneutics with the insights of modern semantic and pragmatic philosophers. It also pays homage to the sophistication of the subject under study, in that the best *uṣūl* discussions are as nuanced and detailed as anything modern philosophy has to offer. Finally, since literal meaning, literalism and literal interpretation are all common phrases, used in everyday parlance as well as secondary literature, the idea of literality can act as a starting point through which a book in the English language can discuss a world expressed almost exclusively through the medium of technical Arabic. The tradition of *uṣūl al-fiqh* is not, I hope, done a disservice by the inevitable compromise involved in describing its ideas to readers outside of the cultural, intellectual and pedagogic context in which the discipline thrived.

This study, then, begins with an exploration of what we mean by literal meaning (Chapter 1) and how this might be applied to the classical theory of language and communication found in works of *uṣūl al-fiqh* (Chapter 2). When and how Muslim writers begin to conceive of the text having a meaning distinct from the intended meaning of the speaker is an interesting historical question, and one which requires the examination of a variety of literary genres, all of which predate the emergence of *uṣūl* as a distinct discipline (Chapter 3). Cast in pragmatic terms, we are concerned with the process by which the distinction between the literal and intended meaning became a fundamental exegetical assumption. A folk assumption that language perfectly expresses the ideas of the speaker hinders the emergence of the idea of a distinct literal meaning. However, once the idea takes hold, particularly when allied with an emerging science of Arabic grammar, it becomes so commonsensical that few subsequent Muslim thinkers felt able to question it. It would seem logical that literal meaning becomes a theoretical requirement when there is an exegetical problem. The extremely useful but contentious notion of the text's literal meaning is surely most likely to come about because it was seen as a useful intellectual tool by which an exegetical problem might be solved. That problem is most likely to be that the text suddenly appears to say something which is at variance with what we have already decided to be the case: this was the staple diet of *uṣūl al-fiqh*, and discussions in this vein are found in the earliest works of legal theory (Chapter 4). In cases of textual ambiguity, one meaning might be preferred to another because it more closely approximates to the text's literal meaning. It could be argued that it is not impossible for a conception of literal meaning to come about purely through a study of the text itself. However, this would posit the idea that there was a pure, isolated exegete, who was so untouched by the external world that she was able to study the text without a consideration of the context of reading. This is not, to my mind, a very persuasive idea. The most plausible working hypothesis, and the one on which I proceed within the following chapters, is that the idea of the literal meaning of a text within early Muslim thought was initially prompted by exegetical problems, and as Muslim hermeneutics gained increasing sophistication, the notion of literal meaning did also.

There were, I argue, various competing notions of literal meaning, and these are linked to both theological doctrine and historical developments. The inherent meaning of the text became an element in the discussions of who has the authoritative interpretation of the revelatory texts and what are the legitimate procedures for identifying this inherent meaning. The former question of interpretive authority is central to one of the distinctive alternatives to the Sunni model (outlined in Chapters 2 and 4). The pivotal role of the Imam as the living embodiment of the divine will in Shīʿī thought gave him the power to determine the true or real (*ḥaqīqī*) meaning of the language of revelation. This meaning was available only through him, and is the only meaning inherent within the text (Chapter 5). All other attempts (even those pursued through the linguistic study of Arabic) are expressions of (at best) human frailty or (at worst) human arrogance. This idea of a secret meaning of revelation was unsustainable in the long term, particularly when some Shīʿī groups decided their Imam was no longer available to consult. Contemporaneous with these discussions of literal meaning was a growing dissatisfaction with the established answers to the second of the above questions concerning the valid procedures for identifying the literal meaning. There was unease concerning, on the one hand, the liberty given to the exegete (in the emerging mainstream Sunni legal theory) and, on the other, the exclusivity and general unavailability of the literal meaning among Shīʿī circles. This reaction provided the impetus for the so-called "literalist" school of the Ẓāhiriyya (Chapter 6). These "literalists", if they can be termed such, went through various phases and the "literal meaning" to which they were devoted was conceived in different ways at different times. The central figure of later Zahirism is the well-known thinker Ibn Ḥazm al-Andalūsī of Cordoba, and his sophisticated system receives particular attention.

The attraction to a text's literal meaning which rules over all fallible human attempts to understand God's message has, if anything, increased in strength amongst modern Muslim legal theorists. This reflects, perhaps, a more general frustration with the abstruse and technical debates of the pre-modern intellectual system and the siren call of most reform movements to return to the forgotten original sources. In legal theory, this has resulted in a series of debates over the processing of legal meaning, in both the increasingly influential Salafī expression of Sunnism and the scholarly hierarchy of modern Shiʿism (Chapter 7). The importance of defining, identifying and promulgating the literal meaning of the central texts of the Muslim tradition shows little sign of diminishing.

There are two studies, which for reasons of time and space are not included here: "'Delaying the Elucidation' (*Taʾkhīr al-bayān*) in Early Muslim Legal Theory: Theological Issues in Legal Hermeneutics" (in a forthcoming collection edited by Gregor Schwarb and Lukas Muehlethaler), and "Literal Meaning in Muslim Hermeneutic Principles (*al-qawāʿid al-uṣūliyya*)" (also forthcoming). They were written alongside the current chapters, and expand upon the themes contained within this book. Furthermore, much of the basic thesis of this book is available (in a single hit, as it were) in "Literal Meaning and Literal Interpretation in Medieval Islamic Hermeneutics" (in a forthcoming collection edited by Mordechai Cohen, Adele Berlin and Meir Bar-Asher). In addition, it is only honest to admit that two portions of this book are based on studies to be published separately. The presentation in Chapter 5 (on Shīʿī conceptions of literal meaning) will appear in slightly different form in the forthcoming festschrift for Professor Bernard Weiss, edited by Kevin Reinhart, Peter Sluglett and myself, whilst the latter part of Chapter 7 (on *ḥaqīqa sharʿiyya* in modern Shīʿī *uṣūl al-fiqh*) forms one element of a study of modern Shīʿī legal theory in a forthcoming volume edited by Ron Shaham and Aaron Layish.

The trouble with taking so long to write a book is that new studies appear, which come to your attention late in the day but which are nevertheless fundamental to your chosen topic. For the current project, the recent work of David Vishanoff (*The Formation of Islamic Hermeneutics* (2011)) and the PhD of Amr Osman ("The History and Doctrines of the Ẓāhirī *Madhhab*" (2010)) are particularly relevant. If I'd read them before I started, along with a clutch of other interesting recent articles on early Muslim hermeneutics, then the book might have been different, as they pose interesting questions. Nevertheless, I try to incorporate their findings into this work at appropriate points. The fact that people are still discovering and devising new ways to approach these questions means that our research is really only a marker for future, more intensive, investigation.

Dates are according to the Hijrī/Mīlādī convention, except for the twentieth century, when only the Mīlādī date is given. The transliteration system is that of the *Encyclopedia of Islam*, Third Edition (with some modifications). In some cases, particularly in Chapter 3, many of the death dates are disputed and should be treated with some caution. Quranic translations are (in the main) my own, since the translation will change, depending on what the commentator or Uṣūlī citing it wants to prove. Transliteration of Quranic passages has been standardised to the prevailing system, rather than the rules of *tajwīd*. Footnotes refer to works in abbreviated form, with full references in the bibliography.

Acknowledgements

As I have been writing this book, I have been collecting debts of gratitude along the way. I am not sure I will be able to repay them, and a simple mention in my acknowledgements section is certainly paltry and insufficient. There are the usual contenders for thanks: my wife, Sarah, and children, Joshua and Samuel ("Has Daddy finished his book yet?") and the publishers ("Further to our last message, could you give us an update on the current state of the manuscript?"). In particular, Nicola Ramsey at EUP has suffered from my inability to keep to a perfectly reasonable (and self-inflicted) timescale. I get the impression she may have encountered academics who work in the timeless zone of "it's nearly finished" before, but, even so, she has demonstrated extreme patience in my case. There are also some unusual suspects, particularly Deanna and Robert Chan, Carolyn Muessig and George Ferzoco, who, when I needed some focused writing time, allowed me to sit in their houses, tapping away on my laptop.

This project started as an idea which came up during an initial period of study leave from the University of Bristol, funded by the Arts and Humanities Research Board, back in 2005; I dropped the idea and focused on something different. I returned to the topic in earnest in 2008, when I had an (albeit truncated) period of study leave from my work at the Institute of Arab and Islamic Studies, University of Exeter; this was followed by a longer period of study leave in 2010. For both of these, I am grateful to all my colleagues in the Institute, as my absence may have meant others had to take up additional duties. I was also fortunate to be one of the RCUK Global Uncertainties Fellows for the project "Legitimate and Illegitimate Violence in Islamic Thought". That project is primarily interested in how particular legal and moral views (specifically involving violence) are justified within a Muslim framework: within the modern period, the literal meaning of scripture has been one of the prime hermeneutic claims employed in discussions over violence and its legitimacy in Islamic law. In a sense, then, this work deals with the fundamental elements of that (still ongoing) research.

As part of that project, and through the kind invitation of Mordechai Cohen and Meir Bar-Asher, I was extremely fortunate to be part of a research group in 2010–11 at the Institute for Advanced Studies in Jerusalem. I owe particular thanks to both group leaders. The group was titled *Encountering Scripture in Overlapping Cultures: Early Jewish, Christian and Muslim Strategies of Reading and their Contemporary Implications*, and in addition to Mordechai and Meir included Adele Berlin, Piero Boitani, Sidney Griffith, Meira Polliack, Stephen Prickett and James Kugel. We were fortunate to have in the group a cluster of scholars interested in questions of literal meaning and interpretation in the three religious traditions, comprising Mordechai, Alastair Minnis, Rita Copeland, Wolfhart Heinrichs and Jon Whitman. Spending time and sharing ideas with this fascinating group of scholars was an intensely rewarding experience, both intellectually and personally, and I hereby record my gratititude to them all, particularly for dealing with my often rather basic questions. Over the years my PhD students have enriched my understanding of this area, through extensive discussions and reflection, and the introduction of new sources into the discussion; many thanks to all of you. Many others have also read parts of this book, including the readers employed by EUP; I would mention them individually, but they may wish to make future comment on it, critically or otherwise, without the burden of an explicit mention, so I thank them all collectively here, and will do so individually when I meet them.

RG, Exeter, January 2012

Note for Paperback Edition

I am grateful to a number of people who pointed out errors and inconsistencies, and made suggestive changes to make my argument clearer. I feel I can now name them here in the paperback edition. In addition to those already named I should add Ahmed Achtar, Camilla Adang, Andreas Christmann, Andrew Rippin, Alex Samely and, of course, Bernard Weiss. Some of these esteemed colleagues may be a little surprised to see their names here, but conversations with each of them, as well comments on draft chapters, have helped my thinking along the way. A few of them have pointed out some egregious technical errors, which I have hopefully ironed out in this paperback edition. Inevitably, any that remain are my responsibility.

RG, Exeter, June 2013

1

Understanding Literal Meaning

In any dispute over the meaning of a text, something called the "literal meaning" of the text invariably crops up in the argument. The parties may agree to reject the literal meaning in favour of a metaphorical or figurative meaning (and then argue over which non-literal meaning is the meaning of the text). Others may argue for the literal meaning, to the exclusion of all non-literal meanings. Yet others may argue that the text can have multiple meanings – amongst which could be both literal and non-literal. Whichever stance the disputants adopt, they share a belief in the *existence* of a literal meaning. They share a commitment to the idea the text has a meaning which is ingrained in its structure, and which stays with it, even when the speaker intends to convey some other meaning. Where they differ is in what the author "actually" means. This "actual" meaning may be identical to the literal meaning, or supplant it, add to it without denying it, but the two are formally distinct. What is clear for the disputants is that the text has a literal meaning which is conceived of as "given" in the text. Their dispute is whether this "given" meaning (which I shall be calling the literal meaning), dictated by the language of the text, is a sufficient account of the text's meaning. They all use this conception (however rudimentary) of the text's literal meaning; it is an intellectual postulate on which subsequent exegetical discussions are based.

This book concerns two related phenomena in the history of Islamic legal theory (or, to give it its generic title, *uṣūl al-fiqh*): literal meaning and literalism. By the first of these ("literal meaning"), I am referring to the meaning the text is believed to have "in itself" solely by virtue of the words used and the rules of the language in which the text is written. In the second chapter, I give an overview of mainstream classical legal theory and the place of literal meaning within it. Muslim jurists constructed various theories as to how the meaning of the text "in itself" can be known and these form the focus of subsequent chapters. By "literalism", the second focus of this study, I am referring to the belief that this literal meaning is somehow privileged. It holds an advantage over all other species of meaning in the interpretation process because it is considered to have a higher level of epistemological security than rival interpretations. Since, it is assumed, intended meanings are potentially many, context dependent, and spring from the whim of the speaker, they hold an epistemological status inferior to the literal meaning. The literal meaning is singular and dictated by an exact science (the science of linguistics); it has a high level of certainty and for many is easily obtained; whilst the intended meaning is conjectural, involves discerning the intentions of others and is, therefore, uncertain. This, in most hermeneutic systems, makes the literal meaning the *prima facie* assumed meaning of an utterance, and this was the view of nearly all classical Muslim writers of *uṣūl al-fiqh* (the Uṣūlīs, as I shall call them). Nearly all classical Muslim writers of Islamic jurisprudence were literalists in that they privileged the literal meaning: they not only believed in its existence but also accorded it a sort of primacy in the interpretation process. Most did not, however, consider the literal meaning insuperable. Even those who were most uncompromising in their promotion of the literal meaning (such as the Ẓāhirīs, discussed in Chapter 6) accepted that there were occasions on which the literal meaning was not the intended meaning of the speaker or author; even for the strictest literalists, the literal meaning's advantage can be overcome when other candidates have sufficient external support. I am aware that my usage of literalism and literalist is a little at variance with commonly accepted understandings of the terms. The term literalist is sometimes reserved for the view of one who proclaims the unacceptability of any deviation from the so-called "literal" meaning of texts. In using both literalism and literalist (the latter as both an adjective and a noun) to refer to the privileging of literal meaning and its presumed pre-eminence (rather than its unassailability), I am adopting the technical employment of these terms in modern linguistic philosophy (more on which below). I do this consciously because those Muslim groups and tendencies commonly called "literalists" (*ḥashwiyya*, *ẓāhiriyya*, *salafiyya* and so on) are simply applying rules concerning non-deviation from the literal meaning with a greater level of rigidity than other so-called "non-literalists". The various groups are not, in truth, operating in a different hermeneutic context. Literalism is, I would maintain, the most useful technical term with which to describe the fundamental assumptions concerning language and communication, as they are presented in classical works of *uṣūl al-fiqh*.

Terminology presents a recurrent difficulty in Western language studies of the Arabic sciences, and in particular finding the "correct" Western language equivalent for technical Arabic terminology has proved problematic. This applies to terms and concepts within the discipline of *uṣūl al-fiqh* which might be candidates for literal meaning; I explore this issue in greater depth in Chapter 2. Ironically, the problem of translating terminology itself gives rise to discussions of literalness and literality: one scholar might object to another's use of an English word for an Arabic technical term because the English word does not capture the Arabic term's meaning within the latter's intellectual context. In an attempt to avoid a rather technical argument about terminology and its translation, I take the idea of literal meaning as my starting point, rather than a term (namely, *ẓāhir*, *ḥaqīqa*, *al-mawḍūʿ lahu* or a host of other possible locutions). As we shall see, terms shift and change their reference points between authors and over time. I believe, though, the idea of a literal meaning underlies much of the hermeneutic debate in Islamic legal theory, even if the terminology used by the participants differs, and even when, as is the case in the works of some thinkers, literal meaning is a background notion within their theories rather than an explicit element of their hermeneutic. A sketch, then, of the general framework (devoid of technical terminology), presaging that given in Chapter 2, will, I hope, enable the reader to see the relevance of my engagement with modern linguistic philosophy in the remainder of this chapter.

In brief, the classical Muslim jurists almost unanimously declare that the significance of a text, that is, the goal to which all exegetical activity is directed, is to be found in the speaker's/writer's intended meaning.[1] In the case of revelatory texts (with which Muslim legal theorists were most concerned), the speaker was almost always considered to be God himself (either directly, in the Qur'ān, or indirectly, through the words and actions of his perfectly obedient messenger, Muḥammad). If intended meaning is the goal, then literal meaning can be a diversion; however, the reason why it was necessary to have a conception of literal meaning for these thinkers was that it constituted, for nearly all of them, the starting point for an investigation into the intended meaning. It was the first contender for the intended meaning. Hence the questions at the heart of the debates described in this book are, then, two: "How does one come to know the literal meaning of a revelatory text?" and "Is this literal meaning, once discovered, an adequate account of God's intended meaning?" On both these questions, Muslims generally, and Uṣūlīs in particular, have differed. A number, amongst them some mystical exegetes, have considered the literal meaning of revelatory texts as an inadequate and perhaps irrelevant account of God's message communicated through a text. Others have considered the literal meaning to be adequate on some occasions, but inadequate on others (and they devised mechanisms whereby one can distinguish between these occasions). A minority have argued that the literal meaning is always (or, put less stridently, "invariably") an adequate account of God's intended message.[2] Of course, the means whereby one comes to know the literal meaning of a text is not divorced from the authority one gives that meaning in one's exegesis. A jurist's responses to the two questions addressed within this book are intimately related; they are linked by sophisticated theories of communication (both how it occurs generally between human beings and how it occurs specifically between God and humanity). In subsequent chapters, even when focusing on one of the two issues, the other is never far away: a jurist's account of how one knows the literal meaning is inevitably related to his assessment of its power within the exegetical process. Furthermore, having literal meaning and literalism as research foci inevitably leads one to discuss other related issues, such as the origin and function of language, the determination of meaning in texts (be they oral or written) and elements of literary theory (such as the

1 There have been recent attempts to incorporate the "postmodern" notion of textual meaning being divorced from authorial intention (the so-called "death of the author") into recent Islamic legal theory. They have not been viewed as acceptable to most Muslim intellectuals, and it is too early to assess their long-term impact. See for example Abou El-Fadl's notion of "Textual Intent" (*Speaking in God's Name*, p. 8, n. 9).

2 The difference between the last two approaches is reduced to one of degree rather than kind. The literalism of Ibn Ḥazm (d. 456/1064), for example, allows non-literal interpretation but within controlled circumstances which are themselves justified by God. See below, pp. 63–5.

function of metaphor and metonym). These are discussed in the course of this work as they relate to an author's conception of literal meaning and his assessment of its value, rather than being a focus of the study itself.[3]

Two tasks immediately present themselves before we begin to trace the development of Muslim juristic theories of literal meaning: an examination of the philosophical coherence of the idea of "literal meaning", and a location of this idea within the developed classical system of Islamic jurisprudence.[4] This chapter explores this first question in the light of modern linguistic philosophy. The next chapter examines which elements of classical *uṣūl al-fiqh* might correspond to our concepts of the literal meaning. Once the general area of enquiry has been established, the technical debates around the mechanisms whereby the literal meaning might be known and how it relates to other potential meanings commence in the third chapter.

The "Literal Meaning" of a Text

Linguistic philosophers usually distinguish the "literal meaning" of a text from two other species of meaning: the meaning the writer intends to convey,[5] and the meaning understood by the reader(s). We have, then, three entities, which I shall refer to as the literal meaning, intended meaning and understood meaning.[6] These may all be identical in content, or they may diverge from one another. Effective communication occurs when the intended and understood meanings converge. The involvement of the literal meaning (it would seem) is not a condition of effective communication. For example, we are watching football, and I say to you, "That centre half is a bit of a handful for the defence." The problem with describing the literal meaning of this statement (that is, giving a "literal interpretation" of it) is that it is overly complex for an ordinary language user: it contains not only metaphor, but also metonym and litotes. "A handful", it might be said, literally means "of sufficient quantity to be held in the hand" as in "a handful of rice" being enough rice to be held in the hand (but whose hand? A child's hand? An adult's hand?) "Centre half" stands for "the footballer playing in the centre-half position" and "defence" similarly is a metonym

3 Two excellent studies of Arabic metaphor, encompassing both legal hermeneutics and rhetoric, have been presented by Heinrichs (*The Hand of the Northwind* and "On the Genesis").

4 I am here excluding the increasing hyperbolic and emphatic uses of "literally" in spoken (and occasionally written) English, such as the sports commentator's comment "the crowd are literally glued to their seats". On this development of the use of the term "literally", see Kjellmer, "Literally: A Case of Harmful Polysemy?".

5 The fact that some medieval Christian exegetes (Thomas Aquinas, for example) argued that the literal *sense* was that which the author intends demonstrates a possible difference between literal *sense* and literal *meaning*. See also below, p. 24.

6 Yunis Ali recognises a similar division in what he calls "Muslim pragmatics" by distinguishing *fahm*, *fiqh* and *ḥaml*. *Fahm* is glossed as *waḍʿ*-based construction, *fiqh* as use-based construction and *ḥaml* as interpretation (see Yunis Ali, *Medieval Islamic Pragmatics*, pp. 44–6).

for "the footballers playing in the defensive positions". "A bit of a handful" would literally mean a part of a handful – that is, an insufficient quantity to make a handful (as previously defined). Finally, the particle "for" (as in "a handful for the defence") cannot be made sense of unless we suppose that it functions as a possessive, being a metaphorical reference to the "hands" of the players in the defensive positions. So a literal meaning of this statement – or rather, my interpretation of its literal meaning, my "literal interpretation" – might be:

> The person playing the role of centre half of one team is of insufficient quantity (weight or volume) to be held in the hands of the players occupying the role of defenders in the opposing team.

This statement is clearly false (unless one imagines the defenders have unnaturally large hands). More important than it being false is the fact that you and I, watching the football, have no connection with this literal meaning. I do not intend it, and you do not understand it.[7] Indeed, the presence of the litotic "a bit of" here means that the intended and understood meanings become a metaphor of the inverse of the literal meaning (the centre half is "more" than can be held in the hands of the defence, being a metaphor for "the defence is unable to control and contain the centre half"). The irrelevance of the literal meaning to the communication process is certainly not common to all instances of communication. At times the literal meaning plays a central role. However, the fact that literal meaning can drop out of the process does indicate that comprehending the literal meaning of a statement (which is simply forming one's own "literal interpretation" of it), even if that meaning is rejected as inappropriate, is not always a precondition for understanding.[8] Another point to note from this frivolous example is that the literal meaning of a statement is not always readily available. The literal interpretation of the statement presented above is arrived at only after some exegetical work, which the "ordinary speaker" of the language (a contested – perhaps fanciful – postulate), desiring as she does to *understand* my words, would consider neither necessary nor worthwhile. The literal meaning is not always obvious: it is sometimes obscure. At times, language use has deviated so far and so often from literal meaning that it is not necessary to have any contact with it

7 Much of the humour of television programmes such as *Mork and Mindy* or, more recently, *Third Rock from the Sun* is based on the application of grammatical rules by aliens to statements which are actually part of a contextualised language system. Goldman sees our mirth as deriving from the aliens' lack of understanding of "deep grammar". See his "Hegemony and Managed Critique in Prime Time Television"; see also below, n. 11, on literal=surface and non-literal=deep grammar understandings.

8 Here, most Muslim jurists differ from the analysis of modern linguistic philosophers, for the jurists insist on the presence of the literal meaning in the understanding process at least in the ideal sense. Literal meaning is the first step towards understanding intended meaning, since there is always a presumption that all meaning must be understood "literally" first, and, if this is found to be inadequate, non-literal meanings are then entertained. See Yunis Ali, *Medieval Islamic Pragmatics*, p. 43, where he cites Shihāb al-Dīn al-Qarāfī (d. 684/1285) arguing that there is always an exegetical assumption that "expressions actualise their implications and designate their meaning".

whatsoever. Furthermore, my construction of the literal meaning of the statement in the above passage is just that: a construction. Another literalist could construct a different literal interpretation.[9]

In Western literary criticism, the usual objection to the exclusive advocacy of the literal meaning is that it forecloses any discussion concerning both the "true" meaning (often associated with the original speaker's intention) and the aesthetic qualities of a text.[10] Rejecting non-literal meaning and advocating literal meaning is, then, an anti-intellectual interpretive position, and hence has rarely found favour amongst those whose task it is to promote intellectual discussion over the meaning of texts (and, perhaps more significantly, whose position in a given society relies upon the legitimacy of such discussions). One aim of this book is to question this assessment of literal meaning and literalism. There are, I argue in the following chapters, a variety of sophisticated conceptions of "literal meaning", and these feed into the primacy of the literal interpretation of revelatory texts in a variety of complex ways. Muslim legal theorists argued over literal meaning, and the complexity of their arguments should put to rest any accusation that literalism (in both its strident and more mild forms, either in its common use or its more specific use in this book) is necessarily anti-intellectual.[11]

Discerning the Literal Meaning

The "given-ness" of literal meaning has, to an extent, been enshrined in the division in Western linguistics between pragmatics and semantics.[12] Semantics, it is said, concerns itself with meaning as determined by language rules or "conventions". It was Paul Grice who introduced into the discussion the now commonplace conception of "conventional meaning".[13] Briefly put, the discipline of semantics has as one of

9 She may, for example, object to my metonymic transfer of "the defence" to "the players occupying the role of defenders", preferring to see "the defence" as referring to an abstract notion such as "the defence of the goal" or even "the defence of the team's game plan" (which is, of course, to win). The defence, for her, is not a collective noun for a group of footballers, but a reference to an element in the team's tactics. It is these tactics which cannot withstand the skill and dexterity of the centre half (which implies that the actual footballers cannot do so either, but that would be a different statement). The fact that the word refers to an abstract notion ("the team's defence plan") does not, it might be argued, make it any less of a literal interpretation. Different literalists, then, may argue for conflicting literal interpretations of the same statement. All this should indicate that literal meaning is not always simple, not always easily accessed, and rarely emerges without both exegetical effort and dispute.

10 Exclusively literalist readings might be characterised as "unjust" in that they do violence to the text in the same way as "delirious" interpretations. On just and unjust readings, see Lecercle, "What Is a False Interpretation?".

11 In Chomskian terms, literal meaning is an element of surface grammar which only occasionally reflects any component of the deep structure. The deep structure is, of course, where true meaning and societal understanding is to be found. See Chomsky, "Deep Structure, Surface Structure" (though he is attempting here to modify some of the positions taken in his classic works *Syntactic Structures* and *Topics*).

12 The literature on the semantics/pragmatics divide is also extensive. For a survey (and an argument for a particular conception of the relationship between the two disciplines), see Carpintero, "Gricean Rational Reconstructions".

13 See below, pp. 8–9.

its (albeit questioned) premises the view that language rules compel a meaning (or meanings, in cases of literal ambiguity) upon a particular sentence irrespective of the speaker's intended meaning, or of the context of the utterance. In contrast, pragmatics discerns a wider context as necessary to interpret meaning, including within its remit factors not immediately associated with linguistic rules. An example used by Muslim jurists neatly illustrates this aspect of the semantics/pragmatics distinction:

> [1] A Bedouin (*aʿrābī*) came to the Prophet (may God bless and grant him peace) and he said to him, "I am doomed and I have caused another to be doomed."
> [2] The Prophet said to him, "What have you done?"
> [3] He said, "I had sexual intercourse intentionally with my wife during the day in Ramaḍān."
> [4] He said to him, "Free a slave."[14]

From a semantic perspective, there is no evidence that the order of the Prophet (line [4] above) is linked to the commission of the act (described in [3] above). The Prophet may have made the order for a reason wholly unrelated to the Bedouin's act of sexual intercourse (he may have been telling everyone, without exception, to free slaves because it was "slave-freeing day"). Semantics, then, cannot provide us with an adequate account of the meaning of the Prophet's statement. It cannot help us reach the conclusion which nearly all Muslim jurists have reached: namely, that the Prophet ordered the freeing of a slave as penance for the transgression of the rules of the fast of sexual intercourse in daylight hours during the month of Ramaḍān.[15] Pragmatic approaches, on the other hand, bring in contextual factors (the Prophet's personality as one who gives orders in a timely and appropriate manner, the manner in which language use implies relevance between consecutive statements and so on). Within the category of these non-linguistic factors, Grice posited an assumption which is present in verbal communication and which language users take for granted. This assumption is the non-linguistic item which enables us to deduce (almost unconsciously and immediately) from the above report that the penance for sexual intercourse during the daylight hours of Ramaḍān is the freeing of a slave. Grice calls this assumption the "maxim of relevance" – speakers expect conversations to be generally *non sequitur* free and they view successive utterances as related to each other. Grice outlines a number of these maxims which in turn are necessitated by (and flesh out) what he calls "the cooperation principle". All speakers of a language assume their interlocutors are following a "cooperation principle" when they enter into communication:

14 This exact version is cited by Sayf al-Dīn al-Āmidī (d. 631/1233; *al-Iḥkām*, v. 3, p. 280). A summary of Āmidī's discussion can be found in Weiss, *The Search*, p. 601.

15 Indeed, semantic analysis brings a further ambiguity not discussed by the Muslim jurists: in the phrase "he said to him", how do we know that the "he" refers to the Bedouin and the "him" refers to the Prophet? The fixing of indexicals is one element of what Recanati calls the "minimalist position" (see Recanati, *Literal Meaning*, p. 7, and his problematisation of minimalism, pp. 8–22). I discuss this further below, pp. 12–14.

> Make your conversational contribution such as is required, at the stage at which it occurs, by the accepted purpose or direction of the talk exchange in which you are engaged.[16]

Hearers of the Prophet's words "free a slave" assume relevance between this and the foregoing statements by the Bedouin. The crucial point for our purposes is that on such occasions, the literal meanings of the component elements of the exchange are an inadequate account of the meaning (that is, the Prophet's intended message in saying what he said). In this case, the jurists argue, the Prophet was instituting the legal rule concerning penance and sexual intercourse, and this cannot be understood from the literal meaning of the exchange alone.

Strict adherence to the literal meaning may help us understand the composition of a sentence. It cannot (always) enable us to understand what was meant by the sentence (as opposed to what the sentence means) when it was uttered or written. If literal meaning is otiose, the question we might ask is whether or not we need it as an operator in the process of understanding, or whether it is merely an invention of the semanticists. In both the football and the fasting examples above, understanding literal meaning constitutes neither a necessary nor sufficient condition of understanding the speaker's intended meaning. Since literal meaning appears potentially redundant, its role in the interpretative process needs to be clearly justified.[17]

Grice's theory, in which literal meaning is distinguished from the speaker's intended meaning, forms a snug fit with the ideas of the classical writers of *uṣūl al-fiqh*. The "conventional meaning" of a word (that is, its literal meaning) provides the speaker with the meaning of the word, which he then assesses, selects and puts to use in a statement. At times, he uses this word or grammatical structure but does not intend the literal meaning, assuming that the listener can understand his non-literal intended meaning. A similar division is made by Austin between "locutionary" and "illocutionary" aspects of a single utterance.[18] Pragmatic discussions since Grice, and his enshrinement of the division between the literal and contextual elements of meaning construction, have been disputes between those who refine his position and those who kick against it. Pragmatists may differ over the utility of literal meaning, but few have questioned its existence. To do so, presumably, brings us to the edge of a precipice, over which lies the anarchy of a language unbounded by rules. Even pragmatists (or, perhaps, *especially* pragmatists), committed as they are to the necessity of contextual factors in understanding a speaker's intended meaning, hold fast to the idea of a literal meaning, inhering in the sentence without reference to context. By being the inherent meaning, the literal meaning has a level of stability over time which other meanings, with their context dependency, are unable to achieve.

A crucial element in pragmatic discussions is that the literal meaning of a

16 Grice, "Logic and Conversation", p. 26.

17 See below, pp. 10–11. To see how the Islamic literalists achieved this end, see below, pp. 42–4.

18 See Austin, *How to Do Things with Words*, pp. 99–106. Tolhurst provides an interesting modification of Austin's view in "On What a Text Is".

statement is assessable as a proposition. So, in the Qur'ān, where it says "your women are a field for you; so approach your field however you wish" (Q2/al-Baqara.223), the literal meaning – namely that the addressees' women are actually a field – is clearly false; crucially, though, the literal meaning forms an assessable proposition once understood. In deciding whether a literal meaning is the intended meaning, this proposition is, according to many theories of metaphor, tested and then rejected as impossible or unlikely. In this case, the proposition that the addressees' women are actually a field is rejected and the speaker is understood to mean that the women are *like* a field in the respect that the man has a licence over them not dissimilar to the owner of property. That the literal meaning can be expressed as an assessable proposition is, for many modern linguistic philosophers, a crucial element in their literalism. When Recanati writes "Literalism is the dominant position in the philosophy of language", he means that most consider it possible to "ascribe truth-conditional content to sentences, independently of the speech act which the sentence is used to perform".[19] That is, most philosophers of language (according to Recanati) believe that sentences (which go together to make texts) mean something *in themselves*, and this thing that they mean can be tested with regard to its truthfulness. The statements are not required to be spoken, written or communicated in some fashion or other before they can be assessed as true or false. Propositional content is a direct result of literal meaning. To purloin another example beloved of the Muslim legal theorists, when one of Joseph's brothers (normally thought to be Reuben) is explaining to the others how to prove their innocence with respect to Joseph's death, he tells them to say to their father:

> Ask the village where we have been, and the caravan in which we returned. We are telling the truth. (Q12/Yūsuf.82)

The meaning of the sentence is, so it is argued, clearly not a command for someone to ask questions to buildings (that is, "ask the village" literally), but instead "village" here means "people of the village". The Muslim jurists differed over whether we have here ellipsis (the phrase "the people of" is missing but understood) or metonymy ("village" stands for "people"), but whichever is the case, it is clear the literal meaning should be discarded (we should not ask buildings). However ridiculous it may be, the literal meaning does form a proposition: namely that the addressees should ask buildings about the speaker in order to ascertain the truthfulness of their claim.

The literal meaning is, then, logically prior to the contextual (pragmatic) meaning because each utterance of a statement is seen as an instantiation of a literal meaning which does not require to be uttered to be discerned. Some have seen this literal meaning as the first tested by the listener, and only when it is found wanting in the communication process is it discarded. The hearer (or reader) is diverted to other possibilities following her immediate recognition of the inadequacy (falsity) of the

19 Recanati, "Literalism and Contextualism", p. 171.

literal meaning of the statement she hears. However, these other possible meanings always bear some relation to the literal meaning of the statement.[20] Meanings characterised as non-literal (contextually generated) are seen as dependent upon the literal meaning, and discerning the literal meaning, though it be discarded, is a first step to understanding the true meaning (usually identified as the intended meaning of the author).[21] The fact that in practice this process happens at imperceptible speed, or that certain constellations of words have, through usage, become immediately associated with certain (non-literal) applications, does not, for literalists, provide evidence against the logical (though not necessarily sequential) priority of the literal meaning. The Muslim jurists, and the modern "literalists", accord the literal meaning a logical priority. The *uṣūlī* idea, about which we learn more in the coming chapters, that the literal meaning is indicated by "whatever is immediate in the mind of the hearer" (termed *al-tabādur* in works of *uṣūl*), is a reflection of the belief in this logical priority of the literal meaning. Asking questions of a set of buildings or a plot of land (the village) may not, in actual fact, enter our minds (though some believed it did),[22] but that is a psychological rather than philosophical observation. The logical priority of "ask the village" meaning "ask buildings" is, for most Muslim legal theorists, established; that it might not enter our minds when hearing the statement does not affect this logical priority.

It is argued by some modern philosophers that the fact we are unaware of having first processed the literal meaning, found it unacceptable and then turned to the diverted meaning is not necessarily an indication that literal meaning does not hold a logical priority. It is, instead, evidence that utterances have diverted non-literal meanings which are so well established in our understanding that they become the immediate understood meaning.[23] Ironically, in order for the speaker in the village example above to establish the *literal* meaning in his listeners' minds, he would probably have to divert the hearers away from the *diverted* (non-literal) meaning to the literal one, saying something like, "No! I actually want you to ask the buildings, not the people, however mad this may sound!" The literal meaning may not be the first to come to mind, but, for Bach, this does not prevent there from being a distinction (and even an implicit hierarchy) between what is said and what is meant:

20 That the non-literal meaning (*majāz*) bears a relation to the literal (*ḥaqīqa*) meaning was a common principle for Muslim legal (and literary) theorists; see below, pp. 40–1. That it holds no priority – logical or otherwise – in terms of participant understanding is argued convincingly, in my view, by Recanati in his "Alleged Priority".

21 For scriptural exegetes, that author is God, perhaps through an intermediary (in Islam, the Prophet Muḥammad) or through an instrumental author (in Christianity, the human writer, acting under the inspiration of God the Holy Spirit). See below, p. 195.

22 That it does not enter our minds was the view of Muḥammad b. Idrīs al-Shāfiʿī (d. 204/820) (on which see below, pp. 109–10).

23 The writers of *uṣūl al-fiqh* were well aware of how the common usage of a phrase or word might not be its literal meaning. Through "customary usage" (*ʿurf*) a word's meaning may change. See below, pp. 38–9.

> It is a mystery to me why facts about what the hearer does in order to understand what the speaker says should be relevant to what the speaker says in the first place.[24]

I am inclined to think that Bach has a point here. The fact that speakers and hearers never come into contact with the literal meaning of a statement does not mean that the literal meaning is somehow irrelevant to an explanation of that statement when uttered. Neither does it mean that the literal meaning does not exist. By this, I am not implying that the literal meaning does exist in the sense Bach wishes to convey, merely that the lack of it appearing in the speaker's mind is not evidence of either its non-existence or its irrelevance. There are other reasons for thinking literal meaning non-existent or irrelevant, but the lack of participant recognition is not one of them.[25] Hence, in the football example above, the fact that neither of us computes the literal meaning of the statement (be it according to my own literal interpretation or someone else's) is not conclusive proof against the existence of the literal meaning. It should, however, prompt us to consider its problematic status.

Philosophical investigations into the idea of literal meaning have revealed the complexity of the notion, and importantly revealed it to be composed of different elements. Since literal meaning has testable propositional content, literalists have had to come to terms with ambiguity, when the literal meaning is unclear from the statement itself isolated from its context. Grice, recognising this, made a distinction between "Sentence Meaning" and "What Is Said".[26] Consider the statement:

> Forbidden to you is carrion, blood and the meat of the swine. (Q5/al-Māʾida.3)

The Sentence Meaning, under Grice's scheme, is that the addressee ("you", plural, undefined) is forbidden from doing something (undefined) with carrion, blood and the meat of swine. The Sentence Meaning is, then, ambiguous: we do not know from this statement alone who is addressed, and we do not know what they are forbidden from doing. Both modern pragmatists and writers of *uṣūl al-fiqh* were well aware of the apparent ambiguity in the literal meaning of statements such as these. Uṣūlīs knew that the intended message was that the believers were not permitted to consume carrion, blood or swine-meat, but they also knew that this is not precisely what the verse said: consumption was implied as forbidden, but it was not explicit. Generally speaking, Uṣūlīs wished to try and deduce the intended meaning within the realms of the literal if they possibly could, and avoid leaving the security of the literal for the uncertainty of the non-literal if they could possibly avoid it. They clearly felt they were, epistemologically speaking, on solid ground with the literal, based as it

24 Bach, "You Don't Say?", p. 25. See also his comment: "Facts about 'pragmatic processing' are not relevant to the semantic-pragmatic distinction … nothing follows from such facts about what is or isn't said, since that's a matter of what a speaker does in uttering a sentence, not what his listeners do in understanding it" (Bach, "Semantic, Pragmatic", p. 7).

25 Participant recognition was, however, an important element in the Muslim juristic account of the meaning of texts; see below, p. 41.

26 I use capitals to indicate their use as technical terms. See Grice, "Utterer's Meaning, Sentence-Meaning, and Word-Meaning".

is in language rather than human deduction. In this case, most argued that there is no ambiguity (*ijmāl*) in the verse over which action is forbidden: clearly it is the consumption of swine-meat which is forbidden, and anyone who knows the Arabic language knows this. Most argued that though there may be suppression or ellipsis of an element ("consumption"), the meaning is entirely clear and does not require any further elaboration. In the technical terms with which we will become more familiar, that it is consumption of swine-meat which is prohibited is part of the true (*ḥaqīqa*), obvious (*ẓāhir*) meaning of the sentence which can be understood without reference to contextual factors (*qarāʾin*). As the great classical Uṣūlī Fakhr al-Dīn al-Rāzī (d. 606/1209) neatly puts it:

> What comes into the mind from the statement of the one who says, "This food is forbidden to you" is that eating of it is forbidden; and from his statement, "This woman is forbidden to you", [it is understood] that having sexual intercourse with her is forbidden. Immediacy of understanding is a proof of literality (*mubādarat al-fahm dalīl al-ḥaqīqa*).[27]

Some had argued[28] that the verse is inherently ambiguous, and that one needs contextual indicators to deduce that it is eating of swine-meat which is forbidden. Most argued that the verse was clear in itself, requiring no knowledge on the part of the listener beyond linguistic understanding.

On occasion, the rules of the language require that an elliptical meaning remain within the literal meaning. Given the potential ambiguity of the Sentence Meaning of many utterances, Grice proposed a second category of literal meaning which he termed "What Is Said". This category refers to the meaning adduced by supplying the referents of those elements of the original sentence which require specification (because of potential ambiguity). "What Is Said" is then an amplified expression of Sentence Meaning, encapsulating its propositional content with a view to testing whether the statement is true or false, and hence discovering whether the words within the statement are being used literally or not. Sentence Meanings typically display "semantic underdetermination": elements which are, in themselves, ambiguous and require specification before precise propositional content can be recognised. These include indexicals, such as "you" (plural) in the Quranic verse "Forbidden to *you*". The "you" here is contextually dependent (the speaker could be addressing various groups, or all humankind), and before we have a proposition to test, we have to fill it (in this case, with "the believers", since that is whom God was addressing). Since the Sentence Meaning was ambiguous, "What Is Said" is "swine-meat is forbidden to the *believers*". The word "believers" has been added by the process dubbed "disambiguation" and reference "assignment" by Grice. However, they are still part of the literal meaning because it is part of the linguistic meaning

27 Rāzī, *al-Maḥṣūl*, v. 3, p. 163.

28 This view is usually attributed to Abū al-Ḥasan al-Karkhī (d. 340/951); see Rāzī, *al-Maḥṣūl*, v. 3, p. 122; Āmidī, *al-Iḥkām*, v. 3, p. 12.

of the pronoun "you" to require disambiguation; whilst the content of "you" is filled by context, the need to fill it is linguistically required. It is this latter characteristic which keeps "What Is Said" within the literal meaning. In a similar manner, most Uṣūlīs argued that the verb "to forbid" requires, linguistically, an action, and the lack of an explicit mention of an action in the Sentence Meaning results in a gap which requires disambiguation (namely, the addition of the word "eating"). "What Is Said" is now expressed "*Eating* swine-meat is forbidden to the *believers*" (where both italicised words are linguistically required but contextually informed). Disambiguated expressions, such as this re-expression of Q5/al-Māʾida.3, are still considered part of the literal meaning of the verse; even though they depart from Sentence Meaning, this departure is minimal. What is clear is that there is a category difference between the minimal process of disambiguation (by inserting "you" and "eating") and a metaphorical reading of the verse in which, for example, "swine-meat" is said to stand for global warming and the verse understood as a demand for an ecological lifestyle.

The inclusion of the disambiguation process in semantic analysis is a limited recognition of the unavoidable need for some sort of contextual information in order to reach a testable expression of a sentence. This information, however, is kept to a minimum,[29] and more crucially its requirement is something which springs from linguistic conventions: that is, the rules of grammar dictate that we need, at a particular point within a statement, to insert a contextual signifier for the statement to have propositional content. By locating these as linguistic requirements (so it is argued), the analysis remains firmly in the realm of semantics (and hence the procured statement remains the literal meaning of the statement under consideration). The identification of both the speaker and the addressee (or pronoun referents) was a textual ambiguity which the Muslim jurists recognised.[30] The debates in *uṣūl* works over the referent of pronouns such as "you" (plural) and phrases such as "O believers" or "O people" in revelation are, in a sense, a recognition of the semantic underdetermination of revelation and the need to fill indexical slots. Some (identified as Ḥanbalīs and Ḥanafīs) considered these locutions within the Qurʾān to apply to all people, or all believers, and not only those present at the time of the Prophet. That is, the Sentence Meaning may identify such phrases as those actually present with the Prophet; "What Is Said" is that the reference is to all people or believers, both those present during the time of the Prophet and those after him. Here, "What Is Said"

29 Hence Recanati's description of this position as "minimalism". See above, p. 15, and the argument against Recanati in Cappelen and Lepore, "A Tall Tale".

30 The common feature of Muslim works of Quranic exegesis (*tafsīr*) in which pronouns in the Quranic text are glossed, and introduced by the words *ay* ("that is"/"i.e.") or *yaʿnī* ("this means"), even when it would seem obvious to whom or what the Qurʾān is referring, can be seen as a means of locating the referents of indexicals. See below, pp. 72–3, for discussion of this phenomenon. Ibn Ḥazm was not alone in proposing a simple rule to solve the indexicals problem which involved the most recent names subject in the passage (see below, pp. 160–2). This rule was, of course, interpreted in various ways, and often broken in exegetical practice. On indexicals generally, see Perry, "Indexicals and Demonstratives".

appears to cover not just "Meaning", but also some elements of "Reference".[31] The crucial point for these Uṣūlīs is that the use of the general grammatical form here makes the application to all periods of time linguistically required (and hence part of the literal meaning). Those who opposed this view (identified as Shāfiʿīs) argued that the general reference is not part of the literal meaning of the phrase. Abū Ḥamid al-Ghazālī (d. 505/1111) expresses it thus:

> Proving that the [Prophet's rules] apply to those who came after him is by an additional indication which demonstrates that every rule which is established during his life time remains until the day of resurrection for every believer. Even if this were the case, it would not be necessitated by the utterance alone. If this was proven, then this would make the statements ["O Believers" and "O People"] general through the attachment of another indicator, and not by the statement alone (*mujarrad al-khiṭāb*).[32]

What this amounts to is the view that whilst indexical slots can be filled in one way ("you" means those present during the Prophet's lifetime), making them apply to a wider group is a non-literal use. In pragmatic terms, the debate here is that what is included in "What Is Said" is, for some Uṣūlīs, highly restricted.

Another example of minimal disambiguation common to pragmatics and classical *uṣūl al-fiqh* is the genitive or *iḍāfa*. In Arabic, as in English, this need not always indicate strict ownership,[33] though its primary meaning would appear to be possession. Similarly, a statement like "John's car" might be considered primarily possessive, but it could (also literally) apply to non-possessive relationships. When I say, "Britain is my country", I am not expressing ownership, and perhaps many would say I am not speaking metaphorically also.[34] Perhaps the genitive in English as well as in Arabic functions as a homonym (expressing both possession and other types of relationship). One can always recognise one application of words as literal and the other as secondary or derivative, it might be argued. Bach, for example, argues that although the meaning of the word "sad" in the two phrases "sad man" and "sad music" are quite different, one can always designate one as literal and the other as non-literal. In this example, only people can have the property of (literally) being sad; saying a piece of music is sad is a non-literal use of the word, referring to its ability to cause sadness.[35] In this, many classical Arabic rhetoricians would have concurred: whilst poets refer to "the cause by the result" (*iṭlāq al-sabab bi-musabbab*), this is quite definitely a non-literal use of language.[36]

31 Meaning being the thing determined internally within language, and Reference being the thing in the real world to which the word refers. The distinction is a shorthand for the intension/extension distinction. See the various studies in Moore (ed.), *Meaning and Reference*. On Ibn Ḥazm's meaning/reference discussion see pp. 165–6 below.

32 Ghazālī, *al-Mustaṣfā*, p. 242.

33 The variety of meanings indicated by the *iḍāfa* in early Arabic grammar are described in Ryding, "Aspects of the Genitive".

34 See Recanati, *Literal Meaning*, pp. 61–4. Bach considers non-possessive uses of genitives to be non-literal, as he argues that "possessive phrases are not so-called for nothing" ("You Don't Say?", p. 39).

35 See Bach, "You Don't Say?", pp. 39–40.

36 This widely recognised rhetorical phenomenon is exemplified nicely by Jalāl al-Dīn al-Suyūṭī (d. 911/1505;

For modern pragmatists, the literal meaning (namely the meaning which is informed by context only in ways which are linguistically determined) encompasses both the ambiguous Sentence Meaning and the propositional "What Is Said". It is clear, though, that not a little exegetical work is required before the latter can be expressed, and this exegetical work (which consists, primarily, of identifying "minimal" contextual elements required by language) moves the resultant statement of propositional content into the category of "non-literal".[37] The statement must be stripped of its variables (both overt and covert) and ambiguities ("semantic underdetermination") must be eliminated. Those who support this view (which Recanati characterises as "minimalism") argue that the final formulation is a semantic statement of the sentence's contents with no reference to the speaker's intended meaning in the context in which it was uttered. What the speaker implies (or implicates) in uttering the sentence on a particular occasion does not play a role in formulating the literal interpretation. Within this "literal meaning" a number of items not explicitly expressed in the statement are included. A contested element amongst the philosophers is whether geographical location implications are part of the literal meaning. The literal meaning of the sentence "It's raining" means (so it is argued by some) that it is raining at the location of the speaker, and this geographical referent is part of the literal meaning. One can imagine circumstances when this is not all of what the speaker means (for example, you ask me if you need a raincoat and I say "it's raining", meaning not only that it is, but also "yes, you do!"). One can imagine circumstances when this is not what the speaker means (for example, the newsreader asks the weatherman what the weather in Manchester is like and the weatherman says "it's raining"). One can imagine circumstances when the speaker's meaning has nothing to do with rain at all (when Buddy Holly says "it's raining", he means "it's raining in my heart" – as, indeed, the song goes on to explain, just so we do not misunderstand). In these circumstances, however, the literal meaning has either been supplemented in context ("you need a coat"), or diverted ("in Manchester but not here"), or used entirely metaphorically ("in my heart"). For Taylor, these are all to be distinguished from "What Is Said" (one element of the literal meaning) which is that it is raining at the location at which the speaker utters the sentence.[38]

---

al-Itqān, v. 2, p. 100): "An example of announcing the caused thing and meaning the cause is 'They could not hear' (*mā kāna yastaṭīʿūna al-samʿ*; Q11/Hūd.20) meaning [they were not able to] accept and act on it; for the latter is the result of hearing." So "hear" does not mean "hear", but means the result of hearing (that is, acceptance of the message and ensuing action). This is clearly non-literal for Suyūṭī, as for most. Ibn Maytham al-Baḥrānī (d. 679/1282–3; *Qawāʿid al-kalām*, p. 90) calls it the "strongest of the different expressions of *majāz*" (*aqwā wujūh al-majāz*).

37 Some, such as Searle ("Literal Meaning"), argue for the impossibility of identifying propositional content (i.e. "What Is Said") without some sort of enrichment by context (and therefore the impossibility of context-free literal meaning). Others, such as Borg, advocate "moderate formal semantics", by which, I take it, she means that literal meaning can include contextual elements of the utterance, not in a "nebulous" manner in which speakers' intentions are guessed ("mind-reading": *Minimal Semantics*, p. 78), but "by recognising the context of a particular utterance as a set of formally described parameters (like speaker and time) against which a sentence-type can be assessed for truth or falsity" (Borg, *Minimal Semantics*, p. 265).

38 This is Taylor's view. See his "Sex, Breakfast", pp. 53–4, where he argues that the statement "it's raining"

The need to "fill the slots" in order to express literal meaning has prompted some to say that unambiguous literal meaning (that is, a meaning entirely free of contextual constraints – Sentence Meaning) is either a myth or useless. All statements require this sort of "variable processing" and demand the introduction of context before becoming assessable and therefore meaningful. Discovering the literal meaning, then, requires a series of interpretive acts, even if some literalists would wish to deny that they are performing exegesis of any sort. In short, unambiguous literal meaning is a rare commodity; what we are left with is interpretations of sentences which claim to be literal (that is, literal *interpretations*).

Perhaps the most developed philosophical model of literal meaning is that proposed by Recanati. He is generally more sceptical about both the existence and the utility of literal meaning, and proposes a typology of three literal meanings (or rather a typology of what might be meant by the term "literal meaning"). The first (which he calls "type-literal meaning" or t-literal meaning) is the meaning which "the conventions of the language endow" upon a particular utterance.[39] This approximates to Grice's Sentence Meaning. Anything which does not correspond to this meaning he dubs "t-non-literal". Within the t-non-literal there is "minimal literal meaning" (or m-literal). The minimal literal meaning is that which departs from the t-literal meaning but in a minimal manner (that is, when indexical slots are filled and perhaps other necessary processes of explication are performed). This minimal departure from the t-literal meaning is "still governed by the conventions of the language"[40] because the conventions of language control the meaning of words like "I" (which literally refers to the speaker) or "she" (which literally refers to a subject of feminine gender). This is Grice's "What Is Said". There is yet a third type of literal meaning, according to Recanati, the "primary literal meaning" (p-literal meaning), and it is this final category which represents his most important philosophical innovation. This is the meaning that directly results from interpreting an utterance in context, but without recourse to "implicatures". For example, the p-literal meaning of the statement "it's raining" refers to the weather at the place where the speaker is located. The p-non-literal meaning of the same statement in certain contexts could be "yes, you need a raincoat" (see above example), or indeed any number of other implied meanings (A: "Can I take the dog for a walk?" B: "It's raining", meaning "it is unadvisable"). Recanati, by instituting this category of literal meaning, is trying to take into account what the ordinary language user "senses" is a literal meaning. The ordinary language user senses that the implication that one should not take the dog for a walk is non-literal; but she does not sense that "it's raining at this location"

contains a "syntactically expressed argument place". Weather descriptions present a particular problem for constructing the literal meaning; "it's raining" begs the question: what exactly is doing the "raining"? If it is a passive, then the agent needs to be explicated, and if not, then something is needed to replace the indexical "it".

39 Recanati, *Literal Meaning*, p. 5.

40 Recanati, *Literal Meaning*, p. 6. Recanati does not consider the minimalist position – that is, the position which posits the priority of the m-literal meaning – to be coherent. See below, p. 55.

is non-literal. Language users (barring perverse examples devised by philosophers) think the assertion that it is raining at the location of the speaker to be part of the literal meaning of the statement "it's raining". It must be "transparent" to the language user that non-literalness is occurring for an expression to be p-non-literal:

> For something to count as non-literal in the ordinary sense, it must not only go beyond the conventional significance of the uttered words (*m*-non-literalness), but it must also be felt as such: the language users must be aware that the conveyed meaning exceeds the conventional significance of the words. That condition I dub the "transparency condition".[41]

Now this introduction of the feelings of the ordinary language user when using words non-literally – a feeling of "discrepancy", as it is described by Bartsch[42] – functions as a sort of criterion whereby p-literal and p-non-literal usage might be determined. For Recanati it means that at times, an m-non-literal usage is so immediately conveyed that an ordinary language user considers it to be a literal meaning. As we shall see, this phenomenon (namely that a meaning can be both non-literal – in the m- sense – and literal – in the p- sense) echoes distinctions between different types of "literal" expressions in works of *uṣūl al-fiqh*. In particular, one thinks of the categories of *haqāʾiq sharʿiyya* and *ḥaqāʾiq ʿurfiyya* and the principle that "what is immediate – *al-mubādar* – is an indicator of literal usage – *al-ḥaqīqa*".[43] The p-literal meaning, then, is what the ordinary language user understands by the phrase "the literal meaning of the statement". How an ordinary language user understands the literal/non-literal distinction is that "non-literal meaning contrasts with ordinary meaning. Non-literal meaning is special, it involves a form of deviance or departure from the norm; a form of deviance or departure which must be transparent to the language users."[44]

Similar understandings of literal meaning function within Islamic exegetical debates; this can be illustrated through an examination of the debate around the meaning of Q5/al-Māʾida.6:

> When you rise to pray, wash your faces and your hands up to the elbows and wipe over your heads, and your feet up to the ankles.

There was, as is well known, major debate concerning the precise ritual performance which would fulfil the order in this verse.[45] Assuming that the text itself is taken as fixed,[46] exegetical debates concerning the meaning (that is, the propositional content)

41 Recanati, "Literal/Nonliteral", p. 271.

42 Bartsch, "Word Meanings", p. 33.

43 See below, pp. 39–40 and 177–9.

44 Recanati, "Literal/Nonliteral", p. 272; *Literal Meaning*, p. 81.

45 Burton's excellent survey of the exegesis of this verse demonstrates the complexity of the tradition, though Burton is using it primarily as an example of his broader thesis concerning the Qurʾān-*Sunna* relationship; see Burton, "The Qurʾān and the Islamic Practice of *wuḍūʾ*". See also Katz, *Body of Text*, pp. 60–86.

46 This was itself a contentious element in the dispute of this verse's meaning. For the variant version of this verse, see Burton, "The Qurʾān and the Islamic Practice of *wuḍūʾ*", pp. 21–4, and below, pp. 138–9.

of the verse alone can be characterised using the above scheme of literal meaning. The t-literal meaning of this verse is ambiguous in that the indexical "you" requires specification. It might be filled by reference to the immediately preceding statement in the verse ("O you who believe"), and hence the believers are identified as the addressees. One can legitimately ask, "believe in what?" since believe is normally understood to be a transitive verb requiring a direct object (that is, "you" stands for "those who believe that there is no god but Allāh and Muḥammad is the messenger of Allāh). By filling indexical slots, we arrive at the m-literal meaning. This is contextually informed, and hence t-non-literal, but the Muslim exegetes do not, normally, consider this "completion" whereby indexicals and free variables are assigned referents as moving beyond the verse itself to a non-literal meaning. Crucial for the t-/m-literal distinction is that this completion is required by the conventions of the language ("you" means the addressee which must be assigned contextually; "believe" requires a direct object – noun or proposition). Whether the "you" means all believers at all times or only those present at the time of the Prophet is a debate we have already encountered; whether or not believers should commit themselves to more than the simple twofold creed of the *shahāda* was, and is, much debated. However, these debates are not about whether filling the slots is a move away from the literal meaning of the verse, but rather about the content with which the slots should be filled. I am yet to find an exegete who is worried about the *process* of filling the slots, though they debate, of course, what might fill them. They do this naturally in their exegesis, with no concern that they are deviating from the meaning of the verse. A further element of the process of moving from t- to m-literal meanings is the notion that an imperative cannot in itself have propositional content ("wash your faces"); it needs reformulation as a statement or rule ("the believers, when they rise to pray, must wash their faces…").[47] Turning the imperatives of revelation into rules is one of the major exegetical tasks of the jurist; what a revelatory imperative might mean in legal terms (obligation, recommendation, permission) is a major pre-occupation of Uṣūlīs.

The real debating ground is over the different m- and p-literal meanings of the verse. For example, the verse says that one should wash "when one rises to pray". Does this mean every time one rises to pray? Muslim law normally decrees that purification is only necessary when one has experienced an impurity infraction (a *ḥadath*) since one's last purification. For some, the verse, on its own, means that the cause of the need to purify is the rising to pray; and so if all we had was the verse, we would have to purify for every prayer, whether or not we had experienced a purity infraction.[48] The requirement to purify only when one has experienced an infraction

47 Searle ("Literal Meaning") sees no need to rephrase an imperative in this way, as he is willing to alter the "truth conditions" of a statement to the "truth or obedience conditions" (see his humorous examples concerning hamburgers and doors, pp. 215–19). Questions such as "when can we say that an order has been obeyed?" are precisely the questions asked by Muslim jurists when examining the literal meaning of the imperative (*ṣīghat al-amr*); see below, pp. 45–7.

48 This was supposedly the view of ʿIkrima b. Abī Jahl: "Every time someone rises to pray, then he must renew his state of purity" (Ṭūsī, *al-Tibyān*, v. 3, p. 449).

is indicated by external indicators, and hence is a non-literal understanding of the verse. The m-literal meaning is that one should purify each time one prays. For others, there is an ellipsis of the phrase "whilst you are in a state of minor ritual impurity" (*wa-antum muḥdithūn*). The Ḥanafī Shams al-Dīn al-Sarakhsī (d. 483/1090) argues that the ellipsis happens "for reasons of eloquence and brevity" (*lil-ījāz wa'l-ikhtiṣār*) which is the normal practice of language users when "there is sufficient indication [of meaning] in the rest" of the utterance.[49] Ellipsis (*taqdīr*, *ḥadhf*), being a "normal practice of language users" (*ʿādat ahl al-lisān*), does not impair understanding, and therefore is an element of the language of the utterance rather than some external factor: that is, it may not be the m-literal meaning, but it is the p-literal meaning. Once we understand this, we realise the requirement to purify is caused by the *ḥadath* and not the rising to pray.

A similar manifestation of p-literal meaning within the examination of this verse is the assumption that the sequence of presentation in the verse requires the sequence of performance. Here there is debate. The Ḥanafī and Mālikī schools are normally credited with the view that the verse lists the actions rather than prescribing a sequence; the Shāfiʿīs, Ḥanbalīs and Imāmīs view the verse requiring order (*tartīb*) and that this is part of the literal meaning of the verse.[50] In both these debates, the nature of the connectedness between two elements of an utterance is considered controversial. "When you rise to pray, wash your faces" would appear to some jurists to have causality as a part of its literal meaning; similarly, "wash your faces and your hands" would seem to have sequence as part of its literal meaning. Others disagree on one or both characterisations of the connections. Recanati argued that causal and sequential connections can be part of the p-literal meaning, even though they are m-non-literal:

> The Queen came to Norwich and the crowds cheered.

Here the p-literal meaning would be that the Queen coming to Norwich was the occasion for the crowds cheering (that is, the Queen's arrival was the "occasioning factor" for the cheering). There is nothing in the m-literal meaning to imply such a connection.

> John and Mary got married and had many children.

The p-literal meaning implies temporal sequence here; the m-literal meaning does not. The dividing line between m- and p-literal meanings, and between p-literal and p-non-literal, then, are at the heart of the debate within works of *uṣūl al-fiqh* concerning the scope of literal meaning, and those occasions when it is to be abandoned.

Underlying the different types of "literal meaning" is a distinction between what

49 Sarakhsī, *Uṣūl*, v. 2, p. 180.

50 For a summary of the various positions, see Ibn Rushd, *Bidāyat al-mujtahid*, v. 1, p. 16, and Ṭūsī, *al-Khilāf*, v. 1, pp. 94–5.

is understood as the literal meaning by specialists (philosophers, linguists) and the literal meaning for ordinary language users. Both conceptions of literal meaning are appealing because of the plausible belief that texts (an utterance, a sentence) have meanings which are inherent within the text, and which exist before the exegete gets to work on them. These meanings are usually seen, from the interpreter's perspective, as epistemologically superior and logically prior to non-literal meanings: we can be sure of the literal meaning, but the non-literal is dependent on the whim of the interpreter. There is some resistance to this idea that the cornerstone of the broad concept of literal meaning, the intuition of the ordinary language user concerning literal and non-literal meaning, is relevant to the process whereby the literal meaning is reached.[51] Along similar lines, there is a rejection of why the process of interpretation carried out by the interpreter should figure in an analysis of what is said.[52] Bach considers the process by which the hearer gains understanding of the meaning of the utterance to be irrelevant in any consideration of Grice's conception of "What Is Said" (even if this is counter-intuitive).[53] As we shall see in the coming chapters, the debate over whether meaning can be determined separately from language use is yet another point of commonality between the modern debates around the pragmatics-semantics boundary and classical *uṣūl al-fiqh*.

Rejections of Literal Meaning

More radical formulations of literal meaning have, though, been proposed by modern linguistic philosophers. Sperber and Wilson have argued that the whole idea of literal meaning belongs to "folk-linguistics", and whilst it may have intuitive appeal, it is actually a red herring, preventing a full understanding of the communicative process.[54] However, even they recognise a need to distinguish between "explicit" and "implicit" content of utterances. When asked if she wishes for some supper, Lisa replies "I have eaten". She is, Sperber and Wilson argue, explicitly stating that she has eaten that evening, and implicitly saying that she does not want any food. Agreeably, she could have stated it more strongly ("I have already eaten" or, more strongly still, "I have already eaten this evening"), but explicitness is a matter of degree for Sperber and Wilson, not a matter of a literal/non-literal category distinction. Measuring a statement against its level of literality as opposed to its explicitness is, perhaps, one of the elements in the classical *uṣūl* distinction, drawn by some authors, between *ḥaqīqa* and *ẓāhir*.[55]

51 Recanati considers the idea of the literal meaning being prior as incoherent. He instead considers it as potentially the most accessible. The manner in which he thinks the most accessible meaning is adopted is outlined in Recanati, "Alleged Priority", and in his *Literal Meaning*, pp. 30–4.

52 See above, n. 24.

53 Bach, "Seemingly Semantic Intuitions".

54 "Arguing about what was said—both its content and its truthfulness—is a social practice conducted within the framework of 'folk-linguistics.' *What is said* and *literal meaning* are folk-linguistic notions" (Sperber and Wilson, "Truthfulness and Relevance", p. 254).

55 See below, pp. 49–52.

The reason why Grice adopted the notion of literal meaning (and part of the reason for its continuing allure amongst pragmatists) was that it was a useful heuristic weapon in his rejection of "ordinary language" philosophy pioneered by the later Wittgenstein. For the later Wittgenstein, "meaning" is located in language use[56] and not in any theorising about (and refining) semantic rules; hence "literal meaning" (that is, a meaning controlled solely by language rules) is a siren which sounds appealing, but is actually philosophically destructive.[57] Wittgenstein's emphasis on use was further employed in discussions around the manner in which use determines meaning and texts (which can be considered extended utterances) have meaning within a tradition of understanding. Fish's "interpretive communities", in which meaning can only be understood within a context of a community of interpreters (past and present), robs the literal meaning of its objective and (therefore) authoritative role.[58] In a different philosophical tradition, Gadamer's rehabilitation of prejudice (or "prejudgement") and his commitment to tradition might also be said to devalue the previously assigned "authority" of literal meaning. Understanding, for Gadamer, is an effect of history, and so it follows that understanding the literal meaning of a text cannot be a simple matter of reading it (or, for m-literal meaning, applying the rules), but is instead an employment of the "horizons" of both the individual and the broader situation in which she embarks on the hermeneutic enterprise.[59] Literalist prejudice occupies no privileged position, consigning others to derivative status – it is itself a tradition, though often (ironically) one which claims to eschew the effects of previous understanding. "What the text says" may be separable from the author's intention, and Gadamer seems to indicate the former's unproblematic status in the here and now.[60] However, I would argue, any understanding of "what the text says" (literal or otherwise) is surely not the result of a "prejudice-free", scientific exercise (as semanticists and literalists claim). If literal interpretation is a "fusing of horizons", to use Gadamer's phrase, it is a fusing of the interpreter's understanding of what constitutes a literal meaning (a historical product) and the text. Literalism undoubtedly has foundationalist (even metaphysical) pretensions, but if Gadamer is right, these are merely an illusion.

56 Wittgenstein, *Philosophical Investigations*, p. 20, #43. Wittgenstein is linking the meaning of any statement to its role in social communication (on which see Habermas, "Intentions, Conventions and Linguistic Interactions", pp. 107–10).

57 This does not deny, however, that Wittgenstein did make some distinction between a primary and secondary meaning, a discussion of which I will not enter into here (but on which see Schulte, "Wittgenstein's Notion of Secondary Meaning").

58 Fish, *Is There a Text in this Class?*, p. 14 ("it is interpretive communities rather than either the text or the reader which produce meanings").

59 See Gadamer, *Truth and Method*, pp. 474–91.

60 "All that matters is what the poem actually says, not what its author intended and perhaps did not know how to say" (Gadamer, *Who Am I and Who Are You?*, p. 68). Gadamer also speaks of the "ideal" meaning of an utterance – that is, the meaning it may have outside of contextual factors on which the speaker draws in utilising it in an utterance. This seems curiously close to the notion Recanati dubs "the eternal sentence" (Recanati, *Literal Meaning*, p. 84) and the general position as "eternalism" (Recanati, "Literalism and Contextualism"), a version of literalism he rejects.

Perhaps the only close analogue to the destruction of the literal/non-literal ideas of literal meaning is the theory of Ibn Taymiyya (d. 728/1328), as expounded by Yunis Ali.[61] Ali terms this the *salafī* version of communication theory, though it really seems to have been restricted to Ibn Taymiyya and Ibn Qayyim al-Jawziyya (d. 751/1350), and even then it has to be pieced together from different works rather than from a sustained discourse by either author. Nevertheless, the presentation is coherent: Ibn Taymiyya considered the distinction between so-called literal and non-literal expression (*ḥaqīqa*/*majāz*) as illusory. With regard to literal meaning, he considered words (for example "lion") to have no meaning independent of context. There is no historical evidence for the institution of the *waḍ*ʿ (in terms of an "event"), and hence no "context less" (*bilā qarīna*) meaning; "immediacy" (*tabādur*) is hardly evidence of *a priori* meaning assignment since this is based on language use (compare with Recanati on the supposed priority of literal meaning);[62] understanding an utterance is always context dependent, and words are never used in an unqualified way; meaning is, then, always context/use generated:

> [Words] when used in isolation are not utterances or parts of utterances, nor do they mean anything; they are nothing in fact but sounds used for cawing.[63]

One is reminded of Wittgenstein's influential position amongst the "ordinary-language philosophers":

> For a large class of cases – though not for all – in which we employ the word "meaning" it can be defined thus: the meaning of a word is its use in language."[64]

This, it might be argued, is a natural extension of Ibn Taymiyya's anti-philosophical stance. Just as universals such as "blackness" do not, for him, exist in abstraction waiting to be realised in individual particulars, so words do not have abstract meanings (assigned in the *waḍ*ʿ) instantiated in particular utterances (which may be used in a literal or non-literal manner). Both abstract meaning and the individual instantiation ultimately compromise the eternal singularity of God.[65] All of this is a welcome corrective to the portrayal of Ibn Taymiyya as a "literalist" who simply rejected *majāz*. Rather, his complaint was against the notions of both *ḥaqīqa* and *majāz* as adequate descriptions of language and communication. When he appears to

61 Yunis Ali, *Medieval Islamic Pragmatics*, pp. 87–140. Yunis Ali indicates that Ibn Taymiyya's *salafī* communication theory is more "radical" than modern reformulation of literal/non-literal distinctions. I am not sure I quite see how; his theory, as Yunis Ali presents it, is certainly challenging in its context, but it seems remarkably similar to, say, the rejection of the literal/non-literal distinction of Sperber and Wilson (see above, n. 54). Whilst Yunis Ali's approach is impressively sophisticated, there is a danger of reading modern use-based linguistic theories into Ibn Taymiyya and Ibn Qayyim al-Jawziyya; see below, pp. 181–3.

62 See above, n. 20.

63 Yunis Ali, *Medieval Islamic Pragmatics*, p. 114, citing a summary of Ibn Qayyim al-Jawziyya's views by Ibn al-Mawṣilī (d. 774/1372).

64 Wittgenstein, *Philosophical Investigations*, p. 20, #43.

65 This, one takes it, is Ibn Taymiyya's objection to "Platonic" forms, described by Yunis Ali, *Medieval Islamic Pragmatics*, pp. 92–3.

be arguing for a "literal" interpretation of Quranic verses (such as God being seated on his throne), he is, in fact, arguing for a use-based understanding of the meaning of the sentence as opposed to the fancifulness of Muʿtazilī interpretations.[66]

Conclusion

The debate around literal meaning in recent linguistic philosophy provides, first of all, a vocabulary with which to explore discussions in *uṣūl al-fiqh*. I employ this vocabulary as and when I feel it illuminates my analysis of the discussion in the following chapters. Recent discussions around literal meaning also provide us with a set of questions which are an interesting echo of the classical discussions in works of *uṣūl al-fiqh*. First, there is the variety of potential literal meanings: a pared-down version of the notion of literal meaning is nicely summarised by Searle in a classic article on the topic:

> The literal meaning of the sentence is the meaning it has independently of any context whatever; and, diachronic changes apart, it keeps that meaning in any context in which it is uttered.[67]

Whilst Searle goes on to argue for the rational incoherence of this idea of literal meaning, his definition does capture something of the idea. One should note the terms he uses to describe the relationship between the sentence and its meaning: they are based around ownership ("the meaning it *has*"; "it *keeps* that meaning"). This imagined close connection between the words/sentence and the literal meaning partly explains its allure: it offers a level of certainty which other "imagined" meanings do not have. Sociological explanations of revivalism often point to the perceived certainty of the ideas within the new movements as opposed to the old order's sophistry. It is, then, no surprise that a devotion to the literal meaning is often an element within such movements, particularly those with a puritanical approach to scriptural interpretation.[68] In the analysis in the subsequent chapters, one of my conclusions is that the appeal to the literal meaning (the so-called "literalism" in the non-technical sense) of movements dissatisfied with the status quo is really an outgrowth of existing hermeneutic structures rather than rejection of them, and this

66 Thanks to Yunis Ali, Ibn Taymiyya's original theory of communication is now more widely known. It will, however, only feature briefly in the following chapters. This is partly because it did not really have extensive influence after him (Ḥanbalīs, for example, generally promoted the mainstream views and did not develop Ibn Taymiyya's theory of communication); also it is not really integrated into a work of *uṣūl al-fiqh*, the principal focus of this book. See below, pp. 176–84.

67 Searle, "Literal Meaning", p. 208. Searle aims to show this conception of literal meaning to be fallacious, and his definition may be a straw man with a lack of nuance – but it is a useful summary. Davidson also provides a useful summary: literal meaning "can be assigned to words and sentences apart from particular contexts of use" (Davidson, "What Metaphors Mean", p. 496).

68 In comparative perspective, see Crapanzano, *Serving the Word*, though it should be noted that the notion of literalism developed here is not identical with that employed by Crapanzano, which is more a form of textual devotion in which (unlike literalism here) authorial intention is not always excluded.

can be seen in the literalism of the Ẓāhiriyya, notably Ibn Ḥazm. Similarly, some of the modern "literalist" movements are offering merely an adjusted version of the classical system. These are best seen as positions along a spectrum rather than entirely separate categories.

The power of the literal is partly linked to the idea of linguistics as a science (in the enlightenment sense: the provider of certain answers to specific questions) through the recognition of eternal grammatical rules. The notion that rules are established before instances of language use (that is, the idea of a primordial language, popular amongst some Muslim jurists) is directly linked to the idea that there is a "decontextualised" literal meaning of a text.[69] Of course, this is empirically questionable: language rules change, and with them literal meanings. This was recognised by the more perceptive Uṣūlīs, and they developed a theory of how new literal meanings could be incorporated into the linguistic system (the *lugha*) through change. When discussing whether phrases like "O believers" applies to all human beings, al-Rāzī makes the insightful comment that he recognises that, because of linguistic development, the ordinary language user's understanding may not always be in tune with the semantic meaning: "The conclusion is that we accept that [applying the phrase to all believers through time] is non-literal in linguistic terms (*majāz fī'l-lugha*) but is literal in terms of language use (*ḥaqīqa fī'l-ʿurf*)."[70] The expansion of the literal has its analogues in other religious traditions,[71] demonstrating the belief that a meaning dictated by language (even when that power of dictation is very broadly conceived) is always more attractive in the quest for religious commitment than the vagaries of the human imagination. A host of questions concerning the changes in epistemological outlook wrought by the spread of literacy and the new technology of the book are raised by the recognition of and commitment to literal meaning.[72] I shall not be able to deal with them in this work, though when relevant I will attempt to make appropriate references. We are dealing here with almost mythological structures, in which modern commentators who attempt to distinguish between interpretive methods which utilise the literal meaning and those which do not often perpetuate the idea that literal meaning is somehow uncomplicated and clear, holding a place of logical priority. Language is posited as capturing the essential nature of ideas, things and events,[73] and, in ideal communication, literal

69 Habermas's approach can, in part, also be helpful in the analysis here. The popularity of his idea that "communicative action" is possible (and desirable) draws on (and is, in part, dependent upon) the notion that there are means of communicating which are free from factors which bring about misunderstanding. See his "Intentions, Conventions and Linguistic Interactions". He speaks not of literal meaning, but of "surface structure" (Habermas, "Reflections", pp. 8–9). Consider also Chomsky's notion of an innate grammar which implies that (literal/grammatical) meanings which clash with true meanings of utterances fail to connect with the "deep structure" of the human mind (which is, for him, the chief interest of linguistics). See above, n. 11.

70 Rāzī, *al-Maḥṣūl*, v. 3, p. 161.

71 See, for example, the extensive survey of Jewish hermeneutic uses of the supposed "literal" sense of scripture (*peshat*) in Cohen, *Opening the Gates*.

72 Stock, *Implications of Literacy*, pp. 326–454.

73 See below, pp. 118–19 (on *ḥaqīqa*).

meaning usage expresses that essential nature. That such a meaning is a construct (created, at times challenging, but certainly "tradition dependent") like other posited meanings does not make it any less appealing. These observations serve to frame the subsequent discussion of the nature of literal meaning and literal interpretation in Islamic legal writings. As we shall see, the English term "literal meaning" (as conceived of in the preceding discussion) had a number of possible analogues in scriptural exegesis generally, and Muslim legal theory in particular.

2

Literal Meaning, Hermeneutics and Islamic Legal Theory

Belief in the "literal meaning", as the term is used in this book, involves the possibly romantic notion that, barring cases of pure homonymity, words (as sounds or "vocables") have singular primary meanings. Regardless of how these primary meanings were acquired, a word/sound and its associated meaning form a very strong, individual relationship. When words are put together into sentences, and then expressed as utterances (that is, they become oral or written texts, the latter being records of the utterance), these composite entities also have a primary meaning, formed from the individual meaning of each word/sound (lexis) combined with fixed rules of grammar which dictate how these elements interrelate to produce meaning (syntax). The strength of the sound-meaning bond is such that when language users perceive the link, they understand a particular meaning (the literal) as being (epistemologically speaking) more secure, relative to other potential meanings. Hence language users naturally tend to adopt this "literal" meaning before any other meaning. The relationship between word/sound and meaning is *sui generis* for literal meanings; other, contextually modified or metaphorically imagined meanings are manufactured rather than natural or fixed, and involve the intention of the speaker or the perception of the listener (or both). Unlike literal meanings, they are not conceived of as inherent within the text. Literalism is the belief that this literal meaning should be prioritised; it demands a primary allegiance, giving it a privileged status in relation to other potential meanings. As we shall see, nearly all Muslim legal hermeneutics is "literalist" in this sense, though different theorists have had different estimations of the strength of the bond, the occasions on which it might be broken, and what mechanisms can bring about the break.

That this conception of literalism, philosophically speaking, might be an incoherent form of foundationalism has been convincingly argued, but my intention here is not to disprove the coherence of the idea of literal meaning, or the theory of literalism. Instead, in the following chapters, I wish to chart the role and employment of the idea of literal meaning (or ideas closely associated with it) in Islamic legal theory (*uṣūl al-fiqh*). Before diving into the early Islamic material in the next chapter, there is an initial task: to understand the "end product", so to speak, of the developments surveyed in this book. I begin, a little ahistorically, with the mature and classical understanding. I do this not because I consider there to have been any inevitability in the intellectual trajectory which led to the hermeneutic system in classical Islamic legal theory and literal meaning's place within in it. The theory could have developed differently, and the early period is not studied simply as an explanation of the eventual hegemony of the later classical model. Rather, if an understanding of the classical theory is reached at the outset, the terms of debate in the early period, and how far the Muslim juristic tradition travelled in a few centuries, are more comprehensible and, in intellectual terms, more impressive.

Muslim Legal Theory

The earliest surviving works which identify their subject matter as *uṣūl al-fiqh* ("the principles/roots of law/understanding") come from the late fourth/tenth century. These works contain records of debates and the arguments of individual authors concerning questions which can be characterised as jurisprudential. That is, these works contain descriptions of how God's law – the Sharīʿa provided for all humanity through the Prophet Muḥammad – has come to be known and will continue to be discovered by the Muslim community's expert jurists (*fuqahāʾ*) in the future. A large proportion of these works focuses on how the accepted "sources" of the law might be interpreted (that is, their subject matter is hermeneutics or the theory of interpretation). These sources are normally conceived of as texts in these works of *uṣūl al-fiqh*: the Qurʾān (or *al-Kitāb*, the book – the text delivered to Muḥammad by God through angelic intermediaries), the Sunna (the way or example of the Prophet, which is recorded in reports called *ḥadīth*) and consensus (*ijmāʿ* – statements and positions which the community has agreed upon since the death of the Prophet Muḥammad in 632). Because of the textual nature of the sources, most *uṣūl* discussions focus on three broad areas of investigation: authority, authenticity and interpretation. Issues discussed within *uṣūl* works range, then, from: (1) the authority of the texts (why should one follow the Qurʾān, or the Sunna, or the consensus of the community?); to (2) a text's authenticity (how do we know this text is part of the Qurʾān, or this report records the Prophet's words or actions; or that the community actually agreed on this or that matter?); to (3) its interpretation (what does the text mean? How should it be interpreted?). This book is primarily concerned with the last of these, that is, hermeneutic questions. It is in these that discussions of the literal meaning of a text, as we understand it here, appear most frequently, either as the object of debate, or as an assumption within a related discussion.

When looking at the earliest surviving works of *uṣūl al-fiqh*, the complex intellectual and juristic context into which they provide a window demonstrates, to my satisfaction at least, that these are not the first Muslim attempts to answer these pressing theoretical questions, neither are they the first works in the discipline which became known as *ʿilm uṣūl al-fiqh* ("knowledge of the principles of the law"). Instead they are, I suggest, the result of development over many years. Unfortunately, texts composed during these earlier years have not survived, with the exception of an early work by Muḥammad b. Idrīs al-Shāfiʿī. The *Risāla* of al-Shāfiʿī may not be a work of *uṣūl* in the strict sense of the term, but its concerns are not irrelevant to those of the mature discipline of the late tenth century CE onwards.[1] Recent research[2] has indicated that quite a few works of *uṣūl al-fiqh* existed in the period before the surviving works (or elements of works) by al-Jaṣṣāṣ (d. 370/980), Ibn al-Qaṣṣār (d. 397/1007) and al-Bāqillānī (d. 403/1013).[3] Even if a postulated pre-Jaṣṣāṣ *uṣūl al-fiqh* is not accepted[4] and we characterise third–fourth/eighth–tenth century *uṣūl* discussions differently, the speed with which the discipline took hold within the centres of Islamic scholarship in the fifth–sixth/eleventh–twelfth centuries is impressive. Literary evidence for the rise of the discipline is found in a stream of works produced by jurist-experts on *uṣūl al-fiqh* ("Uṣūlīs") of different school and theological allegiance over the next 200 years.[5] *Uṣūl al-fiqh* embedded itself within the law curricula of the emerging legal-educational institutions, and the development of the genre follows a familiar pattern in medieval institutions of learning: expansive works were followed by summaries, followed by commentaries on summaries and so on.[6] The result was a reasonably stable structure of a set of texts, containing commonly accepted ideas with well-worn lines of argument laying out established positions, sometimes attributed to individuals, or to groups of scholars associated with both theological and legal schools (*madhāhib*). This stability should not be confused with intellectual stagnation, but is rather a reflection of the level of esteem and respectability in which the genre was held; originality and development certainly occurred in *uṣūl*, but they occurred (as in any field) within limits which defined the field.[7] Within this environment, particular ideas of literalness (or literality) prevailed and formed part of a communication theory propounded by Uṣūlīs. This theory served the purposes of the discipline well, and survived a millennium, well into the modern period.[8]

Classical works of *uṣūl al-fiqh* follow a reasonably consistent structure with a canonical set of questions or issues, namely:

1. Fundamental elements of understanding the discipline: definitions of the discipline of *uṣūl al-fiqh* and its place within the knowledge of the religious sciences (such as logic, theology and *fiqh*) and discussions of language and its operation, providing principles whereby God's law (directly in the Qur'ān or indirectly in the words of the Prophet or the consensus of the community) might be categorised.
2. Provenance: a discussion of the sources we might use to understand God's

1 See Lowry, *Early Islamic Legal Theory*, pp. 359–68.

2 See, for example, Stewart, "Muḥammad b. Dāwūd al-Ẓāhirī" and "Muḥammad b. Jarīr al-Ṭabarī".

3 I examine these works in more detail below, pp. 94–125.

4 Hallaq to an extent initiated this debate with his article "Was al-Shafiʿi the Master Architect?"; see also Schwarb, "Capturing the Meanings", pp. 116–17, n. 23.

5 For a summary of the development of classical *uṣūl al-fiqh*, see Chaumont, *Le Livre des Rais*, pp. 1–17; Hallaq, *A History*, pp. 1–35.

6 See Makdisi, *Rise of the Colleges*, pp. 105–28 for the role of *uṣūl al-fiqh* in the medieval scholastic curriculum.

7 Hallaq, "*Uṣūl al-fiqh*", also argues for originality, though he conceives of it as primarily to be found in novelty rather than reinterpretation of tradition.

8 See below, pp. 175–96.

message including discussions of the Qurʾān, the *ḥadīth* and the consensus of the community.

3. Interpretation: how texts in the sources might be understood as part of a coherent whole including analyses of imperatives and prohibitions and statements (general and particular, unrestricted and restricted, clear and unclear, spoken and implied, apparent and non-apparent). Also included in this section are discussions of how one text might cancel out (rather than simply modify) another through a process of abrogation.
4. Analogy and other procedures bracketed under the term *qiyās*: analogising from the established textual sources (or, to be more precise, the understood message of the established textual sources) is given special attention in works of *uṣūl* as it constitutes the principal mechanism for deciding cases which are deemed (through the interpretive process in 3 above) to be beyond the direct reference of the explicit statements within the source texts. Some other mechanisms of dealing with "unmentioned" cases are also dealt with here.
5. Authority: issues of the skills, identity and qualifications of the jurist interpreter establish a particular theory of hermeneutic authority revolving around the notion of *ijtihād* (the jurist's expenditure of effort in seeking a ruling). Included here are how and when a jurist's opinion should be requested and given (*iftāʾ*) and followed (*taqlīd*).

Nearly all issues (often termed *masāʾil*) of *uṣūl al-fiqh* can be slotted into one of these five headings, and, of course, there is some topic overlap between them. The issues of direct relevance for the discussion of literal meaning concern language (1 and the whole of 3 in the above schema); other sections also occasionally contain elements which are of relevance, but these two sections in classical *uṣūl* works constitute the principal sources for our discussions here.

Literal Meaning within the *Uṣūl* Linguistic System

The notions within the *uṣūl* system which link in with our conception of a text's literal meaning and its status can be usefully explored through exploiting a basic teaching text and *uṣūl* summaries from the mature classical period. In the following summary, I make reference to two such works: the *Mukhtaṣar Muntahā al-Sūl wa'l-Amal fī ʿilmay al-uṣūl wa'l-jadal* of the Mālikī Ibn al-Ḥājib (d. 646/1249), and *Nihāyat al-wuṣūl ilā ʿilm al-uṣūl* of the famous Shīʿī jurist al-ʿAllāma al-Ḥillī (d. 726/1325). Ibn al-Ḥājib's *Mukhtaṣar* became a standard curriculum work of *uṣūl al-fiqh* in medieval teaching institutions, attracting a large number of commentaries by both Shīʿī and Sunni authors.[9] The *Mukhtaṣar* is, itself, an abbreviation of the famous work of the Shāfiʿī writer Sayf al-Din al-Āmidī, on whom Weiss has written extensively.[10] Al-ʿAllāma al-Ḥillī's *Nihāyat al-wuṣūl* was the most expansive of his

9 See Stewart, *Islamic Legal Orthodoxy*, p. 98.

10 See Weiss, *The Search*; Weiss's informative engagement with the use of the word "literal" as a translation

uṣūl works and his ideas set the framework of later Shīʿī jurisprudence; unlike Ibn al-Ḥājib's work, it is not intended to be a brief summary, but a detailed investigation of the different opinions, including those of the Shīʿa, on the major issues of *uṣūl al-fiqh*. Whilst the individual conclusions of the two authors differ occasionally, the overall framework of ideas – the assumptions about how language works and how meaning is created – is consistent across the two works. This remarkable continuity demonstrates how *uṣūl* discussions transcended school and even sectarian differences:[11] Uṣūlīs addressed fundamental questions of understanding and interpretation which stretched across the *madhāhib*, creating a scholarly discourse in which intellectuals of very different theological and legal persuasions participated.

In the classical works of *uṣūl*, meanings are attached to words by an act of "placing" (*waḍʿ*) or "coining", whereby the sound-meaning relationship is established. There is, however, no "natural" relationship between the sound (or the vocable)[12] and the meaning. In this sense, the relationship is arbitrary:

> [Ibn al-Ḥājib]: On the origins of language: between the vocable and the thing it indicates there is no natural affinity (*laysa bayna al-lafẓ wa-madlūlihi munāsaba ṭabīʿiyya*)[13]

Some had argued for a natural affinity between words and meanings, but this was discarded probably sometime in the third/ninth century. This discarded view is normally associated with a Muʿtazilī ʿAbbād b. Sulaymān al-Ṣaymarī (d. 250/854).[14] It was discarded, as al-ʿAllāma al-Ḥillī points out, "because if sounds indicate essentially [that is, by natural affinity], then languages would not differ among the different nations in various places and times … and this is obviously false."[15] A connection which was naturally "within" the sounds and which was connected with the meaning would mean, surely, that all humankind would speak the same language. They obviously do not, so the connection cannot be natural.

The arbitrary nature of the original connection, however, does not lessen the strength of the attachment between sound and meaning. What the sound and the meaning share is a historical event of coining and association known as *waḍʿ*. This event is conceived of as happening sometime in the past, thereby establishing the language system (the *lugha*) that exists in the present. The "accidental" nature of the event by which sound and meaning were linked is widely accepted, and, in Ibn al-Ḥājib's terms, the event was *tawqīf* ("taught", "instructed": arbitrarily fixed) by God. To understand what Ibn al-Ḥājib means by this, it is worth remembering that the

---

of some technical elements of the *uṣūl* lexicon is discussed below, pp. 56–7. See also Weiss, "Exotericism and Objectivity".

11 This has already been noted by Weiss in "*Uṣūl*-related *Madhhab* Differences".

12 I am here following Weiss's translation of the Arabic term *lafẓ*; see Weiss, *The Search*, pp. 95–7.

13 Ibn al-Ḥājib, *Mukhtaṣar*, v. 1, p. 267.

14 On whom, see Van Ess, *Theologie und Gesellschaft*, v. 4, pp. 15–45, particularly pp. 21–2; Weiss, "Medieval Muslim Discussions", pp. 36–8.

15 Ḥillī, *Nihāyat*, v. 1, p. 151.

term *tawqīfī* is also used to describe non-rational ritual performance (*ʿibādāt*).[16] Even for Muʿtazilīs, the number of prayers, or the fast during Ramaḍān, were inscrutable commands (*tawqīfī*) from God. They gained their authority not from anything inherent within them whereby they become appropriate or rational; they are to be done simply because of a specific act in history (God demanding them through his revelation).[17] Languages, like rituals, may be arbitrary, but they nonetheless gain authority through a historical event (real or imagined) by which they were instituted. Whilst the existence of the linguistic system functions as a presumption within the *uṣūl* discussions, its instigator is a matter of some dispute; as Ibn al-Ḥājib says:

> [Abū al-Ḥasan] al-Ashʿarī said that God taught [the *lugha*] by means of revelation, or by creating the sounds, or by some necessary knowledge.
> The followers of Abū Hāshim al-Jubbāʾī [the Muʿtazilī thinker whose followers are called the Bahshamiyya] argue that an individual or a group invented it (*waḍaʿaha*) and learning it was acquired by indication and associations, just as it is with children.
> The *Ustād* [Abu Isḥāq al-Isfarāʾīnī] said: the amount which is needed to understand [the *lugha*] is [simply] declared [by God], and the rest is derived [therefrom].
> The Qāḍī [al-Bāqillānī] said: they are all possible.
> The obvious[ly correct – *al-ẓāhir*] position is that of al-Ashʿarī.[18]

For Ibn al-Ḥājib the view that God taught language is clear from revelatory sources (such as God explaining that he "taught Adam the names, all of them" (Q2/al-Baqara.30). The alternative view that language is a human invention, argued by Abū Hāshim, is supported by the verse "We have not sent a prophet other than with the language of his people" (Q14/Ibrāhīm.4), indicating language pre-existing a prophet's arrival and having been invented by the people to whom he was sent. For al-Ḥillī, as for many Uṣūlīs, the matter is not so clear cut, though he considers attributing the invention to God as the "stronger" position.[19] For both thinkers, however, the linking of sound and meaning is secure because of the historical event of *waḍʿ*:

> If God is the originator [of language, *al-wāḍiʿ*], then his specification [of meaning to vocable] is like his specification of the creation of the world at the time of its creation. If it was a human being, then he specifies it, keeping in his mind that vocable and no other, at that point in time – just as [humans] do with names.[20]

The vocable-meaning link is like the proper names we give to human beings. Notwithstanding the folk notion that given names influence character, a naming is an arbitrary event, chosen by the family on a whim.

Now, if the sound-meaning link was created by God, one might think it was

16 See Weiss, "Medieval Muslim Discussions"; in philological and comparative context, see Shah, "Philological Endeavours Pts I and II".
17 Yunis Ali, *Medieval Islamic Pragmatics*, pp. 15–34.
18 Ibn al-Ḥājib, *Mukhtaṣar*, v. 1, p. 269.
19 Ḥillī, *Nihāyat*, v. 1, p. 158.
20 Ḥillī, *Nihāyat*, v. 1, p. 152.

stronger than any human-made link. The aura of divine connection between sound and meaning could encourage the view that diversion from the divinely ordained (literal) meaning is somehow a deviation from God's created intention.[21] However, postulating that God originally established the vocable-meaning connection does not necessarily lead to strict literalism in this sense. Ibn al-Ḥājib and al-Ḥillī, at least in terms of their legal hermeneutics, are equally eager to assert the validity of non-literal interpretations of texts when the circumstances demand them. Similarly, the Muʿtazila, as is well known, were prone to promoting "non-literal" interpretations of God's words, as literal interpretation led to anthropomorphism.[22] However, this was not because God did, or did not, have a hand in language's invention; rather it was because anthropomorphism (in their view) was rationally incoherent and could not possibly be what God meant when he said he had a hand or sat on a throne. Not all Muʿtazila followed the Bahshamiyya's position of language being simply a human invention, and those that argued this view were not noticeably more "literalist" in their interpretation of rationally problematic Quranic dicta. In the end, it was more important for most Uṣūlīs that the sound-meaning connection was established than who actually established it, since the existence of language as a linguistic code in which sounds/words had meanings attached to them was an assumption on which all subsequent discussion was based. The fact of language's existence mattered more than its origins.

The basic unit of analysis when examining language is, then, the vocable (*lafẓ*) because, as Ibn al-Ḥājib states, "every vocable has been assigned a meaning" (*kull lafẓ wuḍiʿa li-maʿnā*).[23] Being assigned a meaning makes a vocable what it is: after assignation, it is different from a simple sound; by this act of *waḍʿ*, it has a meaning and has been incorporated into the linguistic code, the *lugha*. The Uṣūlīs noticed that vocables are of different types in the *lugha*. Two are to be distinguished at the outset: simple and compound. Simple utterances (*mufrad*) are single-word utterances (for example "house") in which the thing which was assigned the sound (the building itself; "the combination of walls and roofs", as Ḥillī puts it)[24] is "indicated" or "signified" (*dalla*) by the sound.[25] These simple utterances can be names of things (*ism*: "house"), verbs (*fiʿl*: designating an action, for example "run") or particles (*ḥarf*: designating a relation between things such as the preposition "in"). The difference between these three elements relates to their ability to indicate something independently. A particle (such as the preposition "in") cannot "independently" indicate something – its meaning is relational in that it requires other elements

21 This seems implicit in Ibn Ḥazm's championing of God being the agent of language creation; see below, pp. 150–4.

22 On Muʿtazilī theological hermeneutics and their non-literalism in the early period, see Gimaret, *Une Lecture mu'tazilite de Coran.*

23 Ibn al-Ḥājib, *Mukhtaṣar*, v. 1, p. 220.

24 Ḥillī, *Nihāyat*, v. 1, p. 172.

25 For a thorough discussion of "signification" in classical *uṣūl al-fiqh*, see Yunis Ali, *Medieval Islamic Pragmatics*, pp. 141–233.

(names and verbs) to indicate (that is, something has to be "in" something else). A name indicates a specified thing (perhaps at a specific place), but not a time at which the thing exists or happens ("house": we know the sort of thing being indicated, but we do not know what is being said about it). Lastly, without a verb the time is unspecified (*al-zamān hunā ghayr muʿayyan*, as al-Ḥillī puts it); a verb specifies (*yataʿayyan*).[26]

Most of the time the indication process occurs on a "one sound/one meaning" relationship. Sometimes, however, there is a one sound/two (or more) meaning relationship and a homonym is created (*mushtarak*). Other times there is a two (or more) sounds/one meaning relationship, and a synonym is created (*mutarādif*). Compound vocables (*murakkab*) are when more than a single meaning is indicated by the vocable (which can be made up of a single word or a combination of words). So, for example, *yaḍribu* (he hits) is a single word in Arabic, but is nonetheless compound because it contains more than a single meaning. In this single utterance there is the notion of the third person masculine single ("he"), the present tense (the action is happening in the present) and the meaning of the verb (hitting). A compound vocable can be broken down and different elements of meaning (but not necessarily sound) can be recognised.

In both classes of vocable, simple and compound, there is a process envisaged whereby the vocable "indicates" or "signifies" a meaning or an idea – the indication process is termed *dalāla* in the *uṣūl* texts and is the mechanism whereby a sound is linked to an idea or a meaning (*maʿnā*). Once established, these meanings are considered to exist within the vocable: they are all "present" in a text, for example, which is made up of many individual vocables. If one considers the vocable as an individual instantiation of the linguistic system known as the *lugha*, one does not need to go outside of or beyond the vocable in order to discover its meaning. A vocable's meaning precedes any particular instance of use by a language user, and is therefore a meaning free of context: it is the first element of the mature *uṣūlī* linguistic theory which resonates with our notion of literality. Al-Ḥillī describes the three ways in which a word's indication or signification of a meaning might occur, replicating the categorisation found in most works of *uṣūl al-fiqh*. In these discussions it is not always clear whether the Uṣūlīs are describing the meaning which the hearer could derive from the vocable alone, or what the vocable means in and of itself (that is, through *waḍʿ*). The former would assume a context and, it could be argued, is outside of the literal meaning discussed here:

> [1] A vocable could indicate the meaning by means of what it was assigned to. In this case, the indication is equivalent (*muṭābaqa*) – like "house" which is assigned to the combination of walls and roof.

This first would appear the simplest way in which the vocable-meaning connection is conceived – a simple equivalence. The vocable "house" signifies the idea of a

26 Ḥillī, *Nihāyat*, v. 1, p. 177.

collection of walls and a roof. But the Uṣūlīs conceived of other ways of indication and signification:

> [2] [A vocable could indicate the meaning] by means of something within what it was assigned, and in this case the indication is "inclusive" (*tamannin*), like the signification of house to one of its two parts.

This inclusive signification is a little more obscure: it appears to mean that the vocable house refers to the idea/meaning of a house, which in turn necessarily implies the ideas/meanings of walls and a roof. Therefore the individual elements are also signified by the vocable house even though individually they do not mean house. Ḥillī moves on to the third type of signification:

> [3] [A vocable could indicate the meaning] by means of what it necessitates (*luzūmihi*) when it was assigned, and this is called necessary indication (*dalālat al-iltizām*) … as in when the roof indicates the walls.[27]

The vocable "roof" is assigned to the meaning/idea of a roof, but in order to have a roof, you must have a wall: the idea of a roof necessitates the idea of a wall (that is, without walls you would never have roofs, as a roof is a thing which is defined as sitting on top of walls). This is why the relationship between roof and wall is described as "necessary" or "obligated". The meaning of roof is dependent on the separate idea of wall.

The relevance of these rather rarefied discussions for our understanding of literal meaning relates to whether the process of indication described here is considered linguistic or logical/rational. A vocable like "house" is conceived of being attached in the linguistic system to a pre-existent idea (a meaning: *maʿnā*). Included in this idea are additional ideas such as roof; the idea of roof logically necessitates another separate idea, namely walls (the fact that wall is also included in the idea of house is not my point here). Is all of this to be included in the linguistic act of assigned a meaning to a vocable and therefore part of the meaning which inheres in the word "house" (that is, the literal meaning)? The Uṣūlīs answer is, in the main, that these additional elements are not part of the original designation in the *waḍʿ*: the only element of signification which forms part of the assignment of a vocable to a meaning is the "equivalence signification" (*dalāla muṭābaqa*). The other elements are not purely part of the assignment (*waḍʿ*), but include elements of rational deduction. As al-Ḥillī puts it, "The *muṭābaqa* is purely established (*waḍʿiyya ṣirfiyya*). The other two are a combination (*mushārika*) of *waḍʿ* and *ʿaql*."[28] That is, the only meaning or idea which the vocable "house" is "placed on", or "associated with", or "coined for" (all possible translations of *waḍaʿa*) is the idea of house. The constituent elements of a house such as a roof, and, by extension, the items entailed by such a thing as a roof (that is, a wall) – all of these are not purely linguistic features but are formed out of

27 Ḥillī, *Nihāyat*, v. 1, p. 172.
28 Ḥillī, *Nihāyat*, v. 1, p. 172.

a combination of language and rationality. They therefore do not form part of the designation process, and, I would argue, do not form an important element of our investigation of the literal meaning of a term such as "house". This question of the coverage of the designation (that is, whether types of *dalāla* other than *muṭābaqa* are part of the *waḍʿ*) reappears when certain exegetical processes are discussed, and debates emerge over whether they are purely linguistic inferences or examples of analogical reasoning (*qiyās*).[29]

Literal Meaning in Language Use

The Uṣūlīs' prime focus was understanding the manner in which the language system was used by individuals, as understanding this would enable interpreters to comprehend God's meaning when he addresses (*khiṭāb*) his servants. The infrastructure of the *lugha* just described is, then, really an introduction to the task of interpreting God's words because, as has already been mentioned, God is thought to have spoken using the *lugha*, whether or not he was its inventor. Works of *uṣūl al-fiqh* focus on pairs of technical terms used to describe particular phenomena found in language use. These form a matrix through which discourse can be analysed, and its meaning deduced. The aim of the exercise is not, however, to lay out a mechanism whereby the meanings of the vocables, strung together to form texts, might themselves be known, but rather to discover the intended meaning of the speaker (*murād*) who has uttered these vocables. That is, they are not interested in the literal meaning except in so far as it might aid them in understanding what it is the speaker intends to convey. Ideas linked to what we have been calling the literal meaning come into play and feature in the *uṣūl* discussions in as much as they help the interpreter to deduce this intended meaning. There are, of course, theological considerations to take into account here. That God "wills" a particular meaning in a particular utterance raises the question of God's attribute of willing or wanting, and whether or not this attribute is separate from God's essence. Adjunct to this is the idea of God's inner speech (*kalām nafsī*) and its temporal expression in the Qurʾān, which formed the so-called orthodox position associated with al-Ashʿarī.[30] The opponents of al-Ashʿarī, the Muʿtazilīs, saw the Qurʾān as a direct temporal action of God and ended up requiring God to provide definite meaning within the revelatory texts. Whilst these positions affected the evaluation and assessment of the literal meaning, they did not always impact upon its conception. That is, all conceived of the literal

29 See below. As Yunis Ali has demonstrated, there is much debate amongst Uṣūlīs about which types of *dalāla* are entirely *lafẓī* (i.e. present in the text prior to instantiation and context modifying meaning) and which contain external (*khārij*) elements. That there is a meaning in the text is, perhaps, more significant for our purposes here. See his *Medieval Islamic Pragmatics*, pp. 159–87.

30 Vishanoff argues that the conception of an inner speech enables Ashʿarīs to maintain the ambiguity of revelation, as the actual textual expression was seen as quite separate from the will. See, for example, his *The Formation*, pp. 156–8; pp. 172–4.

meaning in a similar way; the dispute emerges when describing the strength of that meaning in relation to other meanings.[31]

Normally, the first pair of hermeneutic terms which are addressed in works of *uṣūl* are *ḥaqīqa* and *majāz*. The term *ḥaqīqa* in works of *uṣūl al-fiqh* has been seen as a candidate for literality.[32] It is important, though, to recognise that the term *ḥaqīqa* itself refers in classical *uṣūl al-fiqh* primarily to the way a vocable has been employed by a speaker rather than the meaning of that vocable:

> [Ibn al-Ḥājib]: *Ḥaqīqa* is the vocable which is used in [accordance with its] primary (or first) coining (*waḍʿ awwal*).[33]

The linking of a vocable to a meaning in the linguistic system before being uttered (that is, in the *waḍʿ*) establishes the attachment. If a speaker then intends this meaning when uttering the vocable, the utterance is classed as *ḥaqīqa*.[34] *Ḥaqīqa*, as a category, does not, then, describe a meaning as such but a type of language use, in which the speaker intends to convey the same meaning as the word's own meaning.[35] If the speaker intends, by using the vocable, to convey some meaning other than the one assigned to it, then the utterance is classed as *majāz*. *Majāz* – which we can gloss by the uninformative negative "non-literal usage" – covers a wide range of matters, some of which are addressed below.[36] Al-Ḥillī uses the philosophical terminology of accident and essence to describe *ḥaqīqa* and *majāz*:[37] "*Ḥaqīqa* and *majāz* are accidents (*ʿawāriḍ*) of the vocables" rather than essential to them. A word is used in a *ḥaqīqa* or *majāz* manner; the meaning assigned to it during the act of *waḍʿ* is somehow linked, after *waḍʿ*, to the vocable's essence (*dhāt*), since (as has already been mentioned) without this act of assignment, the vocable is merely a sound. As Ibn al-Ḥājib puts it, "the vocable, before use, is neither *ḥaqīqa* nor *majāz*" (*al-lafẓ qabl al-istiʿmāl laysa bi-ḥaqīqa wa-lā majāz*).[38] The term *ḥaqīqa*, etymologically linked to notions of right, truth and worthiness, was presumably chosen as the term because it indicated a level of surety on the part of an interpreter. If an utterance is *ḥaqīqa*, the hearer is on solid ground in his attempt to ascertain the speaker's meaning; in the utterance in question, the words are intended to mean what they

31 See my "*Ta'khīr al-Bayān*" for further details.

32 See, for example, Heinrichs, "On the Genesis", p. 115; Yunis Ali, *Medieval Islamic Pragmatics*, p. 27 and *passim*; Vishanoff, *The Formation*, pp. 165–6; Gully, *Grammar and Semantics in Medieval Arabic*, p. 39, amongst many other examples.

33 Ibn al-Ḥājib, *Mukhtaṣar*, v. 1, p. 233.

34 Seeing *ḥaqīqa* as describing a meaning rather than a usage (as is done in some secondary literature, for example Schwarb, "Capturing the Meanings", p. 134) is easily done given the acceptance of a slippage from use to meaning found in some *uṣūl* manuals; see below, pp. 41 and 45.

35 Under the influence of Wittgenstein, modern philosophers have become accustomed to thinking of the meaning of a word being linked to its use. See above, pp. 21–2.

36 See below, pp. 42–4.

37 Ḥillī, *Nihāyat*, v. 1, p. 266.

38 Ibn al-Ḥājib, *Mukhtaṣar*, v. 1, p. 237.

were assigned to mean, making *ḥaqīqa* ("true", "real")[39] a neat terminological fit for this category.[40]

Whilst the term *ḥaqīqa* is reserved as a kind of adverbial description of language use rather than vocable meaning, the phrase *al-maʿnā al-ḥaqīqī* is occasionally found in *uṣūl* texts. It appears to mean the same thing as *al-maʿnā al-waḍʿī*, or *al-maʿnā al-mawḍūʿ* (both of which refer to the meaning assigned to a word in the *waḍʿ*). Phrases such as *al-maʿnā al-ḥaqīqī* have, of course, the connotations of the "true" meaning of a word, a meaning independent of the speaker's intended meaning.[41] Having said this, there is certainly a slippage within the works of *uṣūl al-fiqh* from the strict restriction of *ḥaqīqa* as a description of a term's use to a description of the term's designated meaning (to which I return below in relation to the *ḥaqīqa* of the verbal form of a command).[42]

Ibn al-Ḥājib identifies three types of *ḥaqīqa* usage:

> [The *ḥaqīqa*] is linguistic (*lughawī*) or customary (*ʿurfī*) or legal (*sharʿī*) like the lion, beast and prayer.[43]

The examples described by the coded references to "lion, beast and prayer" are:

1. When a certain predatory feline is described as a lion, this is the meaning it was assigned in the *lugha* and hence when used in this way the expression is

39 Al-Ḥillī, perhaps dryly, observes that *ḥaqīqa* and *majāz* are actually *majāz* usages themselves when describing these categories of meaning: *Nihāyat*, v. 1, p. 242.

40 Bernard Weiss is the only scholar to date to embark on a comprehensive reflective examination of whether or not the term "literal" is an appropriate translation for *ḥaqīqa*, as they are used in *uṣūl al-fiqh*. In his study of al-Āmidī's *al-Iḥkām fī uṣūl al-aḥkām*, Weiss assesses the position of *ḥaqīqa* in al-Āmidī's legal hermeneutics, and whilst it is linked to the idea of the literal meaning, it is not exactly the literal meaning. Al-Āmidī's definition is, naturally, similar to that of Ibn al-Ḥājib: "a vocable is used to convey the meaning to which it was originally assigned [*waḍʿ*] as an item within the lexical code [that is to say within the *lugha*]" (see also Weiss, *The Search*, p. 134). The similarity in wording here should not be surprising – Ibn al-Ḥājib is, of course, providing a summary (*Mukhtaṣar*) of one of al-Āmidī's other *uṣūl* texts, the *Muntahā*). Here, it might be said that the use of *ḥaqīqa* to refer only to expressions differs with the summary of the classical position given by Heinrichs. Heinrichs glosses the term *ḥaqīqa* as "the literal, proper, veridical meaning or use of a given word" (Heinrichs, "On the Genesis", p. 115), giving the impression that in the classical theory, *ḥaqīqa* is used to describe meanings as well as uses (i.e. expressions). Whilst it might be convenient to talk of the "*ḥaqīqa* meaning" of a word or expression, what is really meant by such a phrase is, in al-Āmidī's theory, "the assigned" meaning of the word (*al-mawḍūʿ lahu*). This is the meaning which has been assigned to a sound in the *lugha* and it is this assigned meaning which is the "literal" meaning of a word for Weiss. In this respect al-Āmidī is representative of the *uṣūl* tradition as a whole: an expression is *ḥaqīqa* when a word is used by a speaker to mean the same thing as the assigned/literal meaning. *Ḥaqīqa* describes the use of the word, rather than the meaning, which hints at a medieval understanding of the formal and functional understanding of meaning in modern linguistics (see Yunis Ali, *Medieval Islamic Pragmatics*, p. 15). As with Ibn al-Ḥājib and al-ʿAllāma al-Ḥillī, al-Āmidī's theory is based on the notion (made explicit in the text of the *Iḥkām*) that a word's use is quite different from a word's meaning, in that the former relates to the intended meaning of the speaker, whilst the latter is bound up with the position of the word within the *lugha*.

41 See, for example, Rāzī, *al-Maḥṣūl*, v. 1, p. 349.

42 See below, pp. 45–7; it has been noticed by Weiss, *The Search*, p. 346.

43 Ibn al-Ḥājib, *Mukhtaṣar*, v. 1, p. 243.

ḥaqīqa. It is used to refer to brave people on occasion, but these uses are decidedly not *ḥaqīqa*.

2. Also *ḥaqīqa* are occasions when words may have been given one meaning within the *lugha* (*dābba* = walking animal) but have come to mean something else through prevalent usage (*dābba* = beast). The meaning in customary use has become so ubiquitous that its use is now considered *ḥaqīqa* rather than a non-literal (*majāz*) usage.[44]
3. Finally, the case of *ṣalāt* which, through a designation by God in revelation, came to mean not simply "prayer" but specifically the obligatory prayer of the Muslims, consisting of prostration sequences and is obligatory on a daily basis.

There is some debate as to whether categories 2 and 3 really exist as examples of *ḥaqīqa* usage; some scholars insist these categories ultimately remain *majāz* usages of the expressions in question.[45] To begin with customary *ḥaqīqa*, al-ʿAllāma al-Ḥillī's description of *al-ḥaqīqa al-ʿurfiyya* is remarkably frank about the artificiality of the process here:

> You should know that meanings might appear which have no way of being referenced, for which there are no vocables within the *lugha*, just as we have already shown. So there is a need to invent vocables for them. However, since they disapproved of going beyond the rules of the *lugha*, they resorted to adopting a way whereby the attainment of their desire and the requirement of the rules of the *lugha* were combined. They assigned to each word which was already designated a [new] meaning which was appropriate to it, and for which they were seeking a reference. They transferred [the new meaning] to the word ... When their usage of the second meaning became common place, it became customarily *ḥaqīqa* ... and when the first one became neglected, the usage of the word in this [original manner] became customarily *majāz*, even if it was linguistically *ḥaqīqa*. There is no debate that this is permitted. There is only debate over whether it has happened, and the truth is that it has.[46]

He goes on to say that *ʿurf* can make certain everyday expressions *ḥaqīqa* which are, from a linguistic perspective, deficient in terms of communicating the speaker's intended meaning: they are not (linguistically speaking) *ḥaqīqa*. For example, one category is titled:

> "the ellipsis of the first part of the genitive, but the maintenance of the second". For

44 The reader should recall al-Rāzī's phrase *al-majāz fi'l-lugha walakinnahu ḥaqīqa fi'l-ʿurf* to describe the perspectival aspect of the literal/non-literal distinction. See above, p. 24.

45 I return to the modern debate around *ḥaqāʾiq sharʿiyya* below, pp. 175–96. Some held that God's designation makes words such as *ṣalāt* (supplication generally, Muslim prayer specifically) homonyms; others argued for a continued privileging for the *lughawī* meaning over *sharʿī* and *ʿurfī*; it could be that it is not that new meanings are assigned to vocables, but that new *ḥaqīqa* usages are assigned – which broadens the idea of *ḥaqīqa* to mean not only "words used in accordance with their assigned meaning" but also "words which appear to the language user as if they are used in accordance with their assigned/literal meaning, even though they may not be". This is perhaps what al-Rāzī means by saying that a usage which is *majāz* with respect to the *lugha* is *ḥaqīqa* with respect to *ʿurf*. See above, p. 24, n. 70.

46 Ḥillī, *Nihāyat*, v. 1, p. 244.

> example, "wine is forbidden", when, by *ḥaqīqa*, there is a first part of the genitive which is "drinking" [that is, "drinking wine is forbidden"].[47]

All people understand the phrase *taḥrīm al-khamr* (the prohibition of wine) to mean *taḥrīm shurb al-khamr* (the prohibition of the drinking of wine). Similarly *al-ghāʾiṭ*, which means a hollow in the ground, is taken to mean urination or defecation, because the place is associated (*mutaʿallaq*) with the act. The thinking here is presumably that prevalence of this usage in everyday speech means that understanding the phrase now occurs without computation. It occurs immediately in the mind (*tabādur*, an idea already mentioned).[48] Allowing "customary literal usage" (*ḥaqīqa ʿurfiyya*), then, permits modification of the vocable-meaning relationships through deliberate subsequent acts of designation and their subsequent adoption by the language community. These deliberate changes to designation, however, appear to begin life as *majāz* usages, and then, as they become popular, they "become" (*ṣāra*) customarily *ḥaqīqa*. The *ḥaqīqa* category, then, is now available for modification by initial designation followed by currency within the community. That the literal is somehow linked to the accepted language use of the current (rather than primordial) community will be discussed later.[49] Within this category of "literal" usage established through custom, non-literal meanings of vocables can be seen as *ḥaqīqa*.[50] In order for these to be instances of *ḥaqīqa* usage, there must be envisaged a second act of *waḍʿ* whereby new meanings are assigned to vocables.

The category of *al-ḥaqīqa al-sharʿiyya* is a yet further mechanism for the modification of the original *waḍʿ* meanings, though here there is an identifiable instigator of the new meaning, namely God himself. Al-Ḥillī records that "there is an agreement that [*ḥaqīqa sharʿiyya*] is possible. There is only debate about whether it has actually happened."[51] Some Ashʿarīs (including al-Bāqillānī), he recounts, deny its existence – so for them the word *ṣalāt* had the specific meaning of Muslim ritual prayer in the originally designated code of the *lugha* (or perhaps it gained it through the designation plus currency mechanism of *ḥaqīqa ʿurfiyya*). The Muʿtazilīs accept the category of *al-ḥaqīqa al-sharʿiyya* absolutely and envisage actual occasions of "transference" of meaning effected by revelation: for prayer, there is transference from supplication generally (*duʿā*) to the obligatory prayer (*ṣalāt*); for *zakāt*, from purity to the payment of a specific amount as alms; for *ḥajj*, from "wishing" or "wanting" to the specified pilgrimage of the Muslims.

47 Ḥillī, *Nihāyat*, v. 1, p. 244.

48 Mentioned above, p. 10, and discussed in more detail below, pp. 42–3 and pp. 110–11.

49 See below, pp. 112–16.

50 The category is reminiscent of aspects of Recanati's p-literal meaning, which can, as he argues, include figurative meanings. A figurative meaning can be p-literal because language users will recognise it as the meaning in the utterance and distinguished from any implication. Recanati might term this p-literal with internal duality: his example is "the ATM swallowed the bank card", which is figurative (the ATM cannot swallow like a living being), so there is duality here, but it is p-literal in that the meaning is immediately available. This is to be distinguished from metaphorical use, where the meaning is less available; see above, p. 19.

51 Ḥillī, *Nihāyat*, v. 1, p. 246.

It is interesting that in the introduction of categories of post-(original) *waḍʿ* *ḥaqīqa*, the Uṣūlīs are forced to modify the authority of the original *waḍʿ*. One might legitimately ask why it is necessary to invent these categories, since the *uṣūl* works also contain extensive sections on the perfectly acceptable category of *majāz* expressions.[52] Almost all Uṣūlīs were eager to establish customary and divinely designated meaning as coming about through a new instance of *waḍʿ*: old words were now used with new meanings in a literal (rather than non-literal) manner. There were those who denied that God might speak in a *majāz* manner, perceiving *majāz* usage as somehow less than ideal (and, for some, *majāz* is simply lying). Whilst the controversy with these *majāz* deniers was effectively won before the full elaboration of the *uṣūl* genre in the late tenth century CE,[53] there was still a feeling amongst some Uṣūlīs of an inferiority in *majāz* usage. Even though complex theories of non-literal meaning existed and were promulgated within *uṣūl al-fiqh*, the Uṣūlīs would rather expand literal usage to include these other types of *ḥaqīqa* than leave them as *majāz*.[54]

Whilst our focus here is on literal meaning and literal usage, a note is appropriate on how our authors approach non-literal usage. *Majāz* is not simply the use of a word in a manner at variance with the assigned meaning. For our authors there must be a connection between the literal meaning and the *majāz* usage. Using the classic example, one calls a brave man a lion because lions are generally recognised as brave. If there is no connection, then it should be assumed to be a homonym, in which a vocable has two meanings in the *lugha*, with no connection between them (the example used is *ʿayn*, meaning both "spring" and "eye" – although even here a relationship could be constructed):

> [Ibn al-Ḥājib]: *Majāz* is a [vocable] used not [in accordance with its] primary assignment, in a manner which is sound, and there must be a connection (*ʿalāqa*).[55]

The connection, for al-Ḥillī, must be one of "likeness" or "resemblance" (*mushābaha*): one calls a stupid person a donkey because, like a donkey, he is stupid. Without this quality, it cannot be considered a case of *majāz*.[56] In any particular circumstance, the interpreter has to assess whether the speaker intends a meaning

52 On which, see below, pp. 194–5.

53 Isolated cases remain, such as that of Ibn Taymiyya, although, as we have already argued, his anti-*majāz* stance emerges from a quite sophisticated communication theory; see above, p. 22.

54 The expansion of the category of literal meaning and literal usage – the colonisation of areas of language use previously thought to be non-literal – is not unique to Muslim legal theory; see, for example, Minnis, "Quadruplex Sensus, Multiplex Modus" (with reference also to the work of Beryl Smalley, *The Study of the Bible*). Even though the full-blooded promotion of the literal meaning is seen as dangerously uncompromising by the mainstream hermeneutic tradition, that tradition still wishes to assert the primacy of the literal, and it does this by expanding the category to cover new instances, previously thought to be non-literal. This can also be seen in the development of hermeneutic principles within Muslim legal theory where the primacy of the literal (be it *ḥaqīqa* or the "designated meaning") is put forward as a principle whereby the interpretive enterprise might proceed. See below, pp. 42–4.

55 Ibn al-Ḥājib, *Mukhtaṣar*, v. 1, pp. 233–4.

56 Ḥillī, *Nihāyat*, v. 1, p. 265.

which is connected to the literal assigned meaning (because of a likeness) but is not identical with the assigned meaning. He or she does this by means of external signs or indicators (*qarāʾin*, singular: *qarīna*). Sometimes, the sentence does not make sense if one assumes literal usage (how could a human being be a donkey or a lion?) and our lack of comprehension is, itself, a *qarīna*, a piece of evidence that what is intended here is not the literal meaning: "an utterance which does not make sense except with *qarīna* is *majāz*".[57] Other qarinas are part of the context in which the speaker is addressing, and therefore external to the *waḍʿ*: "the *qarīna* is not assigned (*mawḍūʿa*) such that the combination (of the words and the *qarīna*) makes a single utterance which indicates an assignment".[58] Non-literal usage can come in various forms, according to al-Ḥillī, the most simple division being between individual transferences (lion: brave man; donkey: idiot). It can also happen in a compound manner (*tarkīb*), according to al-Ḥillī:

> Each one of two [or more] words is used in its *maʿnā ḥaqīqī*, but the compound is not equivalent [to the assigned meanings].[59]

This passage is interesting partly because it signals the use of the term *maʿnā ḥaqīqī* for literal (assigned) meaning, which demonstrates the slippage from *ḥaqīqa* being a feature of language use to it being a description of word meaning. More significantly, it reveals a point of difference between our two authors, and within the *uṣūlī* and literary community generally. Ibn al-Ḥājib states categorically that "*majāz* is in simple words, and not in compound [utterances]". This is counted as an unusual opinion by the great Tāj al-dīn al-Subkī (d. 771/1369).[60] Al-Ḥillī gives the following example:

> "They turned the young men's hair white and annihilated the old men, the attack of the morning and the passing of the evening."
> Each one of these individual words is used in its assigned manner, but connecting the attack of the morning to the idea of it "turning the hair white" is not *haqīqī*, because it [turning hair white] is actually done by God.[61]

Once one knows that *majāz* exists as a phenomenon within language use, one needs a mechanism whereby the *ḥaqīqa* might be distinguished from the *majāz*. That is, how is one to deduce from a specific instance of language use, in which vocables are used, whether the speaker is intending something other than the literal meaning? Al-Ḥillī usefully catalogues twelve means whereby *ḥaqīqa* and *majāz* usage might be recognised. They are well-known mechanisms whereby *ḥaqīqa* usage is identified in classic *uṣūl al-fiqh*. It may well be known that literal meanings came about through the act of *waḍʿ*, but scrutinising this act is no longer possible. The community in the present time can only find out the literal meaning through identifying instances of

57 Ḥillī, *Nihāyat*, v. 1, p. 266.
58 Ḥillī, *Nihāyat*, v. 1, p. 266.
59 Ḥillī, *Nihāyat*, v. 1, p. 272.
60 Ibn al-Ḥājib, *Mukhtaṣar*, v. 1, p. 238; Subkī, *Ibhāj*, v. 1, p. 295.
61 Ḥillī, *Nihāyat*, v. 1, p. 272.

ḥaqīqa usage. The tests for *ḥaqīqa* usage found on al-Ḥillī's list are, in effect, the ways in which the present community can gain knowledge that an act of *waḍʿ* took place in the past and that an expression under examination is *ḥaqīqa*. It should be said that al-Ḥillī does not agree that – or at least doubts whether – all of these tests are entirely effective, but they are a good summary of the various (debated) elements of the *ḥaqīqa* in *uṣūl*. I paraphrase the tests here:

1. If the "people of the *lugha*" (*ahl al-lugha*) declare that the instigator of language has designated this as *ḥaqīqa*, then it is *ḥaqīqa*. Here authority is given to a diachronic community of language users, and implicitly those who are experts in the language spoken by that community.[62] The innate expertise of the speakers and experts in the language is the deciding factor.
2. "When they hear the vocable stripped of any context and a meaning appears in the understanding of the *ahl al-lugha*, then this makes it *ḥaqīqa* – because if it was not the assigned meaning (*al-mawḍūʿ lahu*) but something else was, then it would not appear in their understanding."[63] Here the (expert) language users' unreflective understanding is taken as an indication of literal usage (and therefore literal meaning). What appears in the minds of the *ahl al-lugha* is viewed as particularly authoritative since their minds have been saturated with proper language use:[64] they do not simply have expertise in the language (as a science) but are living witnesses to its proper (that is, literal) understanding. As mentioned above, the merging of *ḥaqīqa* meaning with *waḍʿ* meaning in the terminology of the Uṣūlīs probably appears as an abbreviation of the imagined circumstance in which an utterance takes place but without context, and is discussed below in relation to the "literal" meaning of the imperative form. For Ibn Taymiyya, of course, it would seem impossible for the *ahl al-lugha* to "hear" a context-free utterance, because the act of hearing situates them at a particular time and space.[65] The test is clearly a continuation (and restriction) of the more populist (and possibly earlier) notion that "the thing that occurs in the mind" is the literal meaning, or, as expressed here, "an indication of *ḥaqīqa* usage" (*al-tabādur dalīl al-ḥaqīqa*).[66]

62 There is an ambiguity concerning the referent of the "*ahl al-lugha*", both here and elsewhere. It could refer to the current speakers of the language (the reference to the *ahl al-lugha* "hearing" a vocable in real time in the next test might indicate that); it could refer to some past community of language users (the idealised *al-ʿarab*, perhaps, and the third test could be reference to such a community); it could refer to the current experts in the *lugha*, or to those who maintain the "original" Arabic (and this test would seem to indicate this). Al-Ḥillī is not specific, and perhaps the ambiguity is convenient. The general trend, as I recognise it in works of *uṣūl*, is to identify the *ahl al-lugha* as contemporary experts with increasing explicitness. See Weiss, *The Search*, p. 144: *ahl al-lugha* are "the people upon whom we rely for a knowledge of the Lugha and who were themselves noted exemplars of correct usage of the Lugha". The tendency to restrict access to literal meaning to experts, and its link with the promotion of scholarly authority, is discussed below, p. 195.

63 Ḥillī, *Nihāyat*, v. 1, p. 292; cf. Searle's summary of literal meaning (see above, p. 23).

64 See Carpintero's notion of knowledge of utterance meaning coming through "semantic intuitions", "Gricean Rational Reconstructions", p. 127, n. 2.

65 See Yunis Ali, *Medieval Islamic Pragmatics*, pp. 110–11.

66 Ḥillī, *Nihāyat*, v. 1, p. 294

Here, though, rather than all community members having subjective (and hence equal) authority, it is only the *ahl al-lugha* who determine literal meaning.

3. When the *ahl al-lugha* use a word on its own, with the aim of having it understood for a specific meaning, and then use it again with a different meaning but this time they supply external indicators (*qarāʾin*) indicating that a different meaning is intended, then we know that the first is *ḥaqīqa* and the second is *majāz*.
4. If an utterance appears to indicate an impossibility, then it is *majāz*.[67] If not, then it could be *ḥaqīqa*. The example given is the famous "ask the village" example,[68] which would imply asking buildings but means, of course, asking the people of the village.
5. When the *ahl al-lugha* designate a meaning to a vocable, and cease using it on some occasions with that meaning, and then begin using it on other occasions with other meanings, then you know that the second usage is *majāz*. This is clearly the preferred criterion of those who deny the possibility of newly designated meaning (*al-ḥaqīqa al-sharʿiyya*).
6. If there is coherence in a statement, then it is *ḥaqīqa*; incoherence means it is *majāz*.[69]
7. If it is impossible to trace the meaning proposed for a vocable to its linguistic roots (a process known as *ishtiqāq*), then this is a sign of it being *majāz*. If it is possible, then this is a sign of it being *ḥaqīqa*. The point here is that etymology can indicate *ḥaqīqa* usage.[70]
8. If a name is designated to something other than whatever is being referred to in this instance, then this is a sign that its usage here is *majāz*.
9. If a *ḥaqīqī* meaning is dependent on the existence of another thing, and that other thing is not present in the utterance, then it must be *majāz*. This is explained by the example of power (*qudra*), which necessarily requires the person who has power to be powerful over something; when they say "consider God's power" in isolation, without referring to the thing over which he has power, then this is supposedly a case of *majāz*.
10. If you can negate the utterance and it remains true, then this is an indication of *majāz*. For example, "that man is a donkey" can be negated and still be true (for he is not actually a donkey).[71]
11. If it is necessary to provide a caveat or explanation, then this is an indication

67 Cf. Grice's "maxim of truthfulness": "Don't say what you believe to be false"; see above, p. 7. If one knows it is impossible, then one knows it to be false, and therefore a non-literal meaning must be intended. See Grice, "Logic and Conversation", p. 46.

68 See above, p. 9.

69 Cf. Grice's assertion that non-literal interpretation kicks in when there is "categorical falsity" (i.e. incoherence): Grice, "Logic and Conversation", p. 53 ("you are the cream in my coffee").

70 Those who guard this knowledge hold the key to the identification of the literal; see below, p. 195.

71 It is open to negation, of course, but clearly understandable; it is what Lasersohn refers to as the "pragmatic slack" in the use of "donkey"; the "halo" around the word "donkey" includes "stupid person" but not, say, "the Tower of London". "It is, I think, not too controversial to claim that speakers frequently say things

of *majāz*; if not, then it is an indication of *ḥaqīqa*. The example given is "the heat of battle", which requires some sort of explanatory note in order to be understood.[72]

12. If a vocable appropriately rests upon something other than the thing named in the vocable, then this is an indication of *majāz*. The example given is "They play tricks, but God plays tricks" (Q3/Al Imran.54): trick playing is appropriate for humans, but not for God (for theological reasons, given God's justice and truthfulness).[73]

These tests are, taken together, an admixture of literal meaning and its identification which emerged during the early period of Muslim thought generally and in Muslim legal theory in particular. They reflect the thought processes which the early Muslim community went through in order to construct the conception of language, its nature and its use outlined here.

Exegetical Pairings in *Uṣūl al-fiqh* and Literal Meaning

In Ibn al-Ḥājib's *Mukhtaṣar*, the pairing of *ḥaqīqa* and *majāz* is located before the discussion of the provenance of the various "sources" or "indicators" of the law. Later in the work there are extensive discussions of matters of linguistic concern, expressed through further exegetical pairings:

orders and prohibitions (*awāmir/nawāhī*)
general and specific statements (*ʿumūm/khuṣūṣ*)
clarity and obscurity (*mubayyan/mujmal*)
apparent and non-apparent usage (*ẓāhir/muʾawwal*)
expressed and implicated (*manṭūq/mafhūm*)
absolute and restricted (*muṭlaq/muqayyad*)

The discussions are obviously linked, and this set of pairings draws on principles and ideas demonstrated in the earlier discussion of *ḥaqīqa* and *majāz*. The reason for splitting the two discussions in some works of *uṣūl* is not explicitly stated but can be surmised. An obvious reason regarding the division in Ibn al-Ḥājib's *Mukhtaṣar* is his source text, the *Muntahā* of al-Āmidī, which he is summarising: the earlier work is structured in this way and he is merely replicating that structure. That simply shifts the question to an explanation of al-Āmidī's structure, which might run as follows: the earlier discussions concern the architecture of the *lugha* and its relationship with language use; the later discussions are concerned with use (almost) exclusively, setting out a hermeneutic method which supposedly provides practical advice on the

---

that are not, strictly speaking, true, and that many such utterances are neither lies nor mistakes, but a completely normal part of honest, error-free discourse" (Lasersohn, "Pragmatic Halos", p. 248).

72 Cf. the idea of discrepancy as an element of recognition of non-literal meaning: Bartsch, "Word Meanings", pp. 31–3; Recanati, *Literal Meaning*, p. 77.

73 Ḥillī, *Nihāyat*, v. 1, pp. 292–8. For the record, al-Ḥillī is not convinced, or expresses doubts, about tests 2, 4, 6, 7, 8 and 9.

interpretation of the revelatory texts. The difference might be analogous to the meaning/reference distinction in modern philosophy.[74] Interestingly, al-ʿAllāma al-Ḥillī feels no need to divide the discussion in this way, and his discussions of the exegetical pairings follow straight on from the *ḥaqīqa/majāz* discussion with an interesting section on "the operation of [language] use" (*fī kayfiyyat al-istiʿmāl*) sandwiched between them. Both structures are evident in the *uṣūl* tradition.

An exhaustive exploration of all these exegetical pairings, even in the two *uṣūl* works selected here, would be lengthy. However, an examination of the role of literal meaning, usage and interpretation within the different discussions will provide an impression at least of its importance to the hermeneutic principles outlined in works of *uṣūl al-fiqh*.

The primary debate within the chapters on orders and prohibitions is, of course, the verbal form of the imperative and what it might be taken as indicating in terms of legal assessment. When God gives an order, usually in the imperative *ifʿal* verbal form in Arabic, is he saying that we must perform the action, or that it would be good if we did, or that we can if we want? Since the *lugha* is seen as a coherent system for communicating meaning, which (if any) of these meanings of the imperative is the "literal" meaning? That a grammatical form (*ṣīgha*) and not only individual vocables may have a meaning which was designated at the point of *waḍʿ* has been mentioned already.[75] Both Ibn al-Ḥājib and al-ʿAllāma al-Ḥillī use the term *ḥaqīqa* in this and the subsequent arguments to mean not only the use but the meaning of this grammatical form. As mentioned above, *ḥaqīqa* has clearly undergone modification as a technical term and no longer means "the usage of a vocable/form in accordance with the meaning assigned to it in the *waḍʿ*" (as Ibn al-Ḥājib describes it earlier), but simply "the meaning assigned to it in the *waḍʿ*". So, in Ibn al-Ḥājib, we have:

> There is dispute amongst the scholars concerning the imperative form "do!" (*ifʿal*). Most say that it is *ḥaqīqa* for obligation; Abū Hāshim [al-Jubbāʾī (d. 321/933)] says it is recommendation.[76]

Here, as elsewhere, *ḥaqīqa* refers not to usage but to meaning: that is, the designated meaning of the imperative form is obligation.[77]

The citations from other Uṣūlīs given by al-ʿAllāma indicate that he is merely falling in with a standard manner of expression in which *ḥaqīqa* refers to *waḍʿī* meaning and not merely "use in conformity with the meaning assigned in the *waḍʿ*". Why this slippage has occurred when technical terms are available (*al-maʿnā al-waḍʿī*; *al-maʿnā al-mawḍūʿ lahu*; even *al-maʿnā al-ḥaqīqī* would avoid the ambiguity) is not clear, though it probably has something to do with the fact that *ḥaqīqa* has

74 See above, pp. 13–14.
75 See above, p. 18.
76 Ibn al-Ḥājib, *Mukhtaṣar*, v. 1, pp. 651–2.
77 On the use of *ḥaqīqa* to refer to a meaning rather than as an adverb describing an instance of language use, see below, p. 37.

connotations outside of the *uṣūl* discourse which make it particularly attractive as a designator of meaning. It seems also possible that it has become a substitute for an imaginary language situation in which there are no contextual factors. In the case of the imperative this is phrased *al-amr al-mujarrad ʿan al-qarāʾin* (the imperative devoid of external indicators), and it forms the starting point for discussions of whether the imperative demands repetitive or immediate action. In such an imaginary example of language use – when there are no *qarāʾin* to aid in the determination of meaning – then the only meaning available to the addressee is the one designated for the vocables and grammatical forms within the utterance: one assumes, then, that this is an instance of *ḥaqīqa* usage. It is possible that when *ḥaqīqa* is being used to designate a meaning, there is no laziness or lack of awareness of a contradiction between this use of the term *ḥaqīqa* and its clearly stipulated reference to usage in the *ḥaqīqa/majāz* discussions. Instead, we have here a form of abbreviation whereby *ḥaqīqa* = meaning is shorthand for "the meaning of the vocable/form in a context devoid of *qarāʾin* and in which *ḥaqīqa* usage is assumed". The positions of the various groups on this question are well known. Some say *ṣīghat al-amr* means obligation "literally" (that is, it was designated as such) and when used to recommend or permit, these are *majāz* usages. Others choose one of the other categories as *ḥaqīqa*, relegating other meanings as *majāz*. Some, such as Ibn al-Ḥājib, opt for none of these, arguing that the imperative form means "the requirement to act without delay from a higher position" – that is, the imperative meant, literally, that the person speaking was assuming a higher position than the addressee, and is requiring the lower person to perform an action. We shall have occasion to return to this discussion; here it is sufficient to note that the debate is over what the literal meaning of the imperative form might be. It is not a debate over how this literal meaning might be known. The method of discovering the literal meaning is similar across the range of opinions (citations from the revelatory texts or from the canonical corpus of poetry, arguments for the absurdity of the opponent's position, thereby reducing the available options to one, and so on). The debates, though, once again demonstrate that literal meaning was the prime hermeneutic battleground. There exists, within classical *uṣūl* works, a perfectly valid and sophisticated method of recognising non-literal usage, and most Uṣūlīs agreed that God and his Prophet do employ non-literal usage regularly throughout the revealed texts. That there is debate reveals the prestige which the hermeneutic system invested in the meaning the text has in and of itself, independent of context, and how this literal meaning, as I have termed it, was seen as primary, with all others being secondary. The preference for the literal meaning reflects a certain epistemological prejudice (the literal meaning is more certain and true), and also an attempt to control the interpretive process. If one can win the argument and establish one's own conception of the literal meaning as the interpreter's default meaning, then other meanings (the "non-literal") will have a harder task establishing themselves as plausible. In this sense, the classical system is literalist, in that it is constructed to give the literal meaning an advantage over its rivals. For this reason, Uṣūlīs argued over what the literal meaning of the imperative form might be when they had a perfectly acceptable alternative of making individual instances of the imperative form non-literal.

The literal/non-literal usage debate is repeated with Uṣūlīs discussing the general and particular forms (*ʿumūm/khuṣūṣ*) and the unrestricted and restricted (*muṭlaq/muqayyad*). The former normally receives the most comprehensive analysis, and relates to the speech which appears in the form of a general reference (for example, "the thief, male and female, cut off their hands": Q5/al-Māʾida.38) but in fact is not of general reference because exceptions to it are known (the Prophet said, "Do not amputate for a quarter of a dinar or less"). So, unless we are going to impute ignorance to God (which is not particularly theologically desirable), then when he said Q5/al-Māʾida.38 he must have meant not all thieves but only those who steal more than a quarter of a dinar. (There are many other exceptions, such as those who steal out of hunger, but a single exception is enough to demonstrate the point.) So, God spoke in one way, but meant another, which would appear to make the phenomenon one of *ḥaqīqa* and *majāz*. Just as was the case with the imperative form (it may mean obligation, but God at times intends recommendation or permission), the general form is viewed by many jurists as having a fixed set of grammatical forms, which all have the literal meaning of general reference. Words like "all" and "whoever" indicate general reference; grammatical forms like plurals ("the Muslims") indicate general reference; and there are other such coded formulations in language. This is the view that is attributed by al-Ḥillī to "the Muʿtazila, Shāfiʿī, and a large number of jurists".[78] For this group, then, when a general reference form is used in a revelatory text but it is clear that the general reference is not meant, then this is *majāz*. For these jurists, general reference is presumed to be the speaker's intended meaning when a general reference form is used. There is a group mentioned by al-Ḥillī who believed the reverse: that the forms which appear to indicate general reference in fact have been designated particular reference; that is, even though "the thief" verse looks like it refers to all thieves, its literal meaning is that it applies to some thieves. If it is to mean all thieves, then *qarāʾin* are required. This rather unusual position is not attributed to anyone in particular. Then there are those (such as, according to one transmission, Abū al-Ḥasan al-Ashʿarī (d. 324/935)) who consider the forms of general reference to be homonyms – that is, they have been assigned, through the *waḍʿ*, two meanings: general reference and specific reference. Finally, there are those (al-Bāqillānī and al-Ashʿarī's other opinion) who suspend an opinion on this, and adopt no default position. Those who have suspended holding an opinion are not, practically speaking, in a very different situation from those who argue for homonymity. For both groups, additional evidence (*qarāʾin*) is necessary before an opinion is formed as to whether an individual instance of a general form indicates a general or specific reference. There are those, whom al-Ḥillī mentions, who argue that general reference has no particular form within the Arabic language (*lughat al-ʿArab*),

78 Ḥillī, *Nihāyat*, v. 2, p. 121.

amongst whom is the great Shīʿī Uṣūlī al-Sayyid al-Murtaḍā (d. 436/1044).[79] For this group, since there is no general reference form, there is no real problem of the literal meaning of those forms and the issues which occupy the pages on *ʿumūm* and *khuṣūṣ* are sidestepped.

The mirroring of questions regarding general and particular reference in the discussions of unqualified and qualified reference is noted by both our authors. Ibn al-Ḥājib states:

> What has been said about particularisation [of general statements], what is agreed upon, what they differ over, what they prefer or dislike, applies here [to *muṭlaq* and *muqayyad*].[80]

Of *muṭlaq* (unqualified), al-Ḥillī and Ibn al-Ḥājib offer similar definitions:

> [Ibn al-Ḥājib]: The *muṭlaq* is that which indicates an individual item generally applicable to its class (*al-muṭlaq mā dalla ʿalā shāʾiʿ fī jinsihi*).[81]
> [al-Ḥillī]: [The *muṭlaq*] is the vocable which indicates a thing which is generally applicable to its class (*al-lafẓ al-dāll ʿalā madlūl shāʾiʿ fī jinsihi*).[82]

By these rather opaque definitions, our authors are concerned with statements such as "a slave" in the order "free a slave" (*taḥrīr/iʿtaq raqaba*) found in the Qurʾān with reference to penance (*kaffāra*) for transgressions of the law, the point being, as the statement stands, any slave will fulfil the demand. However, if a subsequent text is discovered in which the *kaffāra* is stipulated as "free a *believing* slave" (as it is in Q4/al-Nisāʾ.92), then this second text is said to operate as a qualification (*muqayyad*) on the early text. When the speaker said the first text, he intended a qualified meaning even though he used the unqualified verbal form (that is, the indefinite noun). As with the general and the particular, there is a literal meaning to the form of words in the statement (as laid down by the act of *waḍʿ*) which is at variance with the intended meaning of the speaker: that is, we have here a case of *majāz*.

The questions around the operation of general and unqualified reference in the revelatory texts, and their relationship with particularising and qualifying statements, form a large element of the hermeneutic discussions in *uṣūl* texts. These are not directly relevant to our purpose at this point, though it should be noted that they are instances of *bayān* (elucidation) – that is, how one piece of revelation, standing alone, is either ambiguous or inaccurate, and how God provides elucidation in order to prevent misunderstanding.[83] As a whole, the *ʿumūm/khuṣūṣ* and *muṭlaq/muqayyad* discussions indicate how the aim of the *uṣūl* hermeneutic system is to discover the intended meaning of the author (God) through bringing together his various statements on an issue and postulating a means of marrying them. The importance

79 Ḥillī, *Nihāyat*, v. 2, p. 121; see Murtaḍā, *al-Dharīʿa*, 1, pp. 201–2.
80 Ibn al-Ḥājib, *Mukhtaṣar*, v. 2, p. 860 (see also Ḥillī, *Nihāyat*, v. 2, p. 380).
81 Ibn al-Ḥājib, *Mukhtaṣar*, v. 2, p. 859.
82 Ḥillī, *Nihāyat*, v. 2, p. 387.
83 See below, pp. 99–101.

of the literal meaning of those texts, and the means whereby it might be discarded, are discussed later in the context of the assessment rather than the delimitation of the literal meaning.

A set of hermeneutic issues is associated with the hermeneutic pairing of *mujmal/mubayyan* (ambiguous/clarifying). A text, which is made up of utterances employing vocables, can be ambiguous for numerous reasons. The vocables within it may have been allotted more than one literal meaning in the act of *waḍʿ*, and there are no *qarāʾin* to indicate which literal meaning is preferable. This is likely to happen if *ḥaqīqa sharʿiyya* or *ḥaqīqa ʿurfiyya* has taken place, as their new literal meanings may appear to clash with their original established meanings. Perhaps it is clear from a *qarīna* that the literal meaning is not the intended meaning (that is, the utterance is *majāz*), but it is not clear which possible *majāz* usage is intended. In all these instances, and in others not mentioned here, the text (or rather the information within the text) is insufficient in itself to determine what is intended. What is needed is an elucidating item, and this is called the *mubayyan*, which establishes one amongst the possible meanings as the preferred one or, in the case of radical obscurity (when no sense at all, even a ridiculous one, can be made of the text), it points the way to a meaning. This process of elucidation (*bayān*) and the role of the literal meaning within it are examined in greater detail in a later chapter.[84] It is enough to record here that the phenomenon of ambiguity within the revelatory texts – as it was recognised by the Uṣūlīs generally and our two authors in particular – represents a failure of the literal meaning of a text to convey that intended by the speaker. It could be argued that the need for a *bayān* risks an implicit accusation that the speaker has failed to use the language system correctly.

Finally we come to two pairs of hermeneutic terms which would appear to have central importance for the understanding of the literal meaning:

apparent/interpreted (*ẓāhir*/*muʾawwal*)
what is said/what is implied (*manṭūq*/*mafhūm*)

As has been mentioned already, the term *ẓāhir* has regularly been translated as "literal meaning", and the group that are supposed to have promoted its adoption as the legitimate interpretation of revelatory texts – the Ẓāhiriyya – are usually described as the "literalists". The appropriateness of these translations form an element of a later chapter,[85] but for now our two authors (as do most Uṣūlīs) begin with definitions:

> [Ibn al-Ḥājib]: [*al-ẓāhir*] in technical terms is whatever indicates a presumptive proof (*dilāla ẓanniyya*), whether it is by *waḍʿ*, as in the case of the *asad* (lion), or by *ʿurf*, as is the case with the privy (*ghāʾit*).[86]

84 See below, pp. 164–5.
85 See below, p. 146.
86 Ibn al-Ḥājib, *Mukhtaṣar*, v. 2, p. 908.

The brevity of this definition, of course, requires unpacking (indeed, this unpacking is, in some ways, the point of writing a *mukhtaṣar*). The *ẓāhir* is the interpretation of an utterance which does not identify the intended meaning of the speaker with certainty, but it does bring a presumption (that is, it is *ẓannī*) as to that intended meaning. It does this through a correspondence of the *ẓāhir* meaning with what we have up to now been calling the "literal meaning" of the utterance (acquired either through *waḍʿ* – the original act of assignment – or through *ʿurf* – a subsequent acquired assignment). Ibn al-Ḥājib's point here is that the *ẓāhir* is the meaning of an utterance which draws ahead of other possible meanings because it emerges from a consideration of the meanings assigned to the utterance's word and which inhere in the words, and not through any contextual evidence.

Al-Ḥillī does not make reference to Ibn al-Ḥājib's definition of *ẓāhir* directly, but he does quote al-Āmidī (whose *Muntahā al-sūl* Ibn al-Ḥājib is summarising):

> The *ẓāhir* utterance is one which indicates a meaning by reference to either the original or the customary *waḍʿ*, whilst maintaining, as a less preferred possibility, something other than [the *ẓāhir*] may be [the intended meaning].[87]

Ibn al-Ḥājib's definition of *ẓāhir* is, I suspect, a combination of al-Āmidī's definition, cited above, and the much-cited definition of al-Ghazālī:

> The *ẓāhir* is the utterance from which the understanding of meaning forms the strongest presumption [of being the intended meaning] without being certain.[88]

Ibn al-Ḥājib appears to combine the epistemological references to presumption (*ẓann*) with al-Āmidī's reference to *waḍʿ* (original and customary).

Al-Ḥillī is, however, unhappy with al-Āmidī's definition because:

> The *ẓāhir* is not restricted to whatever is indicated by the original [*waḍʿ*] or by convention. Rather every utterance in which there is a meaning which establishes itself as preferred (*tarajjaḥ*) is *ẓāhir* in relation to [the intended meaning].[89]

A meaning may establish itself as the preferred meaning not only through reference to the meaning assigned to the words in the *waḍʿ*, but also, for al-Ḥillī, through other mechanisms. Al-Āmidī's linking of the *ẓāhir* to a *waḍʿī* meaning – one of our candidates for literal meaning in *uṣūl al-fiqh* – is, in al-Ḥillī's view, unjustified (neither does it appear to be an essential element of al-Ghazālī's definition). Al-Ḥillī, then, appears to broaden the potential reference of *ẓāhir* to a meaning which is obvious or apparent from the utterance, whether it accords with the meaning assigned to it in the *lugha* or not. His point here is, I think, linked to his argument that each word within a statement may be being used in a *ḥaqīqa* manner but the whole statement be *majāz*. The *ẓāhir* meaning of an utterance may be technically *majāz*. What is "apparent" may not be the linguistic meaning established in language; it

87 Ḥillī, *Nihāyat*, v. 2, p. 489; see also Āmidī, *al-Iḥkām*, v. 3, p. 36.
88 Āmidī, *al-Iḥkām*, v. 3, p. 48.
89 Ḥillī, *Nihāyat*, v. 2, p. 489.

could just as easily be a non-linguistic meaning. Al-Ḥillī, then, asserts that *ẓāhir* is not a fixed entity linked to a technical feature of language (as al-Āmidī wishes to determine it), but rather something which can be perspectival (what is apparent for an individual person in a specific context) and is comparative (one meaning beats other meanings as being more apparent):

> The conclusion is, therefore, that [*ẓāhir*] is a relative matter (*min al-umūr al-iḍāfiyya*) which varies according to the different things it is used for. It might, at one point, be relative to individuals; and at another time in relation to meanings.[90]

Al-Ḥillī, though, seems unwilling to allow *ẓāhir* to become entirely subjective, thereby reducing it to simply "the meaning that appears to the individual interpreter". He admits this is one aspect of a text's *ẓāhir*, but what he is more interested in is *ẓāhir* in relation to meanings. In this definition the *ẓāhir* of a text is not simply what appears to be the meaning to the individual interpreter, but rather is obtained when the "indication of [a particular possible meaning] becomes preferred (*tatarajjaḥ dalālatuhu*)".[91] The process of "becoming the preferred meaning" is not subjective, for al-Ḥillī, but the result of scientific analysis taking into account not only linguistic meaning, but textual and other elements of context. Out of this assessment an individual meaning becomes apparent.

Even though these different strands of *uṣūlī* thinking have different conceptions of the meaning of *ẓāhir*, they all subscribe to the same basic framework: that is, the *ẓāhir* of a text, its "apparent" meaning, is not necessarily the intended meaning of the speaker. The *ẓāhir* only forms a presumed intended meaning; it may well be that wider factors (such as the overall context of the Sharīʿa and other known demands within it) make it necessary to move away from the *ẓāhir* to a self-consciously "interpreted" meaning (*muʾawwal*). This interpreted meaning is definitely not what the text appears to mean, but what the speaker probably does mean after a separate and non-contiguous textual indicator elsewhere within the revelatory corpus is taken into account. Al-Ghazālī described the process of *taʾwīl* (that is, identifying the non-*ẓāhir* meaning as the intended meaning) as "an interpretation, supported by a *dalīl*, by which it [the interpretation] becomes a more probable view [as to the intended meaning] than the meaning which the *ẓāhir* indicates".[92] This definition, which is criticised by some Uṣūlīs, describes the basic elements of the concept:

> The *ẓāhir* of a text indicates a probable intended meaning.
> A *dalīl* (from outside of the text under consideration) indicates a different meaning.
> *Taʾwīl* is the process whereby this different meaning is discovered and vested with authority.
> The *muʾawwal* is the new meaning, which is put forward as now the more probable meaning of the text, when the *dalīl* is taken into account.

90 Ḥillī, *Nihāyat*, v. 2, p. 489.
91 Ḥillī, *Nihāyat*, v. 2, p. 489.
92 Ghazālī, *al-Mustaṣfā*, v. 2, p. 49.

Ta'wīl under this scheme becomes a mechanism whereby the "true" meaning of an utterance (that is, the intended meaning of the speaker) is separated from the apparent meaning of the text. Most of the Uṣūlīs who conceive of the *ẓāhir/mu'awwal* dichotomy in this manner see the apparent meaning as intimately linked with the assigned and linguistically determined meaning of the individual words and grammatical components of the text. Al-Ḥillī perhaps draws the *ẓāhir* further away from the literal meaning by saying that the *ẓāhir* is, from one perspective, relative to the individual interpreter's perception (for it to be apparent it has to be apparent to someone); from another perspective, it can be applied to meanings, and one meaning can be seen as "objectively" preferred over others, and this need not be the linguistically determined meaning, but it remains a strictly textual meaning. Nevertheless, for al-Ḥillī, as for all the other Uṣūlīs in this tradition, the *ẓāhir* is not certain to be the speaker's intended meaning: a *dalīl* external to the text may render the *ẓāhir* irrelevant and an alternative (*mu'awwal*) will, on consideration, be preferred.[93]

This brief account does not exhaust the uses of the term *ẓāhir* in *uṣūl al-fiqh*,[94] but it does indicate the generally accepted linkage between it and what I am calling the literal meaning, and it establishes the *ẓāhir* (as we saw with the *waḍʿī/ḥaqīqī* meaning) as the presumed or default meaning of a text. The burden of proof falls on other potential meanings. They are to dislodge the *ẓāhir*. The relationship between the *ẓāhir* and the *waḍʿī/ḥaqīqī* meanings is, as we have seen, debated. Some Uṣūlīs, perhaps the majority, argued for the *ẓāhir* being the more probable and preferred meaning on account of it being in accord with the *waḍʿī/ḥaqīqī* meaning. The fact that a potential meaning of a text is in accord with (or derived from) the meaning assigned to it in the *waḍʿ* makes this meaning *ẓāhir*, which in turn makes it preferred over other potential meanings. It does not make it invincible (*ta'wīl* is always possible with the *ẓāhir*), but it does establish it as not only the default meaning but the interpretation of a particular text which can be adopted with the soundest justification before other texts are taken into account.

The final hermeneutic pairing which has a bearing on our discussion of the literal meaning is *manṭūq* ("what is expressed" or, perhaps, with resonances of modern pragmatics, "what is said") and *mafhūm* ("what is understood" or "what is implicated").[95] In classical form, Ibn al-Ḥājib defines the two terms as follows:

93 There is, however, another conception of the *ẓāhir* present in *uṣūl* works which deserves mention here, and it is related to the (primarily) Ḥanafī method of categorising the clarity with which a text expresses its meaning. In this schema, *ẓāhir* describes a linguistic meaning of a text which is free of ambiguity. This *ẓāhir* may not be the intended speaker's meaning, but as a linguistic meaning it is clear. Whilst Ḥanafīs slot it into a different framework, I do not see this definition of *ẓāhir* as substantially different from that proposed by al-Āmidī and Ibn al-Ḥājib. In both the "mainstream" (as Yunis Ali calls it) and the Ḥanafī system, the *ẓāhir* is defined in relation to the *waḍʿ*. In al-Ḥillī's system, the *ẓāhir* is the textual meaning, but it is not necessarily linked to the *waḍʿī* meaning of either the text's components or its composite features. See Yunis Ali, *Medieval Islamic Pragmatics*, pp. 128–30; see also Kamali (*Principles*, pp. 91–4), who presents a semi-synthesised view of the different approaches.

94 Other meanings emerge in the subsequent chapters; see below, pp. 108–12.

95 The line between these is, of course, controversial; see the Ḥanafī/Shāfiʿī categorisations which reflect the

> *Manṭūq* is that which a vocable indicates at the point of expression.
> The *mafhūm* is the opposite: that is, what is not [expressed] at the point of expression.[96]

What vocables indicate is normally taken to be meanings, and so the *manṭūq* is the meaning which is indicated at the point of expression or utterance. *Mafhūm*, it would appear, is something external to this, something implicated by the statement but not present within it. The *manṭūq* naturally, then, resonates with some elements of "literal meaning", as we are using the term here.

Ibn al-Ḥājib goes on to say that the *manṭūq* meaning is "explicit" (*ṣarīḥ* – when "it is what the vocable was assigned to") and the *mafhūm* meaning is not explicit but necessitated by the statement (*mā yalzamu ʿanhu*). Al-Ḥillī's definitions are similar (unsurprisingly, since both authors are drawing on al-Āmidī), but his glosses are instructive here, as they highlight elements of the "literal meaning" which will reoccur in the coming chapters. The *manṭūq* is glossed as "what the vocable indicates by its explicitness on the first indication (*dalāla awwaliyya*)"[97] – chiming with the requirement of immediate comprehension for the literal meaning discussed earlier. On the *mafhūm*, al-Ḥillī glosses it as going beyond the "understanding of the meaning which is known to/currency amongst the people" (*al-fahm bi'l-maʿnā al-mutaʿārif ʿinda al-nās*).[98] That is, the *mafhūm* goes beyond popularly recognised meanings, also mentioned as an element in the literal meaning.

Examples of things required by the text but not present within it are divided by al-Ḥillī into four categories, and in this his typology is typical of classical *uṣūl* works following the Shāfiʿī classification schema:

1. Meanings necessitated by the text for it to be rationally or theologically sound (termed *dalālat al-iqtiḍā*):[99] the missing word "people" in the "ask the village" example is required to make sense, as we cannot ask buildings.
2. Meanings which emerge from the explicit meaning of the text such that as soon as one understands the utterance, one understands this new meaning (termed *dalālat al-tanbīh wa'l-īmā*): when the Prophet said "free a slave" to the man who had had sexual intercourse with his wife during the day in Ramaḍān, we understand that the freeing of a slave is a penance for the transgression of the law.
3. Meanings which were not part of the intended meaning of the speaker at the point of utterance, but which are revealed through understanding the utterance (*dalālat al-ishāra*). The implication that the maximum amount of time that a

different Ḥanafī and Shāfiʿī notions of what is "in" and what is "outside of" the text (Yunis Ali, *Medieval Islamic Pragmatics*, pp. 159–87); cf. the discussion in modern pragmatics – Bezuidenhout, "Metaphor and What Is Said" – where even certain basic metaphors are included in "what is said".

96 Ibn al-Ḥājib, *Mukhtaṣar*, v. 2, p. 924.

97 Ḥillī, *Nihāyat*, v. 2, p. 513.

98 Ḥillī, *Nihāyat*, v. 2, p. 513.

99 One could attempt to translate the various technical terms here, but I doubt it would serve much purpose; see, for example, Hallaq, *A History*, pp. 96–101.

menstrual period might be said to occur is one half of the month is deduced from the statement of the Prophet that women are deficient in religion because they can spend half their lives (*shiṭrat dahrihā*) not praying.[100]

4. Meanings which were not part of the utterance, but may well have been part of the intention of the speaker (*dalālat al-mafhūm*): for example, the implication that we should not beat our parents by the Quranic verse "Say not *uff* to your parents" (Q17.23). Since we are forbidden from saying *uff* to them, we are surely also forbidden from beating them.

Now these four types of implication can be categorised in different ways, and they were so by Uṣūlīs in the classical period. In all cases, something is understood from the utterance which is not explicitly (literally?) stated. In all these cases, though, an understanding of the text leads immediately and without ambiguity to an understanding of the implication, even though, from a linguistic perspective, the implication is not "in" the text. The implied meaning here is textual (in the sense that the existence of the text requires the existence of the implication) but not explicit. One might argue that the implications are textual but not literal, in the sense of "linguistically required". Then again, and bringing in other elements of our concept of literality, these meanings are viewed by the Uṣūlīs as present within the text, simply not explicitly expressed. Indeed, the debates amongst Uṣūlīs about the correct categorisation of some of these implications are, in a sense, debates over whether they can be seen as text-based or deduced by the reader through a consideration of external factors. For example, Shāfiʿīs viewed (2) above (*dalālat al-tanbīh wa'l-īmā*) as properly discussed under the rubric of *qiyās* (generally analogical reasoning), since the implication (in the example, the *taʿlīl* – identification of the reason for the ruling) is a central element in the procedure of analogy. The Shāfiʿīs also generally considered (4) – which was seen as *mafhūm* proper – as essentially analogical and not strictly linguistic. Even if it was obvious upon hearing the verse that one should not beat one's parents, the process whereby one reaches that conclusion is deductive and analogical. They may be still legitimate deductions, but they are certainly no longer literal. Ḥanafīs generally viewed the example cited in (4) as a linguistic inference, though they rejected other types of implication. Most famously, this was debated regarding the *mafhūm al-mukhālafa*, in which a specific mention in a text is viewed as evidence that those elements not mentioned carry an opposite ruling. The debate here, as elsewhere, concerned whether a meaning might be thought of as "in" the text or deduced from the text. The textualism of *uṣūl al-fiqh* usually meant the former was a stronger position from which to argue, and jurists often wished to cram the desired meaning into the text through an expanded notion of "what the text says". What is interesting about the *manṭūq*/*mafhūm* pairing is that the Uṣūlīs were generally arguing that what distinguished the two types of meaning was not their connection to the text (in both cases, the *manṭūq* and the *mafhūm* meanings were intimately connected to the text). Rather, it was, in a sense, how obvious the

100 Ḥillī, *Nihāyat*, v. 2, pp. 513–17.

meanings were and how explicitly they were expressed which dominated the discussions here.[101]

Translations and Literal Meaning

Turning to secondary literature, the term "literal meaning" is used extensively, but generally uncritically, in the secondary literature on medieval Islamic hermeneutics. A brief examination of these will situate my own approach within this field. Two technical terms in classical *uṣūl al-fiqh* are frequently associated with the literal meaning (or literal understanding, literal definition or literal interpretation): *ẓāhir* and *ḥaqīqa*. As we shall see in the next chapter, in the formative period of *uṣūl* (that is, from al-Shāfiʿī onwards), these two terms (and derivatives of them) had little stable intellectual referent in juristic discussions.[102] To use them as glosses for literal meaning, or to translate them as such, without caveats and explanation, though, is commonplace in the secondary literature but, I would argue, potentially misleading. Even in the classical period where the structure of the discipline is much more stable, the literal meaning (as we use the term here: the meaning a text/utterance has in itself or which it owns regardless of author/speaker intentions and context) can be associated with a bundle of elements within the system, as just demonstrated. *Ḥaqīqa* or *ẓāhir* are amongst these, but they are not the only contributors.[103]

Within theological debates, of course, there was extensive discussion of the interpretation of particular Quranic verses and whether they mean what they appear to say. The most debated terms are those in which God is described in anthropomorphic terms. Those who considered these to be references to real or physical elements of God's body are invariably called "literalists" in the secondary literature, as they adhere to the "literal" meaning of the Quranic text. Though not the focus of this book, it is useful to consider the terminology heresiographers have used to describe this belief which most secondary literatures have chosen to translate with terms associated with literality. Amongst the early groups associated with this anthropomorphism are the *ḥashwiyya* or *ahl al-ḥashw*, often categorised as a subsect of the Mushabbiha.[104] The Mushabbiha are those who subscribe to a doctrine of

101 Sperber and Wilson, as already mentioned (p. 20), view the literal/non-literal distinction as fallacious but based their analysis around an understanding of "explicitness": in *uṣūlī* terms, the *manṭūq* might be considered to be the most explicitly indicated meaning, whilst the *mafhūm* is much less so, and the non-literal meaning is hardly explicit at all. The division in Recanati's scheme between m- and p-literal meanings also applies here: m-literal meanings are *manṭūq*; p-literal meanings are *mafhūm*. As al-Ḥillī says, the members of the language community understand the *mafhūm* immediately; they consider it the message conveyed by the text, even though this meaning is technically speaking m-non-literal. See above, p. 17; Recanati, *Literal Meaning*, pp. 68–82; Sperber and Wilson, "Loose Talk". As mentioned above, the debate over whether particular understandings are linguistic or not (Ḥanafīs vs Shāfiʿīs over *a minori ad maius: tanbīh bi'l-adnā ʿalā al-aʿlā*, for example) is, I suggest, a debate over whether they are understood as non-literal or p-literal; see above, p. 19.

102 See below, p. 112.

103 Larcher, "Quand, en arabe (I)", p. 126.

104 Little work has been done on the Ḥashwiyya since Halkin's article "The Ḥashwiyya".

tashbīh ("likening") – that is, God is likened to a human being, being described in the same terms and conceived of as having the same characteristics. The usual term for their mode of interpretive understanding is *ẓāhir*. As the great heresiographer Abū al-Fatḥ al-Shahrastānī (d. 548/1153) puts it:

> As for what is revealed in scripture concerning sitting, and the face, and the two hands, and the side, coming and going, and being above something, and other things, then [the *ḥashwiyya*] reckon them according to their *ẓāhir* – meaning whatever is understood by bodies in an unrestricted/general manner (*ʿinda al-iṭlāq*).[105]

Here the term *ẓāhir* is glossed as the general or unrestricted (as opposed to special or unusual) meaning. What is meant is the commonly understood meaning of sitting, face, hands and so on. Kazi and Flynn translate *ʿalā al-ẓāhir* as the "literally" here,[106] though the term within the context of Shahrastānī's account is used to designate a meaning located in ordinary everyday speech, which does not exclude an "original meaning", but does not necessarily include it.

In studies of *uṣūl al-fiqh*, scholars have also suggested a plethora of alternative translations for both *ẓāhir* and *ḥaqīqa* (from "obvious" and "uncritical" for *ẓāhir* to "veridical" and "proper" for *ḥaqīqa*), though "literal", by my estimate, is the most popular for both terms. Most of this usage has been unreflective, with little discussion of why "literal" may or may not be an appropriate translation of *ẓāhir* or *ḥaqīqa*.[107] More recently, scholars examining the development of *uṣūl al-fiqh* have used the term "literal" within their account of *uṣūl al-fiqh* with a little more discrimination. Three recent studies stand out as having a particular interest in the text as a bearer of meaning in itself: namely, those of Weiss, Yunis Ali and Vishanoff.

Weiss tackles the term *ẓāhir* and its relationship with *ḥaqīqa* as a means of describing an expression in his study of the influential Uṣūlī Sayf al-Dīn al-Āmidī. For Weiss, literality is linked with the terms *ẓāhir* and *ḥaqīqa*; they interrelate as follows: a *ẓāhir* expression is a particular type of *ḥaqīqa* expression, namely one which has a single literal (assigned; *al-maʿnā al-mawḍūʿ lahu*) meaning. The initial reason for this subcategory being necessary is the phenomenon of homonymity –

105 Shahrastānī, *Milal*, v. 1, p. 105.

106 Shahrastānī (trans. Kazi and Flynn), *Muslim Sects and Divisions*, p. 90; see also Shahrastānī (trans. Gimaret, Monnot and Jolivet), *Livre des religions et des sects*, v. 1, p. 242, "au sense literal"; see also n. 103. For Muʿtazilī, *ḥashwiyya* refers to the *aṣḥāb al-ḥadīth* generally; for Ashʿarī it is the name of ignorant Sunnis who take the anthropomorphisms of the Qurʾān "to the letter".

107 For a selection, consider the following: *ẓāhir*: "literal" (Dutton, *The Origins of Islamic Law*, p. 79; Bernard, "Ḥanafī *uṣūl al-fiqh*", p. 625); "obvious" (Winkel, *Islam and the Living Law*, p. 40); "apparent" (Sands, *Ṣūfī Commentaries on the Qurʾān*, p. 60); "immediate implication" (Bedir, "An Early Response to Shāfiʿī", p. 298); "overt manifestation" (Gully, "Implication of Meaning", p. 462). Zamah runs through the possible meanings in her "Master of the Obvious". *Ḥaqīqa*: "literal" (Heinrichs, "On the Genesis", p. 115; Gully, *Grammar and Semantics in Medieval Arabic*, p. 39); "veridical" (Heinrichs, "On the Genesis", p. 115; Wansbrough, *Qurʾanic Studies*, p. 236; Lowry, "The Legal Hermeneutics of al-Shāfiʿī and Ibn Qutayba", p. 36); "strict sense" (Frank, *Beings and their Attributes*, p. 157); "real" (Peters, *God's Created Speech*, p. 79; Wild, "We Have Sent Down", p. 151). This does not exhaust the translations in English of either term, without even mentioning the terms' translation into other languages.

that is, particular vocables having more than one meaning assigned to them. Weiss uses the word "bank" as an illustration of this (it has two assigned definitions: financial institution/side of a river).[108] Homonymity exists quite extensively in Arabic and, when it does, an expression using a word (or words) with two (or more) assigned meanings can now be simultaneously ambiguous and *ḥaqīqa*. The frequency of this occurrence is not a matter of concern for al-Āmidī – its existence establishes the need to have a theory which accounts for such an eventuality. A *ẓāhir* expression is one which is not troubled by homonymity. Each word/phrase within the *ẓāhir* expression has a single literal meaning, which when combined give us a single literal meaning of the expression. When this occurs, we can say that the expression is *ẓāhir* – it is "univocal", in Weiss's terminology. Its univocality engenders the probability that the intended meaning of the expression is its literal meaning (that is, the meaning assigned to its component parts in the *lugha*). When used to describe a meaning rather than an expression, Weiss wishes to translate *ẓāhir* as "apparent". The meaning of an expression (as opposed to the expression itself) can also be described as *ẓāhir*: it is "the apparent intended meaning by virtue of its being the sole literal meaning of the expression and by virtue of the preponderance of literal meaning over non-literal meaning".[109] The result of all this is that the rather lax use of the term "literal" in the secondary literature on hermeneutics is ripe for re-examination. Weiss remarks:

> [In presenting al-Āmidī's thought in this way,] I am obviously taking exception to the common practice of translating *zāhir* as "literal." A *zāhir* meaning is, of course, a literal meaning, but it is more than that: it is a literal meaning that has no competitors and thus has an *ab initio* claim to be the meaning intended by the author.[110]

Now Weiss ties down his use of the term "literal" here, and this may reflect his focus on the functions of *ẓāhir* and *ḥaqīqa* within the legal theory of al-Āmidī. His employment of the term "literal" simply for a meaning designated or coined (*mawḍūʿ*) within the linguistic system called the *lugha* may work well when talking about a single thinker, such as al-Āmidī, who prized consistency in the application of technical terminology. However, considering the *uṣūl* discipline more generally, "literal meaning", along the lines developed in modern linguistic philosophy and which I have elaborated so far, covers a wider remit than simply the designated, coined meaning of a word.

The limited linking of *ḥaqīqa* with "literal meaning" is maintained by Yunis Ali, who uses it interchangeably with "normative" as a translation of *ḥaqīqa*. He also follows Weiss in using "apparent" for *ẓāhir*. Unfortunately, this framework is somewhat compromised by his reference to the Ẓāhiriyya as "literalists".[111] Yunis Ali's

108 Weiss, *The Search*, p. 139.
109 Weiss, *The Search*, p. 140.
110 Weiss, *The Search*, p. 140.
111 Yunis Ali, *Medieval Islamic Pragmatics*, p. 44; he, perhaps ironically, glosses Ẓāhiriyya with "lit. literalists". What else he might have used is not obvious, though we should not feel the need to translate every technical term into English.

study, though, is particularly useful for its exposition of the Uṣūlīs' thinking on clarity and immediacy in meaning. That there is an association between the literal/non-literal distinction as it is used here and the clear/obscure dichotomy within *uṣūl al-fiqh* has already been explored above. The clearest expression is one in which the words are used with their literal meaning – and the interpretive process, according to the dominant linguistic theory of *uṣūl al-fiqh*, is easiest when the expression is clear. The link here, as Yunis Ali nicely points out, is the need for determinacy which underlies the literalism of the Uṣūlīs. Most relevant here is Yunis Ali's exposition of immediacy and its relationship with literal meaning. Recanati, one recalls, built immediacy into his notion of literal meaning, only then to deconstruct it as a mistaken presumption.[112] The Uṣūlīs, following Yunis Ali's analysis, saw immediacy as an indication of literalness. That is, using once again one of the tests mentioned above when citing al-Ḥillī, the meaning of an utterance which occurs in the mind of the hearer immediately (*tabādur*) is the literal meaning (*ḥaqīqa*), according to the Uṣūlīs. After considering this meaning, and finding it irrelevant or nonsensical, the hearer turns to non-literal meanings. One of the non-literal meanings becomes more plausible than all others because of the contextual factors (*qarāʾin*), and the hearer selects this one. The similarity of the process as described by Yunis Ali and the position Recanati sets out to undermine is noteworthy. It is important to remember that once the literal meaning has been discarded, the interpreter's epistemological position has changed and his personal involvement in constructing the meaning of the utterance increased. Yunis Ali's most important contribution, however, is his construction of Ibn Taymiyya's critique of the established parameters of the literal/non-literal distinction. As already mentioned, Ibn Taymiyya, according to Yunis Ali, rejects the Uṣūlīs' construction of the interpretive process and argues for a contextualised approach, in which the meaning which is immediate to the hearer will not necessarily be the literal.[113] In this sense Ibn Taymiyya is a non-literalist, under Recanati's typology.[114]

112 See above, p. 16.

113 See above, p. 22. Instead, on the basis of a presumption that the speaker is intending to "make his manifest", and that the two belong to the same language community, and that the speaker is following an established habit, the meaning which might be immediate to the hearer will not necessarily accord with the imagined literal meaning established in the linguistic code – given these contextual factors, the hearer will, most likely, never process the literal meaning and instead jump to the non-literal. Yunis Ali is, perhaps, a little too keen to present Ibn Taymiyya's analysis in pragmatic terms, but the exposition does reveal a powerful analogy between the critiques of literalism by Ibn Taymiyya and some modern philosophers and, as in Recanati's case, the critique signals a general dissatisfaction with the literal/non-literal:*ḥaqīqa*/*majāz* dichotomies. It seems that Ibn Taymiyya's critique was only really understood by his discipline Ibn Qayyim al-Jawziyya; Yunis Ali lumps the two thinkers together as "the Salafīs", though it is not clear whether any subsequent "Salafīs" understood or subscribed to Ibn Taymiyya's position. Subsequent tradition, even those who viewed Ibn Taymiyya favourably, understood his rejection of *majāz* as a sign of an anthropomorphic literalism rather than as a proposal of a whole alternative model of communication. The implications of this are explored below, pp. 176–84.

114 Ibn Taymiyya would, I suppose, concur with Sperber and Wilson's view: "Literal talk, loose talk and metaphorical talk are often seen as different in kind. We … argue that they differ not in kind but only in

The final example of recent commentary on literal meaning and its importance in *uṣūl al-fiqh* is the work of David Vishanoff, in which the development of early Islamic hermeneutics is given detailed and careful exposition. With regard to the Ẓāhiriyya, they are termed "literalists" (to the exclusion of other groups), though they are also demonstrated to be operating in a similar hermeneutic structure to the so-called "non-literalists".[115] Vishanoff, like Weiss and Yunis Ali, employs "literal" as a translation of *ḥaqīqa* (usually), and uses it with regard to both usage and meaning; in this sense it is interchangeable with "normative" (following Yunis Ali). He also refers to "literal meaning" in different contexts by different terms: "ordinary", "linguistic", "normative", "literal" or "apparent" meaning.[116] Whilst the focus is the development of what he calls "transgressive" usages and meanings (*majāz*), the variation in terminology for literal meaning reflects the imprecision amongst the early writers not only concerning transgressing the normal bounds of language but also in sticking to them. To be fair to Vishanoff, his interest is not in how a text's inherent meaning is established in the minds of the Uṣūlīs, but in how the author's intended meaning might be understood. Of these, one indicator (but not the only one) is the text's own meaning, and when we reach the early classical period (fourth/eleventh century), one finds "literal" and "understood literally" being used to refer to the various forms of assignment (linguistic, customary, revelatory) described as forming *ḥaqīqa* usages.[117] As Vishanoff rightly notes, not all thinkers accept widespread and common customary usage (*ʿurf*) as a means of making a new assigned meaning for a word or phrase; instead widespread and customary usage is treated in the same way as literal usage within, say, al-Bāqillānī's system, but is not literal in the sense that *al-ḥaqāʾiq al-ʿurfiyya* in the classical system described above was conceived.[118] By maintaining the use of literal for the originally assigned meaning, Vishanoff maintains Weiss's designation of literal (*al-maʿnā al-mawḍūʿ lahu*: the meaning assigned to/coined for/placed upon a vocable/sound).

My use of the term "literal meaning" in this book both encompasses and is distinct from the use of the term in these recent studies. In using this conception, I am influenced by recent philosophical discussions in which the term is used to refer to a pragmatic phenomenon, namely the idea that the text owns, or carries, or "has" in and of itself a meaning which sits firmly within the text and which is, in essence,

degree of looseness and they are understood in essentially the same way" (Sperber and Wilson, "Loose Talk", p. 153).

115 It should be noted that Vishanoff's use of literalist is more restricted, and perhaps less technical, than the one I am using here. Literalism, as I use it, is a belief in the existence and privilege of a literal meaning in the exegetical process: some, such as the Ẓāhiriyya, considered its position to be insuperable (or nearly so); others allowed it to be dislodged with varying degrees of rigidity. In this sense, they were all literalists (taking my cue from modern pragmatic uses of the term; see above, pp. 1–2).

116 All these are in evidence to refer to the same thing over four pages examining the early development of *majāz* (Vishanoff, *The Formation*, pp. 19–23).

117 Vishanoff, *The Formation*, p. 125.

118 Vishanoff, *The Formation*, p. 167. We shall have cause to return to Vishanoff's important study in future chapters.

distinct from the author's intended meaning, even when in content the two are identical.[119] This almost anthropomorphic notion of a text (where texts "own", "carry" or "bear" meanings) became standard quite early in Muslim intellectual history, in part as a natural outgrowth of the dogma of a scriptural revelation, but also possibly under the influence of existing notions of text and meaning. The text's meaning was an assumed proposition in many exegetical discussions, and when it was addressed explicitly, different terms were used. The emergence and professionalisation of the various sciences in the ninth and tenth century CE resulted in a more consistent use of technical terms, eventually leading to the hermeneutic structure I have described in this chapter and the notions of literal meaning which nestle within it. Issues which were given various answers in the early period included what the literal meaning of a text was, how it might be known, and which external elements (such as context) might intrude into its definition. The writers of legal theory used the findings of other sciences, particularly the emerging discipline of Arabic linguistics, and naturalised them in an *uṣūl* environment, producing the general structure described above. The use of "literal meaning" in the works of Weiss and Yunis Ali, then, is more specific than that used here (tied to meanings which are *ḥaqīqa* when used); Vishanoff's use of a cluster of terms to describe the idea of a text's own meaning ("ordinary", "linguistic", "normative", "apparent") perhaps unintentionally reflects the basic notion of the literal meaning I wish to isolate here, with all its debated and contested elements. The questions analysed above, then, are canonical elements of *uṣūl* discussions and are linked to literal meaning, as conceived here. Literal meaning may in the later classical tradition be restricted to a particular notion (meaning assigned in the *waḍʿ*), but, as we shall discover in the coming chapters, the idea went beyond any single technical convention.

Conclusion

My investigation into literal meaning in *uṣūl al-fiqh* brings together a number of conflicting ideas present within Muslim legal theory. The notion of a linguistically determined system is found in the imagined foundations of language and the designation of sounds to meaning. The signs of when this meaning is employed are found in the tests for recognising *ḥaqīqa* as opposed to *majāz* usage. Within these tests, and in more detail elsewhere in the *uṣūl* discussions, further elements of literality are developed. The commonly accepted meaning amongst the language's user community can be identified in the Quranic idea of a Prophet being sent to deliver the message in the prosaic language of his audience. The meaning which is immediately present in the hearer's mind is revealed in the idea of *tabādur* (immediacy); what occurs immediately in the mind of the language user is an

119 I readily accept that a term such as "textual meaning" could have been selected for this meaning; "textualism" is the label for a trend in legal studies which is linked to the idea of literal meaning. See below, p. 150, n. 19, and Manning, "Textualism and Legislative Intent".

indication (*dalīl*) of the *ḥaqīqa* usage, which in turn reveals the meaning which was assigned to the word in the *waḍʿ*. This may be another way of saying the "commonly accepted meaning", but, as we shall see, this was not always the case. Sometimes the distinction was expressed technically, in terms of *ḥaqāʾiq ʿurfiyya/sharʿiyya/ lughawiyya*. Furthermore, the notion of a meaning which belongs to the text – which the words own and which they never relinquish, even when that meaning is overruled in the process of interpretation – is not always coincident with the obvious or immediate meanings, or with the obvious or apparent criterion of literality which comes through the discussions of *ẓāhir*. The idea of the articulated rather than the unarticulated meaning, found in the *manṭūq/mafhūm* division, also raises the possible distinction between textual and literal meanings. Running through these discussions is a belief in literalism: that is, the text has a meaning, and there is a preference for this meaning identified as "in" the text or inherent within an utterance. There is a general promotion of this meaning (as default, or as superior, or as certain). As the intellectual structure developed and the text's meaning became more precisely identified as the meaning assigned in the *waḍʿ*, other elements of our concept of literal meaning (common usage, the meaning immediate in the hearer's mind, the obvious meaning and so on) changed their role. They became evidence or indicators (*dalāʾil*) of the literal meaning, but they have to an extent been subordinated to the technical, "scientific" linguistic meaning, which becomes the gold standard.

We could, of course, pick one or other of these technical notions in mature *uṣūl al-fiqh* and designate it as the literal meaning, thereby distinguishing it from other types of meaning (translation of technical terms is, rather like the original *waḍʿ*, arbitrary). Previous commentators on *uṣūl al-fiqh* writing in English have done this; the more careful have done so self-reflectively, aware that they are not doing much more than choosing an English term with which to refer to an Arabic technical term. I prefer, at this stage at least, not to tie the term "literal" to any specific term or concept used in classical *uṣūl*. My reason for doing so is partly that no translation is a perfect equivalent and therefore will always be, to an extent, artificial. More importantly, though, I wish to keep hold of the various ways in which literal interpretation, literal meaning and literalism are employed both in technical (philosophical) discourse and in everyday English, and examine how they might be found in Muslim legal discourse. The variety of connotations associated with literal was well demonstrated by Recanati and examined in the previous chapter.[120] The general preference for the literal which one finds in modern pragmatics and in classical *uṣūl* reflects, as I argue in the coming chapters, an assumed certainty and surety invested in meanings located in a text. This does not mean that Uṣūlīs condemned excursions beyond strictly textual meanings. Indeed, most accepted and even encouraged these interpretations. It should be noted, though, that the results were often accorded a "less than certain" status. However, in order even to discuss the different possible grades and nuances of the literal meaning of texts, the idea that

120 See above, p. 16.

the text had a meaning in and of itself which is distinguishable from the intended meaning of the author needed first to be embedded within the intellectual system. The process in early Muslim thought whereby texts (oral or written) were invested with this independent, and independently knowable, meaning forms the subject of the next chapter.

3

The Emergence of Literal Meaning in Early Islamic Thought

The development of the literal meaning in early Islamic thought can be traced to the belief (implicit in some Muslim discussions, explicit in others) that, once established, meaning is intimately connected to an assigned sound. The Arabic verb often used to describe this relationship is *taʿalluq* – to cling to, or be attached to something. In classical legal theory, the literal meaning is a meaning the utterance/text has which may have been arbitrarily assigned originally but, once assigned, is present in the text, even when the author's intended meaning is something quite different. In early Islamic thought, this conception of the meaning-sound connection was still being developed.[1] As we have already seen, the term "literal meaning" can be stretched from its raw literal meaning to cover the elimination of potential ambiguities arising out of linguistic features of the text, and yet further to encompass what ordinary language users understand to be the meaning inherent in the utterance. This typology of related (but distinct) notions of literal meaning is debated within modern linguistic philosophy, but remains a useful lens through which to view the competing conceptions of literal meaning in Islamic thought, since authors (particularly in the early period, as we shall see) often exhibited a vague understanding of literality which is nicely congruent with these different conceptions of literal meaning.

Whilst our principal aim in this work is to examine ideas of literal meaning in Islamic legal theory, this science did not develop in a vacuum. Indeed, Muslim legal hermeneutics generally shows the imprint of other discussions in the exegetical, grammatical and rhetorical sciences. Influence is particularly evident in ideas of literal meaning, where the competition between different conceptions within early legal theory reflects earlier discussions in these other disciplines. In all these fields, literal meaning can be identified when contrasts are drawn between what a text or utterance says (or appears to say) and what the author is presumed to mean. This happens in the cases of idiomatic expression, but also elision, allusion, inference and the various types of metaphor. On such hermeneutic occasions, literal meaning is defined, often simply to be rejected. An awareness of the distinction between literal and non-literal, in a sense, enables literal meaning to be defined. Without this distinction, meaning is of a single genus, and discerning it does not usually present

1 That this identity is, philosophically speaking, a fiction is irrelevant to understanding the power of the idea of literal meaning and tracing its development through the history of Muslim jurisprudence; see above, pp. 20–3.

a problem.[2] In this chapter, I trace the emergence of the literal/non-literal distinction and the concomitant notions of literal meaning it contains.

Quranic Literal/Non-literal Distinctions

It could be said that there are hints of the literal/non-literal distinction in the Qurʾān itself. Amongst the Quranic terms relevant to our investigation here are the juxtaposition of *ẓāhir*/*bāṭin*, *tafsīr*, *taʾwīl*, *muḥkam*, *mutashābih*, *ʿarabī mubīn* and the verb *ḥarrafa*. An examination of their Quranic usage informs any account of how the distinction emerged within Islamic literature more generally.

The *ẓāhir*/*bāṭin* distinction is, of course, well known and is employed in many later Islamic sciences. The two terms are used in a contrasting sense within the Qurʾān:

> Q6/al-Anʿām.120:
> Avoid the *ẓāhir* of a sin and its *bāṭin*.
>
> Q6/al-Anʿām.151:
> Do not come near to sinful actions, both that which is *ẓāhir* of them, and that which is *bāṭin* of them.[3]
>
> Q31/Luqmān.20:
> He showers his graces upon you, both the *ẓāhir* of them and the *bāṭin*.
>
> Q57/al-Ḥadīd.3:
> [God] is the first and last, the *ẓāhir* and the *bāṭin*.

Certainly, *ẓāhir* and *bāṭin* are seen as a contrasting pair, perhaps one of the most stable within the Quranic vocabulary. The traditional translation of "outer" and "inner" would seem the appropriate sense in most instances. With regard to sinful actions (*fawāḥish*, *ithm*), the actual performance of the action (*ẓāhir*) and the inner intention (*bāṭin*) could be indicated; with respect to God's graces, they are said to have both an outer benefit and an inner one; with respect to God being the *ẓāhir* and the *bāṭin*, a simple epithet of all-inclusivity is employed (the antithetical pairing is employed to indicate God's all-encompassing dominion). Words using the root ẓ-h-r are quite frequent in the Qurʾān, and are used in the sense of "to appear", "to become apparent/manifest" and "to prevail over".[4] The last of these is evident in references to battle and the victory of the Muslims (for example, Q9/al-Tawba.8 and Q18/al-Kahf.20). The idea that to be or to become *ẓāhir* is to prevail over one's opponents is comparable to the use of *ẓāhir* as a preponderant meaning in later Muslim

2 I am aware that in the case of incomprehensible words within an utterance, meaning does become problematic. As we shall see, in early Quranic exegesis this problem is normally overcome by supplying etymologies for words on a one-to-one lexical basis. In such an exercise, however, there is little (even implicit) evidence of a theory of literal meaning; see below, pp. 86–7.

3 Here I construe the verbs *ẓahara* and *baṭana* to mean "to be *ẓāhir*" and "to be *bāṭin*" in order to avoid prejudging what the *ẓāhir* and *bāṭin* might mean.

4 See Wansbrough, *Qurʾanic Studies*, pp. 152–3.

jurisprudence.[5] The *ẓāhir* of an utterance or a text would potentially be a cognate of the notion of literal meaning. The phrase *ẓāhir min al-qawl* (following the translation, the "outward appearance of the statement") in Q13/al-Raʿd.33 is a possible candidate. The opponents of God's message are challenged regarding the partners they ascribe to God:

> So name them, or do you point him [God?] to something on earth of which he is unaware? Or [do you point him] towards a *ẓāhir min al-qawl*?

The phrase was immediately viewed as problematic, as the subsequent dispute amongst exegetes indicates. The questions appear rhetorical. There is, of course, nothing which God can not know. Since the opponents clearly have nothing to teach God, they are pointing him towards a mere *ẓāhir min al-qawl*. Context indicates that the phrase refers to an empty claim. The *ẓāhir* is the outer shell of a hollow statement. Every statement may have a *ẓāhir*, but its truth lies not in its appearance, but in its accord with reality (hence the mock surprise that they assert something God may be unaware of). Whilst this is not a precise reference to a useful hermeneutic pairing of *ẓāhir* and *bāṭin*, the Quranic examples clearly set the scene for the exploitation of these terms in subsequent exegesis.

The common translation of both the Quranic terms *taʾwīl* and *tafsīr* as "interpretation" might also imply an awareness within the Qurʾān itself of a textual/literal meaning which is then subjected to exegesis. *Tafsīr* appears in a single Quranic verse (Q25/al-Furqān.33):

> *wa-lā yaʾtūnaka bi-mathalin illā jiʾnāka biʾl-ḥaqq wa-aḥsan tafsīran.*
> And they bring to you (sing.) nothing similar; but we bring you (sing.) the truth and a better *tafsīr* (*aḥsana tafsīran*).

The usage here does not seem to fit with the later usage of the term *tafsīr*, and subsequent attempts to establish such a link are, from a historical perspective, artificial.[6] However, the use of *tafsīr* here is of interest to the later tradition, and deserves some further analysis. Q25/al-Furqān.33 appears within a passage in which God (the usual Quranic voice) seeks to reassure his messenger (*rasūl*) that even though the Qurʾān is being rejected by the audience, every prophet (*kull nabī*) has sinful enemies. The messenger should not feel undermined by the enemies' challenge over the piecemeal revelation of the Qurʾān, rather than in one session (*jumlatan wāḥidatan*). This serial revelation is the most appropriate arrangement and is done for the messenger's own benefit (in order "to settle his mind"). We then have the reference to *tafsīr*: the enemy can bring nothing like the Qurʾān, but God brings the truth (*al-ḥaqq*) and a better *tafsīr*. Leaving aside any possible linguistic definition of the verbal noun *tafsīr* and the implied verb *fassara*, the context could indicate that *tafsīr* here refers to the Qurʾān itself – it is far superior to any attempted similar text

5 See Weiss, *The Search*, pp. 134–8.
6 Wansbrough, *Qurʾanic Studies*, p. 154 ff.

(*mathal*) brought by the enemies. *Tafsīr* could, with some licence, be said to be not an interpretation of a text as such, but the text itself (the recitation) which God provides to his messenger in order to counter the pathetic attempts of the enemy to produce a viable contender to the Quranic revelation. Such an account, however, may be unduly influenced by subsequent notions of the inimitability (*iʿjāz*) and the events of the Prophet's life normally associated with Quranic passages such as Q25/al-Furqān.30–3 (and the following verse in the *sūra*). An alternative explanation could have the term *tafsīr* be a reference to God bringing a better "explanation" as to the serial revelation of the Qurʾān; "explanation" for *tafsīr* would certainly have a closer link to subsequent semantic and technical understandings of *tafsīr*/*fassara*. The enemies have an explanation (a *tafsīr*?) as to why the Qurʾān is revealed piecemeal – the implication here, it would appear, is that a piecemeal process might be seen as evidence of the messenger inventing rather than receiving his text. But, comes the reply, if he were simply inventing the Qurʾān, then the enemy could bring something similar. Since they cannot (implying inimitability once again), their arguments fail. *Tafsīr* here is the alternative explanation for the piecemeal revelation of the Qurʾān which trumps the opponents' explanation of this phenomenon (namely, that the messenger is fabricating his Qurʾān). If this reading is adopted, then we do have, in the Qurʾān's use of the term *tafsīr*, an initial starting point for the later explorations of literal meaning, but in reference not to a text but to events. The piecemeal uncovering of the Qurʾān might appear to be an indication of its manufacture by Muḥammad rather than it being a divine revelation. This explanation, even though it comes from a belligerent source, is natural and perhaps, on the face of it, the most obvious account. God, however, has provided a better *tafsīr* (explanation), namely that piecemeal revelation settles the Prophet's mind, and the enemies' inability to produce anything similar to the revelation (a *mathal*) means the "natural" explanation of the enemies (fabrication) is to be replaced with God's "better" (but not initially obvious) *tafsīr*. *Tafsīr* is associated here with providing an alternative explanation of a phenomenon which could, almost without malice, be understood differently. It is not a huge leap from here to the notion of *tafsīr* as scriptural/textual exegesis.[7]

In contrast to the occasional references to *tafsīr*, *taʾwīl*, a term common in exegetical literature, is found frequently in the Qurʾān. Its verb, *awwala*, could be understood as "to return to the beginning/first/original", or "to restore – return to its original state" (in the Quranic citations below, it could be argued it refers to the act of "returning to the original intended message/meaning").[8] There is what appears to be a cognate expression to the *aḥsan tafsīran* ("finer in terms of *tafsīr*" in Q25/al-

7 My point here aims to temper Wansbrough's assertion that the connection between the genre of *tafsīr* and Q25/al-Furqān.33 is manufactured (*Qurʾanic Studies*, p. 154). I do not posit a causative link here between verse and genre, or even between verse and technical term. My point is merely that the verse reveals a Quranic usage of *tafsīr* which is not completely alien to the subsequent understanding of the term in (and the practice of) Muslim exegetical writings.

8 Wansbrough, *Qurʾanic Studies*, pp. 154–7.

Furqān.33) in *aḥsan taʾwīlan* ("finer in terms of *taʾwīl*") found at Q4/al-Nisāʾ.59 and Q17/al-Isrāʾ.35 in the phrase (identical in both locations) *dhālika khayr wa-aḥsan taʾwīlan*: that is good (or "the best") and the finest in terms of *taʾwīl*. The phrase is used on both occasions after a command addressed to the believers ("Obey God, his Prophet and those in authority"; "Use correct measures and balances"). Here *taʾwīl* appears to refer to an appropriate way of responding to God's command – or perhaps, more interpretively, a correct understanding of the command as a preparation for obedient action. A slightly different use of *taʾwīl* is prominent in Q12/Yūsuf, where it is used loosely as "understanding the significance of" something. For example, the phrase *taʾwīl al-aḥādīth* (the understanding/message of the events) is always used in connection with the verb "to teach" (*ʿallama*) – God will teach Joseph the *taʾwīl al-aḥādīth* (the "meaning" of the events, perhaps) in Q12/Yūsuf.6, 21 and 101 (in each case, *taʾwīl* could refer more specifically to dream interpretation). One can also refer here to the words of Moses's companion (often identified extra-Quranically as Khidr) who explains the meaning (*taʾwīl*) of his actions (the scuttling of ships, the killing of an apparently innocent boy and the repairing of a wall in a hostile town; see Q18/al-Kahf.60–82). That history has a message and should not be understood simply as a collection of (random) events is, of course, an underlying presumption of the historical references in the Qurʾān (as is the case in other scriptural and non-scriptural contexts). *Taʾwīl* is most prevalent in relation to the understanding of dreams in Q12/Yūsuf (see verses 36, 37, 44, 45 and 101), and this merges into the notion of the fulfilment of a prediction/dream as in Q12/Yūsuf.101, where Jacob identifies Joseph's invitation to come to Egypt as a "*taʾwīl* of my vision (*raʾī*)": one does not know the meaning/*taʾwīl* of a dream/prediction until the events occur which act as its fulfilment (also referred to as its *taʾwīl*). One passage from Q12/Yūsuf in particular is relevant to my purpose here:

> v. 35: Two young men entered prison at the same time – one of them said, "I saw myself [in a dream] pressing wine," and the other said, "I saw myself carrying bread on my head which the birds were eating." Tell us the *taʾwīl*. We see you are one of the good.
>
> v. 36: *lā yaʾtīkuma ṭaʿāmun turzaqānihi illā nabaʾtukuma bi-taʾwīlihi.*
> No provisions from which you might gain sustenance will come to you – but I will tell you its *taʾwīl*.

Joseph here tells his prisoner companions that they should not take the dreams "literally" – they will not have the actual wine or bread, even though the dreams portray them as having these provisions. *Taʾwīl* here refers to the non-obvious meaning of a thing; the *taʾwīl* is not apparent from the thing itself – once again, a basic notion in the exegetical framework in which literal meaning plays a major role.[9]

9 I am, I suppose, pointing out that Versteegh's assertion that *taʾwīl*'s meaning in early Quranic commentaries was "to apply a verse to a given situation" (*Arabic Grammar*, p. 63) does not appear to apply to the Qurʾān itself. A radical break between Quranic and post-Quranic usage of a term such as *taʾwīl* seems perfectly

Perhaps the reference to *ta'wīl* best exploited in later hermeneutic tradition is in Q3/Āl ʿImrān.7:

> He is the one who sent down to you the Book, in which there are clear/decisive signs/verses (*āyāt muḥkamāt*) – and these are the foundation/mother (lit. mother) of the book. Others are unclear/inconclusive (*mutashābihāt*). And as for those in whose hearts there is deviancy, they follow what is unclear/inconclusive, seeking discord and seeking its *ta'wīl*, and no one knows its *ta'wīl* except for God, and those who are secure in knowledge (who) say "we believe in it; all of it is with our lord". Only those of understanding will heed the warning.

My translation is interpretive (as all are): the verse is ambiguous both lexically and syntactically.[10] There is, of course, an identification in the later tradition of the *āyāt* (both *muḥkam* and *mutashābih*) as a reference to textual segments ("verses") rather than real world phenomena awaiting treatment by an interpretive process; but this later identification need not control our understanding of the verse's meaning. As is well known, *āya* invariably refers to "signs" in the Qur'ān (in Q2/al-Baqara.151, the *āyāt*/signs are actually distinguished from the *kitāb*/book); the *āyāt* in the verse could be signs in the Book as easily as they are later technical names for verses; there is a lack of explicit self-reference in the verse (that is, there is no statement that this is the Book talking about itself, as is often presumed – "the Book" could be something other than the text in front of us);[11] and, finally, the context of the verse does not indicate that the passage from which the verse is extracted is a thematic treatment of textual, interpretive or hermeneutic themes. In any case, whether the *āyāt* are seen as textual segments or events through which God wishes to communicate, the basic hermeneutic paradigm is employed: the *āyāt* are signs which indicate a meaning which is not always apparent at first encounter. Those which have an apparent meaning do not need a *ta'wīl* (that is, an interpretive meaning) to be supplied – they are the *muḥkamāt*; those that are not apparent (*mutashābih*), require a *ta'wīl* to be supplied, and a warning is made against those who attempt to find this *ta'wīl* independently. Interestingly, elsewhere in the Qur'ān, the book which God "sends down" is identified as *mutashābih* (Q39/al-Zumar.23), which is not normally taken as an admittance of ambiguity on the part of the Book. Returning to Q3/Āl ʿImrān.7, only God (and possibly "those secure in knowledge" depending on

---

possible to me. However, the most persuasive examples adduced by Versteegh relate to *ta'awwal* meaning "apply" rather than *ta'wīl*/*awwala*. For *ta'wīl* specifically, the examples he quotes concur with the Quranic usage more or less – *ta'wīl* refers to a meaning (of an event, and, in exegesis, to a text) which is other than a natural meaning. For example, for a hungry prisoner's dream concerning bread to "come true" it would seem natural that receiving food would be part of the fulfilment of the dream; but Joseph says the *ta'wīl* of the dream is that he will not see the food. Versteegh's examples of *ta'wīl* (*Arabic Grammar*, p. 64), as opposed to those of *ta'awwala*, seem approximately in tune with this Quranic usage.

10 See Kinberg, "*Muḥkamāt* and *mutashābihāt*", pp. 43–5.

11 Wild, of course, views the Qur'ān as being self-referential here – and that is the traditional interpretation of the verse. I agree that it is possible that this is a case of self-referentiality, but it is not the only possible understanding of the verse. See Wild, "Self-referentiality", pp. 432–3.

syntactic and sectarian understanding of the verse)[12] can know the *taʾwīl.* Even though not all the Book is known, all of it should be accepted and trusted ("believed in"). Hence, knowing the meaning of a verse is not crucial to accepting it as a scripture. Once again, *taʾwīl* is the end product of an interpretive process in which something puzzling (be it a text or an event) is explained. The resultant meaning is its *taʾwīl.* Despite its grammatical appearance as a verbal noun, its Quranic references appear to be as the end product of a process rather than the process itself (no one appears to "do" *taʾwīl*; instead they know or learn or teach the *taʾwīl* of a thing).

Other examples support this reading, such as when *taʾwīl* is connected with the verb *atā* (to come): the *taʾwīl* of the day of reckoning will come (become clear, possibly) to those who are sinful (Q7/al-Aʿrāf.53); some reject the Apostle's message even before its *taʾwīl* has come (Q10/Yūnus.39).[13] If we are to enforce consistent usage of the term across the Quranic corpus (a potentially artificial exercise, admittedly), *taʾwīl* is more likely to refer to the end product of an interpretive process (for example, Joseph gives the *taʾwīl*/meaning of the dreams to his prisoner companions) than the process itself (compare with the ambiguous reference to teaching *taʾwīl al-aḥādīth* – it could mean the process, and it could mean the end product). In any case, the true meaning of a dream or event is not the apparent, immediate meaning but an interpreted message.

This privileging of a non-immediate understanding could be said to contrast with at least two themes presented within the Qurʾān: its clarity claims and its attitude towards other scriptures. In the first of these, the self-representation of the Qurʾān as a text of "clear Arabic tongue" (Q16/al-Naḥl.103 and Q26/al-Shuʿarāʾ.195) is a claim that it is easily understood, and the failure to hear and respond is, therefore, a denial of the obvious made against the non-Quranic religious communities. It is unsurprising then that these claims occur in the course of polemics against the enemies of the messenger. Whether this amounts to a special claim for Arabic as supremely expressive and clear was debated by later writers, but the message of such verses does appear to make a special claim for the Qurʾān as superior: due to its style, it requires little exegetical effort on the part of the (Arabic-speaking) listener. Past scriptures are also expressed clearly, even if their custodians have sought to obfuscate their meaning (constituting a second Quranic theme in which a text's meaning is contrasted with its interpretation). The recipients of past scriptures (primarily Christians and Jews) refuse to accept the new Muslim ethical, legal and religious order, and amongst their failings is the supposed textual adjustment of their scriptures for community (rather than divine) purposes. The key term here in later exegesis is *taḥrīf,*[14] though the verb *ḥarrafa* appears within the Qurʾān only in reference to the

12 For a discussion of the sectarian Imāmī understanding, see Bar-Asher, *Scripture and Exegesis*, p. 100.

13 See also Wild, "Self-referentiality", p. 428.

14 See Nickel, *Narratives of Tampering*, for a comprehensive examination of the ideas surrounding alteration and corruption.

Jews (both ancient and contemporary to the Prophet), and is possibly unconnected with its later doctrine of scriptural alteration. Q2/al-Baqara.75 reads:

> Do you hope that they [the Jews] will be true to you? A group of them used to listen to God's word (*kalām Allāh*), and then twist it knowingly after they had understood it (*ʿaqalūhu*).

The Jews (or, more precisely, a group – *fāriq* – of them) understand the meaning of scripture (a process signified by the verb *ʿaqala*), but twist it (*yuḥarrifūnahu*) intentionally/knowingly. The verb *ḥarrafa* here need not be understood as alteration of scripture (as per later dogma), but could equally refer to the deliberate misrepresentation of its message. This construal would be consonant with at least some of the other appearances of *ḥarrafa* in the Qurʾān. *Taḥrīf* is clearly a corruption of some sort and is a charge explicitly aimed at the Jews, though what it entails is not explicitly stated. Q4/al-Nisāʾ.46 reads:

> Some of those who are Jews (*al-ladhīna hādū*) twist words out of their places (*yuḥarrifūnahu ʿan mawāḍiʿihi*) and say, "we hear and we disobey" and "listen to one who does not hear" and "observe us", twisting their tongues and defaming religion.

The translation of this verse is, of course, problematic, but we need not immediately jump to meanings such as "to alter" or "to change" for *ḥarrafa*. The Jews hear the Prophet's message, understand it, but refuse to follow it. The verse continues to represent a parallel to the three exhortations:

> If they had said, "we heard and we obeyed" and "hear!" and "look at us", it would have been better for them, and more correct. (Q4/al-Nisāʾ.46)

So, the three statements in this latter part of the verse are partners to the three earlier statements by the (or some) Jews. The Jews, then, deliberately gave an inappropriate response to God's word – it appears as mocking the messenger. Is this what is meant by "twisting God's speech out of its place"? It is possible that *ḥarrafa* is unconnected with the doctrine of scriptural alteration (as it is later understood), or even deliberate misunderstanding/misinterpretation (as per Q2/al-Baqara.75). It is simply a reference to the alleged perfidy of the Jews.

In Q5/al-Māʾida.13, the same locution *yuḥarrifūn ʿan mawāḍiʿihi* appears, but here, I would argue, it is better understood as referring to deliberate misinterpretation or wilfully ignoring the meaning of scripture. In reference to the people of Israel, the Qurʾān states:

> And because of them breaking their covenant, we have cursed them and made their hearts hard. They twist words out of their places, and forget a part by which they were warned.

And, later in this *sūra*, Q5/al-Māʾida.41:

> And amongst the Jews [there are those] who listen to lies, listen to another people who did not come to you (sing.) – they twist the word *after their places* [their placements? *yuḥarrifūna al-kalim min baʿd mawāḍiʿihi*].

The last phrase is peculiar perhaps, and could refer to the coinage of terms. Although it would seem anachronistic to be referring to even an embryonic theory of *waḍʿ* here,[15] the idea that the words are "placed", or that they have proper "placements" which the Jews are then accused of altering, remains a possible reading. In these instances, however, deliberate misinterpretation (following Q2/al-Baqara.75) is a likely intended reference, rather than deliberate and malicious alteration of the text. Whatever is the case, for our purposes the fact that these references to *taḥrīf* refer to an understanding of the text (a process represented by the verb *ʿaqala*), which is relatively easily obtained and then deliberately corrupted (*ḥarrafa*), is sufficient – the meaning is changed, the text is ignored or forgotten, an inappropriate response is given; the text itself, however, is not necessarily changed. This reasoning is, of course, speculative given the opacity of Quranic expression, though it is noteworthy that lexicons record *ḥarrafa* as meaning not only substituting one text with another (*tabdīl*) but also "diverting it away from its meaning".[16] Notwithstanding the lack of precision over the meaning of *ḥarrafa* and the fact that the technical apparatus is not developed, the *kalām/kalim Allāh* is seen in these references as having a readily available meaning which the Jews are misrepresenting. For our purposes, the crucial point here is that within the Qurʾān itself, there is an acceptance of the basic hermeneutic division between obvious meaning and real signification.

This presentation does not exhaust the Quranic material, nor does it establish a causal link between the Quranic ideas and later Muslim hermeneutics. However, we can say that there is not yet a purely textual focus within the Quranic material in terms of the literal/non-literal distinction. A word such as *taʾwīl* refers really to the "thing signified" by a phenomenon which might otherwise be seen as inconsequential or incomprehensible. The *taʾwīl* of Joseph's dreams are what they signify for the individuals concerned ("what they mean", in one sense of the phrase). When the Qurʾān records that the *taʾwīl al-aḥādīth* will be taught, the reference is clearly not to teaching a bare chronological listing of events, but the underlying message of historical happenings. It is their significance for the life of the believing community which is important; their status as signs (*āyāt*) requires identification and interpretation. I am not unaware of a close proximity between these ideas and textual interpretation: what a sign means slips into what a text means, since a text is a kind of sign itself (hence the term *āya* for verse). However, my purpose here is simply to indicate the continuities and dissonances between the Qurʾān and later exegetical models. The Qurʾān's recognition of an interpretive process (mostly of things generally rather than texts specifically) provided a context for the more specific

15 Ambros sees this as a hybrid with *min baʿdi waḍʿihi* (*Concise Dictionary of Koranic Arabic*, p. 291). It seems more likely to be a hybrid of *ʿan mawāḍiʿihi* and *min baʿd mā ʿaqalahu* of Q2/al-Baqara.75.

16 See, for example, Ibn Manẓūr, *Lisān al-ʿArab*, v. 9, p. 43: "*al-Taḥrīf* in the Qurʾān and in talking is to change a *ḥarf* from its meaning, or a word from its meaning … The Jews used to change the *meanings* (*maʿānī*) of the Torah with similarities (*ashbāh*)" (emphasis added – it is the meanings that are changed rather than the text). In a similar vein, see Burton, "Corruption of the Scriptures"; on *ḥarrafa* specifically see Nickel, *Narratives of Tampering*, pp. 57–9.

hermeneutic explorations of later writers. The Quranic vocabulary of interpretation (*ẓāhir, bāṭin, tafsīr, taʾwīl, muḥkam, mutashābih, taḥrīf, mawāḍiʿ* and so on) is not expressly technical, even if the words are shared with later Muslim exegesis and hermeneutics. Nevertheless, the recognition of an interpretive process in the Quranic text provided (at the very least) lexes (though perhaps not the refined concepts behind the terms) with which the interpretive act could be described. Implicit in this recognition was the basic binary distinction between an uninterpreted and an interpreted meaning of events, which segues into both the notion of a text being an event in itself (for example, the Qurʾān) and the interpretation of texts which record those events.

Literal Meaning in Early Muslim Writings

There are, then, general dichotomies of outer/inner and obvious/hidden found within the Qurʾān and here applied to events, narratives, individuals and (more rarely) words and texts. Sometimes the inner/hidden meaning is elevated to the position of the real; at others it is the outer/obvious meaning which is crucially important and which the unbelievers deny in their obstinacy. I am not suggesting these notions constitute the cause of later doctrines of the literal/non-literal distinction in Muslim jurisprudence; they do, however, create a context for the later intellectual exploration of the distinction, and to an extent they provide some key elements of the terminology of the later exegetical and juristic sciences. The Quranic ideas of a bifurcated understanding are hardly surprising in a context rich in scripturalism, even if the Muslims were not, *ab initio*, in possession of a scripture. They do not, however, amount to a subtle conception of literal meaning, or to the literal/non-literal distinction which came to dominate later Muslim legal hermeneutics. To chart the emergence of that particular hermeneutic device, the primary source is early Quranic exegesis.

Rippin has characterised some of the later exegetical material as "Arabic translations" of the Qurʾān.[17] Much of the exegesis found in the *tafsīr* works attributed to Ibn ʿAbbās (d. 68?/688–9), Mujāhid (d. 102?/720), Sufyān al-Thawrī (d. 161?/777–8) and others, and a substantial portion of the orally transmitted exegesis of early figures outside of these attributed texts, consists of simple assertions of the type:

> Qurʾān says X; and it means Y.

X is a Quranic phrase, and Y is the exegete's interpretation (or perhaps translation) of that into his own words – and they are sometimes connected by a phrase (*yaʿnī, ay, maʿnāhu*).[18] At other times there is no connector ("X is Y"). Examples of this are found with great regularity within the early material (both in supposed *tafsīr* works

17 Rippin, "Lexicographical Texts", p. 164.

18 An examination of these connectors, and a history of the term *maʿnā* in early Islamic writings, can be found in Versteegh, *Arabic Linguistic Tradition*.

and in orally transmitted material); indeed, this style of exegesis appears the dominant one. For example:

> Q38/Ṣād.26:
> Those who have gone astray from the path of God will have a great punishment concerning what they have forgotten of the day of reckoning.
> Sufyān: the day of resurrection.[19]
>
> Q4/al-Nisāʾ.46:
> They hear and they disobey.
> Zayd b. ʿAlī: its meaning (*maʿnāhu*) is "they hear your words and they disobey your orders".[20]
>
> Q3/al-Māʾida.54:
> God will bring forth a people whom he will love and who love him.
> Ibn ʿAbbās: *God will bring forth* he will come with *a people whom he* God *will love and who love him* they will love God.[21]
>
> ʿAbd al-Raḥmān>Ibrāhīm>Ādam>Warqāʾ>Ibn Abī Najīh>Mujāhid said:
> [*Adam to God*]: *I will wait for them on your straight path* (*ṣirāṭuka al-mustaqīm*) *yaʿnī* Islam, the true religion.[22]

The usual explanation for the popularity of this technique was that rapid Arabic language change has rendered words within the Qurʾān as obscure, ambiguous or meaningless in everyday Arabic.[23] This may indeed account for some of the proposed equivalents by early exegetes. However, in many cases (such as the examples above), the meaning proposed in each gloss does not seem outlandish when one reads the Quranic text. Indeed, the glosses seem quite unremarkable in this sense (accepting that our reading of the Quranic text may have been conditioned). Versteegh points towards the swift expansion of the Muslim community in the early period, and hence the scarcity of linguistic knowledge of "Bedouin" Arabic (in which the Qurʾān is presented), as the reason for this exegetical technique.[24] But many of these glosses would not immediately appear to require extensive knowledge of "Bedouin" Arabic. The identification of anaphora[25] (as in the Ibn ʿAbbās example) or objects governed by verbs (as in Zayd b. ʿAlī's text) would not, I suggest, require detailed knowledge

19 Sufyān, *Tafsīr*, p. 258.
20 Zayd b. ʿAlī, *Tafsīr*, p. 119.
21 Ibn ʿAbbās, *Tanwīr*, p. 126. Here, as elsewhere, the italics are the source text (usually a Quranic passage) which is repeated and glossed with the author's comments.
22 Mujāhid, *Tafsīr*, v. 1, p. 232.
23 See, for example, Versteegh, *Arabic Grammar*, p. 86.
24 Versteegh, *Arabic Grammar*, p. 88. Such a view assumes a historical development analogous to a so-called "Salafī" framework – that there was a time when the Qurʾān was perfectly clear in meaning, after which the community gradually lost its (linguistic) purity, making the original message of the Qurʾān unrecoverable. It also assumes a certain account of the formation of the Quranic text.
25 Or "lexical slots", as Recanati puts it; see above, pp. 15–16.

of the language of the *badw*. In some texts, such as those given by Ibn ʿAbbās, the coverage is almost total – almost no phrase in the Qur'ān is left unglossed; we should not conclude from this that Ibn ʿAbbās thought the whole Qur'ān to be obscure and its meaning forgotten.[26] Instead, the technique should, I believe, be seen as an expression of the message of scripture, most of which is already known. This creative rewriting was not developed simply because scripture had, *in toto* or in part, become obscure. Rather, the rewriting was primarily a mixture of piety, the creative impulse and the beginnings of the scholastic enterprise in Islam. It should not be viewed as initiated solely for the pragmatic purpose of understanding the Quranic text in order to establish the correctness of communal belief. Instead, the emergence of an industry of scholarship during the Umayyad period, and subsequently enhanced after the ʿAbbāsid revolution, involved the development of particular disciplines of learning. The techniques and methods of each discipline develop at times in response to a communal need, but also out of the creativity of its participants. This "lexical paraphrasing" is one such technique.[27] Clarifying obscure phrases in the Qur'ān was only one element of the technique (and could be seen as a useful by-product of its adoption). A fuller analysis would probably identify other factors which explain the emergence of this exegetical technique, including the demonstration of academic virtuosity; a pietistic desire to express the mind of God; the emergence of elementary theories of communication and language; and a movement towards disciplinary completeness, as the whole Qur'ān is restated. Eliminating obscurity and worries about the disappearance of the meaning of certain Quranic terms are only part of the explanation.[28]

However the appearance of this technique is explained, our concern here is primarily its relationship with literal meaning. It seems unlikely to me that the exegetes believed their rewording to be the literal meaning (in the sense of the meaning the text owns). This is because, as will become clear below, there is a different (albeit rudimentary) awareness of literal meaning within this early exegetical corpus, and it is recognised as separate from the meanings presented in the glosses. In short, the glosses focus on how a word or phrase is used within the Qur'ān

26 There was an appeal to Bedouin Arab usage which became popular in later *tafsīr*s and in Sībawayh. I deal with this below (pp. 120–4). But its use is a technique, and it does not explain the emergence of the glossing process exemplified here.

27 Using the locution "lexical paraphrase" to describe the technique is, I submit, not quite accurate since the exegetes, generally speaking, are not discussing what the text means, but what the author intends by the text. As Versteegh points out (perhaps inconsistently with his use of "lexical paraphrasing"), "the commentators were not interested in the language of the Qur'ān as such" (*Arabic Grammar*, p. 84). He does recognise the difference between lexical and other forms of paraphrase, but a paraphrase is, it seems to me, a paraphrase of a text (that is, what a text says), modulated by reference to the intentions of the author (often in an unsystematic manner). The textual focus causes me to doubt whether the English word "paraphrase" is the correct term here.

28 It is possible that it grew out of perceived obscurities within the Quranic text; the glossing became necessary for those words and phrases, and then it became a habit for the whole text. On this *tafsīr* style, see Versteegh, *Arabic Grammar*, pp. 55–61.

with an eye to the author's intended meaning. This may or may not coincide with the exegetes' notion of what the words "literally" mean. Literal meaning, as we are using it here, is most in evidence in these *tafsīr*s when it is rejected in favour of a non-literal meaning. At these points, the exegetes are required to express a phrase's literal meaning, and distinguish it from its non-literal (intended) meaning. In order to demonstrate the employment of literal meaning in early Quranic exegesis, I focus below on three linked issues: literal meaning in early Quranic *tafsīr*s (in particular those ascribed to Ibn ʿAbbās, Mujāhid and Zayd b. ʿAlī (d. 122/740)); the emergence of a hermeneutic awareness (in particular the *kull shayʾ* rules); and the relationship between literal meaning and *kalām al-ʿArab*. Following this, I consider the rise of grammatical learning and its impact on the ideas of literal meaning current at the time when Islamic legal theory emerged (that is, in the early third/ninth century with the work of al-Shāfiʿī).

Literal meaning and "early" *tafsīr*

One does find in the earliest (attributed) exegetical statements an occasional call on the distinction between the Qurʾān's literal and non-literal meaning. The tradition supposedly begins with the companion and relative of the Prophet Muḥammad, ʿAbd Allāh Ibn ʿAbbās. It is highly debatable whether we can trace a body of teaching back to Ibn ʿAbbās, let alone whether he authored a book as such.[29] What we have is a large number of exegetical *ḥadīth* in which Ibn ʿAbbās is said to give the meaning of this or that Quranic passage or phrase cited by later exegetes. To supplement this material, we have a full(ish) work, one recension of which has been published under the title of *Tanwīr al-Miqbās min Tafsīr Ibn ʿAbbās.* This work has, at various times, been attributed to Ibn ʿAbbās, transmitted through an *isnād* to a later scholar (al-Kalbī [d. 146/763], al-Fīrūzabādī [d. 817/1414], and so on). Let us call the reports and the *tafsīr* text attributed to Ibn ʿAbbās the "oral" and "written" tradition regarding Ibn ʿAbbās respectively. A comparison of these two exegetical sets is instructive. Within the oral tradition (the corpus of *ḥadīth* citations from Ibn ʿAbbās), there is a sensitivity to the literal/non-literal meaning distinction. For example, there is a collection of traditions attributed to Ibn ʿAbbās through different *isnād*s, and presented by al-Ṭabarī in relation to Q2/al-Baqara.223 – "Women are your fields, go into your fields as you wish":

> (from ʿIkrima): Ibn ʿAbbās said: "go into your fields" means the birthplace of the child.
> (from Saʿīd b. Jubayr): Ibn ʿAbbās said: "go into your fields as you wish" means enter her however you wish, as long as you do not enter her *in ano* or *in menstruo.*
> (from Saʿid b. Jubayr): Ibn ʿAbbās said: "women are your fields – go into them as you wish" means you can enter them from the front or the back, as long as you do not enter them *in ano* or *in menstruo.*
> (from ʿAlī): Ibn ʿAbbās said: "go into your fields as you wish"; he means, by field, the

29 On Ibn ʿAbbās and his *tafsīr* see Berg, "The Isnād and the Production of Cultural Memory", and, more generally, his *The Development of Exegesis in Early Islam.*

vagina, and is saying, "you go into it however you wish, from the front or from behind – in any way one wishes after the vagina has been disallowed to someone else. This is why he says: "go into them in the way God has ordered you" (Q2/al-Baqara.222).[30]

There are, for Ibn ʿAbbās (as for later commentators), two concurrent and related tropes in this Quranic verse:

fields: women
fields: female genitalia

The first is well signalled by the divine author ("Women are your fields"); the second is less obvious. The move from the first metaphor to the second in the course of the verse (as Ibn ʿAbbās seems to do in the above citation) is, one presumes, to prevent the verse from becoming a possible permission for supposed sexual deviancy. The apparently unrestricted order implied by the statement "as you wish" in v. 223 is restricted by reference to various prohibitions by Ibn ʿAbbās, the most general one being the order in the preceding verse "go into them in the way God has ordered you" (v. 222). In accordance with "God's commands" means that only vaginal intercourse is permitted, and then only after the woman has been disallowed to anyone else (that is, it is an exclusive sexual relationship with the addressee of the verse) and when it occurs outside of her menstrual period. The collection of statements from Ibn ʿAbbās demonstrate an awareness of the literal/non-literal distinction in the form of metaphor (women are not actually fields), and also of metonymy built on metaphor: the first part is reasonably straightforward ("women are your fields"); in the second part, "fields", which had stood for "women", is now used to refer to a part of a woman (*farj*). Furthermore, there is an understanding that the apparently unrestricted nature of the permission in the verse (signalled by the phrase "as you wish") needs to be restricted by the non-metaphorical statement in the preceding verse ("go into them in the way God has ordered you"). This restriction is in turn filled out with the various restrictions known from other elements of the law. It is possible that an unrestricted statement of the law, derived through an understanding of a metaphorical expression within the Qurʾān, stands on less solid epistemological ground (and is therefore more vulnerable or in need of restriction) than an unrestricted statement gained through a non-metaphorical phrase. There is, then, in these simple statements from Ibn ʿAbbās some quite sophisticated, and at times contradictory, assumptions. Al-Ṭabarī, as usual, weaves these reports (and others) together with technical skill.

In the written tradition attributed to Ibn ʿAbbās (the *Tanwīr al-Miqbās*), the metaphor in the verse is recognised, but it is presented with much-reduced nuance:

"Women are your fields" – it is said that the genitalia of women are the plantations for your children; "go into your fields", your plantations; "as you wish", however you like – from the front or the back – as long as it is in a single aperture.[31]

30 Ṭabarī, *Jāmiʿ al-Bayān*, v. 2, pp. 532–3.
31 Ibn ʿAbbās, *Tanwīr*, p. 39.

Here the complexity of having a metaphor in the first part of the verse followed by a metonym in the second is somewhat flattened. Only one of the restrictions is presented, and there is no hint of recognition of the relative epistemological status of rulings derived through metaphor or by other means. There is no development into the list found in the oral tradition attributed to Ibn ʿAbbās. It would seem that the treatments of the literal/non-literal distinction seem less accomplished in the written tradition than in the oral, which could indicate the order of the emergence of the various elements of Ibn ʿAbbās's supposed exegesis of this verse.[32] However, in both cases, the glossing technique is used: the presented exegesis is not the literal meaning of the Quranic phrase (the idea that women are actually fields is not even entertained). The focus is squarely on the meaning of the passage rather than the manner in which its literal meaning is acquired. In both cases the literal meaning is not subjected to any detailed analysis, but it is recognised to exist. It is taken as uncomplicated and obviously incorrect. The presumption is, I would suggest, that everyone knows what a sentence of the type "X are your Y" usually means, but it is so obviously incorrect in this verse that there is no need to explore how we come to know it.

Within Mujāhid's *tafsīr* text, the literal/non-literal meaning division is also clearly present, though once again in embryonic form. Mujāhid's *tafsīr* (in its published edition) consists, in the main, of exegetical statements traced back to Mujāhid through *isnād*s. There is a recognition within these collated reports that the author's meaning may be distinct from the text's meaning. In Q2/al-Baqara.65, God speaks concerning those Jews who have ignored the Sabbath: "We said to them, 'Be apes, despised' (*faqulnā lakum kūnū qirada khāsiʾīn*)." In Mujāhid's *tafsīr* it states:

> ʿAbd al-Raḥmān>Ibrāhīm>Ādam>Warqāʾ>Ibn Abī Najīh>Mujāhid concerning his words *kūnū qirada khāsiʾīn*: They did not turn into monkeys – rather it is like his statement "[they are like] a donkey who carries books" (from Q.62/al-Jumʿa.5).[33]

In this short passage, at least two exegetical operations are present. First, there is the simple recognition that the phrase is problematic ("Be apes" appears to indicate that those addressed should metamorphose). Second, there is an appeal to stylistic unity of the Qurʾān by saying that the expression here is "like" (*ka-*) the expression in another verse. That the subject matter in the two verses is the same (Jews who fail to keep the commandments) strengthens Mujāhid's case for linking the approach to the two verses.[34] In the corroborating reference, Q.62/al-Jumʿa.5, God likens those who received commandments from God but failed to keep them to "a donkey who carries books" (that is, they possess the books but, like a donkey, are unable to

32 Of course, the difference could be due to the intentional brevity of the *tafsīr* text, and the more expansive nature of later *tafsīr*s (such as the *Jāmiʿ al-Bayān* of al-Ṭabarī (310/923)). A comparison of the exegetical citations and published *Tafsīr* of Muqātil (d. 150/767) has been carried out by Koç ("A Comparison"), though he does not view the differences as significant.

33 Mujāhid, *Tafsīr*, v. 1, pp. 77–8.

34 I return to this notion with the *kull shayʾ* rule below, pp. 79–84.

understand or obey them). However, there is no recognition that the imagery in the two verses is, in fact, expressed through different figures. The simile in Q.62/al-Jumʿa.5 is signalled by the phrase *ka-mathal* ("as the likeness of" – the comparison between the Jews and the donkey is heightened by the play on the root ḥ-m-l: *ḥummilū*; *lam yaḥmilūhā*; *yaḥmilu*). In this verse there is no deviation from the literal meaning because the simile is well flagged. The problem with Q2/al-Baqara.65 is that the metaphor is not flagged but simply stated; the exegetical problem posed by it is, I suggest, unlike that posed by Q.62/al-Jumʿa.5. The two verses are alike in that they both use figures of speech, but they are quite unalike in that one uses simile and the other straightforward metaphor. Clearly the hermeneutic sense is not so well developed here – there is a recognition that something is happening which involves a non-literal understanding of the words donkey and ape, but there is no typology of metaphor on which Mujāhid draws.

In the equally problematic *Tafsīr Gharīb al-Qurʾān* ascribed to Zayd b. ʿAlī, there is no real understanding of metaphor in this verse at all,[35] which might tempt us to think that we have here an even earlier exegetical form than that found in Mujāhid. But this would be hasty, since elsewhere the literal/non-literal meaning distinction is understood, though it does not dominate, and nor is it theoretised. As with Mujāhid, most of the exegetical comments are glosses, definitions of words, clarifications and additions to Quranic narratives. The notion that the message somehow differs from the meaning of the text is not examined in detail, and is certainly not explained. There is not, as far as I can tell, any real hermeneutic sophistication (such as technical terms or the expression of general rules of interpretation). It is, however, clearly understood and implicit in some of Zayd's exegetical teachings found within the current text of the *tafsīr*:

> Q2.al-Baqara/255:
> His *kursī* stretches over the heavens and the earth.
> He [Zayd] said: His knowledge stretches over heaven and earth … and it is said that the *kursī* is the place where the throne is placed.[36]

Both the non-literal and the (more) literal meanings are given, though neither is given a technical category. The (incorrect) literal understanding is introduced by *yuqāl* ("it is said"). Zayd uses this phrase to introduce overruled (and not always literal) alternatives. Similarly, less controversial metaphors are explained by the word *maʿnā* or *yaʿnī*:

> Q88/al-Mursalāt.8:
> "When the stars are obliterated": meaning their light disappears.

> Q88/al-Mursalāt.9:
> "and the skies are split open": its meaning is that they are uncovered.[37]

35 Zayd b. ʿAlī, *Tafsīr*, p. 84.
36 Zayd b. ʿAlī, *Tafsīr*, p. 103.
37 Zayd b. ʿAlī, *Tafsīr*, p. 364.

Literal meaning is clearly understood in the background, as it were, and this has prompted the need for exegesis. Zayd picks verses for this treatment; his *tafsīr* does not cover every verse. However, there is no hint here as to how the literal meaning emerges and how the reader comes to perceive it. The exegetical framework is, I suspect, less sophisticated than that displayed in Mujāhid.[38]

Literal meaning and the *kull shayʾ* rules

Zayd in his *tafsīr* is said to recognise a problem with Q9/al-Tawba.30 in which it says "May God fight them" (that is, the Jews and Christians who make claims of messianic status for particular pre-Muhammadan prophets):

> *qātalahum Allāh: maʿnāhu laʿanahum Allāh.*
> "May God fight them": its meaning is "may God curse them".[39]

In this simple statement, the meaning of a word (for example *qātala* – "to fight") is not the meaning to be understood; there is an alternative, correct meaning (designated *maʿnā*, namely *laʿana* – "to curse"). The referent of the *-hu* in phrases like *maʿnāhu laʿanahum Allāh* is important but difficult to tie down: whose meaning is being attributed here, the author's intended meaning or the text's meaning? In Zayd's *tafsīr* the *maʿnā* of the text appears to be the intention of the author (a position not unique to him, but which seems to be the usual employment of the term in early *tafsīr*s). An alternative (sometimes literal) meaning exists, but it is not called *maʿnā*. Indeed, as far as I can tell, it is not yet given a name.

In the Ibn ʿAbbās corpus is the following, once again found in al-Ṭabarī's *Jāmiʿ al-Bayān*, and once again representing a relatively developed hermeneutic sense:

> Q9/al-Tawba.30:
> The Jews say ʿUzayr is the son of God; the Christians say the Messiah is the son of God; this is what they say with their mouths, imitating what those in the past have said. May Allāh fight them (*qātalahum Allāh*) – how they have been turned away.
> Muthannā>Abū Ṣaliḥ>Muʿāwiya>ʿAlī>Ibn ʿAbbās who said: "*qātalahum Allāh*" – it means "May God curse them". And every time killing (*qatl*) is [mentioned] in the Qurʾān, it is *laʿn* (cursing).[40]

Here the phrase "May God fight them" is interpreted as meaning "May God curse them"; this was (later) accepted as the meaning of a standard idiomatic expression of the Arabs. Ibn ʿAbbās is recorded as saying that when this phrase is used within

38 A more thorough comparison would be necessary to confirm this, and the precise dating or order of these texts is not essential to my purposes here. On the possibility of dating early *tafsīr* texts, see Rippin, "*Tafsīr* Ibn ʿAbbās".

39 See Zayd b. ʿAlī, *Tafsīr*, p. 150; the phrase is also used in Q63/al-Munāfiqūn.4, glossed with identical wording (see Zayd b. ʿAlī, *Tafsīr*, p. 334).

40 Quoted from Ibn ʿAbbās in Ṭabarī, *Jāmiʿ al-Bayān*, v. 10, p. 145. On the rule "and every time … is [mentioned] in the Qurʾān" (*kull shayʾ fī al-qurʾān*), and its attribution to Ibn ʿAbbās, see Versteegh, *Arabic Grammar*, pp. 86–7.

the Qur'ān, it means cursing. Such an interpretation of an idiomatic expression is, perhaps, unremarkable. It does, though, establish a distinction between textual meaning and idiom, which (in itself) forms the basis for a literal/non-literal distinction. Ibn ʿAbbās's attributed employment of a hermeneutic rule, namely *kull shayʾ fī al-qurʾān* … ("every time a phrase is used in the Qur'ān it means …" – the *kull shayʾ* rule), is particularly noteworthy. He is not the first to have (supposedly) employed the rule. The companion Ubayy b. Kaʿb (d. 29/649) is said by Ibn Abī Ḥātim (d. 327/938) to have used it in relation to the word *al-riyāh* ("clouds": for example, Q2/al-Baqara.164 – every time it is used it means *raḥma*).[41] Ibn ʿAbbās is credited with using the rule on various occasions, transmitted through Mujāhid (but, interestingly, never in his written *tafsīr*).[42] The principle, when attached to a phrase, indicates that every time that phrase is used in the Qur'ān, it has a particular meaning. The rule's aim is clearly to establish a unified discourse for the Quranic text; that is, the rule is formed as a response to a theological doctrine (and perhaps a historical reality of the establishment of a canonical text).

At first blush, the *kull shayʾ* rule present in early exegetical texts establishes the literal meaning, and its history could inform a history of the literal meaning. Versteegh has made reference to the *kull shayʾ* rule's employment, describing it as something "close to a linguistic rule",[43] by which he means that it establishes a linguistic (literal?) meaning of the word or phrase in question. *Kull shayʾ* is, in my view, a hermeneutic rule rather than a linguistic one; or rather it is a convention which establishes a whole set of individual hermeneutic rules. A collation of the various instances in which the *kull shayʾ* rule is employed in early exegesis indicates that its purpose is not to establish literal/lexical meaning (a linguistic rule), but rather to establish interpretive practice ("this is how the construction/word/phrase is used in the Qur'ān"). That is, it is a means of identifying reference rather than meaning. Nonetheless, the idea of a literal meaning is often embedded within the individual presentations of a *kull shayʾ* rule. *Qātalahum Allāh*, for example, is clearly a case of deciding for the non-literal meaning over the literal meaning: on such occasions, the supposed meaning of the phrase and the intended meaning of the author diverge. The unanimity in terms of the gloss "God curse them" amongst the exegetes shows that the divergence was accepted as natural and eventually explicable through the positing of an idealised idiom of the Arabs (on which, see below). Despite the unanimity, however, the exegetes still felt the need to mention it on every occasion. Al-Ṭabarī's work usefully marks the end point of this early period of Quranic exegesis. He first records the equivalence attributed to Ibn ʿAbbās of *qātalahum Allāh: laʿanahum Allāh* (God fight them: God curse them). He says this is the Arabs' way of talking (*kalām al-ʿArab*), and compares it with other similar phrases (*qātaʿahum Allāh*). He also entertains the equivalent: *qatalahum Allāh: qātalahum*

41 Ibn Abī Ḥātim, *Tafsīr*, v. 1, p. 275.
42 Ibn Abī Ḥātim, *Tafsīr*, v. 1, p. 133; p. 196.
43 Versteegh, *Arabic Grammar*, p. 87.

Allāh (God kill them: God fight them), and gives similar examples where the verbal form changes (from *faʿala* to *fāʿala*) but eventually retains the notion that forms have distinctive meaning. His conclusion is that the phrase *qātalahum Allāh* is really an expression of amazement (*taʿajjub* – it does not literally constitute an exhortation for God to fight them, but is instead a figure of speech expressing amazement at their obstinacy), because such a usage is clearly recorded in the practice of the original Arabic-speaking community. It breaks the usual operation of linguistic conformity based around the comparison and analogy (*qiyās*) of different derivative forms and patterns.[44]

Here the speech of the Arabs is brought to the fore, but it is speech in which analogy (*qiyās*) operates. The *qiyās* referred to here is the notion that new language forms are based on patterns of established language conventions (such as the distinctive meaning of different verbal and nominal forms). That is, the *kalām al-ʿArab* is based on regular patterning of verbal forms, each with distinctive meanings. The fact that some linguistic experts (*ahl al-maʿrifa bi-kalām al-ʿArab*) claim that meaning can be shared between verbal forms (perhaps an appeal to contemporary language usage) is discarded. The debate here is over what counts as the *kalām al-ʿArab* – the perfect linguistic system in which *qiyās* can operate without exception, or the posited language use of a past community (*al-ʿArab*) in which *fāʿala* forms (III) can mean the same as *faʿala* (I).[45]

The *kull shayʾ* rule's attribution to Ibn ʿAbbās is, of course, spurious, and "Ibn ʿAbbās" does not, in al-Ṭabarī's passage, tell us how the rejected (literal) meaning of the passage is known. As mentioned above, that particular filling out of the theory of literal meaning was not the primary concern of the early *tafsīr* tradition. It is not that there is no conception of the literal meaning present in these texts: all "know" that the literal meaning of *qātalahum Allāh* is "God fight them", just as all know this cannot be the intended meaning (both theological dogma and Arabic idiom require otherwise).[46]

The *kull shayʾ* phrase also does not appear in the published *tafsīr* text ascribed to Mujāhid either, even though (if we trust the oral reports) he must have known about it. He is supposed to have transmitted the rule from Ibn ʿAbbās:

44 Ṭabarī, *Jāmiʿ al-Bayān*, v. 10, p. 145.

45 I discuss the appeal to *kalām al-ʿArab* in more detail below, pp. 84–8.

46 Incidentally, when we turn to Ibn ʿAbbās's attributed (and published) *tafsīr* text, *Tanwīr al-Miqbās min Tafsīr Ibn ʿAbbās*, Q9/al-Tawba.30 is glossed as "May God curse them" (Ibn ʿAbbās, *Tanwīr*, p. 597). The phrase *qātalahum Allāh* is also present in Q63/al-Munāfiqūn.4: "They are enemies, so beware of them. May Allāh fight them (*qātalahum Allāh*) – how they have been turned away." The *Tafsīr* of Ibn ʿAbbās records it, once again, as meaning "May God curse them" (*Tanwīr*, p. 597). Clearly there is no doubt about the interpretation (*qātalahum Allāh* means *laʿanahum Allāh*, and it means this on both occasions the phrase appears in the Qurʾān). However, neither here nor elsewhere in the published *Tafsīr Ibn ʿAbbās* is there a mention of the *kull shayʾ* rule (the reference to the rule in *Tanwīr*, p. 288, appears outside of the *isnād-matn* structure, and would seem not even to be attributed to Ibn ʿAbbās). To return to the question of relative dating, an attempt to theoretise about the interpretive exercise is absent from the textual tradition; the oral tradition, with its employment of the *kull shayʾ* rule, appears more accomplished.

> Sufyān>Layth>Mujāhid>Ibn ʿAbbās, who says: Every time in the Qurʾān there is "or … or" (*aw aw*), as in the statement "the compensation is to fast or give charity or to sacrifice" [Q2/al-Baqara.196 – referring to one who cannot shave his head at the end of *ḥajj*], it means one can choose.[47]

This report is found in the *tafsīr* text attributed to Sufyān al-Thawrī and also in the *Muṣannaf* of Ibn Abī Shayba (d. 235/849).[48] The example, previously identified by Versteegh,[49] is not a reference to when the text means one thing and the author means another. Instead, it is an identification of one of the possible meanings of *aw* (that is, choice, the *aw al-takhyīr* of later Arabic grammar) as the author's meaning. There is no rejection of a literal meaning in favour of a non-literal one, but an assertion of how the Quranic author uses words, phrases and constructions which are potentially ambiguous (that is, it is not a linguistic rule, but a hermeneutic one). The underlying premise is that either there is no single literal meaning of *aw*, or, if there is, it does not determine Quranic usage. The *qātalahum Allāh* example, on the other hand, is used to demonstrate that the Qurʾān can consistently use a particular phrase to mean something other than its literal meaning, and the glossing technique enables Quranic usage to be asserted.

In the Shīʿī tradition, Mujāhid is attributed with using the *kull shayʾ* rule himself on occasion:

> ʿAbd Allāh b. Kharrāsh>al-ʿAwām b. Ḥawshab>Mujāhid who said: Every time it says in the Qurʾān "O you who believe", then it refers to ʿAlī's priority and superiority because he was before all of them in Islam.[50]

Here the *kull shayʾ* rule is used for purely sectarian advantage, in order to establish Mujāhid as one who respected the Ahl al-Bayt. But it confirms the view that it is unlikely that Mujāhid would transmit the *kull shayʾ* rule from Ibn ʿAbbās, and use it himself (according to some reports), but fail to make any mention of it in his Qurʾān commentary. As with Ibn ʿAbbās, the Mujāhid oral tradition appears more sophisticated than the written tradition, which may indicate a relative dating.

Attributions of using the *kull shayʾ* rule abound in the attributed reports, indicating a seminal level of hermeneutic awareness on the part of those attributed with its use. After Ibn ʿAbbās, al-Ḍaḥḥāk (d. 105/723) is said to have used it in relation of *jaʿala* ("to make"; for example, Q2/al-Baqara.22 – it means "create"); ʿAmr b. Dīnār (d. 126/744) uses it (in relation to *aw* along the lines outlined above), as does ʿAṭā b. Abī Rabāh (d. 114/732);[51] Qatāda uses it in relation to the word *taṣbīḥ* (which

47 Sufyān, *Tafsīr*, p. 71.

48 Ibn Abī Shayba, *al-Muṣannaf*, v. 3, p. 497.

49 Versteegh, *Arabic Grammar*, p. 87.

50 Furāt al-Kūfī, *Tafsīr*, p. 49. Compare this with the usual rule that every time this phrase is used, it means it is Medinan; when *yā ayyuhā al-nās* is used, it could be Meccan or Medinan (Zayd b. ʿAlī, *Tafsīr*, p. 288).

51 Shāfiʿī, *Aḥkām*, v. 1, p. 129.

always means *ṣalāt* in the Qurʾān).[52] Imams Muḥammad al-Bāqir (d. c. 117?/735) and Jaʿfar al-Ṣādiq (d. 149?/766) amongst the Shīʿa also used it on numerous occasions:

> Imam Muḥammad al-Bāqir: God delegated to the people in the expiation for the [broken] oath just as he delegated to the Imam in war that he can do what he wishes. Every time it says *aw* in the Qurʾān then its partner is a choice.[53]

Imam Jaʿfar al-Ṣādiq is credited with the same opinion on *aw*, and adds:

> Every time it says "and whoever cannot afford it", it means that he must, but the thing before it is a choice.[54]

Jaʿfar al-Ṣādiq is credited with delineating exceptions to a *kull shayʾ* rule. For example, in relation to Q24/al-Nūr.30 he is recorded as having said:

> Q24/al-Nūr.30:
> And say the believing women that they should lower their gaze and preserve their *furūj*.
> He [Jaʿfar] said: Everywhere in the Qurʾān the preservation of the *farj* is mentioned, it means [protection] "from *zinā*" except in this verse, where it means "from sight".[55]

Ibn Jurayj (d. 150/767) is also credited with exceptions:

> Dīnār said: Everywhere in the Qurʾān that there is *aw* … *aw* then one can choose which ever one wishes.
> Ibn Jurayj said: Except in the statement of God, the punishment of those who wage war against God [… is execution or crucifixion, or the cutting off of hands from opposite sides, or exile; Q5/al-Māʾida.33].[56]

What is clear is that most of these instances of the *kull shayʾ* rule are not assertions of even proto-linguistic rules, but are collectively an expression of an early hermeneutic understanding with regard to the intended meaning of the utterance recorded in the text, namely that each speaker has a particular style which must be delineated before his speech can be understood. He uses phrases in a consistent manner, but his intended meaning may not always be clear from this usage; at times there will be an individual use of a homonym; at other times, there will be idiosyncratic use of a word which would normally be understood to mean something else. Hence there is a need for *kull shayʾ* rules. However, there is also a need to formulate exceptions to these rules when appropriate – but this, presumably, would be a secondary stage of development.

In Muqātil's *tafsīr*, the *kull shayʾ* rule is used extensively and seems securely part of the hermeneutic context.

52 ʿAbd al-Razzāq, *Tafsīr al-Qurʾān*, v. 3, p. 182.
53 Thamālī, *Tafsīr* (reconstructed), p. 161.
54 Ṭūsī, *al-Istibṣār*, v. 2, p. 195.
55 Kulaynī, *al-Kāfī*, v. 2, p. 36.
56 Bayhaqī, *Sunan*, v. 5, p. 185.

Q67/al-Mulk.30:
Put away behind them.
Muqātil: Every time "behind them" is used in the Qur'ān, it means (*ya'nī*) in front of them (*amāmahum*).[57]

Q95/al-Tīn.8:
Is not God (*a-laysa Allāh*) the wisest of judges?
Muqātil: Every time *a-laysa Allāh* is used in the Qur'ān, it means "I, God, am ..." (*anā Allāh* ...)[58]

In sum, the oral attributions of the rule (to whichever early exegete) would seem most appropriately treated as contemporaneous with Muqātil's *tafsīr*,[59] when the formula becomes common currency. I doubt it was in use during Mujāhid's time, and certainly not for Ubayy b. Ka'b and Ibn 'Abbās. As has been noticed by others, Muqātil's *tafsīr* represents a significant leap from *tafsīr*s of only a generation before him in a variety of ways, the employment of the *kull shay'* rule being just one of them.[60]

However, in terms of the literal-meaning notions present within these *kull shay'* examples, up to and including Muqātil, there does not seem to be an understanding of what it is that non-literal meaning diverges from. The meaning which the text has before its specification by a *kull shay'* rule does not receive much attention, and therefore it is not clear how one attains this "pre-interpretive" meaning. As with the Ibn 'Abbās tradition, the implicit assumption is that the normal reader can grasp this literal meaning through simply hearing or reading the text. The *kull shay'* rule is, in effect, a statement that this commonly understood meaning may not be the specific usage of the phrase within the Qur'ān. The fact that the exegetes are described as using the *kull shay'* rule is evidence, if you like, that Quranic statements might, if understood without this hermeneutical brake, be taken to mean something other than their intended meaning. Whilst the non-literal/interpreted meaning receives an increasingly sophisticated hermeneutical treatment, the literal meaning is left assumed as commonly understood and uncontroversial. Nevertheless, in Muqātil, one does find the introduction of another variable in the hermeneutic equation introduced and exploited: the notion of the normative speech of the Arabs. This, in time, contributes to the apparatus by which the notion of literal meaning might be tied down.

The *kalām al-'Arab* and literal meaning

The notion that the meaning of an obscure Quranic phrase might be cleared up by

57 Muqātil, *Tafsīr*, v. 3, pp. 433, 478, 499, 512.
58 Muqātil, *Tafsīr*, v. 3, p. 499; see also pp. 313, 478, 512 (on which see Versteegh, *Arabic Grammar*, pp. 137–8).
59 Though whether that is most appropriately understood as during the lifetime of Muqātil is a different matter; see Rippin, "Studying Early *Tafsīr* Texts".
60 There is also the evidence from *al-Ashbāh wa'l-Naẓā'ir* of Muqātil which Wansbrough (*Qur'anic Studies*, pp. 208–12) considers a false attribution on similar grounds; and also the *Kitāb al-Mutashābihāt* of al-Kisā'ī (on which see *Qur'anic Studies*, pp. 214–17).

reference to the linguistic norms of the Arabs (*kalām al-ʿArab*) is at the fore in the *tafsīr* of Muqātil b. Sulaymān. The appeal to *kalām al-ʿArab* as a hermeneutic method is not, as we shall see, an attempt to establish the literal meaning of a text (in particular the Qurʾān). In its initial employment it was to explain deviations from the literal meaning; only later was it used to establish linguistic norms which control the literal meaning.

The use of *kalām al-ʿArab* is not absent from the *tafsīr* material attributed to figures before Muqātil. In Mujāhid's *tafsīr*, the phrase "the Arabs used to say" (*kānat al-ʿArab taqūl*) is occasionally employed. In the description of the inhabitants of hell in Q88/al-Ghāshiya.5 – "they shall be served with drink from a 'ripe' spring (*ʿayn āniyya*)" – Mujāhid says:

> ʿAbd al-Raḥmān>Ibrāhīm>Ādam>al-Mubārak b. Faḍāla>al-Ḥasan who said: The Arabs say for a thing that has reached such a heat that there is nothing hotter than it, "its heat has already ripened (*ānā*)". So God says, "from a ripe spring".[61]

"Arab" usage here determines a superlative understanding of the water from the spring: it is not merely boiled, but heated to the maximum possible heat. The construction *min ʿayn āniyya* is taken to refer to this excessive heating process brought about by God. One would not understand this from the phrase itself; the hyperbolic usage of the construction by the Arabs enables this inference to be drawn.

Similarly, in the *Tafsīr Zayd b. ʿAlī*:

> When a war or some other matter, more serious than any other, afflicted the Arabs, they used to say *kashafat al-ḥarb ʿan sāqin* ["literally": "the war has uncovered a shin"]. So God says, "On the day, a shin will be uncovered and they shall be summoned to bow" (Q68/al-Qalam.42).[62]

The use of the Arabs' idiom here, once again, is to draw attention to a non-literal meaning by which God's intended meaning might be known.

In Muqātil's *tafsīr*, there are two principal ways in which *kalām al-ʿArab* is employed. The first is a continuation and expansion of the usage in *tafsīr*s attributed to figures before Muqātil where an idiomatic expression of the Arabs is not to be taken literally. Examples of this are numerous, and also instructive as to the conception of literal meaning present in Muqātil's *tafsīr*.

> Q55/al-Raḥmān.31:
> We shall "charge" for you, O two weighty ones.
> Muqātil: Meaning (*yaʿnī*): we will charge the account of both men and *jinn* … This is the speech of the Arabs when they say, "I will charge for you; and he was uncharged before that". It is a warning: nothing actually concerns God [concerning the thing charged].[63]

61 Mujāhid, *Tafsīr*, v. 1, p. 753.
62 Zayd b. ʿAlī, *Tafsīr*, p. 340.
63 Muqātil, *Tafsīr*, v. 3, p. 306.

A phrase in the Qur'ān (*wa'afgharu lakum*) makes it sound as if God is owed something which he needs to claim back. This is just idiomatic Arabic (*kalām al-ʿArab*) for someone claiming back a debt.[64] God is not impoverished and in need of repayment.

> Q23/al-Mu'minūn.78:
> He has created for you hearing, sight and feeling – little (*qalīl*) do you show thanks [to him for it].
> Muqātil: It means (*yaʿnī*) by *qalīl* that they do not show thanks to the Lord of this bounty who in his goodness created them, and [they do not] recognise his unity. The Arabs say: "He is 'little of understanding'" (*qalīl al-fahm*), meaning he does not understand and does not comprehend.[65]

Here the phrase *qalīl mā* in the Qur'ān could mean having a little understanding, but it is interpreted according to the *kalām al-ʿArab* to mean he has no understanding at all. Sometimes it is not idiom which means a departure from the literal, but metaphor:

> Q31/Luqmān.19:
> The most unpleasant of sounds is the braying of a donkey [Luqmān's advice to son concerning arrogance].
> Muqātil: It means (*yaʿnī*) that the most ugly of sounds is the sound of the donkey on account of the strength of their voice. The Arabs say, "these are the sounds of the donkey", and "this is a donkey's voice", and they say, "this is the sound of chickens", or "these are the sounds of chickens".[66]

Here the voice of the arrogant is described as the braying of a donkey. The metaphor (constructed as a plural followed by a singular – *ankar al-aṣwat li-ṣawt al-ḥumayr*) is explained, as is the unusual grammatical construction, by reference to the speech of the Arabs.[67] At times, the grammatical meaning is overruled due to an idiomatic meaning of a linguistic phenomenon:

> Q50/Qāf.24:
> Throw (dual) into hell …
> Muqātil: This is in the speech of the Arabs "grab (dual) him" – when one person speaks to another single person with the speech of the dual.[68]

Here the dual being used as an emphatic denoting repetition ("grab, grab him", "throw, throw him") in ordinary Arab speech is used to explain a Quranic grammatical

64 Similarly, see Muqātil, *Tafsīr*, v. 2, p. 157, where the phrase "a necessity in the heart of Jacob" (*ḥāja fī nafs Yaʿqūb*: Q12/Yūsuf.67) is understood *min kalām al-ʿArab* as meaning "an unpalatable/disquieting matter".

65 Muqātil, *Tafsīr*, v. 3, p. 27.

66 Muqātil, *Tafsīr*, v. 3, p. 21.

67 Similarly, see Muqātil, *Tafsīr*, v. 3, p. 413, where the phrase "and your clothes are purified" (Q74/al-Mudaththir.4) is explained by reference to the Arabs (the Arabs used to say – *kānat al-ʿArab taqūl*) saying when a man sins, he has soiled his clothes, and when he dies (and therefore his sins are expiated), "they say: his are now 'pure of clothes'".

68 Muqātil, *Tafsīr*, v. 3, p. 271.

anomaly. As has been noted by others, Muqātil's use of the term *iḍmār* (suppression) is one of the few examples of technical terminology within his *tafsīr*,[69] and this is probably also due to the conventions of the speech of the Arabs.

In all these cases, the *kalām al-ʿArab* provides the non-literal meaning for an expression in the Qurʾān – a literal meaning is left behind in the interpretive process. It is possible that Muqātil is explaining these idioms and figures because he fears they will be misunderstood; that is, they have a clear meaning but it is not the intended meaning of the speaker. The *kalām al-ʿArab* facilitates access to the intended meaning, and can be seen here to be a much-exploited tool in exegesis. There is, however, no *theory* of literal meaning expressed here (there is, incidentally, no comprehensive theory of non-literal meaning either). There is, however, a general presumption that the text has a meaning from which idiomatic Arabic (of the type used by the ideal imagined language community of *al-ʿArab*) sometimes diverges. Most of the time, this assumed literal meaning appears constructed around a natural understanding of the text; though never expressed, Muqātil appears to be working on the basis of the literal meaning being what a contemporary speaker of the language might think the meaning is, before he deals with the deviations from that meaning. At times, this literal meaning is given grammatical expression (as in the Q50/Qāf.24 example above),[70] but normally it is left simply assumed or baldly stated.

However, there is, to my mind, a second category of uses where *kalām al-ʿArab* is employed to elucidate the literal meaning of the text. Muqātil, at times, appears to be providing meanings for words which would otherwise not be understood at all:

> Q5/al-Māʾida.97:
> God made the Kaʿba the sacred house.
> Muqātil: It is called the Kaʿba because it is an isolated building, and every isolated building, in the speech of the Arabs, is a *kaʿba*.
> Abū Muḥammad says that Thaʿlab said: the Arabs call every four-sided house *al-kaʿba*.[71]

> Q13/al-Raʿd.29:
> Those who believe and do good works, *ṭūba* is for them.
> Muqātil: It means goodness (*ḥusnā*) is for them, and it is in the language of the Arabs (*bi-lughat al-ʿArab*).[72]

> Q15/al-Ḥijr.72:
> By my life!
> Muqātil: It is a statement/oath (*kalima*) in the speech of the Arabs.[73]

69 Versteegh, *Arabic Grammar*, pp. 146–51.

70 I do not intend to underestimate the importance of the introduction of grammatical meaning as literal meaning in Muqātil's *tafsīr*, simply to state that it is the minor notion of literal meaning operative within the *tafsīr*. The major notion is linked to the everyday understanding of the words.

71 Muqātil, *Tafsīr*, v. 1, p. 322.

72 Muqātil, *Tafsīr*, v. 2, p. 176.

73 Muqātil, *Tafsīr*, v. 2, p. 208.

Finally, there is triangulation of evidence, with one element being the *kalām al-ʿArab*:

> Q8/al-Anfāl.12:
> So strike above the *aʿnāq*.
> Muqātil: It means the neck. The Arabs say, "so strike above your head", meaning the neck.[74]

This last use of *kalām al-ʿArab* is, I suggest, a significant departure from its use in *tafsīrs* and usually dates from a period prior to Muqātil. In those *tafsīrs*, and for most of Muqātil's *tafsīr*, *kalām al-ʿArab* is the manner in which the intended meaning is understood as separate from the literal meaning of the text. However, in this last example, we have the *kalām al-ʿArab* being used to establish the literal meaning of strange words (or words used in strange ways). That is, *kalām al-ʿArab* is being used lexicographically and with the intention of establishing the literal meaning of words by reference to the idealised language use of the past community of Arabs. Upholding the language system of the Arabs before and contemporary with Muḥammad, and using it as the source of not only lexicographical but also linguistic knowledge more generally, enabled the emergence of a science of grammar. It is clear from Muqātil's *tafsīr* that we are encountering a more sophisticated use of *kalām al-ʿArab* than that used in the corpus of material attributed to writers before him.

Arabic grammar and literal meaning

The employment of the "language of the Arabs" as a criterion of good linguistic practice was central to the project of constructing a grammar of Arabic. Correct Arabic speech was identified by Sībawayh (d. 177/793) with the speech of *al-ʿArab*, and he apparently gathered informants from the tribes who (he believed) still spoke the pure language. *ʿArab* language use forms one of his three main sources for his description of proper language use (the other two being the Qurʾān and Arab poetry). Does Sībawayh have a sophisticated concept of literal meaning, in the sense understood here? Establishing and describing such a meaning does not appear his main concern.[75] From his *Kitāb*, his main concern appears to be a description of the Arabic grammatical system, garnered from his sources, and the occasional correction of a grammatically defective expression. In most examples, the intended meaning of the speaker is not in doubt; the question which seems to consume Sībawayh is whether or not the utterance is correct Arabic. So in the oft-quoted example:

> Amongst that which comes from the extension of speech and its abbreviation is God's statement "so ask the village where he have been and the caravan in which we came back" (Q12/Yūsuf.82). It only means "ask the people of the village". It is abbreviated, and the governance of the verb on "village" is just as it would be on "people", if the latter were there.[76]

74 Muqātil, *Tafsīr*, v. 2, p. 8.
75 On this see the collected articles of Aryeh Levin in his *Arabic Linguistic Thought and Dialectology*.
76 Sībawayh, *al-Kitāb*, v. 1, p. 212.

Here what is left when the word *ahl* ("the people of") in the phrase "ask the village" is omitted (that is, the literal meaning of *was'al al-qarya*) is not a matter of enormous concern to Sībawayh. He clearly recognises that it is an unusual linguistic feature since otherwise he would not propose the solution that God simply "abbreviated", as good Arabic speech allows. It is elision rather than omission, because (as Sībawayh points out) the verb acts on village (to make it accusative) just as it would have done on "people". The fact that village is not in the genitive (as it would be in "people of the village") means there is elision here rather than simple omission. However, Sībawayh is not, I think, worried that someone may misunderstand the meaning here and proceed to imagine Jacob asking buildings rather than people. Speech (*kalām*) can go beyond the boundaries of grammatically correct Arabic (a process known as *ittisāʿ* – "broadening") without doing violence to the intended meaning (signified by variants of the verb *arāda* – "to wish/intend"). In a section entitled "Using a verb in expression but not in meaning on account of their [the Arabs'] broadening of speech", Sībawayh lists various examples of texts (taken from the Qurʾān, poetry, everyday speech and the *kalām al-ʿArab*) in which the utterance (*lafẓ*) and the meaning (*maʿnā*) diverge. For example:

> They say "We hunted the Qanawayn[77]". It only means "We hunted in the Qanawayn", or "We hunted the wild animals of the Qanawayn" – Qanawayn is simply the name of a plot of land.[78]

The syntax here enables us to tie down the subject of *yurīd* in other examples in Sībawayh. The subject in one part is plural and the other singular: *they* say something, but *it* only intends (*yurīd*) something else. The implication here is that their statement (*qawl*) or the text itself has an "intention" (*murād*, possibly "meaning"); and, interestingly, the thing that it means is the author's intended meaning (namely, that you hunted in the area, or you hunted the beasts of the area). The use of the exclusive particle *innamā* ("only"?) here is characteristic of Sībawayh. He uses it to introduce the intended meaning of a statement, as in:

> Of this type is their saying, "I ate of the land of such and such" and "I ate of the town of such and such" – and it *only* means he came across its produce, and ate and drank of them.[79]

Innamā indicates that the utterance intends this meaning and nothing else (that is, the literal meaning could never have been intended by the utterance). This appears as the most likely understanding, though one says this with caution, given the various uses of *innamā*.

In these examples, and the others in the section on *ittisāʿ*, the utterance itself has gained a category (*lafẓ*), and clearly the *lafẓ* can have a meaning in and of itself

77 Probably a reference to two mountains in Oman, east of al-Ḥajir (see Ḥamawī, *Muʿjam al-Buldān*, v. 4, p. 408).

78 Sībawayh, *al-Kitāb*, v. 1, p. 213.

79 Sībawayh, *al-Kitāb*, v. 1, p. 214.

(otherwise these examples would not be thought of as ambiguous or potentially defective). Furthermore, the text itself is almost "ensouled" and given an intention, which it indicates to the exclusion of any other possible intention (*innamā*). However, in these examples, the meaning which the text has "in itself" (that is, its literal meaning) is not distinguished from its utterance (*lafẓ*). The surface level of *lafẓ* points towards a deeper level of meaning which has to be reconstituted by the grammarian from the *lafẓ*.[80] The *lafẓ*, it seems, could make sense, or it may be grammatically defective and therefore have meaning only after deductive work carried out by a trained grammarian. Sībawayh does not seem to distinguish between these two categories where the *lafẓ* diverges from the *maʿnā*. That is, there is no systematic distinction between utterances which have no literal meaning because they fail to follow the rules of grammar, and utterances which have a literal meaning but this does not accord with the *maʿnā*. He examines, for example, the omission/elision of elements of a sentence (*iḍmār*), but he does not really examine what the sentence might mean without the omitted element. His interest is purely in the meaning that the words point to – the intended meaning. For example,

> This is the chapter on "when the operative verb elides becoming clear in enunciation". This is when you say:
> [1] "the people are rewarded for their actions – if good [accusative], then good [nominative], and if bad [acc.], then bad [nom.]" and
> [2] "the man is killed by whatever he kills with – if a catapult [acc.], then a catapult [nom.], and if a sword [acc.], then a sword [nom.]".
>
> If you want to express the verb (*aẓharta al-fiʿl*) then you say:
> [3] "if *it was* a catapult [acc.], then a catapult [nom.]" and
> [4] "if *it was* evil [acc.], then evil [nom.]".
>
> Amongst the Arabs, there are those who say:
> [5] "if a catapult [acc.], then a catapult [acc.]" and
> [6] "if good [acc.], then good [acc.]; and if evil [acc.], then evil [acc.]"
> as if he was saying:
> [7] "if what he did was good, then he is rewarded with good; and if it was evil, then he is rewarded with evil" and
> [8] "if the one who kills did so with a catapult, then he is the one who will be killed by a catapult".[81]

Here, abbreviated sentences [1] and [2] are expanded to [3] and [4] by the insertion of (presumed) missing elements. A variant expression is recorded [5] and [6], which are subjected to an even greater extent of full expression (*iẓhār*) in [7] and [8]. There is no exploration of what the words might mean without the expansion and the elimination of *iḍmār*. The focus, as one would expect in a grammar book, is on

80 On this see Versteegh, "The Arabic Tradition", pp. 244–51.
81 Sībawayh, *al-Kitāb*, v. 1, p. 258.

acceptable Arabic usage which deviates from the fullest expression (the norm), rather than literal meaning.

The general direction of Sībawayh's argumentation was carried on in the subsequent grammatical tradition. There is a general emphasis on how to match *lafẓ* and *maʿnā* through "broadening" language use (*kalām*) to cover idiomatic, grammatically incorrect or omitted (or suppressed) elements. The (intended) meaning of an utterance is rarely in doubt; it is the dissonance between meaning and utterance which causes consternation and leads the grammarian to elaborate mechanisms whereby one set of words (be they meaningful in their own right or not) can indicate this *maʿnā*. The idea of a literal meaning is not entirely absent from such a project, and indeed the *Kitāb* does give numerous rules whereby particular meanings can be inferred from particular linguistic phenomena, rather than words. The *Kitāb* is not, in this sense, a lexicographical text. However, we are not here dealing with an exposé of literal meaning, but rather an explication of how meaning comes from utterances, often when those utterances appear to break grammatical rules which were previously thought invariable.

Conclusion

There were, then, a number of notions of literal meaning current in the emerging Islamic intellectual tradition at the end of the second/early ninth centuries. The Qurʾān certainly has an implicit notion that events (happenings, dreams, perhaps texts in the more technical sense) have a superficial (and ordinary) significance and a spiritual (and specialised) significance. The latter is promoted, and the former is seen as the realm of the ignorant and uninitiated. However, there is also within the Qurʾān a commitment to the obvious truth of its message, and it is at least possible that the criticism of other religious communities (Jews mainly, but Christians also) is that they have ignored the obvious sense of their scriptures. In this sense, the hidden (the non-literal) and the manifest (the literal) are in tension, with each being promoted in the Qurʾān at different points. All this provides a background, but not a determining cause, for the discussions in early Quranic exegesis. There, I have argued, one finds two principal notions which revolve around language use and grammatical/lexical meaning respectively. With regard to the former, a natural, plain understanding of the text by a speaker of the language was assumed, and at times made explicit in early *tafsīr* of the Qurʾān. This meaning comes to the fore in the exegetical process when the exegete concludes that the Quranic text does not do the work (that is, presenting a clear meaning) which is usually expected of a communicative utterance. When the text means one thing and God obviously means another, there is an exegetical problem. What the text "means" (as distinct from the speaker's intention), in such circumstances, is identified in much of early *tafsīr* as what would normally be understood by the listener. It does not receive extensive examination and is assumed to be obvious and uncontroversial. The attitudes towards this literal meaning, and the manner in which it might be discarded, vary in their sophistication and show a clear line of development which enables us to propose a tentative sequence of emergence of these different strands of *tafsīr*, though determining dates for the various stages in this process is more difficult. In general terms, the material which is attributed to an early exegete in individual reports is of greater hermeneutic sophistication than the material found in the *tafsīr* work attributed to that exegete. This appears to be the case when one compares the oral tradition with the "written" tradition and the *tafsīr* texts attributed to Ibn ʿAbbās, Mujāhid and Zayd b. ʿAlī. The "oral" tradition (sometimes only known through the work of exegetes such as al-Ṭabarī) had some time to emerge, develop and be embellished. The written tradition seems to have been reasonably fixed at an earlier point. This, at least, is what the passages relating to literal meaning seem to indicate.

Part of this developing sophistication is the intrusion, one might say, of the idea that a text's "grammatical meaning" is its literal meaning (that is, the meaning that is there before we interpret). The grammatical emphasis can be seen in some of Muqātil's comments, and lies in the background of Sībawayh's examination of *ittisāʿ* and *iḍmār*. Here the notion of a grammatically determined meaning is sometimes absent from an utterance: the deviations from grammar within some utterances mean that they do not really have a meaning in and of themselves. What the utterances intend (*maʿnā*) or what they wish (*irāda*) to communicate are clear. The grammarian's task is to explain how this or that utterance can be understood to have this or that meaning. Sībawayh does not distinguish between utterances which have a meaning in their raw state ("ask the village") and utterances which, due to defective expression, do not ("if good, then good; if bad, then bad"). Whilst the literal meaning is generally understood to be grammatically determined, it does not receive detailed attention in Sībawayh.

Due to the unsystematic development of the literal meaning in this early period, writers (if we can talk of independent authors at this stage) might employ different notions in a single work, sometimes in a single passage. It was a matter not of a devotion to one or other idea of literal meaning, but rather of a tendency to employ this or that notion more regularly. The lack of reflection on how texts come to have meanings independent of authorial intention encouraged this lack of precision. In the idea of the *kalām al-ʿArab* we have a tool with which the two notions could be brought together. At first, the normative speech of the Arabs was used to identify the meaning of ambiguous or misleading utterances. Gradually, the *kalām al-ʿArab* was employed to determine literal meaning, in the sense we are using the term here. This is evidenced in Muqātil as a significant phenomenon; *kalām al-ʿArab* becomes the major "source" of Arabic grammar for Sībawayh. Sībawayh's *Kitāb* does not necessarily reflect a universally held intellectual stance; nevertheless, in his work a basic framework for Arabic grammar does emerge, and within that framework a certain notion of literal meaning is developed. An utterance's literal meaning is defined by rules which are established through deduction; observing the usual speech of the Arab is the primary fieldwork activity. However, deviations from the literal meaning are also to be understood by observing the *kalām al-ʿArab*. In this sense, both usage meaning and grammatically determined meaning are encapsulated in the employment of the language use of a grammatically perfect past community as the criterion of literal meaning. In Sībawayh, there is an implication that access to this linguistic knowledge will reduce over time, and hence the rules must be recorded for current and future language use and understanding. Three notions of literal meaning can, then, be sketched at this stage: (1) the current language user's ordinary understanding, (2) the grammatical rules of the language and (3) the language use of a (mythical) past community which defines the grammatical rules. All three could clearly be employed by a single author without discrimination; to an extent, the notions are not mutually exclusive. Current language use could follow the grammatical rules and be understood as a continuation of a previous ideal language practice. There were potential combinations of these three which could form interesting new versions of the literal meaning. Their importance for this study lies in the scene they set for the considerations of literal meaning to be found in early Islamic jurisprudence, to which I now turn.

4

Literal Meaning in Early Islamic Legal Theory

Presenting a description of the early development of Muslim jurisprudence is both potentially controversial and historically problematic. It is not necessarily germane to my purpose here to rehearse the arguments which have dominated the field of early Islamic legal studies.[1] It is important to note, however, that prior to the writings of al-Shāfiʿī, there is very little evidence of any explicit interest in legal theory. By this I mean that the extant texts of early Islamic jurisprudence contain many references to and refutations of the opinions of the great scholars of the early period, but there is little discernible systematic concern with the method by which one legal view might be demonstrated as superior to another. We do not, before al-Shāfiʿī, find extensive reflection on how the law, *in toto*, is to be justified and what makes a good argument in the context of the law. Instead, much of the legal literature that survives from this period, rather like the exegetical material surveyed in the last chapter, contains views of scholars and authors, cited with approval or disapproval. When argumentation is present, it is not always obvious whether or not it could be combined into a coherent theory in which sources are assessed and considered authoritative, and in which certain processes of legal reasoning are deemed acceptable and convincing and others rejected. The evidence from the early pre-Shāfiʿī texts is, then, that the whole legal enterprise was not reified, and thereby forced into a coherent framework. Since it is within these discussions that a theory of literal meaning might emerge, it is perhaps not surprising that early juristic writings contain no detailed or subtle understanding of the operation of language, expressed explicitly or implicitly, in which a notion of literal (or textual) meaning might sit.

Having said that, some material within the pre-Shāfiʿī juristic corpus, consisting as it does of legal dicta attributed to scholars, early luminaries and the Prophet himself, does, at times, display an interest in language as a hermeneutic tool. For example, amongst the responses of the Iraqi jurist Ḥammād b. Abī Sulaymān (d. 120/738) it is recorded:

> A man said to his wife ,"You are divorced." She said, "What did you say?" He said,

1 For a useful summary of research in the modern era, see Motzki, *Origins of Islamic Jurisprudence*, pp. 1–49.

> "You are indeed divorced." Ḥammād said, "If he merely wishes (*arāda*) to help her understand, then there is no problem here."[2]

The man had uttered the divorce formula ("you are divorced": *anti ṭāliq*) twice. A literal reading of his utterance is that his wife is now divorced two times (for an irrevocable divorce, the formula must be announced three times). However, Ḥammād distinguished between what the man said and what he meant, and therefore the pair are not bound by the literal meaning of the words.

In the section on oaths in Muḥammad al-Shaybānī's (d. 189/804) *al-Jāmiʿ al-Kabīr*, a slightly more nuanced understanding of literal meaning is presented. We find a reference to a general/specific distinction in the section on oaths, using the terms common in the later *Risāla* of al-Shāfiʿī, *ʿāmm* and *khāṣṣ* ("Chapter on liability for an oath which can be in both specific and general forms"). For example:

> A man says, "my slave is free if I eat fowl," and he eats cock … or he makes an oath that he will not eat meat of a "slaughter camel" (*jazūr*) and he eats the meat of a "camel" (*baʿīr*), male or female, or he will not eat the meat of male or female cattle, and he eats an ox … In all these cases, he is liable [for breaking an oath].
> If he makes an oath that he will not eat a hen and he eats a rooster, or he will not eat the meat of a rooster and he eats the meat of a hen, or he will not eat the meat of a she-camel and he eats the meat of a he-camel … then he is not liable [for breaking an oath].
> A man orders another man to buy a cow, and he buys an ox, or for him to buy a he-camel, and he buys a she-camel, then the order remains [unfulfilled].[3]

The issue at stake here is not what the person intended by making his oath, or what the term is commonly understood to mean, but what the word means "literally". By using certain words, the person is committing himself to one course of action irrespective of his own intention when uttering these words.[4] A general term (for example, fowl – *dajāj*) covers both male and female "literally" even though it is often used to refer to female chickens only; eating a cock breaks the oath. The term for camels for slaughter (*jazūr*) is often understood as referring to female camels (since they are the ones usually slaughtered), but "literally" it is not gender specific; hence the eating of a *baʿīr* (a camel, male or female) breaks the oath not to eat *jazūr*. Using a gender-specific term (*dīk* – cock; *nāqa* – she-camel) is exclusive, and eating the opposite does not break the oath. Al-Shaybānī gives us an analogous case (*qiyās*, though the term is not used – "A man orders another …"). The reasoning is not made explicit, but there is here clearly an underlying notion that words have very specific literal meanings, which differ from what is in common currency, or what the hearer might understand by them, or what the speaker might intend by them.

Significant as these juristic understandings of language were, they do not prepare

2 Ibn Abī Shayba, *al-Muṣannaf*, v. 4, p. 22.

3 Shaybānī, *al-Jāmiʿ*, pp. 72–3.

4 For an exploration of the oaths within this section of *al-Jāmiʿ al-Kabīr*, see Calder, "*Ḥinth, Birr, Tabarrur, Taḥannuth*".

one for the sophistication and level of self-reflection available in the *Risāla* of Muḥammad b. Idrīs al-Shāfiʿī (d. 204/820). This work, which has rightly been the subject of quite extensive academic analysis, contains numerous passages on language and its role in the legal exegetical process. Al-Shāfiʿī is famous, of course, for establishing the primacy of the Prophetic Sunna, alongside the Qurʾān, as found in *ḥadīth*, as the essential source and justificatory mechanism for the law. This important aspect of al-Shāfiʿī's thought system is not really my concern here. In the *Risāla*, al-Shāfiʿī also sets out a reasonably coherent hermeneutic theory, in which he identifies a meaning which texts have in and of themselves, which is distinguished from the intended meaning of the speaker (in the case of revelatory texts, this is God himself or the Prophet). In this, his work can be seen as a formalisation for the purposes of legal derivation of the trends already seen in Quranic exegesis and grammatical works examined in the last chapter. Here, I begin with an analysis of al-Shāfiʿī's conception of how revelatory language should be interpreted, and the elements of that theory which resonate with the component parts of literal meaning as we understand it here.

That there is no immediate successor to al-Shāfiʿī's *Risāla* to provide the link between his work and the leap in theoretical thinking evident in early works of *uṣūl al-fiqh* is unfortunate as it makes construction of the thought processes around literal meaning challenging. However, in the clutch of surviving early *uṣūl* texts, I recognise three conceptions of meaning which act as candidates for the literal meaning and which form the basis for some of the arguments in the earliest surviving *uṣūl* texts. Abū Bakr al-Jaṣṣāṣ (d. 370/980), the author of the important early Ḥanafī Muʿtazilī text of *uṣūl al-fiqh* entitled *al-Fuṣūl*, was a pupil of Abū al-Ḥasan al-Karkhī. Some have credited al-Karkhī with being the "real" founder of the Ḥanafī school of Muslim jurisprudence,[5] since the supposed founders Abū Ḥanīfa (d. 150/767), who acts as school eponym, and his pupils Muḥammad al-Shaybānī and Abū Yūsuf (d. 182/798), can hardly be said to have provided a consistent body of legal opinions or a distinctive legal methodology. Al-Jaṣṣāṣ's *al-Fuṣūl*, then, preserves the legal methodology of the early Ḥanafī school (particularly that found in Baghdad, where al-Karkhī and al-Jaṣṣāṣ were active). In this work, I argue below, al-Jaṣṣāṣ develops a view of a meaning which clings to the text which is primarily bound up with the understanding of ordinary language users and how the community understands the words they hear in the text. This, if you like, is his conception of the literal meaning, and it is, relatively speaking, popularist, non-technical and, one might say, "parole" based. Beneath this view lies a tendency to regard the passage of time (and the attendant potential for language development) as not particularly problematic.

Roughly contemporary with al-Jaṣṣāṣ, one has the great Mālikī jurist and theologian Abū Bakr al-Bāqillānī (d. 403/1013). His main surviving work of *uṣūl al-fiqh*, *al-Taqrīb wa'l-Irshād*, is, like al-Jaṣṣāṣ's work, an impressive accomplishment, revealing a working through of Ashʿarī theology into legal theory. Along the

5 Melchert, *The Formation*, pp. 125–9.

way, he develops a notion of language, communication and the role of literal meaning in which grammatical considerations play a major role. For al-Bāqillānī, the primary determinant of the meaning a text "owns" and which should act as the presumed meaning when attempting to derive laws from the sources is that dictated by the linguistic and grammatical rules. This, it would seem, takes the construction of literal meaning away from the community and places it in the hands of the grammatical experts. Where it goes from there is a matter for jurists, but what an ordinary language user might think of as the literal meaning of a text is marginalised in al-Bāqillānī's hermeneutic construct.

The third trend in the conception of literal meaning examined in this chapter is found within ʿAlī b. ʿAmr Ibn al-Qaṣṣār's *al-Muqaddima fī uṣūl al-fiqh.* Ibn al-Qaṣṣār (d. 398/1008), also a Mālikī, composed this brief summary of the rules, as he calls it, of legal hermeneutics, and in it he clearly draws on developments common in the academy at the time. Amongst these is an assertion that the primary determinant of the literal meaning in revelatory texts is the meaning dictated by the original utterance situation – that is, the language of Arabs. The *lughat al-ʿArab*, in which God spoke to the Prophet and in which the Prophet and the companions communicated with the people, determines the meaning which a revelatory text, in isolation, should be taken as having at the outset of the hermeneutic enterprise. It is not necessarily what the text means; other revelatory texts may adjust this meaning and, as Ibn al-Qaṣṣār describes in some detail, do so quite frequently. However, the starting point for meaning is the *lughat al-ʿArab.*

These three trends in the idea of literal meaning (in the sense of "text-owned" meaning) are evident in al-Shāfiʿī's work, but are not really differentiated or the subject of extensive reflection. Even in these three later *uṣūl* works, the trends are not exclusive. The meaning inherent within an utterance constitutes for all of them the presumed intended meaning at the outset of the exegetical process, but it is still the case that we have here only general emphases in each work that this or that item constitutes the literal meaning for a particular author. As we have seen, there is a distinction (which is much clearer in subsequent *uṣūl al-fiqh*) between, on the one hand, popular language use or grammatical meaning or the *lughat al-ʿArab* and what came to be the primary contender for the literal meaning (namely, the *maʿnā mawḍūʿ lahu*). These three ideas of "literal meaning" become, instead, *indications* of the literal meaning. This, as we have seen, means the literal meaning is defined (as created in the act of *waḍʿ*), but at the same time removed, as the jurist now works with evidence for the *waḍʿ* having taken place rather than pure knowledge of literal meaning.[6] This distinction is only hazily presented in al-Shāfiʿī's *Risāla* and appears more developed in these early *uṣūl* texts. Here the authors do not always distinguish between the meaning which, due to evidence, is a presumed literal meaning (which is in turn a presumed intended meaning) and the literal meaning itself. The ideas of literal meaning within these early *uṣūl* texts mark, then, an intermediate stage

6 See above, p. 61.

between the (relatively) rudimentary notions of literal meaning found in the *Risāla* and the full-blown, and consistently successful, theory found in mature *uṣūl al-fiqh*.

This change in methodological focus reflects broader developments in early Muslim legal theory, as jurists gradually systematised their linguistic thinking under the influence of the grammatical, exegetical and rhetorical sciences.[7] As we have seen in Chapter 2, literal meaning, as we use the term here, is almost exclusively understood in classical *uṣūl al-fiqh* as the meaning "established by the *waḍʿ*" (*al-maʿnā al-mawḍūʿ lahu, al-maʿnā al-waḍʿī*), and this forms part of a clearly defined set of hermeneutic categories shared by nearly all works of classical *uṣūl*. In the earlier texts, linguistic notions are not described with such refined clarity. As we shall see, the literal meaning (that is, the meaning which "clings to" and "is owned by" the text) is at times identical with the intended meaning of the author/speaker; at other times the literal and intended meanings are quite definitely distinct for these early authors. This lack of conceptual clarity was cleared up in classical *uṣūl*: the literal meaning is not so easily obtained, and is accessed through indicators (*ʿalamāt, adilla*, including popular language use, grammatical understanding, the archaic linguistic community of *al-ʿArab*). These indicators are, themselves, subjects of dispute and discussion, and so literal meaning is moved back in the process, and known with reduced certainty. Hence the *uṣūl* maxims in which literal meaning forms a strong exegetical presumption are nearly universally held at a hermeneutic level, but nearly always debated and contentious at the level of specific exegesis. With the removal of easy access to literal meaning in classical *uṣūl*, the intended meaning is made yet more distant, since in the classical system one must travel through the literal (often rejecting it along the way) before reaching the intended meaning. It might be said that this development is marked terminologically: the prevalent use of *ẓāhir* (apparent, obvious) for the literal gives way to *ḥaqīqa* (true, real) in early and classical *uṣūl* and *ẓāhir* is reassigned to a technical element of the hermeneutic process.

Whilst the early legal theorists devised mechanisms to discover the intended meaning, the jurists of the more mature *uṣūl* tradition added to them methods of determining the literal meaning as a distinct category. It was the literal meaning which, for them, formed the starting point for the exegetical exercise. The endpoint remained, of course, the discovery of the author's/speaker's intended meaning, and so the aim of the exercise was not fundamentally changed. The methodological alteration came about gradually, and under the influence of the increasingly popular conception of language as an independent, objective system of meaning-sound relationships. Unlike other imagined meanings, these relationships remain present within an utterance in an almost ontological fashion. Even when discarded as the speaker's intended meaning, the "literal" meaning has an indissoluble link to the utterance or text. It is the emergence of how this powerful idea of a text's "literal" meaning came to be a central element of Islamic legal theory which is traced below.

7 See, in particular, Heinrichs, "Contacts".

Literal Meaning in al-Shāfiʿī's *Risāla*

The *Risāla* attributed to al-Shāfiʿī probably represents the earliest surviving attempt to describe the exegetic principles which underpin the appropriate derivation of legal rulings from the authoritative texts. It might be described as the first proper attempt at outlining a general Muslim hermeneutic theory. Unlike its contemporary texts, the *Risāla* is more than a collection of solutions to problems (legal and theological) with *obiter* comments revealing some self-reflection. Rather, it is an attempt to delineate a typology of interpretive methods through the investigation of particular legal examples, regularly utilising the literary device of an interlocutor in order to demonstrate the need for consistency in the application of these methods. This is not to say that it qualifies as a work of *uṣūl al-fiqh* as understood in subsequent Muslim scholarship, but it is the case that many of the interpretive methods outlined in the *Risāla* are found in the later *uṣūl* tradition in more elaborate and sophisticated formulations. The conception (or conceptions) of literal meaning which emerge in the *Risāla* could be used as a means of dating the text.[8] However, even if Calder's ambitious assertion that the *Risāla* post-dates the work of Ibn Qutayba (d. 276/889) is accepted,[9] the work still represents a first attempt at a comprehensive description of the modality of juristic interpretation, and a categorisation of approved hermeneutic devices in the derivation of the law.

Central to al-Shāfiʿī's description of the manner in which meaning is derived from texts is the concept of *bayān*. This term can be translated as "elucidation", and refers to the manner in which the intended meaning of one element of revelation (principally the Qurʾān and the Sunna of the Prophet) might be known (that is, elucidated, become clear) through its juxtaposition with another. Other cognate terms are also employed in the *Risāla*, such as *bayyana* (as a verb meaning "to elucidate", describing the activity of one element of revelation upon another) and *bayyin* ("clear" or "elucidated" but also the item which performs the clarification or elucidation). Al-Shāfiʿī's typology of *bayān* has been well described by Lowry,[10] but, briefly put, *bayān* is divided by al-Shāfiʿī into a number of types which are described in the early sections of the *Risāla*. They include:

1. The Qurʾān elucidating (that is, acting as a *bayān* upon) itself. For example, God says of Moses's enforced seclusion: "We designated thirty nights for Moses, and completed them [or it, i.e. the time] with ten. Thus, the time of his Lord was forty nights" (Q7/al-Aʿrāf.142). The last phrase ("forty nights") acts as an elucidation (*tabyīn*) of the earlier part of the verse, and the statement is clear (*bayyin*) for the "one to whom it is addressed" (*ʿinda man khūṭiba*).[11] Here the Qurʾān elucidates itself. One supposes that the mention of "forty

8 Al-Shāfiʿī's ideas do not seem wildly out of step with contemporary (or earlier) grammatical writings, for example. See above, pp. 88–91.

9 Calder, *Studies in Early Muslim Jurisprudence*, pp. 223–43.

10 Lowry, *Early Islamic Legal Theory*, pp. 23–59.

11 Shāfiʿī, *al-Risāla*, #76 and #77, p. 27.

nights" rules out the possibility that the phrase "completed them with ten" refers to the last ten nights of the thirty. That the elucidating statement is connected (*mutaṣṣil*) to the elucidated statement was an element of later discussions of the operation of *bayān*.[12]

2. The Sunna elucidating the Qur'ān, making something unclear in the Qur'ān clear. God commands ritual purification before the performance of prayer and describes the actions involved in the performance (Q5/al-Mā'ida.6). However, it is not clear whether the actions should be performed once or more than once.[13] Whilst the wording of the verse at the very least indicates that it should be performed once, al-Shāfiʿī argues that the verse's wording (its literal meaning, perhaps) does not exclude the possibility (*iḥtimāl*) that elements of the ritual purification should be performed more than once. The Sunna makes this clear (that is, a certain element of the ritual should be performed three times).
3. The Sunna elucidating the Qur'ān, by providing the details of how to carry out an order expressed in the Qur'ān. The Qur'ān establishes the duty to perform prayer, whilst the Sunna gives the number of prayers and their times. This differs from 2 above, for in that case there was an ambiguity (does the verse mean one or more than one performance?), and the Sunna confirms one of the possible interpretations. In this type there is no ambiguity: there is total ignorance of the details, followed by the subsequent provision of further details.
4. The Sunna elucidating the details of duties of which there is no mention in the Qur'ān. When this occurs, the Sunna acts as a *bayān* of the general Quranic injunction to obey the Prophet.
5. Both the Qur'ān and the Sunna are ambiguous concerning the details of a particular duty, but these can be determined through a comparison of the relevant revelatory texts with unrelated revelatory texts or external sources (such as ordinary language use). Through this, the meaning of the texts is clarified (*bayyana*) and the operation is termed *qiyās*.[14]

This delineation of al-Shāfiʿī's categories of *bayān* could be refined (for example, different types of comparison in category 5 could be distinguished), or indeed simplified (for example, categories 2 and 3 could be combined), but this is not necessarily relevant to my objective here. What is relevant, however, is the underlying assumption that whilst in al-Shāfiʿī's schema the texts may at times be equivocal, there is always one meaning which achieves initial prominence over the others. This prominent meaning is not necessarily what was meant by the utterance (that is, located in the speaker's intent), but it is, nonetheless, present in the text. That a text can "say" one thing but, through *bayān*, be understood to have a different meaning is, of course, one mechanism which hints at what we have been calling the

12 See Gleave, "*Ta'khīr al-Bayān*".

13 Shāfiʿī, *al-Risāla*, #86 and #87, p. 29.

14 This is not, necessarily, identical with the later *uṣūlī* understanding of the term *qiyās* mentioned in the previous chapter. Here it seems simply to refer to a process of "comparison" between texts in order to achieve understanding of the intended meaning of one of them.

"literal meaning".[15] In addition, the meaning which is distinct from the understood meaning may or may not require a *bayān* amongst the types described by al-Shāfiʿī. It would appear that this meaning, for al-Shāfiʿī, is an initial candidate for what I have been calling the literal meaning and is invariably termed *al-ẓāhir* in the *Risāla*.[16]

The term *ḥaqīqa* is not used in the *Risāla*.[17] *Ẓāhir* (and its cognates), however, is commonplace. Lowry mentions in passing that the use of *ẓāhir* (and cognates) in the *Risāla* is, in his view, not "hermeneutic technique".[18] The evidence rallied below does, I feel, demonstrate that the employment of *ẓāhir* cognates in the *Risāla* is technical and encompasses many of the elements of literal meaning. Though al-Shāfiʿī does not enter into extensive theoretical reflection on the nature of *ẓāhir* meaning, there is enough here to determine that his is a reasonably coherent conception. His usage of the term certainly contrasts both with later technical definitions and with *ẓāhir* as understood by later *uṣūl* writers, indicating the fluidity of the application of technical terms in early Muslim hermeneutic theory.[19]

As with many other technical terms, al-Shāfiʿī does not provide a handy definition of *ẓāhir*. In order not to prejudice the construction of its usage in the *Risāla*, I have left the term untranslated in the analysis below, with the aim of producing an attempted definition at the conclusion of the analysis.[20] One type of passage in which the term *ẓāhir* is used regularly is summaries of what appear to be hermeneutic maxims or exegetical principles. These appear as general presumptions which the hearer should adopt when hearing or reading a text of revelation in order to aid his/her interpretation.[21] These maxim passages often come at the end of an exchange between al-Shāfiʿī and his interlocutor: for al-Shāfiʿī they appear to end the debate, as if no further questioning is required as the explanatory maxim has been cited. For example:

15 The clarity or otherwise of a statement's meaning is not a feature of the text itself for al-Shāfiʿī (it is not an inherent characteristic of the text that it is clear or unclear). Rather, a text's clarity, or lack of it, is "an interpretive claim" (Vishanoff, *The Formation*, p. 54).

16 Vishanoff's exposition of al-Shāfiʿī's hermeneutics introduces a number of terms for the broadly conceived literal/textual meaning which is technically expressed as *al-ẓāhir* within the *Risāla* (*The Formation*, pp. 36–47): "plain meaning", "face value", "apparent meaning", "obvious meaning", a meaning "transparently expressed by its verbal form". See above, p. 59.

17 There is a reference to *ḥaqīqa* (*al-Risāla*, #577, p. 213), where it is used to argue that reports from the Prophet may be answers to questions which are not transmitted. The true nature of the answer (*ḥaqīqat al-jawāb*) can only be understood when one knows the "cause" (*sabab*) of the statement (i.e. the question). The usage here can hardly be described as technical, and certainly is not influenced by contemporary usage of *ḥaqīqa* and *majāz* (on which see Heinrichs, "On the Genesis").

18 Lowry, "The Legal Hermeneutics of al-Shāfiʿī and Ibn Qutayba", p. 35. Osman ("Ẓāhirī *Madhhab*", pp. 173–82) embarks on an analysis of al-Shāfiʿī's use of *ẓāhir* and also argues that it has technical elements, though I am not convinced al-Shāfiʿī exclusively understood the term as tied to generality (*ʿumūm*), as Osman argues.

19 See above, pp. 49–52.

20 The reader may wish to use as a working definition Lowry's "apparent or plain (pre-interpretive) meaning" (though this will be refined somewhat below).

21 I discuss these maxims in greater detail in "Literal Meaning".

> The Qur'ān is according to its *ẓāhir* (*ʿalā ẓāhirihi*) until an indication within it (*dalālatun minhu*) or a *sunna* or an *ijmāʿ* comes [indicating] that it is according to a *bāṭin* not a *ẓāhir*.[22]

This maxim, it would appear, indicates that the Qur'ān is to be understood or interpreted as *ẓāhir* (though it could refer to its being expressed in a *ẓāhir* mode) as its default. The term *bāṭin*, which has been translated as "hidden" (but seems to mean simply "non-*ẓāhir*"), appears to be a catch-all term to describe any understanding of a text which is reached by a consideration of evidence extraneous to the text under examination. Hence the *ẓāhir* is a meaning which emerges from consideration of the text itself, whilst the *bāṭin* is a meaning brought about through the consideration of external evidence (be it from elsewhere in the Qur'ān, or a *sunna* or an *ijmāʿ*). Elsewhere, al-Shāfiʿī characterises this extraneous evidence as "elucidating" (*bayyana*) a passage, thereby linking the *ẓāhir*/*bāṭin* dichotomy with his ever-prevalent conception of *bayān*. The *ẓāhir* is, then, a meaning of the word or phrase under analysis without taking into account the revelatory context (envisioned in a limited or broad manner) in which it was uttered.

Ẓāhir and the *ẓāhir*/*bāṭin* dichotomy are not used exclusively in relation to the discussion of Quranic texts. In line with al-Shāfiʿī's general promotion of the Sunna of the Prophet as a revealed source, the texts of the Sunna should also be understood as *ẓāhir* unless there is extraneous evidence. In an important passage, after discussing a *ḥadīth* concerning times of prayer, al-Shāfiʿī states:

> This is like other *ḥadīth* of the Prophet of God. It is [to be understood?] according to the *ẓāhir* of generality (*al-ẓāhir min al-ʿāmm*) until an indication concerning it comes, as I have already described, or there is a consensus of the Muslims that it should [be understood] according to its *bāṭin* not its *ẓāhir*, and being particular rather than general (*khāṣṣ dūna ʿāmm*).[23]

Here the link between the *ẓāhir*/*bāṭin* and the *ʿāmm*/*khāṣṣ* dichotomies is expressed. A word or phrase is "general" (*ʿāmm*) when it applies to all members of its class.[24] For example, God in the Qur'ān states: "O people (*al-nās*)! A story has been set down – so listen to it. Those [gods] on whom you call, other than God, cannot even create a fly" (Q22/al-Ḥajj.73). Al-Shāfiʿī states that the verse could be understood as a general address to all people – that is, "what comes out of the utterance" itself (*makhraj al-lafẓ*).[25] However, it is clear that not all people are addressed here, but only those who call on gods other than Allāh (that is, the believers are excluded). Hence even though a general term is used, a particular subset (*khāṣṣ*) of the reference of that term is meant. The subset-meaning is the *khāṣṣ* in the above citation and is,

22 Shāfiʿī, *al-Risāla*, #1727, p. 580; for similar usages of *ẓāhir* see #923, p. 341; #610, p. 222; #624, p. 226.
23 Shāfiʿī, *al-Risāla*, #882, p. 322.
24 See Osman, "Ẓāhirī *Madhhab*", p. 173. Here al-Shāfiʿī's notion of *ʿāmm* is not so different from that developed in later *uṣūl al-fiqh* texts; see above, pp. 47–8.
25 Shāfiʿī, *al-Risāla*, #203, p. 60.

on this occasion, the *bāṭin* of the utterance *nās*; the *ʿāmm* (all people) is the *ẓāhir* of the word *nās*. This depiction of the *ẓāhir* as "what comes out of the vocable" itself (*makhraj al-lafẓ*) anchors it within at least one element of literal meaning, namely the meaning a word has in and of itself.

An expression in a revelatory text, al-Shāfiʿī informs us, is to be taken as having general reference until some other piece of evidence particularises it.[26] This general reference is *ẓāhir* (as an adjective). The nominal use of the *ẓāhir* of an utterance (a noun referring to a particular meaning of an utterance) appears regularly, but as an adjective, *ẓāhir* is normally linked with the notion of generality (for example, *ʿāmman ẓāhiran* – a general meaning which is *ẓāhir*). For example:

> God, through his book [the Qurʾān], addressed the Arabs in their own tongue, in accordance with what they understood of its meanings. Amongst what they understood of its meanings was the "breadth" of their language (*ittisāʿ lisānihā*),[27] and that [God's] usual way (*fiṭratahu*)[28] of speaking of a thing from within [the book] is:
>
> 1. a *ẓāhir* general [manner] (*ʿāmman ẓāhiran*) by which the *ẓāhir* general [meaning] was intended
> 2. a *ẓāhir* general by which the general was intended, but within which the particular was included
> 3. a *ẓāhir* general by which the particular was intended
> 4. a *ẓāhir* when it is known from its context (*siyāqihi*) that something other than the *ẓāhir* is intended
>
> All of this is known to exist at the start of speech, in its middle and at its end.[29]

Ẓāhir is used in this passage both as an adjective (to describe a particular interpreted meaning) and as a noun (as the meaning itself), though the distinction does not seem to be crucial in comprehending the categories of text. Al-Shāfiʿī here outlines the operation of *ẓāhir* within the revelatory texts, and therefore a few preliminary comments are in order. First, the "breadth" of the language of the Arabs is, I take it, the ability of language to go beyond the *ẓāhir* and express meanings other than its "literal" meaning.[30] Amongst these modes of expression are categories 2 to 4. These are not the only examples of God's usage of Arabic's breadth (*ittisāʿ*), but they cover many of the examples presented by al-Shāfiʿī in the *Risāla*. Second, *fiṭra* – which I have translated as "usual way" ("original nature") – could, of course, imply "only way", and it is possible (but unlikely, in my opinion) that al-Shāfiʿī considers God to express

26 Vishanoff phrases this as "a text's meaning could be modified by another text" (*The Formation*, p. 55), but it is not the text's meaning which is modified; it is the meaning understood from the text in the context of the total revelatory data.

27 See pp. 89 and 93 for the notion of *ittisāʿ* in grammatical thinking.

28 There is some debate about the reference of the pronoun in *fiṭratahu* here. Montgomery translates it as Arabic's "very nature" ("Al-Jāḥiẓ's *Kitāb al-Bayān*", p. 105); Osman sees this as a reference to the "Arab knowing by nature" ("Ẓāhirī *Madhhab*", p. 174); Lowry considers it to be a reference to "God's habit" (*Early Islamic Legal Theory*, p. 73). Lowry's interpretation seems the most convincing to me in context.

29 Shāfiʿī, *al-Risāla*, #173, pp. 51–2. The numbering is mine.

30 See Versteegh, "Freedom of the Speaker".

himself in ways outside of his *fiṭra*. Finally, "the language of the Arabs" determines how a text should be understood – be it *ẓāhir* or *bāṭin*. It remains unclear how the *ẓāhir* meaning is determined, though it is clear the language of the Arabs is central to the understanding process, which may, at times, require us to reject the *ẓāhir* meaning.[31]

These comments aside, a number of interesting points emerge from this passage. First, there is a distinction mentioned earlier between the *ẓāhir* and the intended meaning. On some occasions, they may coincide (category 1), but on other occasions they will not (categories 2, 3 and 4). We have already noted this distinction in early works concerned with the interpretation of the Qur'ān, in early grammatical theory and, to a lesser extent, in the *ḥadīth* collections.[32] The distinction, then, seems to have been an assumption of much Muslim hermeneutic activity before al-Shāfiʿī. Second, there is also an assertion that all parts of the Qur'ān have a *ẓāhir* meaning – that is, there are no parts of the Qur'ān where a *ẓāhir* meaning cannot be discerned, even if, on consideration of all the evidence, the *ẓāhir* meaning is not the one intended by the speaker in the passage. Third, it is unclear here whether or not there is a distinction between *ẓāhir* and *ʿāmm*. In this passage, *ẓāhir* is used both as an adjectival qualification of *ʿāmm* (*ʿāmman ẓāhiran*) and as a noun in its own right (as in category 4), though the extent to which the nominal and adjectival usages are distinct is unclear. One interpretation could be that *ẓāhir* is a broad category of which *ʿāmm ẓāhir* is a specific subcategory, though this interpretation may be unduly influenced by subsequent *uṣūl al-fiqh*.

This rough and ready categorisation of God's modes of communication with his people is exploited throughout the *Risāla*. Whilst the first category is not subject to further comment (it could be argued that it is unnecessary, since the *ẓāhir* is both the intended and the understood meaning), categories 2, 3 and 4 are the focus of the next three sections of the *Risāla* respectively. The term therefore appears in the subsequent section headings:

> "An elucidation of what has been sent down in the Book which is general of the *ẓāhir* and combines both generality and particularity."[33]
> "An elucidation of what has been sent down in the Book which is general of the *ẓāhir* and by which, on each occasion, the particular is intended."[34]
> "The type [of speech] in which its expression indicates its *bāṭin* rather than its *ẓāhir*."[35]

In the first two headings we have the locution *ʿāmm al-ẓāhir* ("general of the *ẓāhir*"),[36] where both elements are definite nouns. The last of these headings employs the most common oppositional term to *ẓāhir* in the *Risāla*, namely *bāṭin*.

31 See pp. 84–8 and below. Montgomery characterises al-Shāfiʿī as promoting an Arabic which was viewed as "sacral" (see "Al-Jāḥiz's *Kitāb al-Bayān*", pp. 103–7). See also Wansbrough, *Qur'anic Studies*, pp. 215–16.
32 See above, pp. 75–91.
33 Shāfiʿī, *al-Risāla*, p. 56.
34 Shāfiʿī, *al-Risāla*, p. 58.
35 Shāfiʿī, *al-Risāla*, p. 64.
36 This is not the only locution; we find *al-ẓāhir min al-ʿāmm*, *ʿāmm al-ẓāhir* and *ʿāmm fī'l-ẓāhir* at various points within the *Risāla*. See below, pp. 107–8.

Another example is annexed to al-Shāfiʿī's analysis of whether the Prophet's prohibition on selling an item not in one's possession covers selling something which one owns but which is not actually present with the seller at the time of sale. In a concluding maxim, al-Shāfiʿī states:

> Every expression which is *ẓāhir* general (*ʿāmm ẓāhir*) in the Sunna of the Prophet of God is [to be understood] according to its *ẓuhūr* [its "*ẓāhir*-ness"?] and its generality, until a *ḥadīth* proven to be from the Prophet of God is known which indicates that what is intended by a general statement in the *ẓāhir* is actually some of [that indicated by the general statement] and not others.[37]

When Ḥākim b. Ḥizām states that "the Prophet of God prohibited me from selling what was not with me (*mā laysa ʿindī*)", it means anything that was not "with one" at that moment and anything which one could not count as amongst one's property (*maḍmūn ʿalayka*).[38] The *ẓāhir* general meaning is that both types of "having" (that is, being present with and having amongst one's property) are included in the prohibition ("having" here is, perhaps, a homonym, though al-Shāfiʿī does not use the technical term of *ishtirāk*).

These maxim statements are useful in that they bring to the fore the importance of the *ẓāhir* category (and the *ẓāhir*/*bāṭin* dichotomy) for al-Shāfiʿī's hermeneutic system. They do not, however, precisely explain what is meant by the *ẓāhir*. Al-Shāfiʿī, at least in the *Risāla*, offers no definition of the *ẓāhir* (or rather he offers no definition similar to those found in later *uṣūl al-fiqh* for other elements of the vocabulary of literalism, such as *ḥaqīqa*). His conception of the *ẓāhir* meaning can, however, be explored through the examples in which it forms a central element of his argumentation. One who is ignorant of the Arabic language (or the Arabs' language: *lisān al-ʿArab*) will, most likely, misunderstand intended meaning of utterances because they will only understand the *ẓāhir*, and the contrast here is between those who understand the *lisān al-ʿArab* (and hence can detect the *bāṭin*) and those who do not (*man yajhal lisān al-ʿArab*). That the *lisān al-ʿArab* enables one to go beyond the *ẓāhir* contrasts with later *uṣūlī* systems, in which the *lisān al-ʿArab* is a primary mechanism for discovering the literal meaning.

For example, al-Shāfiʿī discusses how clear (*wāḍiḥ*) or otherwise three uses of *nās* might appear to one who is ignorant of the Arabic language:

1. Those to whom the people (*al-nās*) said, "the people (*al-nās*) gather against you" (Q3/Āl ʿImrān.173).
2. O people (*al-nās*)! A story has been set down – so listen to it. Those [gods] on whom you call, other than God, cannot even create a fly (Q22/al-Hajj.73) (referred to above).
3. [Whilst on *ḥajj*] Pass on quickly where the people (*al-nās*) usually pass on quickly (Q2/al-Baqara.199).

37 Shāfiʿī, *al-Risāla*, #923, p. 341.
38 Shāfiʿī, *al-Risāla*, #914–15, pp. 336–7.

> [The third] verse is like the two preceding ones in meaning. Amongst the Arabs they are all the same, but for one who is ignorant of the Arabic language the first is clearer than the second, and the second clearer than the third. Amongst the Arabs, however, there is no difference in the clarity of these verses.[39]

First, al-Shāfiʿī does not mean here someone who does not know Arabic (clearly for someone completely illiterate in Arabic all the verses are meaningless sounds). He means someone who is not well versed in the ways of the Arabic language: *al-ʿArab* gain this naturally; others can learn it, it appears. For the one ignorant of the *lisān al-ʿArab*, the use of *nās* (people) in the first verse clearly does not mean all people. In this verse, the first use of *nās* addresses another set of individuals ("those to whom"), so it cannot mean all people; and the second use of *nās* refers to those "gathering against you", and this clearly does not refer to all people either, but rather a group of people. The need to divert the meaning from a general to a particular reference of *nās* is obvious from the verse itself. In the second verse, the use of *nās* is also clearly restricted and not general, though less so as the restrictive passage ("those [gods] on whom you call") is somewhat separated and distant from the word *nās*, and more work is required to recognise the particularisation. The third verse is the least clear, as "people" here could, quite possibly, be of general reference. However, for someone who knows the *lisān al-ʿArab* – by which al-Shāfiʿī means not only the grammar of the Arabic language but the actual discourse of the Arabs – all these verses are equally perspicuous. The *ẓāhir* of *nās* is that it applies to all people, and that is what someone who is ignorant of the *lisān al-ʿArab* will understand from these verses. However, the *bāṭin* of each use of *nās* (that is, its intended meaning) can be recognised, with varying levels of ease, by this ignorant one because of clues within the text. In 1 there are more clues than in 2, and in 2 more than in 3. For the one who knows *lisān al-ʿArab*, however (in particular the Arabs themselves), the *bāṭin* is equally accessible in all three cases. The *ẓāhir* meaning is, then, the meaning which a grammatically informed (but "uncultured"?) individual will understand – and that may be all he or she understands, as without knowledge of Arabic discourse, the hearer may remain entirely within the *ẓāhir*. The *ẓāhir*, then, is accessed through grammar and not through historic language use.[40]

As is well known, according to al-Shāfiʿī, the Quranic texts "The thief, male and female, cut off their hands" (Q5/al-Māʾida.38) and "The fornicator, female and male, beat each of them with 100 lashes" (Q24/al-Nūr.2) are subject to "particularisation" by Prophetic Sunna. As al-Shāfiʿī puts it:

> The Prophet of God made a *sunna* that amputation is [obligatory] for [or possibly

39 Shāfiʿī, *al-Risāla*, #206, p. 61. Vishanoff cites this passage (*The Formation*, p. 47) as part of his promotion of the thesis that al-Shāfiʿī's main preoccupation is to demonstrate the ambiguity of the revelatory canon.

40 Vishanoff considers al-Shāfiʿī to have a vague notion of what meaning was dictated by linguistic form, and he implies that this was kept vague in order to allow ambiguity to remain within the system; ambiguity being maximised allowed for flexibility in interpretation since the meaning the text has in itself is less determinate. See Vishanoff, *The Formation*, p. 61.

"enacted upon"] him whose theft amounts to a quarter of a dinar or more, and lashing is [obligatory?] for free virgins, not free non-virgins and slaves. The Prophet of God's *sunna* indicates that God meant by them the particular meaning (*al-khāṣṣ*) of fornicators and thieves, even though what can be extracted from the speech (*makhraj al-kalām*) "in the *ẓāhir*" is of general reference concerning thieves and fornicators.[41]

"In the *ẓāhir*", what is "extracted" from the speech (*makhraj al-kalām* – which seems undifferentiated from the term *makhraj al-lafẓ*, mentioned above) is that thief (*sāriq*) and fornicator (*zānī*) are of a general reference (*ʿāmm*). God, however, intends to convey the particular reference (*arāda Allāh bihā al-khāṣṣ*). Once again, the distinction between intended meaning and what is understood "in the *ẓāhir*" is drawn. The examples of the "thieves" and "fornicators" verses are used elsewhere in the *Risāla* to exemplify the operation of particularisation of one revelatory text (in this case, the Qurʾān) by another (in this case, an element of the Prophet's Sunna) as an archetypal instance of *bayān*.[42] However, only on this occasion is the term *ẓāhir* employed to describe the means whereby the general reference is understood. By comparing the use of these examples elsewhere in the *Risāla*, an idea of what al-Shāfiʿī means by *ẓāhir* in this instance emerges. For example:

When the Prophet of God stoned a non-virgin for fornication and did not lash him, then the Sunna of the Prophet of God indicates that the intended [recipient] of the one hundred lashes for *zinā* was free non-virgins, and that the intended recipient of the amputation for theft was he who steals out of greed and his theft amounts to a quarter of a dinar, and not anyone else to whom the terms of theft and fornication apply.[43]

The implication here is that the words "thief" and "fornicator" are necessarily applied to all those who perform the associated actions. In the above quotation,[44] this is what is meant by "understanding the utterance in the *ẓāhir*". If one presumes consistency within the *Risāla* in the interpretation of this problem, "to understand an utterance in the *ẓāhir*" might be initially glossed as "to understand an utterance with the meanings which are *necessitated* by the words the speaker is using". This idea that certain words have a meaning which is necessarily bound to their expression, this *ẓāhir*, is, of course, one of the elements of "the literal meaning" developed in the first chapter.

Later in the *Risāla*, the theft verse is used as an example of a ruling on which it is not permitted to perform *qiyās*. For al-Shāfiʿī, if a ruling has been altered in some way from its original (*ẓāhir*?) meaning, this alteration acts to prevent any analogical reasoning from being performed in reference to the verse according to its new meaning. For example, God commanded that one perform ritual ablution by washing

41 Shāfiʿī, *al-Risāla*, #616, pp. 223–4.

42 Other citations of these verses which do not deal with the interpretation of it "in the *ẓāhir*" are #333, p. 111, and #648, p. 233. There are also instances where the fornicator verse is used as an example of abrogation (#376, p. 129, and #683, p. 236).

43 Shāfiʿī, *al-Risāla*, #227, p. 67. I see *lazima* here to mean that the qualities of being a thief and being a fornicator are necessarily associated with the individuals categorised as thieves and fornicators.

44 Shāfiʿī, *al-Risāla*, #616, pp. 223–4.

one's face, hands and feet in Q5/al-Mā'ida.6. However, the Prophet, on one occasion, wiped his shoes rather than washing his feet. Now, al-Shāfiʿī argues that one cannot then perform *qiyās* on this new ruling (which he calls a "lightening" of the original demand – *takhfīf*). It is not the case that one can, under certain circumstances, merely wipe one's turban (or *burquʿ*) or gloves in place of washing the head or hands. What God meant when he said that we should wash our feet is made clear by the Prophet's Sunna, which delineates times when we can wipe our feet in place of washing them.[45] That is, because particularisation can occur on any individual ruling in revelation, the same term can be intended with two different meanings, even in a single verse: the term *ghusl* (wash) when applied to feet does not mean the same as *ghusl* when applied to head or hands. *Ghusl* with respect to feet encompasses an exception (on certain occasions one can wipe); with respect to head and hands there is no exception. The Prophet's Sunna shows us that a single word in revelation (the verb *ghusl*) can have a particular and a general meaning simultaneously depending on the object (feet or head/hands) for which one is attempting to draw up a ruling. When asked if such reasoning is permitted in language (*a-wa-yajūzu hādhā fī'l-lisān?*), al-Shāfiʿī answers that it is. The example cited is the thief verse: "The Sunna indicates that God did not intend that all thieves undergo amputation."[46] Wash usually means X but in this verse, and when related to feet, it means Y; thief normally means X but in this verse, when related to the amputation punishment, it means Y. That is, a meaning can be intended by the utterance of a word which is at variance with the "unmarked" meaning necessitated by the word itself. When a marked meaning is intended, this is indicated by another piece of revelatory evidence.

From the various instances of al-Shāfiʿī's usage of the "thief" and "fornicator" verses, then, one can deduce that *ẓāhir* means "unmarked", "necessitated" (*lāzim*) and coming from the utterance itself (*makhraj al-kalām*), all of which can be conceptualised as elements of the literal meaning. The non-*ẓāhir*/*bāṭin* meaning is marked, derivative and comes about through consideration of external factors. Other instances of al-Shāfiʿī's use of *ẓāhir* amplify and confirm this description. Usually the term is used in relation to particularisation:

1. The *ẓāhir* of various verses on *jihad* is that it is a duty upon all the people (*fa-ammā al-ẓāhir min al-āyāt, fa-l-farḍ ʿalā al-ʿāmma*). However, Q4/al-Nisā'.95 demonstrates that it is not a general duty but a collective one (*bi'l-kifāya*), and this is what God intended when he revealed the other Quranic verses.[47] Here the general reference is *ẓāhir*, and is particularised by another Quranic verse.
2. After a discussion concerning on which materials (including the ore of various metals, gold, silver, buried minerals and so on) the religious taxes are due, al-Shāfiʿī notes that most of the specific rulings come from the Sunna not the Qur'ān and "If there had been no indication from the Sunna, the *ẓāhir* of the

45 Shāfiʿī, *al-Risāla*, #1616, p. 546.
46 Shāfiʿī, *al-Risāla*, #1620, p. 548.
47 Shāfiʿī, *al-Risāla*, #982, p. 364.

> Qurʾān would have been that all wealth was the same in this regard, and zakat was due on all of them, not on some rather than others".[48] This is where a general ruling in the Qurʾān that one should pay tax on one's wealth is particularised by the Sunna.

That a text says one thing (its *ẓāhir*) but a knowledge of language reveals the meaning to be otherwise (*bāṭin*) is illustrated by the well-known "village" example:

> *The type* [*of speech*] *in which its expression indicates its* bāṭin *rather than its* ẓāhir
>
> God, may he be blessed and glorified, when he was relating the statement of Joseph's brothers to their father, said,
>
> > We do not bear witness except to what we know and we do not preserve what we have not seen. Ask the village in which we have been and the caravan in which we returned. We are indeed telling the truth. (Q12/Yūsuf.81–2)
>
> This verse is like the previous verses[49] in meaning. Amongst those who are knowledgeable about language (*ʿinda ahl al-ʿilm bi'l-lisān*) there is no dispute that [the brothers] demanded that their father ask the *people* of the village and the *people* of the caravan because the village and the caravan [themselves] could not testify to their honesty.[50]

The brothers must have meant the people of the village and caravan and not the buildings or the caravan baggage, because they wished their father to believe their story concerning Joseph, and to do so they needed witnesses to the truth of their statement. Buildings and caravan baggage could not perform this function. Grammatically the text demands that one ask buildings and caravan baggage. In terms of sense, these cannot be the references of "village" and "caravan", and hence the meaning is taken to be "the people of the village" and "the people of the caravan". The "context" (*siyāq*) has demanded that the *ẓāhir* understanding be set aside, and the ellipsis inserted, making the new meaning *bāṭin*.[51]

Al-Shāfiʿī recognises that when one hears phrases in which there is obvious ellipsis, such as "How many villages which were immoral have we destroyed?"

48 Shāfiʿī, *al-Risāla*, #534, p. 193.

49 Whilst this verse is an example of the category of "the type [of speech] in which its expression indicates its *bāṭin* rather than its *ẓāhir*", it is likened here to other verses in which "village" is used to refer to "the people of the village" rather than the buildings or the baggage of a caravan. These are called "the type [of speech] in which its context (*siyāquhu*) elucidates (*yubayyin*) its meaning" (Shāfiʿī, *al-Risāla*, #208–11, pp. 62–3). Whether these two represent distinct categories for al-Shāfiʿī is debatable. I notice that the first is headed by *Bab al-ṣinf alladhī* and the second by *al-ṣinf alladhī*, and Shākir (the editor) considers them part of the same section. There is, though, a manuscript variant which makes the second a *bāb* in itself (see Shāfiʿī, *al-Risāla*, p. 64, n. 1). I see no real difference between the examples and the reasoning in the two sections.

50 Shāfiʿī, *al-Risāla*, #212–13, p. 64.

51 This is category 4 in al-Shāfiʿī's categorisation cited above, n. 29. Osman ("Ẓāhirī *Madhhab*", p. 179): "The *bāṭin* meaning here, therefore, is the correct meaning, which is indicated by the wording (*al-lafẓ*) of the verse." I am not sure *al-lafẓ* necessarily refers to "wording" here, but there is an indication that al-Shāfiʿī viewed ellipsis in cases such as these as a natural consequence of a linguistic understanding of the text (see above, pp. 43 and 53, for this discussion in mature *uṣūl al-fiqh*).

(Q21/al-Anbiyāʾ.12), "the hearer will [understand] that the *only* (*innamā*) immoral ones are the people [of the villages], not [the villages'] houses which cannot be immoral".[52] Al-Shāfiʿī is stating here that the hearer gains one, and *only* one, meaning when he hears the vocable "village" in these verses: he understands the people of the village. In a related example, he describes this process of understanding as when "knowledge encompasses" (*aḥāṭa al-ʿilm*) the hearer.[53] If the hearer *only* understands the people and not the buildings, and if he is "encompassed by knowledge" that this is the case, and (most importantly) these immediately understood meanings are, for al-Shāfiʿī, *bāṭin*, it seems clear that the "apparent" meaning will not be the *ẓāhir* on all occasions. It may seem counter intuitive, but at times the meaning which appears to the hearer will be the *bāṭin*.[54] Instead, the *ẓāhir* meaning, for al-Shāfiʿī, at times approximates to the linguistically demanded meaning (that is, "ask the buildings of the village") and not the one which would necessarily be immediate in the hearer's mind.[55] On occasion, of course, the *ẓāhir* will be the same as what the hearer immediately understands, but in the "village" examples (and these for al-Shāfiʿī are just examples of types of speech) this is not the case, and therefore there is a distinction between *ẓāhir* and apparent or obvious meaning.

There are also hints elsewhere in the *Risāla* that there may be more than one possible *ẓāhir* meaning of an utterance. In his discussion of what the word "like" (*mithl*) means in the Quranic demand that one who intentionally hunts and kills in the Ḥaram area must make a sacrifice "like" the animal he has killed (Q5/al-Māʾida.90), al-Shāfiʿī entertains two possibilities. One is that "like" here refers to the value of the kill, and the other that it refers to size (*al-ʿizm min al-badan*). Al-Shāfiʿī says that the "more general *ẓāhir*" understanding (size) is the preferred of the two meanings, implying that there is a less general *ẓāhir* (value).[56] Al-Shāfiʿī discusses the verse:

> Say, I do not find, in what has been revealed to me, anything forbidden to be consumed by one who eats, other than carrion, or spilled blood, or swine-meat, for [these are] unclean (*rijs*) or impious things over which the name of God has not been recited (Q6/al-Anʿām.145).

There are, he says, two interpretations: (1) that nothing is forbidden to the "one who eats" except those things mentioned here, and (2) that because God is ordering the Prophet here to give an answer to a question when asked, it could be an answer to a

52 Shāfiʿī, *al-Risāla*, #211, p. 63 (my emphasis).

53 Shāfiʿī, *al-Risāla*, #211, p. 63.

54 Vishanoff (*The Formation*, pp. 46–7) explains how al-Shāfiʿī's example choice is deliberate: he wishes to demonstrate the obvious ambiguity of normal (literal) Arabic expression, which then enables him to explain contradictions within the revelatory canon.

55 That is, the *ẓāhir* is roughly equivalent to Recanati's t-literal rather than m-literal meaning; see above, p. 16.

56 This should not be taken as definitive proof: al-Shāfiʿī also says that it is a "disapproved *bāṭin* reading" (*mustakrahan bāṭinan*) – so it would seem (quite naturally, perhaps) that a *bāṭin* reading is less *ẓāhir* than the *aẓhar*.

specific question or set of questions posed to the Prophet, and therefore is not describing all things which are forbidden. What probably underlies this second interpretation is not only that there is Prophetic Sunna which mentions other items that it is prohibited to eat,[57] but also that God has said that the mentioned foodstuffs (carrion, blood and swine-meat) are prohibited for a reason (they are unclean and impious) and this might be the basis for future analogical reasoning. In any case, al-Shāfiʿī includes an interesting description of the first possible meaning:

> This meaning, when a man recognises himself to be addressed by it, is what comes to him (*yasbiqu ilayhi*): nothing is prohibited other than what God has named as forbidden. [Meanings] like this are what one calls "the most *ẓāhir*" of meanings, the most general of them and the most overwhelming of them (*aẓhar al-maʿānī, aʿammuhā wa-aghlabuhā*). When a verse has a meaning like this, it is the meaning which the people of knowledge are obliged to support (*yalzamu ahl al-ʿilm al-qawl bihi*). However, if the Sunna of the Prophet points towards a meaning other than this one, [and] this is a possible interpretation of the verse, then one says that this is the meaning which God, the most high and blessed, intends.[58]

A statement may have a number of *ẓāhir* meanings, of which one is more "*ẓāhir*" than others. This "most *ẓāhir*" meaning is the one the scholars must support, in the absence of extraneous evidence (such as the Sunna). This passage would seem to contradict al-Shāfiʿī's view concerning the "villages" verses outlined previously. There the *ẓāhir* is a meaning which was "compelled" by the rules of language (the village itself is to be asked and so on), and this may differ from what the hearer (*al-sāmiʿ*) immediately understands. Here the most *ẓāhir* meaning is the one which "comes to" (or "proceeds to" – *yasbiqu ilayhi*) a man when he recognises that he is being addressed. This sounds close (but not identical) to the idea of a literal meaning discerned through an immediate comprehension (*al-mutabādir*) and can, of course, be distinguished from a grammatically determined meaning, as it was for the early Quranic exegetes.[59]

57 Two examples of the *sunna* are given in Shāfiʿī, *al-Risāla*, #571 and #572, p. 208.

58 Shāfiʿī, *al-Risāla*, #557, pp. 206–7.

59 One could try, in the fashion of a determined exegete, to enforce consistency between the two passages. Pursuant to this, one could argue that the rule concerning "what proceeds to a man when he recognises he is being addressed" is only relevant when there is more than one possible *ẓāhir* meaning. In many cases, this will not happen (that is, there will be a single *ẓāhir* meaning). So one might reformulate the rule expressed by al-Shāfiʿī here as "When there is more than one *ẓāhir* meaning (i.e. more than one meaning which is compelled by linguistic rules), the one which 'comes to' the addressee by the utterance is the *aẓhar* and the one which the scholars must support". In this particular case (forbidden foodstuffs), the Prophet is being addressed, and he already knows that what is meant by God in these words is *not* that forbidden foodstuffs are restricted to this list; hence the meaning which comes to the "one who is addressed" (in this case, the Prophet) is the authoritative one, and this already incorporates an element of modification by the *Sunna*. We are, if you like, listening in on a conversation between God and the Prophet and any meaning we take from this conversation must be tempered by that fact. I give this reasoning here not because I am particularly convinced by it (I prefer to see here an example of the underdevelopment of ideas within the *Risāla*), but as an example of the sort of measures which would be necessary if one was to argue that al-Shāfiʿī (or whoever is responsible for the text) has a conception of *ẓāhir* which he uses with unerring consistency.

The analysis here could be extended through further examples from the *Risāla*, and possibly from al-Shāfiʿī's other writings as well. However, from the above selection of citations, *ẓāhir* as a noun refers to a meaning of an utterance/text which is present within the text itself but which may be left behind in the exegetical process due to extraneous evidence. Extraneous evidence also means the context of the discourse in which the utterance takes place. This notion, which has to be constructed from the occasions on which the term *ẓāhir* is used in the *Risāla*, fulfils the principal characteristics of the literal meaning. The question remains, however, how this *ẓāhir* meaning is to be grasped, and here al-Shāfiʿī is not entirely clear. At times (as in the analysis of Q6/al-Anʿām.145) the *ẓāhir* meaning is located in the immediate understanding of the listener. Regularly, however, al-Shāfiʿī explicitly rejects immediate understanding as an indication of the *ẓāhir* (compare the village cases above). In such examples, the hearer immediately understands the *bāṭin*, and the *ẓāhir* is that necessitated by a simple application of the rules of Arabic grammar and lexicography. Is it possible that al-Shāfiʿī is assuming that the hearer is not the ordinary language user, but one versed in *lisān al-ʿArab*? Such a person would immediately access the *bāṭin* without reference to the *ẓāhir*. In any case, it is not expressed explicitly and the lack of precision here is, perhaps, an example of the underdevelopment of ideas within al-Shāfiʿī's *Risāla*. As we shall see, *uṣūl* writers of future generations formulated their ideas with more precision.

The matter is complicated further by the use of *ẓāhir* as an adjective to describe a particular interpretation or understanding of a verse. Here, in line with the general understanding of the term *ẓāhir*, phrases such as *ʿāmm ẓāhir* describe utterances whose literal meaning (that is, the meaning necessitated by the utterance itself, without reference to external contextual factors) is general. This may not be the apparent meaning, in the sense of the meaning which appears to the ordinary Arabic-skilled listener, but it could be the meaning which appears in the mind of someone skilled in the grammar but not the language of the Arabs. Suffice it to say, in terms of the *ẓāhir*, al-Shāfiʿī's usage appears technical (use in maxims, consistent employment of the term in hermeneutic discussions), but elements of the discussion (how to/who can access the *ẓāhir* and the *bāṭin*; what is its relationship with the *lisān al-ʿArab*?) are not satisfactorily resolved within the *Risāla*.[60]

Language Use and Literal Meaning: al-Jaṣṣāṣ's *Fuṣūl*

The surviving portions of al-Jaṣṣāṣ's text of *uṣūl al-fiqh*, *al-Fuṣūl fī ʿilm al-uṣūl*, represent both a continuation of and a development from the notion of literal meaning developed in al-Shāfiʿī's *Risāla*. It is a continuation in that al-Jaṣṣāṣ picks up the notion of the utterance meaning which appears to the ordinary listener and develops this into a defining element of his conception of literal meaning. Al-Jaṣṣāṣ's work,

60 And this, perhaps, demonstrates that al-Shāfiʿī has recognised an intuitively persuasive idea of literal meaning but did not have the tools to flesh it out as the later Uṣūlīs did.

however, presents a more developed lexicon of terminology for the hermeneutic task, and we should not expect this to replicate al-Shāfiʿī's terminology. Within that lexicon, we find a more careful delineation of what is and is not the literal meaning of a text. He tackles, for example, the question of contrary implication which contrasts what a texts says (that is, its supposedly literal meaning) with the information conveyed by it implicitly (that is, the author's intended meaning).

> Yaʿlā b. Ummaya said to ʿUmar b. al-Khaṭṭāb, "'There is no sin for you if you shorten your prayer if you fear those who disbelieve might attack' (Q4/al-Nisāʾ.101). The people have made peace [so we cannot shorten prayer]." He [ʿUmar] said, "I pondered on this like you did. I asked the messenger of God about this and he said, 'God has given you a gift (*ṣadaqa*); so accept his gift.'"[61]

Here the question is whether God's permission to shorten prayer when attack is feared is removed when the fear of attack is eliminated (that is, when there is a treaty between the Muslims and the enemy). Clearly, Yaʿlā and ʿUmar expected it to work in this way. Since the reason for shortening the prayer was the fear of attack, when the reason disappears, the permission does also. Instead, however, the Prophet indicates that shortening the prayer is still permitted even when fear is eliminated (or at least reduced) due to the treaty. It is argued by the Shāfiʿīs that even though the Prophet is actually rejecting a conclusion reached through contrary implication (*dalīl al-khiṭāb/mafhūm al-mukhālafa*) in this instance, the report actually confirms the validity of contrary implication. The Prophet's companions, ʿUmar and Yaʿlā, had used contrary implication, and their implied surprise on hearing the rule is otherwise is evidence not of the invalidity of *mafhūm al-mukhālafa*, but of its default validity until God or the Prophet decrees otherwise.

Al-Jaṣṣāṣ, setting the tone for subsequent Ḥanafī discussions on this issue, wishes to reject the validity of *mafhūm al-mukhālafa*, and he does so by reassessing what it is that ʿUmar and Yaʿlā are asking here:

> The matter is not as you think. Those two are not saying that the verse prohibits shortening [prayer] during the period of a treaty, they are only saying, "How can we shorten when we have concluded a treaty when God has ordered us to complete prayer during the period of a treaty?"... This is the meaning (*maʿnā*) of what the two are asking, in our view. And when ʿUmar asks the Prophet about this, he [the Prophet] informed him [ʿUmar] that this is a "lightening" (*takhfīf*) from God to you in both situations even though it is not mentioned in the Qurʾān – rather it is in the form of direct revelation (*waḥy* – to the Prophet] and not through the Qurʾān.[62]

That is, ʿUmar and Yaʿlā were not, in fact, employing *mafhūm al-mukhālafa* at all. Instead, they were saying that God has, elsewhere in the Qurʾān, commanded us to perform complete prayers (and not shorten them), and God makes an exception for when one fears an attack. What they are asking is whether there are other

61 Muslim, *al-Ṣaḥīḥ*, v. 2, p. 143, amongst other references.
62 Jaṣṣāṣ, *al-Fuṣūl*, v. 1, pp. 304–5.

circumstances in which prayers might be shortened (and, indeed, there are – namely when an individual is travelling). The counter argument of the Shāfiʿīs is then presented:

> One of the opponents argues that al-Shāfiʿī supported [*mafhūm al-mukhālafa* on the basis of this report], and he was one of the *ahl al-lugha*; he claims that Abū ʿUbayd, Thaʿlab and al-Mubarrad said this also.

The Shāfiʿī argument, then, is that since these persons were experts in language, their opinion on the companions' alleged use of *mafhūm al-muwāfaqa* is authoritative. Al-Jaṣṣāṣ's response is almost vitriolic:

> This person's view is that al-Shāfiʿī was one of the *ahl al-lugha*, and that [al-Shāfiʿī] said so, and so his proof is demonstrated – if someone takes refuge in proofs like this against his opponents, then all that is left is the extent of his bankruptcy …
> As for his report about Thaʿlab and al-Mubarrad – it is a useless story (*hikāya bāṭila*) without foundation, and this one who tells you this is not to be trusted. And as for what he relates about Abū ʿUbayd – it is meaningless because Abū ʿUbayd was not particularly distinguished above anyone else in knowledge [of the *lugha*].[63]

So the first element of the rebuttal consists of a rejection of the qualifications of the intellectuals claimed to be experts in language. But the argument is actually more fundamental than that:

> The *ahl al-lugha* and the rest [of the people] are equal in knowledge of this matter. The *ahl al-lugha* are only expert in the knowledge of names and the vocables placed upon items to be named, such that they can say "the Arabs call this such and such". As for meanings (*maʿānī*) and the indications of speech, then the *ahl al-lugha* are not experts superior to anyone else in their knowledge … If the *ahl al-lugha* have no particular expertise over and above anyone else in this knowledge, then their [the Shāfiʿīs'] claim that one of the *ahl al-lugha* says this or that is void and pointless.[64]

Knowledge of the meaning of speech (referred to here by both terms *kalām* and *lafẓ*) is not something particular to the experts (*ahl al-lugha*). All they can tell you is the names of things according to the *lughat al-ʿArab*. The way utterances are composed in order to create meaning is beyond their expertise. This popularism in al-Jaṣṣāṣ's theory is explicitly extended to what might be called the literal meaning:

> If it is said:
>
> > It is known from the way people speak (*khiṭāb al-nās*) and their forms of knowledge that if someone says, "If Zayd enters the house, then give him a dirham", then the handing over of the dirham is necessitated by the entering. If he does not enter, then it is not permitted to give.
>
> Then it is said to him:
>
> > This is actually a point against you – for every rational person (*ʿāqil*) when he

63 Jaṣṣāṣ, *al-Fuṣūl*, v. 1, pp. 306–7.
64 Jaṣṣāṣ, *al-Fuṣūl*, v. 1, pp. 307–8.

> hears this statement understands from it that he is not forbidden from giving the dirham when [Zayd] does not enter [the house]. The entering is simply a stipulation that the dirham should be handed over. And so, it is permitted to give a dirham freely.[65]

The meaning of a statement, then, is whatever the sensible speaker of the language takes it to mean. In the Zayd-house-dirham example, the opponent is arguing that the discourse of the people is such that they are unable to understand the literal meaning since they would immediately understand that if Zayd does not enter the house, then he should not get a dirham. Al-Jaṣṣāṣ argues the opposite: people understand the literal meaning quite well – indeed, their understanding defines it, since they know a ruling that Zayd should not get a dirham if he does not enter the house is a meaning external to the text and not present within it. In his rejection of the right of those who claim to be *ahl al-lugha* to arbitrate utterance meaning, al-Jaṣṣāṣ's position represents a continuation of the notion that literal meaning is identified with the meaning as it appears to current language users.

This is not to say that al-Jaṣṣāṣ demands adherence to the literal meaning in all circumstances, even if he does reject *mafhūm al-mukhālafa*. In his section on *ḥaqīqa* and *majāz*, he outlines the ways in which the meaning of a statement can diverge from the meaning assigned to words in the *aṣl* (that is, in the original act of assignation). His view is, however, that divergence from *ḥaqīqa* to *majāz* (and *isti*ʿ*āra*) is permitted in the language of the Arabs. When God says he will use "clear Arabic language" (*lisān* ʿ*arabī mubīn*; Q16/al-Naḥl.103) and when he says "I have made it for you a Qurʾān ʿ*arabī*"(Q43/al-Zukhruf.3) he is saying he will use Arabic with all its flexibility (*ḥaqīqa, majāz, isti*ʿ*āra* and *ittisā*ʿ), since these things exist in Arabic. For al-Jaṣṣāṣ, that an utterance is non-literal does not make it any less clear than the literal – the ability of the language user to derive meaning from non-literal expressions is as efficient as it is from literal expressions. However, meaning acquisition from non-literal expressions is only unproblematic when the usage remains within the *lughat al-*ʿ*Arab*. In another swipe against the *ahl al-lugha*, al-Jaṣṣāṣ says, in terms which are themselves rather elliptical, that it is "not because the *ahl al-lugha* have called [an example of metaphor] *isti*ʿ*āra* which necessitates God employing metaphor with regard to something. But rather, it is because he addresses us with something that is *isti*ʿ*āra* in language, or *majāz* or *ittisā*ʿ and not according to the *ḥaqīqa* laid down for it in the *aṣl*."[66] I think what al-Jaṣṣāṣ means here is that some understand God's usage of *isti*ʿ*āra* as him employing a rhetorical technique involving deviation from literal meaning which has been cleverly identified (or devised) by the *ahl al-lugha*. This understanding is, however, incorrect: God is, in fact, employing a mode of speech which is perfectly acceptable in the *lughat al-*ʿ*Arab* and was recognised as such well before the *ahl al-lugha* gave it a name.

For al-Jaṣṣāṣ, on occasion language use also determines whether a particular

65 Jaṣṣāṣ, *al-Fuṣūl*, v. 1, pp. 316–17.

66 Jaṣṣāṣ, *al-Fuṣūl*, v. 1, p. 367.

instance is *ḥaqīqa* or *majāz*. In the famous "ask the village" case, for example, some have argued that the word *qarya* ("village") can refer to people and not simply to buildings, and therefore the statement is not *majāz*, but *ḥaqīqa*. Al-Jaṣṣāṣ replies:

> If it is said, "the people of the village are sometimes called 'the village' when they are in it", then it is said:
> If this were the case, it would be permitted for us, when we are referring to some men in the village, to say "they are a village" and mean by this the men and not the buildings. This is not allowed, absolutely, with any of them. And [furthermore] it would be permitted to refer to these men, after they have left the village, and say that they are a village because the name for them would be *ḥaqīqa* according to the statement of this one who does not permit *majāz*. Them leaving the [village] would not prevent the unconditional reference to them being a village, just it does not prevent them being unconditionally referred to as men wherever they may be. The impossibility of an unconditional use of the word "village" to refer to a group of men indicates that the village cannot be a name for men under any circumstances, and that his statement "ask the village" necessitates the ellipsis (*iḍmār*) of its "people".[67]

The term *ḥaqīqa* receives a formulaic definition at various places in al-Jaṣṣāṣ's *Fuṣūl*: *al-ḥaqīqa hiya al-lafẓ al-mustaʿmal fī mawdiʿihi al-mawdūʿ lahu fī al-lugha* – *ḥaqīqa* is an expression used in the way given to it in language. However, as the above (and other) examples show, the primary manner in which "the way given to it in language" is known is by reference to language users' understanding of what the words mean in and of themselves. Al-Jaṣṣāṣ, and a number of Ḥanafī Uṣūlīs after him, are, then, the natural inheritors of the pre-Sībawayh view of literal meaning (which is also marginal – but present – in al-Shāfiʿī's *Risāla*), namely that everyday language use is the primary criterion for determining literal meaning.

Grammatically Determined Meaning in al-Bāqillānī's *Taqrīb*

Al-Bāqillānī, in his *al-Taqrīb wa'l-Irshād*, divides the information one gains from discourse (*khiṭāb*) into three types, distinguished by the extent to which understanding is gained independently and without the need for interpretation. The first category is defined as information the acquisition of which is "independent by virtue of itself (*mustaqill bi-nafsihi*) in revealing everything which is under its categorisation, and there is no uncertainty in a single element of its meanings".[68] This category of information is in turn divided into two subcategories, the first being information which is "independent by virtue of itself by explicating the intended meaning by univocal and explicit speech"; the second is the same, except its intended meaning is explicated by an apparent grammatical irregularity or by an implication. Of these two subcategories, the first would appear linked to our concept of "literal meaning" in that in this type of discourse, the literal meaning is intended by the

67 Jaṣṣāṣ, *al-Fuṣūl*, v. 1, pp. 361–2.
68 The other two categories are, predictably, "entirely non-independent" and "mixed independent and non-independent" – and need not concern us here.

speaker and understood by the audience. Al-Bāqillānī's examples and description of this category are instructive:

> As for that which is independent by virtue of itself because of its *naṣṣ*,[69] then it is like the statements of the Most High:
> Muḥammad is the Prophet of God (Q48/al-Fatḥ.29)
> Do not go near to *zinā* (Q17/al-Isrāʾ.32)
> Do not kill yourselves (Q4/al-Nisāʾ.29)
> Do not kill your children through fear of want (Q17/al-Isrāʾ.31)
> These, and examples like them, are *ẓāhir* texts which are unproblematic and unambiguous in terms of what they mean (*lā ishkāl wa-lā iḥtimāl fī al-murād bihā*). This category is called *naṣṣ*, and the reason why it is termed this is because the meaning comes about without ambiguity/the need for interpretation (*ẓuhūr maʿnāhu min ghayr iḥtimāl*) and the thing that is mentioned is pronounced with its name which was given to it, and it is explicit without any elision or metaphorical usage (*dūna al-iḍmār lahu wa'l-kināya ʿanhu*).[70]

Al-Bāqillānī here introduces the category of *naṣṣ*, which is often defined as "text", but here it refers to the quality of a text. *Naṣṣ* texts are those that are clear or apparent (*al-nuṣūṣ al-ẓāhira*) and which convey their meaning in an unambiguous fashion. They do this because they use words (or names – *asmāʾ*) in their assigned fashion (*al-mawḍūʿ lahu*). In this sense, *naṣṣ* for al-Bāqillānī describes those texts/expressions in which there is a single literal meaning for each element/word; the words are used in this literal manner, and there is no implied meaning within the statement which might lead to ambiguity. *Naṣṣ*, then, is the mode of expression in which only literal meanings are employed, and every element of meaning is expressed through some feature of the text. They are "independent by virtue of themselves" in that no external indicators are necessary in order to understand the text's meaning.

The other type of "independent by virtue of itself" text is glossed as "on account of its implication" (*mafhūm*). This includes, for example, the notion that one should not hit one's parents from the statement that one should not "say *uff* to them" (Q17/al-Isrāʾ.23). Al-Bāqillānī believes these implied meanings are so obvious that there is no reasoning process involved in gaining their meaning:

> Every speaker of a language, and those who know about the discourse of the people who speak it, agree that the meaning immediately proceeds into the understanding of the hearer by statements such as this; and the understanding which is not mentioned explicitly is more immediate than the understanding which is explicitly expressed in the [statement]. And if it is not more immediate, then they are simultaneous.[71]

69 For this term, see al-Bāqillānī's definition, below. Al-Bāqillānī's system of language and communication is discussed in more detail in Vishanoff, *The Formation*, pp. 152–86.

70 Bāqillānī, *al-Taqrīb*, v. 1, pp. 340–1.

71 Bāqillānī, *al-Taqrīb*, v. 1, p. 342.

Al-Bāqillānī is, then, staking out his position on the well-known debate about whether the acquisition of an implied meaning (such as not to hit one's parents from Q17/al-Isrāʾ.23) is a purely linguistic matter, or whether there is a reasoning process (*qiyās*) involved here. Al-Bāqillānī is not, he says, disputing whether the implied meaning is actually written (*manṣūṣ*) in the text. He accepts that, in some way, it is not "there" in the text. However, "anyone who knows the rules of discourse (*ʿālim bi-aḥkām al-khiṭāb*) does not need analogical reasoning and deduction (*qiyās wa-istinbāṭ*) in order to understand" the text's meaning.

Two things emerge from the way in which al-Bāqillānī is arguing here. First, there is clearly a focus on what the text means in and of itself, and the notion of the intended meaning of the speaker is not the operative tool in determining textual meaning. This is not to say that the intended meaning is irrelevant in al-Bāqillānī's scheme, but rather it is understood, at least at the initial stage, through (that is, after) the meaning gained from the text "by virtue of itself". This has major implications for the way in which the literal meaning functions within his discourse theory. The text, and hence the language within it, has become the object of study for al-Bāqillānī, which represents a significant difference from al-Jaṣṣāṣ's hearer-orientated approach. Second, al-Bāqillānī is explicitly breaking the link between immediate understanding and the literal meaning, which was to reoccur within the *uṣūl* tradition.[72] The thing that is immediately understood by the speaker of the language is not always the literal meaning; instead it can be an implied meaning which, while not written in the text, is immediately understood. The result is that, for al-Bāqillānī, literal meaning is not necessarily gained from the testimony of the language user; it must be discovered by different means.

His use of the stock phrase "the meaning to which they have been assigned" (*al-mawḍūʿ lahu*) indicates that his conception of literal meaning is identified with the notion of *ḥaqīqa*, even though he does not use the term in the section on distinguishing different types of discourse. However, the *Taqrīb* does contain chapters relevant here: one on the meaning of *ḥaqīqa* and *majāz* (*al-qawl fī maʿnā al-ḥaqīqa wa'l-majāz*), and the other on means of distinguishing between them (*maʿrifat al-faṣl bayn al-ḥaqīqa wa'l-majāz*). In the first, most of the discussion relates to *majāz*, though al-Bāqillānī interestingly distinguishes two meanings of *ḥaqīqa*. In the first, *ḥaqīqa* is the "quality of a thing by which it is specified and upon which it rests, in itself". So when one refers to someone as a scholar, the *ḥaqīqa* is that he has the quality of knowledge (*ʿilm*). In this sense, *ḥaqīqa* means something like "the truth conditions of a defining characteristic". It refers to the reality of the individual rather than a fact of language. The second meaning of *ḥaqīqa*, however, is familiar from other works of jurisprudence: "the quality of speech in which [one can say] that the statement is used in the way to which it was assigned originally".[73] The difference between the two meanings, al-Bāqillānī explains, is that the first deals with reality

72 See above, p. 39.
73 Bāqillānī, *al-Taqrīb*, v. 1, p. 352.

(that is, is a matter of reference), whilst the other is a linguistic (meaning-related) phenomenon which, unlike reality, can be negated by a non-*ḥaqīqa* use (that is, *majāz*).[74] How, then, does one know a *ḥaqīqa* usage when one sees one? Al-Bāqillānī outlines four mechanisms for identifying *ḥaqīqa*:

1. *Ḥaqīqa* applies to the items which were assigned to it in a general manner. That is, the *ḥaqīqa* refers to when the general meaning of a word like "horse" or "man" applies truthfully in all instances.
2. *Ḥaqīqa* can be derived etymologically from the roots of the word. For example, the term *amr* has a large number of different meanings: when it refers to a matter or affair it is *majāz*, but when to a command, the opposite of a prohibition, then it is *ḥaqīqa* because it comes from the root meaning of ʾ-m-r (meaning to order or require action from another).
3. *Ḥaqīqa* can be identified by the plural of the word in question. So the plural of *amr*/command is *awāmir*, whilst the plural of *amr*/affair is *umūr*. Al-Bāqillānī does not, however, state that one plural form indicates *ḥaqīqa* and the other *majāz*. It appears that this is merely an indication that we have a *ḥaqīqa* and a *majāz* usage here, for if they were both *ḥaqīqa* (that is, *amr* was a homonym meaning both order and affair) they would have the same plural.
4. *Ḥaqīqa* can be identified as applying to all cases within a category. Power (*al-qudra*), for example, is used in a *ḥaqīqa* way when there is something over which there is power (*maqdūr*). Furthermore, when God says "the wall wanted to fall" (Q18/al-Kahf.77) it is clearly *majāz* because you cannot say that all walls have a "desire" to fall. The *majāz* is, then, the unusual, marked usage of a word.

Ḥaqīqa, it would seem, describes the manner in which a word is used (*istiʿmāl*), and these four criteria are mechanisms for discovering that *ḥaqīqa* has taken place.[75] A *ḥaqīqa* expression has occurred when words are used in accordance with the meaning they have been assigned, and for al-Bāqillānī it is the meaning assigned to a word which is its literal meaning. *Ḥaqīqa* describes speech (*kalām*) rather than meanings (*maʿānī*) for al-Bāqillānī. However, when one has identified an expression as *ḥaqīqa*, and one knows what the expression means, then one has, indirectly, discovered its literal meaning, since a *ḥaqīqa* expression is one in which words are used in accordance with the meaning assigned to them (*al-mawḍūʿ lahu*). The link between assigned/literal meaning and a *ḥaqīqa* mode of expression is so strong that, as we have seen, some writers allow the two categories to blur and they occasionally speak of *ḥaqīqa* meanings. Formally speaking, however, they are distinct, and this should be borne in mind when comparing terms such as *ẓāhir* (which does refer to the meanings of expressions) and *ḥaqīqa* (which refers to a way of speaking).[76]

74 See above, pp. 13–14, for the meaning/reference distinction.

75 They can be usefully compared with the twelve mechanisms for identifying *ḥaqīqa* meaning mentioned and assessed by al-Ḥillī in the more mature tradition; see above, pp. 42–4.

76 See above, pp. 45–9.

If identifying the *ḥaqīqa* implies an identification of the literal meaning, then these four criteria relate to the literal meaning as well as the *ḥaqīqa* expression. What is of interest, of course, is that all four are technical and contain an extremely limited recourse to ordinary language users; two of them are specifically grammatical/etymological (2 and 3). Identifying the expression as *ḥaqīqa* (that the words within it are used with their literal meaning, and so by implication the literal meaning itself is discovered) emerges from the application of scholarly method (in particular, grammatical techniques) to the expressions' individual elements.

Ibn al-Qaṣṣār and the Ossified but Correct Language of the Arabs

Ibn al-Qaṣṣār, also a Mālikī *uṣūlī* and writing at around the same time as al-Bāqillānī, employs a similar categorisation scheme to that found in the *Taqrīb*. What is understood from the language of the text alone (something which one might consider a gloss for the literal meaning) includes implicated meaning. For example, *mafhūm al-mukhālafa* (referred to as *dalīl al-khiṭāb* by Ibn al-Qaṣṣār) is perfectly valid (*maḥkūm bihi*) primarily because Mālik b. Anas (d. 179/795) himself approved of its use. In reference to Q4/al-Nisāʾ.101 and the vexed issue of shortening prayer for reasons other than fear (the reason explicitly mentioned in the verse), he writes:

> The companions of the messenger of God asked about the shortening of prayer when there is a peace treaty, as they had heard God's words, "There is no sin for you if you shorten your prayer because you fear that those who disbelieve will attack you" (Q4/al-Nisāʾ.101). For them it was the case that whenever there was no "fear", there was a "peace treaty" with the opposite [ruling]. The messenger of God said to them, "God has given you a gift (*ṣadaqa*); so accept his gift." He does not refute what they thought, and he does not say they have erred in what they had assessed. This proves that [*dalīl al-khiṭāb*] was in his language and theirs (*lughatuhu … wa-lughatuhum*). This indicates the validity of *dalīl al-khiṭāb*. And God knows best.[77]

Ironically, then, the fact that the Prophet rejects the application of *dalīl al-khiṭāb* in this instance is proof for Ibn al-Qaṣṣār that, for the Prophet, normally *dalīl al-khiṭāb* is a valid hermeneutic mechanism. The Prophet reveals a new rule (God's gift of shortening prayer, *taqṣīr al-ṣalāt*) in order to validate it, and there is a presumption that *dalīl al-khiṭāb* operates unless there is an indicator (that is, another *dalīl*) which proves otherwise. The choice of technical terminology here is revealing. *Mafhūm al-mukhālafa* employs the notion of an implication within the speech which is not in the text; *dalīl al-khiṭāb* hints at the discourse itself (*khiṭāb*) indicating something which is present within the language. For Ibn al-Qaṣṣār (as for al-Bāqillānī, and for subsequent Mālikīs and Shāfiʿīs), the opposite meaning of the expressed order (in Q4/al-Nisāʾ.101, that prayer cannot be shortened for reasons other than fear of attack) is a matter of language alone. For al-Jaṣṣāṣ, it is beyond the text, and hence cannot

77 Ibn al-Qaṣṣār, *al-Muqaddima*, p. 86.

be justified by it. What is most telling is that for Ibn al-Qaṣṣār, it is the *lugha* of the Prophet and the companions which requires us to accept the opposite of an expressed order as forbidden. This is expanded to include the language of the ancient Arabs:

> Discourse (*khiṭāb*) can come in different ways; the *ẓāhir* of [*khiṭāb*] is that when it comes context-free (*tajarrada*), it indicates that its opposite is the opposite of it [that is, *dalīl al-khiṭāb*], unless there is an indicator to the contrary. The proof of this opinion of [Mālik] in favour of *dalīl al-khiṭāb* is that, when it comes context-free, this was [included in] the language of the Arabs (*lughat al-ʿArab*). For [divine] discourse only comes in the Arabic language (*al-lisān al-ʿarabī*), and its explanation is attained from [the Arabic language]. We see the experts in language (*ahl al-lisān*) distinguishing between *muṭlaq* and *muqayyad*, and between *mubham* and whatever is conditional. When someone says
>
> [1] "Whoever from the Banū Tamīm enters my house, give him a dirham"
>
> then what is understood is different from what is understood from the statement
>
> [2] "Whoever enters my house, give him a dirham".
>
> What is understood from the statement
>
> [3] "Whoever does not enter my house, give him a dirham"
>
> is [also] different.[78]

The three formulations have three distinct meanings which were understood by the Arabs and formed part of their *lugha*. In order to discover the meanings found in the text (be they explicit or implied), one needs to understand this *lugha*, and that, in the current times, is the task of the *ahl al-lisān*/*ahl al-lugha*. The location of the true meaning of discourse within the language of the Prophet, the companions and, more generally, the Arabs is a dominant feature of Ibn al-Qaṣṣār's account of the text's literal meaning.

On the question of the general and particular, Ibn al-Qaṣṣār treats statements such as Q2/al-Baqara.187, "Do your retreat in the mosques", as intended by God to be an order of general reference: that is, the Ramaḍān retreat (*iʿtikāf*) can be carried out in any type of mosque (congregational or otherwise). In order to identify this general meaning as the intended meaning, Ibn al-Qaṣṣār states that one must first carry out a search of the sources to see if there is any indicator (*dalīl*) which might particularise (*takhṣīṣ*) the statement.[79] So, in the famous example of Q5/al-Māʾida.40 ("the thief, male and female, cut off their hands"), Ibn al-Qaṣṣār states that the Prophet explains (*bayyana*) what is intended when he states that it refers to thefts of a quarter of a dinar or more only. Ibn al-Qaṣṣār accepts that in linguistic form a statement such as Q5/al-Māʾida.40 is general – *ʿāmm*/*ʿumūm*; in form, it applies to all thieves. However, this linguistic form is to be distinguished from what can be taken to be the presumed intended meaning (*murād*) of the statement. A statement which is general in form is, in the original linguistic system (*fiṭrat al-lisān*), "susceptible to particularisation" (*iḥtimāl al-khuṣūṣ*). That is how it functioned in the language of the

78 Ibn al-Qaṣṣār, *al-Muqaddima*, pp. 85–6.
79 Ibn al-Qaṣṣār, *al-Muqaddima*, p. 55.

Arabs, and the dictates of subsequent grammatical analysis of linguistic form do not give the linguistically required, grammatical meaning any privileged position. Grammar and linguistic rules might dictate that the general form indicated general meaning, but for Ibn al-Qaṣṣār, this is a foolhardy assumption on which to embark upon the understanding of the revelatory texts. Since, in the speech of the Arabs, the general form is susceptible to particularisation, then to assume a general meaning without any investigation would be incorrect, not to say reckless. So even though a statement may have the linguistic form of a general statement, it cannot be assumed to be general until after "examination and investigation".[80] A statement which, under the analysis of grammar, has a general form does not necessitate a general meaning (*ʿayn al-lafẓ lā tūjibu al-ʿumūm*) because the *fiṭrat al-lisān* demands something different (namely, that general statements are subject to particularisation). Linguistic forms, then, do have grammatically determined meanings, but these meanings should not be seen as presumed intended meanings when approaching a text. For grammatical meanings to be taken as the text's intended meaning, evidence is required (in the form of indicators – *adilla*). Amongst the *adilla* – perhaps principal amongst them – is the requirement that a search be carried out to discover if there is a particularising statement. In this sense, "the Book, the Sunna and the *uṣūl*, all of them, are like a single verse (*kal-āya al-wāḥida*)".[81] Whilst each verse has its own meaning derived from its particular linguistic form, meaning can only become a legitimate "assumed intended meaning" after a thorough search has provided evidence that this can be the assumed intended meaning.[82]

That Ibn al-Qaṣṣār demands a search before a general meaning can occupy the prized position of being the assumed intended meaning of the utterance indicates that the meaning dictated by grammatical form is, for him, not primary. Instead, the meaning which is present within the text, which inheres within it, is the meaning in the *fiṭrat al-lisān* ("the original/natural state of language"). Within these discussions, such a locution would appear to refer to an idealised (past) linguistic context, and this is identified as the *lughat al-ʿArab* for Ibn al-Qaṣṣār. For example, he discusses the general term which has been subject to partial particularisation, and whether all other usages of this general term must be understood to be particular. Some say that one must suspend judgement (*tawaqquf*) in such instances until one finds an indicator which indicates whether this or that usage is specific or general. The *madhhab* of Mālik, according to Ibn al-Qaṣṣār, is that if they have been demonstrated to be

80 Ibn al-Qaṣṣār, *al-Muqaddima*, p. 55; the Arabic reads: *lam yajuz al-iqdām ʿalā al-ḥukm bihi dūna al-baḥth wa'l-naẓr fī al-murād bihi wa'l-maʿnā al-ladhī yakhruj ʿalayhi.*

81 Ibn al-Qaṣṣār, *al-Muqaddima*, p. 56. The slogan that all of revelation is a single verse is used for different effect by Ibn Ḥazm; see below, p. 166.

82 It is, I think, important to point out that for Ibn al-Qaṣṣār the other texts do not change the meaning of the linguistic form of the text; they simply adjust the manner in which the text operates as an indicator of intended meaning. This, it could be said, distinguishes his use of the "one verse" slogan from Ibn Ḥazm's use where the other texts change the linguistic meaning of the text under consideration, since for him all revelation is not "*like* one verse" (that is, is not to be treated *as if it were a single* verse); rather, for Ibn Ḥazm, all of revelation actually is one verse, or one utterance. See below, p. 166, n. 72.

general, then they remain so unless another indicator shows them to be particularised also. The reason for this judgement is explained:

> The indicator for this [position] is that God speaks to us in the language of the Arabs (*lughat al-ʿArab*) and we find them, when they command someone who should obey them saying, "Give the Banū Tamīm such and such" (or orders like this). This obligates the one ordered to give [the Banū Tamīm] whatever it was that was ordered. When he says to them later, "Do not give the old men of the Banū Tamīm a thing", then there is nothing within this which prohibits you giving [something] to the remaining young people. This is because giving to all was proven by the order, and the extraction of some from the whole does not indicate the invalidity of the whole. This is known for them [the Arabs], and was common in their language (*mashhūr fī lisānihim*), and it is obligatory that [one] should not depart from [the *lisān al-ʿArab*].[83]

To be sure, Ibn al-Qaṣṣār is attempting to set out rules whereby the intended meaning of utterances might be understood – and in this enterprise it is the meaning dictated by the language use of the Prophet, the companions and the Arabs which acts as the primary criterion when opting for an assumed intended meaning. In this he resembles al-Shāfiʿī's position referred to above. However, this meaning, once determined, is fundamental and holds pole position in any attempt to discern the meaning of the text. It can be relegated, modified or discarded under the influence of other elements of God's revelatory texts, but it is the starting point for interpretive understanding. Ibn al-Qaṣṣār, then, has a tendency to see the interpretation of revelatory texts as revolving around a past system of language which bears some relationship to either the language in current use or the artifice of the grammarians. However, it is not controlled by (or even primarily known through) these sources. Perhaps this makes it slightly more difficult (practically speaking) to determine God's intended meaning in the revelatory texts.

Whilst in al-Bāqillānī's system, this linguistic meaning has a priority claim to be the intended meaning, Ibn al-Qaṣṣār demotes this meaning. It can only occupy this position once a thorough search of the potential indicators (*adilla*) has been carried out. The linguistic, grammatical meaning can only become the assumed intended meaning when it is confirmed, by evidence from the *lughat al-ʿArab*, that it is reasonable for it to do so. Whilst for a number of early Uṣūlīs the *lughat al-ʿArab* formed one amongst a number of sources in the determination of meaning, for Ibn al-Qaṣṣār it is a (perhaps the) crucial test. Ibn al-Qaṣṣār implies a distinction between "us" and the Arabs who spoke the original language. The experts in language (*ahl al-lisān*) should really be experts in the language of the Arabs (and, of course, amongst them was Mālik himself). That a meaning is demanded by the (modern) science of grammar does not necessarily give it privileged status for Ibn al-Qaṣṣār; that a meaning is current amongst the current spoken language similarly does not, in itself, recommend it as the assumed intended meaning of God when he addresses us in revelation. The position – the hermeneutic default, if you like – is a text's meaning

83 Ibn al-Qaṣṣār, *al-Muqaddima*, p. 126.

as discovered through our knowledge of the *lughat al-ʿArab* in which God, the Prophet and the companions conducted their discourse. Most of the qualities of the literal meaning are, for Ibn al-Qaṣṣār, to be found in this meaning: it is the "original", in that the Arabs, including the Prophet and the companions, were the ones who operated this (past) language system; the meaning inheres within the language itself (in so much as implications are part of linguistic meaning rather than derived through analogy or extension); he appears to see this as the text's isolated, context-free meaning (indicated by his use of the verse *tajarrada* and its derivatives – by which I think he means "without reference to other revelatory indicators", rather than "without reference to *qarāʾin*"). The meaning dictated by linguistic form (for example, *ʿumūm* form indicating *ʿumūm* meaning) is secondary here; it does not have the strength to become the assumed intended meaning by itself, and is activated only when the *lughat al-ʿArab* allows it to come to the fore in the interpretive process. Literal meaning (the meaning contained within the text) is, for Ibn al-Qaṣṣār, most appropriately found in an ossified language use of the past Arabian community, recoverable by experts who preserve this usage (and hence control its knowledge). Grammatical analysis, and possibly the meanings determined thereby, is not necessarily irrelevant to this process but is, in essence, a modern science, and to allow it to determine textual (that is, literal) meaning would, one suspects, be anachronistic in Ibn al-Qaṣṣār's view.

Conclusion

These three trends in the construction of literal meaning all come out of the hermeneutic thinking begun before al-Shāfiʿī but summarised in his *al-Risāla*, and I do not mean to suggest that the *uṣūl al-fiqh* of al-Jaṣṣāṣ, al-Bāqillānī or Ibn al-Qaṣṣār were single-mindedly dedicated to declaring their own conception of literal meaning at the expense of the others. I present evidence here of these three trends in these early works of *uṣūl al-fiqh* from which the great classical edifice of the *uṣūl* hermeneutic theory of literal meaning, which I outlined in Chapter 2, emerged. In that system, the literal meaning of a statement is primarily identified with the meaning assigned to a word in the *lugha*, through an act of *waḍʿ*. These three trends were formalised into *evidence* of the *waḍʿ*. The *lughat al-ʿArab*, the grammatical meaning and current usage (through use or through "immediate understanding") were all indicators of the *maʿnā waḍʿī*. That is, they were not the *waḍʿī* meaning, but they were the mechanism by which one comes to know the *waḍʿī* meaning. This distinction, clear in later *uṣūl*, and sometimes in evidence here, is not yet fully formed. The writers tend to allow their preferred location of meaning (ordinary language use, technical grammar, *lughat al-ʿArab*) to spill over and define rather than indicate the literal meaning. This is particularly evident in the writers' assumption that the meaning indicated by one or other of these three sources of meaning is the presumed intended meaning of the speaker. The literal meaning is, of course, only useful in so far as it informs a judgement about the speaker's intended meaning; otherwise it is a fanciful scholarly diversion. In many cases, that original act is irrecoverable, and all we have are signs of *ḥaqīqa* usage (that is, usage in conformity with the *waḍʿ*). The conceptions of the literal meaning analysed in this chapter were, in the developed theory, transformed into "signs of literal usage" (*ʿalamāt/ʿalāʾim al-ḥaqīqa*); that is, pieces of evidence for literal meaning rather than the defining element or "home" of literal meaning itself. This process of transformation was under way when these *uṣūl* texts were written, and the works of al-Jaṣṣāṣ, al-Bāqillānī and Ibn al-Qaṣṣār already show evidence of how the encroaching textualism of mature *uṣūl al-fiqh* was to develop. However, they also bear witness to the variety of literal meanings in *uṣūl* thought in the early period between al-Shāfiʿī and the first "full-blown" works of *uṣūl al-fiqh* which were eventually incorporated (and ultimately downgraded) in the dominant model of classical *uṣūl al-fiqh.* These were not the only intellectual casualties in the formalisation of the *uṣūl* discipline. In the next chapter, I present another such lost conception of literal meaning during this period found in early Shīʿī writings, and which also eventually dissolved in the dominance of the mature paradigm.

5

Early Shīʿī Conceptions of Literal Meaning

The famous Arabic lexicographer Ibn Durayd (d. 321/933) wrote a wonderful book of Arabic homonyms entitled *Kitāb al-Malāḥin*. He wrote it "so that one who is forced, unjustly, to make a vow which is repugnant to him might take refuge in [the book] … he can secretly [vow] something different to what he outwardly says so as to stay safe from the wrongs of the oppressor".[1] In the book he provides words which have more than one meaning, and which the individual forced to make a vow can use intending one thing, whilst the oppressor understands another. The meaning which the individual outwardly expresses and which the oppressor takes the individual to mean is, interestingly, a cognate of *ẓāhir* (*yuẓhiru*). So, for example, someone could say, "By God I will not break so-and-so's shin (*sāq*), and I will not touch it".[2] *Sāq*, Ibn Durayd explains, can (amongst other things) mean the trunk of a tree. So one can make this vow if forced, and not commit oneself to not breaking the person's shin, but instead to not breaking the trunk of his tree. The general rule in vows is that words are presumed to be used in their "literal" sense, and the one making the vow cannot claim that he meant something non-literal when uttering the words. That is, the vow-maker's intention is less important than the literal meaning of the words he is using. For Ibn Durayd, the words listed in his book have to be homonyms, having at least two literal meanings. If they were not, and the vow-maker could use words in his vows in a non-literal manner, he could use whatever words he liked and be bound by his intended meaning. However, since the vow is a public promise, it has to be publicly accessible, and hence the "literal" meaning must be used as that is the publicly agreed meaning. If, however, there is more than one literal meaning, there will be more than one way of fulfilling a vow. Ibn Durayd is claimed by the Twelver Shīʿa as one of their own, and his promotion of the notion that one can deliberately say a thing which the oppressor will hear and understand in one way, but which you will mean in another, brings to mind the Shīʿī doctrine of *taqiyya* or dissimulation. The implications of the doctrine of *taqiyya* for an understanding of literal meaning in Shiʿism are not entirely clear from Shīʿī legal literature, but one can note here that there is a difference between Ibn Durayd's proposal and that countenanced under the classical doctrine of *taqiyya*. In the classical doctrine, a vow taken under *taqiyya*

1 Ibn Durayd, *al-Malāḥin*, p. 2.
2 Ibn Durayd, *al-Malāḥin*, p. 14.

has no legal effect, and need only be fulfilled in another act of *taqiyya*. *Taqiyya* vows are not intended, and therefore need not be respected: no atonement (*kaffāra*) is required from breaking a *taqiyya* vow under *taqiyya*, other than the atonement required to keep up the appearance of conformity which caused the *taqiyya* in the first place.

From this, one might think that the intention of the vow-maker is the crucial thing, but this does not extend to non-*taqiyya* vows. There, for the Shīʿa, the primacy of literal meaning predominates, as it does in Sunni jurisprudence. The importance of using literal meaning in vows across the schools is probably a result of the seriousness with which they are taken in Muslim jurisprudence. Consider the following two legal issues from the famous *Kitāb al-Mabsūṭ* of the Shīʿī jurist Muḥammad b. al-Ḥasan al-Ṭūsī (d. 460/1067):

> If [a man] vows that he will not ride the slave's beast, and the slave does indeed have a beast which the master named in [the slave's] inventory which he then rides, then he has not broken his vow. Some say he has broken his vow because [the beast] is associated with [the slave]. The former opinion is stronger because it is *ḥaqīqa* and the second is *majāz*.[3]
>
> If he vows that he will not smell rose, and he smells a rose itself, then he has broken his vow; if he smells rose oil, then he has not broken his vow. If he vows not to smell violet, and he smells the flower of a violet, he has broken his vow, but if he smells the oil of [a violet] he has not broken his vow. Some of them say he has broken his vow because its oil is sometimes called "violet". The former opinion is stronger because it is *ḥaqīqa*, and what they say is *majāz*.[4]

In the first example, the man owns the slave and the slave owns the beast – so the man, in reality, owns the beast. He has not, then, ridden the slave's beast as the slave does not really own a beast. The slave only "has" a beast in a non-literal manner. The genitive construction (*iḍāfa*) with which the ownership of a thing is expressed cannot apply to slaves in a literal manner as they are not free and cannot truly own anything. In the second example, the oil of a rose is sometimes called "rose", and the oil of violet is sometimes called "violet", but both usages are non-literal (*majāz*) and the one taking the vow has not broken his vow. On the other hand, when we call a violet's flower a violet we are doing so in a literal (*ḥaqīqa*) manner, and hence the smelling of that flower constitutes a breaking of the vow. Al-Ṭūsī's notions of *ḥaqīqa* and *majāz* here represent the endpoint of a process of development within Shīʿī legal literature concerning literal and non-literal meaning. Here the notion of literal meaning seems to concur, generally speaking, with that current in the mature Sunni tradition, but it was not always so. In this chapter I explore the various distinctive notions of literal meaning amongst the Shīʿa, and their role in the development of their early jurisprudence, and how they ended up adopting the framework of *uṣūl al-fiqh* developed by the Sunni jurists from al-Shāfiʿī onwards.

3 Ṭūsī, *al-Mabsūṭ*, v. 6, p. 244.
4 Ṭūsī, *al-Mabsūṭ*, v. 6, p. 248.

Notions of Literal Meaning in Early Imāmī *Ḥadīth* Literature

Potential evidence for an early reflexive Shīʿī understanding of literal meaning can be found in a report attributed to Imam ʿAlī in an early Shīʿī source, the *Kitāb Sulaym b. Qays.*[5] The report presents the Imam as well aware of at least some of the standard hermeneutic categories of later *uṣūl al-fiqh*. Imam ʿAlī says:

> In the hands of the people there is valid and invalid (*ḥaqqan wa-bāṭilan*), truth and falsehood (*ṣidqan wa-kadhib*), abrogating and abrogated (*nāsikhan wa-mansūkhan*), general and particular (*ʿāmman wa-khāṣṣan*), clear and ambiguous (*muḥkaman wa-mutashābihan*), preserved and whimsical (*ḥifẓan wa-wahman*) … The orders of the Prophet and his prohibitions are like the Qurʾān – with abrogating and abrogated, general and particular, decisive and ambiguous. The speech which comes from the Prophet is of two types. There is particular speech and general speech, just as in the Qurʾān. Someone who does not know what God means by [this speech], or what God's messenger means by it, may hear it. Not every companion of the messenger would ask him questions, and understand. There were amongst them [i.e. the companions] some who did not ask or enquire. Hence they loved it when a stranger or a Bedouin used to come and ask the Prophet [a question] so that they might listen to him.[6]

Within this passage, some of the constituent elements of the later theory of literal meaning are to be found. In particular, the idea that one may hear what God or the Prophet says and misunderstand it is fundamental. The reason for the misunderstanding is that one takes it as *ʿāmm* when it is *khāṣṣ*, or *muḥkam* when it is *mutashābih*, and *nāsikh* when it is *mansūkh*. Dealing with these pairings in turn, the last (*nāsikh/mansūkh*) operated entirely within the realm of the literal: the literal meaning of one revelatory segment cancels out the literal meaning of another. *Naskh* can be seen as a rather rudimentary effort at solving revelatory contradiction between the literal meanings of two parts of the revelatory corpus. It is, to an extent, an abandonment of exegesis; an admission that the two segments cannot be reconciled by reinterpreting one or the other (as, for example, *ʿāmm* and *khāṣṣ*). Activating *naskh* could signal a failure to produce a convincing combination through the application of the common literal/non-literal operations (*ʿāmm/khāṣṣ*, *muṭlaq/muqayyad*, *ḥaqīqa/majāz* and so on). In either case, an awareness of the process of abrogation does not necessarily imply a commitment to an advanced theory of literal meaning and its operation in revelatory texts.

The presence of the pairings *ʿāmm/khāṣṣ* and *muḥkam/mutashābih*, on the other hand, might indicate a theoretical awareness of literal meaning (presuming, of course, the pairings are used in a manner congruent with their employment in later exegetical writings). However, it is not at all clear from the report in the *Kitāb Sulaym* that the terms are used in the same way as in a later classical work of, say, *uṣūl al-fiqh* or *tafsīr*. When the report was transmogrified into one of ʿAlī's speeches in the *Nahj*

5 An assessment of the authenticity of the *Kitāb Sulaym* can be found in Modarressi, *Tradition and Survival*, pp. 82–6, and I discuss this particular report further in my "*Kitāb Sulaym*".

6 Raḍī, *Nahj al-Balāgha*, v. 2, p. 623.

al-Balāgha, the commentators naturally assumed that the meanings of these terms are quite stable and unproblematic. By doing this they imply that ʿAlī, in the early years of the Rāshidūn, had mastery over the technical categories of the later science of *uṣūl al-fiqh*. Ibn Abī al-Ḥadīd (d. 655/1257 or 656/1258) writes:

> The statement concerning the interpretation of *uṣūlī* terms, such as *ʿāmm* and *khāṣṣ*, *nāsikh* and *mansūkh*, *ṣidq* and *kadhib*, *muḥkam* and *mutashābih*, is all related to the discipline of *uṣūl al-fiqh*, and I have already discussed this [discipline] when I covered the *uṣūlī* books. To lengthen my commentary [on this speech] at this point [by repeating this] would be improper.[7]

Another early commentator on the *Nahj al-Balāgha*, this time from within the Shīʿī tradition, Ibn Maytham al-Baḥrānī (d. 679/1280), also assumes the terms are used with their technical meanings. According to him, they refer to "types of speech" (*anwāʿ al-kalām*) and the "understanding of these notions (*mafhūmāt*) has already been established".[8] In the treatment of this passage by both exegetes, the only pairing which needs particular mention is *ḥifẓ*/*wahm*, since this is not present in subsequent hermeneutic thought (though the meaning of the two terms need not concern us here).[9] But this, on both the commentators' parts, is probably wishful thinking.

When read on its own terms, what can be deduced about the meaning of *ʿāmm*/*khāṣṣ* and *muḥkam*/*mutashābih* in the report? It is clear that a proper recognition of *ʿāmm* and *khāṣṣ* relates to an accurate understanding of "what God or the Prophet means". That is, within the report revelatory texts (specifically the Qurʾān and Prophetic reports) are devices through which God and the Prophet make their intended meaning known. But the report also recognises that an individual exegete may, due to inadequate understanding, identify an incorrect intended meaning of a statement by assuming that the text is general when it is particular (or vice versa). The procedure is familiar to those acquainted with *uṣūl al-fiqh*, and I need not go into it here,[10] but the relevant point is that even the "rough and ready" understanding of *ʿāmm* and *khāṣṣ* which can be gleamed from the report assumes the notion that the text has one meaning (*ʿāmm*) which could, potentially, differ from the speaker's intended meaning. One who does not understand what God and the Prophet intend

7 Ibn Abī al-Ḥadīd, *Sharḥ Nahj al-Balāgha*, v. 9, p. 40.

8 Ibn Maytham al-Baḥrānī, *Sharḥ Nahj al-Balāgha*, v. 2, p. 109.

9 *Ḥifẓ* refers to "that which is preserved from the Prophet exactly as it is"; *wahm* is when it is misunderstood – for example, it is thought to be *ʿāmm* when it is *khāṣṣ*, or secure (*thābit*) when in fact it is *mansūkh* (Ibn Maytham al-Baḥrānī, *Sharḥ Nahj al-Balāgha*, v. 2, p. 109). What is notable about the pairing is that they seem ill-matched: the first refers to a technical ability of transmission, the latter to a skill in interpretation – one could, surely, preserve something the Prophet said accurately, but misunderstand its legal significance entirely. Ibn Maytham's assumption seems to be that the Prophet's words are sufficiently clear in and of themselves that to transmit them is to provide their wording and their meaning simultaneously. The other pairings would seem to be mutually exclusive (either *ʿāmm* or *khāṣṣ*, either *nāsikh* or *mansūkh* and so on).

10 The operations of the pairings *ʿāmm* and *khāṣṣ* in classical *uṣūl al-fiqh* are described by Zysow, "Economy of Certainty", pp. 128–51; also by Hallaq (*A History*, pp. 45–7) and Weiss (*The Search*, pp. 389–441). See also above, pp. 47–9.

to convey may "hear" the revelatory segment but not understand it, and they will not understand it until they can correctly distinguish the *ʿāmm* from the *khāṣṣ*. What is missing is explicit evidence within the report that *ʿāmm* as a category is used to cover general statements as it is in later *uṣūl al-fiqh* (for example, Q5/al-Māʾida.38, "the thief, male and female, cut off their hands") and *khāṣṣ* is used for particular statements (for example, "the hand should only be cut for a quarter of a dinar or more"[11]). This is not ruled out, but there is no indication that the later understanding of *ʿāmm*/*khāṣṣ* is operative within the report. Nevertheless, the report does indicate a number of presumptions: the *ʿāmm* meaning of a statement is its primary meaning; an exegete will understand this *ʿāmm* meaning naturally when reading or hearing the text; the *ʿāmm* meaning may not be the intended meaning, but taking it as the meaning is an understandable error on the exegete's part.

The report, in typical Shīʿī fashion, takes a side swipe at the companions (*aṣḥāb*) of the Prophet, who failed to enquire about, or understand, the Prophet's words. The *aṣḥāb*, it appears, merely transmit the Prophet's words like a rote learner. In order to understand God and the Prophet they needed a Bedouin to come and converse with the Prophet. Through listening to the Bedouin's account of what the Prophet said, the *aṣḥāb* gain access to the intended meaning. This appears to be a reference to the familiar motif of the Bedouin's pure Arabic being the code whereby the perfect language of revelation is to be understood. The implication is that this "high"/"original" Arabic is, of course, characterised by tropes which need explanation for the less sophisticated. The report, if genuine, would be an indication of the seminal state of the Imam's hermeneutic understanding (including a notion of literal meaning). I have argued elsewhere that the report (on the basis of both its *matn* and its *isnād*) is probably best dated to the early or mid ninth century.[12] However, even with this speculative dating, the report is still an indication of the development of a notion of literal meaning amongst the Shīʿa which ran alongside, and perhaps predated, those present within early Sunni literature.[13]

The report in *Kitāb Sulaym* does, at least, demonstrate that Shīʿī self-reflection on the interpretive process led before the Occultation (that is, before 329/939) to the employment of a more sophisticated technical apparatus to aid the exegete. Some of this apparatus was taken from the wider intellectual environment (probably *ʿāmm*/*khāṣṣ* falls into this category); some was perhaps more exclusively Shīʿī (the *taʾwīl*/*tanzīl* distinction found in early Imāmī *ḥadīth* and examined below). Our understanding of this emerging Shīʿī awareness of the linguistic aspect of the communicative process can be enhanced, I believe, by a broader perspective on early Shīʿī views on language, and how these relate to the later classical understanding of *waḍʿ*. There is within the Imāmī *ḥadīth* corpus a dominant view that language is quite definitely created:

11 Bukhārī, *al-Ṣaḥīḥ*, v. 8, book 81, #780.
12 Gleave, "*Kitāb Sulaym*".
13 See above, pp. 112–24.

> Imam Jaʿfar al-Ṣādiq said: "God's name is separate from him. On all things there is the name of a thing, and that is a created thing, except God. Whatever the tongue utters, or the hand makes, that is created."[14]

This would appear to conform to the Imāmī-Muʿtazilī convergence on the created nature of speech (and hence the created nature of the Qur'ān). The way the doctrine is expressed here seems appropriate to the mid-Abbasid period at the earliest (that is, early to mid ninth century CE). Similarly, there is an absolute distinction between God and any of his "names", and this is expressed in Imam Jaʿfar's (d. 149/766) reminder to the Imāmī theologian Hishām b. al-Ḥakam (d. c. 179/795):[15] "God is a thing (*maʿnā*) which is indicated by these names, and all of them are separate from him."[16] On the timing of the creation of language, the Imams do, in places, explore the *locus classicus* of later writings: Q2/al-Baqara.31 – "He [God] taught him [Adam] all the names". The glosses attributed to the Imams variously describe how God taught Adam the names of mountains and their passes, seas, valleys, plants, animals and so on.[17] But the Quranic verse is not used as a springboard to a full account of the creation of language. Rather, it appears to refer to the invention of proper names. In some reports, ʿAlī is seen as knowing the "name" of every "thing", just as Adam did. When the Prophet showed ʿAlī a collection of unknown seeds, for example, ʿAlī was able to name them all. The Prophet, in response, said:

> Gabriel had told me that God had taught you all the names, just as he had taught Adam.[18]

A special linguistic knowledge accorded to ʿAlī is reproduced in reference to the Imams, who are also described as knowing all languages of the world.[19] Once again, there is no systematic account of how these languages came about, merely that the Imams knew them. There is, however, a hint here of a linguistic knowledge reserved for the Imams, a theme which is present but imperfectly developed elsewhere in the early corpus of reports attributed to the Imams. This is also linked to the notion that the Imams know the special/secret name of God, and have access to a concealed knowledge. These doctrines, which some commentators have termed "esoteric",[20] are not strictly relevant to the topic of the legal hermeneutics of literal meaning. However, they may be an appropriate background from which to explain occasional manoeuvres of legal exegesis found within the Imāmī *akhbār*. Take, for example, the debate around Q5/al-Mā'ida.6: "if you have touched women" (*lāmastum al-nisā'*), found amongst the list of actions which cause ritual impurity and the need for ritual

14 Kulaynī, *al-Kāfī*, v. 1, p. 113.
15 On Hishām and his divergence from other trends within early Imāmīs, see Bayhom-Daou, "Hishām b. al-Ḥakam".
16 Kulaynī, *al-Kāfī*, v. 1, p. 115.
17 See the reports in ʿAyyāshī, *Tafsīr al-ʿAyyāshī*, v. 1, pp. 32–3.
18 Ṣaffār, *Baṣā'ir al-Darajāt*, p. 438.
19 See Ṣaffār, *Baṣā'ir al-Darajāt*, pp. 357–60; Amir-Moezzi, *Divine Guide*, p. 112.
20 Amir-Moezzi, *Divine Guide*, passim and p. 207, n. 427.

ablutions before prayer. The classical legal debate concerns whether God, by this phrase, means sexual intercourse or mere skin-to-skin contact (or both), and, if the former, then is he using *mulāmasa* (usually translated as "touching") in a *ḥaqīqa* or *majāz* manner?[21] A report from Imam Muḥammad al-Bāqir (d. 114/732 or 117/735) deals directly with this linguistic issue:

> From Abū Maryam: I said to Imam Muḥammad al-Bāqir: What do you say about a man who does his *wuḍūʾ* and then calls to his slave girl; she takes him by the hand until he reaches the mosque? There are those amongst us who say this is *mulāmasa*.
> He said: No! By God! If he does this, what is the problem here? Nothing is meant by this "*lāmastum al-nisāʾ*" other than the introduction [of the penis] into the vagina.[22]

The example of holding the slave girl's hand is probably hypothetical (a clever student's test case, perhaps), and exaggerated for effect. As to the interpretation of *mulāmasa*, it is possible that the phrase "nothing is meant … except …" (*mā yaʿnī bi-hādhā … ilā*) is an attempt to give a linguistic definition of *mulāmasa* generally and *lāmastum al-nisāʾ* in particular. There are at least three possibilities here. First, the Imam might be saying that *mulāmasa* (that is, Form III of *lams*) means to have sexual intercourse in a literal manner (that is, what might anachronistically be called the *mawḍūʿ lahu, waḍʿī* or *ḥaqīqa* meaning). Second, the Imam might be proposing *mulāmasa* to be a homonym (in technical terms *mushtarak*) with two, equally literal meanings, "to touch" and "to have sexual intercourse", and announcing that (due to his particular legal knowledge) he can decree the latter to be the intended meaning on this occasion. Finally, he could be arguing that he is able to speak authoritatively about the intended meaning of *mulāmasa* as a *majāz* because he has peculiar knowledge of the relevant *qarāʾin* (that is, he has special access to God's intended *majāz* expressions). The most theoretically interesting of these possibilities is probably the first, and that this is at least a possible understanding is strengthened by another report, this time attributed to Imam Jaʿfar al-Ṣādiq:

> From al-Ḥalabī: I asked Imam Jaʿfar about God's statement "or if you have touched women" (*lāmastum al-nisāʾ*). He said, "It is intercourse, but God is the concealer (*satīr*) who loves to conceal things. He does not give names in the same way that you give names (*fa-lam yusamma kamā tusammūna*)."[23]

Taking these reports together, they seem to form a view that God (at least at times) has given a name (*tasmiya*) which is generally unavailable, and therefore functions like the tropic language found in the Qurʾān. The meaning of the verses, which include verses with legal relevance such as this one, can only be made publicly available through the Imam. The Imam, with his knowledge of God's law in general, and the true meaning of the Qurʾān as a legal source in particular, is essential for us

21 Summaries of the debate can be found in a number of secondary sources: Katz, *Body of Text*, pp. 86–92; Maghen, *Virtues of the Flesh*, pp. 133–282.

22 Ṭūsī, *Tahdhīb*, v. 1, p. 22, and Ṭūsī, *al-Istibṣār*, v. 1, p. 88.

23 Kulaynī, *al-Kāfī*, v. 5, p. 555.

if we wish to gain access not only to theological truth, but also to the legally relevant meaning of the Qurʾān. Such a doctrine would probably be classed by later Shīʿī theologians as associated with the *ghulāt* and not the Imams themselves. It is possible, of course, to understand these reports, and others like them, in a more mundane fashion,[24] but whilst the Imam in such cases appears to have exclusive access to God's intended meaning, there is a hint here that this intended meaning represents God's designated linguistic meaning of the words. If so, there is here an indication of a "real" designation of words (*ḥaqāʾiq*), given by God and revealed to us through the Imams. The theory was never fully worked out, and was rapidly overtaken amongst the Imāmiyya by the more usual (and orthodox) theory developing in the nascent science of *uṣūl al-fiqh*.[25] Nonetheless, the above citations are evidence of this theory's percolation into legal discussions amongst the Imāmiyya in the pre-occultation period (that is, before 329/941). The notion that the Imam is the only true interpreter of God's speech, and that the meaning of revelation was in some way impenetrable without the Imam's interpretation (both linguistic and theological), was naturally attractive to some Shīʿī groups. This is particularly the case for those which have an extensive ("exaggerated") doctrine of the Imam's powers.[26] In the history of Twelver legal theory, one sees the idea re-emerge in the Akhbārī movement and also in modern debates around *al-ḥaqāʾiq al-sharʿiyya* (legal-literal meanings).[27]

Indications of a more conventional view of literal meaning (at least by later standards) are also present within early Imāmī *ḥadīth* literature. As with the more esoteric reports, the material here is extremely tricky to date, but much of it clearly predates the greater occultation as it is found in works securely dated to that period.[28] A more recognisable notion of literal meaning[29] forms a presumptive background for much of the exegetical material. Exegetical reasoning in this material is rarely explicitly expressed, with the interpretation simply being presented alongside the revelatory segment. Examples of this method of presenting an interpretation abound, in relation to both legal and non-legal topics. Once again, the approach within the *akhbār* to non-legal topics forms the background for our understanding of legal exegetical processes.

24 The phrase *Allāh satīr yuḥabbu al-satr* could, admittedly, be merely a reference to God's desire to be euphemistic; though recognising when God is being euphemistic is, in itself, a particular knowledge not necessarily available to all. Such a reading would, perhaps, raise the issue of where the notion of such a euphemistic God might have come from, given the lack of bashfulness elsewhere in revelation; but other uses of the term *satīr* within the *ḥadīth* do link it to the related idea of a respect for privacy. The Prophet is supposed to have said: "God is a living concealer – he loves life and he loves to conceal. So when any of you want to wash, cover yourself" (Abū Dāwūd, *al-Sunan*, v. 2, pp. 250–1, #4012).

25 See above, pp. 29–35.

26 See Bayhom-Daou, "Hishām b. al-Ḥakam", p. 87.

27 See Gleave, *Scripturalist Islam*, pp. 275–82; Gleave, "Approaches to Modern Shīʿī Legal Theory (*uṣūl al-fiqh*)"; below, pp. 184–94.

28 Such works include the *Baṣāʾir al-Darajāt* of al-Ṣaffār (d. 290/902–3) and *al-Maḥāsin* of al-Barqī (d. 274–80/887–94).

29 "Recognisable", that is, from a later *uṣūl* perspective; see Heinrichs, "On the Genesis".

For the sake of illustration, one can consider Imam al-Bāqir's exegetical statement concerning Q39/al-Zumar.9 found in the *Baṣā'ir al-Darajāt* of al-Ṣaffār:

> Say: Are those who know equal to those who do not know? Only those who possess [faculties of] understanding (*ulū al-albāb*) shall be warned (Q39/al-Zumar.9).
> From al-Bāqir: We are the ones who know; our enemies are those who do not know; and our Shīʿa are the *ulū al-albāb*.[30]

The simple identification of Quranic referents hardly constitutes sophisticated exegetical reasoning, but the employment of this technique indicates that such reports did not emerge in an environment where these interpretations needed to be defended. That is, the report is most likely composed for affirmation of already established doctrine, rather than persuasion of an intellectual opponent. Nonetheless, this form of presentation, repeated in many reports and perhaps the most prevalent exegetical style in the Imāmī *ḥadīth* corpus, is based on the notion that the Quranic text has a meaning independent of its exegesis. This meaning is, perhaps, unspecific rather than ambiguous: the phrase "those who know", for example, has a perfectly recoverable meaning through which it is understandable. Leaving it as it is, though, and understanding it solely in textual terms will inevitably lead to a failure to comprehend the intended meaning of the text. That is, what the phrase means in itself does not contradict the speaker's (God's) intended meaning, but to limit one's understanding of the verse to this meaning is, in some way, deficient. The report's message appears to be that one cannot fully (or adequately) understand the Quranic passage simply by reading the text in isolation (that is, by acquiring its "literal" meaning). One has need of an Imam to provide the referent of the unspecified phrases, which in this verse are "those who know", "those who do not know" and "those who possess understanding".[31] But, and this is central to our concerns here, the shift between the literal meaning and the intended meaning is not due to any feature of the text (that is, usual linguistic exegetical methods are useless here). Instead one needs to discover an almost arbitrary link between a Quranic phrase and an intended referent, and for that one needs the Imam. This distinguishes this literal/non-literal meaning relationship from those of a more literary quality and characterised as *ḥaqīqa* and *majāz*.[32]

Such a process of arbitrary linkage is, of course, particularly useful in the development of a sectarian reading of the text and can be combined with a belief in the alteration of the Quranic text itself (*taḥrīf*).[33] The role of literal meaning in reports referring to supplementation and emendation of the Quranic text is a little more complex. A central hermeneutic pairing is *tanzīl/ta'wīl*:

1. Muḥammad b. Fuḍayl, from Abū al-Ḥasan [the tenth Imam ʿAlī al-Hādī]. [Ibn

30 Ṣaffār, *Baṣā'ir al-Darajāt*, p. 17.
31 One could, perhaps, link this to the reference/meaning distinction, on which see above, pp. 13–14.
32 See Weiss, *The Search*, p. 135.
33 Bar-Asher, *Scripture and Exegesis*, pp. 101–4; Amir-Moezzi and Kohlberg, *Revelation and Falsification*, pp. 24–30; above, pp. 69–71.

Fuḍayl] said: I asked him about the statement God makes, "They intend to extinguish the light of God with their mouths" (Q61/al-Ṣaff.8).
He said: They intend to extinguish devotion to the Commander of the Believers (*walāyat amīr al-muʾminīn*) with their mouths.

2. I asked [about the statement]: "But God is the one to complete his light" (Q61/al-Ṣaff.8).
He said: "God is the one to complete the Imamate" in accordance with his words, "Those who believe in God, his Prophet and the light which he has sent down" (Q64/al-Taghābūn.8). The "light" here is the Imam.

3. I said: [What about] "He is the one who has sent his messenger with the guidance and the religion of truth" (Q61/al-Ṣaff.9)?
He answered: He is the one whose messenger has ordered [us] to show devotion (*walāya*) to his successor, and the *walāya* is the religion of truth.

4. I said: [What about] "So that he may make it apparent to all religion[s]" (Q61/al-Ṣaff.9)?
He replied: He will make it apparent to all religions (*jāmiʿ al-adyān*) when the one who rises up appears (*qiyam al-qāʾim*).

5. Then he said: "God will complete his light" with the *walāya* of the *qāʾim* even if those who do not believe detest the *walāya* of ʿAlī (Q61/al-Ṣaff.8).

6. I said to him: Is this *tanzīl*?
He said: Yes, this statement (*hādhā al-ḥarf*) is *tanzīl*, and the rest of it is *taʾwīl*.[34]

The precise meaning of *taʾwīl* and *tanzīl* is not clear from this report, and deserves further (separate) investigation. However, in reference to the notion of literal meaning and exegetical technique, the first four elements are identified as *taʾwīl*, in which the identification of the intended referent of a Quranic phrase takes place, but the text remains unchanged. In 1, "light" does not mean (linguistically) "devotion to the Commander of the Believers", but it is what God means by it. If the use of this *taʾwīl*/*tanzīl* terminology was rolled out across the corpus (admittedly a rather artificial process), then al-Bāqir's identification of "those who know/don't know/possess understanding" (in Q39/al-Zumar.9) would also be classed as *taʾwīl*. The last segment (5 in my numbering), however, is described as *tanzīl*, implying that this is how it was revealed but that the text has been subject to corruption, and (perhaps) requires correction. So now the Quranic phrase, instead of reading "and God will complete his light, even though the unbelievers may detest [it]", should now read "and God will complete his light *with the walāya of the qāʾim* even if those who do not believe detest *the walāya of ʿAlī*". Here the Imam is not content to leave the text

34 Kulaynī, *al-Kāfī*, v. 1, p. 435. The paragraph numbering is mine.

having a literal meaning which is, in itself, inadequate to discern the intended message (how might one know from the earlier text, for example, that *ulū al-albāb* refers to the Shīʿa?). Instead the Imam changes (or restores) the text, so that a text with the inadequate literal meaning is replaced with a text with a new literal meaning, more obviously in line with the intended meaning of the speaker.[35] The process of textual adjustment is, in a sense, a piece of exegesis, but one which changes the literal meaning by altering the text.

In both these processes (referent identification and textual improvement), the literal meaning is either deliberately ignored or altered; hence establishing it is essential in the exegetical equation. Referent identification and textual improvement are explicitly marked in legal reports, and these can be usefully contrasted with the theological-exegetical reports mentioned above. Literal meaning forms a fundamental, if perhaps unspoken, element of the message in reports such as the following, from Imam Muḥammad al-Bāqir:

1. It is reported from Zurāra and Muḥammad b. Muslim that they said, "We said to Abū Jaʿfar [Muḥammad al-Bāqir], 'What do you say about the prayer when you are travelling? How is it and how many is it?'"[36]

2. He said, "God says, 'If you go on a journey, there is no blame on you (*laysa ʿalaykum al-junāḥ*) for shortening your prayer' (Q4/al-Nisāʾ.101). So it is obligatory when travelling, just as a complete [prayer] is obligatory when stationary."

3. [They continue] So we said, "God only says *there is no blame on you.* He did not say, 'Do it!' So how can this become obligatory, just as a complete [prayer] is obligatory when stationary?"

4. He said, "Has not God said concerning Ṣafā and Marwā, 'He who is doing pilgrimage to the House or *ʿumra*, then there is no blame on him (*lā junāḥ ʿalayhi*) if he go around them both' (Q2/al-Baqara.158)? Do you not see that going around both of them is obligatory-commanded (*wājib mafrūḍ*), because God mentions it in his Book, and his Prophet did it? And in the same way, shortening [prayer] is something that the Prophet did, and God mentions in his Book."[37]

The hermeneutical tenor of the argument here is resonant of later *uṣūl* discussions. In this exchange, a number of legal theoretical issues are intermingled. The Imam's companions play the role of the picky students, perhaps testing the Imam. Their

35 See once again the meaning/reference distinction, above, pp. 13–14.

36 The wording here is interpreted in the following way: "how is it?" – i.e. "is it a *rukhṣa* or an *ʿazīma*?" and "how many is it?" – i.e. "how many *rakʿāt* are there in it?" or, alternatively, "how far does one travel before it becomes obligatory?". See Ibn Bābawayh, *Man lā*, v. 1, p. 434, n. 2.

37 Ibn Bābawayh, *Man lā*, v. 1, pp. 434–5, #1265 (extract).

demand for a justification from the Imam for his interpretation jars somewhat with the later Imāmī doctrinal requirement of unconditional obedience to the Imam. That aside, literal meaning is more apparent here than in the brief exegetical comments in the above examples. The believer may, when travelling, perform a shortened prayer on the basis of Q4/al-Nisāʾ.101. There was debate around whether this is an option available to the believer, or whether one is obligated to perform a shortened prayer. Al-Shāfiʿī is attributed with the view that it is an option; Mālik with the view that it is recommended to shorten, but not obligatory; Abū Ḥanīfa with the view that it is obligatory. The Imāmīs, on this occasion, adopt the view of Abū Ḥanīfa, as reflected here in the statement of Imam al-Bāqir (2 above), and they based this on Q4/al-Nisāʾ.101. The Imam's disciples object, saying that the phrase "there is no blame on you" does not mean "it is obligatory". Their argument relies on the assertion that natural (literal?) understanding of *laysa ʿalaykum junāḥ* ("there is no blame on you") is permission only (making the action minimally optional). For obligation, something more direct would be required (such as an imperative *ifʿal*). Zurāra and Muḥammad b. Muslim are clearly operating with the understanding that the imperative has the literal (that is, the primary, decontextualised) meaning of a command creating an obligation (a position associated with the Ḥanafīs in classical *uṣūl*)[38] and the phrase *laysa ʿalaykum junāḥ* has a literal meaning which falls short of that.

The Imam's reply is most interesting in that he does not deny that this is the natural (literal) understanding of the phrases in question, but, he adds, the phrase *laysa ʿalaykum junāḥ* (or *lā junāḥ ʿalaykum*), when used in the Qurʾān and then supported by the actions of the Prophet, makes an action obligatory; indeed, such actions have their own subcategory of the obligatory spectrum in the form of "obligatory-commanded (*wājib mafrūḍ*).[39] The Quranic phrase has a natural meaning of permitting the action in question, but when the action is confirmed by Prophetic practice, the intended meaning of the original phrase is now understood as being obligation. In the terminology of later *uṣūl*, Prophetic practice acts as a *qarīna*, with which we can recognise that the intended meaning of the phrase differs from its literal meaning. The underlying hermeneutic structure in the report is much closer to the developed *uṣūl* theory, and tempts one to date the statement sometime later than the early eighth century.

On occasion the Imams are attributed with the ability to employ their knowledge of Arabic grammar in their exegesis. On a non-legal matter, grammatical knowledge lies behind the asserted meaning of Q53/al-Najm.3:

> *It was at a distance of two bow-lengths or (aw) nearer* (Q53/al-Najm.3).
> From Imam al-Ṣādiq: That is (*ay*), rather (*bal*), it was nearer.[40]

38 See Zysow, "Economy of Certainty", p. 101 ff – though, as Zysow notes, the position is not as straightforward as a simple equation of linguistic form with ethical-legal assessment, and is linked with particular elements of Māturīdī doctrine prevalent amongst the Samarqandī Ḥanafīs.

39 The meaning is not spelled out, but this would appear to be a reference to actions which attain obligatory status through the confirmation by the Prophet of a possible interpretation of a Quranic injunction.

40 Qummī, *Tafsīr*, v. 1, pp. 246–7.

Here the Imam is employing a particular function of the particle *aw* (*aw bi-maʿnā bal*). Normally understood to mean "or" (in particular, that there is a choice, *takhyīr*, between the antecedent and subsequent items), the particle *aw* can also mean (that is, it is permitted for it to be used to mean) "rather" – that is, the antecedent is rejected in favour of the subsequent. This alternative meaning of *aw* is already known from the *Tafsīr* of Muqātil b. Sulaymān.[41] It is, of course, not possible to deduce from the report alone that the *aw al-takhyīr* use is conceived of as the actual (literal) meaning by the Imam, whilst other usages (of which *aw bi-maʿnā bal* is just one) are non-literal. Alternatively, there might be some conception of homonymity at work (*aw* means both *al-takhyīr* and *bi-maʿnā bal*). However, *aw bi-maʿnā bal*, here and elsewhere, is certainly marked (that is, unnatural but comprehensible), otherwise Imam al-Ṣādiq (or, probably before him, Muqātil b. Sulaymān) would not be required to provide the gloss. The process is much closer to the *ḥaqīqa*/*majāz* contrast of later *uṣūl*, though the technical terms are not employed. Instead the intended meaning is signalled by the particle *ay*.

The interpretive techniques used for theological-historical Quranic passages, such as this one, were not sealed off from the practice of legal exegesis. Concerning the exegesis of Q5/al-Māʾida.6 (on the practice of *wuḍūʾ*):

> Zurāra said: I said to Abū Jaʿfar, "Can you tell me how I can know and declare that one should wipe part of one's head and part of one's feet?" He laughed and said, "The Prophet said so, and the Book was sent down from God saying so, for God says, *wash your faces* and we know that all of one's face needs to be washed. And then he says, *and your arms up to the elbows.* Then he makes a break in the statement and says *wipe* (*bi*) *your heads* and we know when he says [*bi*] *your heads* that one wipes part of one's head by the position of the [preposition] *bi.* Then he connects the two feet to the head in the same manner as he had connected the two hands to the face. Then he says, *and your feet up to the ankles* and we know when he connects this to the head that the wiping is over part of them."[42]

Not unlike the Q53/al-Najm.3 example above ("two bow-lengths or less than that"), the Imam here is attempting to describe a particular use of the preposition "*bi*" (the "b" of division; *bāʾ al-tabʿīḍ* or *al-bāʾ lil-tabʿīḍ*, though he does not use the technical term). When "wipe" takes a direct object, so the argument goes, the order is to wash all of the object; when *bi* is used, only part of the head is signalled. The Imam is arguing that the grammatical meaning of the verse (that is, the combination of *amsaḥū*/wipe and the preposition *bi*) means that only part of the head is being used. The phenomenon of *bāʾ al-tabʿīḍ* (but not the technical term) is known to the Imam. The argument does not appear in either Mujāhid or Muqātil b. Sulaymān, though it

41 Muqātil, *Tafsīr*, v. 3, p. 108, where it is cited analogously with Muqātil's interpretation of Q37/al-Ṣāffāt.147, "and we sent him to a hundred thousand or more (*aw yazīdūn*)". Here the *aw* is *bi-maʿnā bal*, as Yūnis was sent to more than a hundred thousand. See also above, p. 138.

42 Kulaynī, *al-Kāfī*, v. 3, p. 30; also found in Ibn Bābawayh, *Man lā*, v. 1, p. 103, and Ṭūsī, *Tahdhīb*, v. 1, p. 61.

had clearly entered circulation by the time of al-Shāfiʿī,[43] so it is possible that the report emerged just prior to that; pushing it back to the mid second/mid eighth century would, in my view, require supplementary justification.

The use of grammatical arguments is tied into the emergence of a particular (linguistic) notion of the literal meaning.[44] This is in evidence in other reports related to the understanding of Q5/al-Māida.6, including the debate over whether the verse requires one to wash or to wipe one's feet during the purification ritual (*wuḍūʾ*). As is well known, part of the argument here revolves around whether the word for "feet" is in the genitive (and therefore an indirect object of wipe) or accusative (and therefore a direct object of wash). Imam Muḥammad al-Bāqir is portrayed as being well aware of the debate:

> Ghālib b. al-Hudhayl says: I asked Abū Jaʿfar [the fifth Imam Muḥammad al-Bāqir] about God's statement, *wipe your heads and your feet up to the ankles* (Q5/al-Māʾida.6) and whether [feet] is in the genitive (*al-khafḍ*) or the accusative (*al-naṣb*). He said: "It is in the genitive."[45]

Once again, the use of grammar to establish a verse as evidence of a particular legal position contributes towards the linguistic notion of literal meaning. It is this that the Imam supposedly employs in this report. There are even some phonetic opinions ascribed to the Imams, on occasion. In a controversial report in the *Fiqh al-Riḍā*, attributed to Imam ʿAlī al-Riḍā (d. 203/818), he is reported as saying:

> If you wash your two feet, and you forget to wipe them, then that will suffice you because you have done more than what is required of you. God has already mentioned all this in the Qurʾān, both the wiping and the washing, when he says "and your feet (*arjalakum*) up to the ankles", meaning by it washing with an "a" vowel on the *lām* (*bi-naṣb al-lām*); and when he says "*arjalikum*" with an "i" vowel on the *lām* (*bi-kasr al-lām*), he means by it wiping. Both are permitted – the washing and the wiping.[46]

The presence of this report in the *Fiqh al-Riḍā* is one of the reasons why subsequent Shīʿī scholars considered it a dubious source of legal doctrine: the legal position justified through this phonetic/grammatical exegesis is contrary to the standard Shīʿī doctrine. That aside, both of these reports (from Imams al-Bāqir and al-Riḍā) present the Imams as capable of employing grammatical arguments in support of legal doctrine, which in turn requires a notion of literal meaning as linguistically generated.

The exegetical procedures described in the above citations indicate that there was no single notion of literal meaning amongst the pre-*ghayba* Imāmiyya. Instead one finds a variety of meanings which the texts are seen to "own" distinct from their interpretation. In some instances these are the "true" meanings assigned to words within a revelatory text (such as the Qurʾān) which only the Imams are able to

43 Shāfiʿī, *Kitāb al-Umm*, v. 1, p. 41.
44 See above, p. 92.
45 Ṭūsī, *Tahdhīb*, v. 1, p. 60.
46 Riḍā (attrib), *Fiqh al-Riḍā*, p. 79.

understand/interpret and communicate to the wider community. The sources are not univocal here: when the Imam says that *lāmastum al-nisāʾ* means "nothing other" than sexual intercourse, is he saying that God has designated that a particular word/phrase has a particular meaning (that is, an act of *waḍʿ* preceding a *ḥaqīqa* usage), or is he saying that the word/phrase has the meaning, but God is using it figuratively (a *majāz* usage)? Evidence for the former reading includes the doctrine (also found throughout the Imāmī *ḥadīth* corpus) that Imam ʿAlī (who, for Shīʿīs, passes on all knowledge to his successor Imams) has access to the names of all things, taught to him by Gabriel. The Imams also know God's special name, constituting one element in a secret language in which the true names of things are used. One of the central elements of sectarian exegesis is that revelatory texts appear to mean one thing, but in fact mean another. Such an exegetical stance assumes that the text has a meaning which is obvious to an uninitiated reader but diverges from the hidden/true meaning of the text. This results in the interesting phenomenon in which the true (*ḥaqīqa*) meaning of the text is actually not obviously available, but hidden (*bāṭin*).[47] It is possible to identify the influence of this idea in the normally drier discourse of the law, even when developed in a sectarian environment such as Shiʿism. This idea of the literal meaning as the (ontologically) "real" meaning possessed only by the Imams appears to have quickly lost ground as Imāmī Shiʿism began to develop its own juristic stratum, and notions of literal meaning became more scholastic.[48] In any case, this notion of a secret language known to God and the Imams and through which the Qurʾān was expressed was not left unchallenged in the Imāmī *ḥadīth* corpus. There is the notion of the literal meaning being the obvious meaning: *lā junāḥ ʿalaykum* (on its own) does not mean the action is obligatory, as Muḥammad b. Muslim and Zurāra point out; it appears to mean the action is, at best, permitted. However, states the Imam, one can recognise "obligation" as God's intended meaning when the phrase is combined with evidence from the actions of the Prophet. Then there is the notion of a linguistically permitted meaning as one of the competing literal meanings (for example, the *aw bi-maʿnā bal* and *al-bāʾ lil-tabʿīḍ* – where these prepositions could be interpreted in another manner). Finally, there is the linguistically determined literal meaning (for example, "feet" is genitive not accusative, and therefore they must be wiped). The lack of coherence in the notion of literal meaning in Imāmī *ḥadīth* is not surprising. The reports emerged in different contexts (and, most likely, at different times), absorbing different intellectual presumptions as they did so. In fact, given that the formulation of a widely accepted (and coherent) doctrine of the "literal meaning" was some way off in the ninth

47 Whilst not pertinent to my interest here, it might be possible to trace a linkage in Imāmī sectarian exegesis between the true meaning (*ḥaqīqa*) and the allegorical rather than either the linguistically determined or obvious meaning (which are also normally understood to be the *ḥaqīqa*). It would seem reminiscent of the phenomenon noticed by Heinrichs when examining Abū ʿUbayd's *Majāz al-qurʾān*: *majāz* in this text appears to mean both the figurative expression and its translated "natural" equivalent. See Heinrichs, "On the Genesis", p. 125 ff.

48 See above, p. 30.

century, it would be more surprising if the Imāmī *ḥadīth* literature did present a universally agreed notion of what might be termed in English the "literal meaning".

Early Imāmī *Fiqh* and Literal Meaning

The distinction between *ḥadīth* and *fiqh* was blurred in the Imāmī literature of the tenth and early eleventh centuries. This was not simply because many of the most influential (so-called) *ḥadīth* collections were actually either works of *fiqh* or commentaries on works of *fiqh*.[49] It is also because, as indicated above, the Imams (in particular Imams Muḥammad al-Bāqir, Jaʿfar al-Ṣādiq, Mūsā al-Kāẓim and ʿAlī al-Riḍā, to whom most reports were attributed) were also understood to be jurists, and hence their statements reflected not only simple statements of the law (such as "this is *ḥalāl*", "that is *ḥarām*") but also elements of legal reasoning in which evidence in support of particular legal doctrines is given. Early works of Imāmī *fiqh*, such as *al-Muqniʿ* by Ibn Bābawayh (d. 381/991), display little legal reasoning – legal doctrine is pronounced but rarely justified in any meaningful sense. Discerning any notion of literal meaning is, then, not really possible from such a text. In Ibn Bābawayh's *Man lā yaḥḍuruhu al-faqīh*, though, there is more evidence of legal reasoning. For example:

> The Prophet said, "There is no *raḍāʿ* after weaning (*fiṭām*)." And he means by this that if a child is wet-nursed (*raḍāʿ*) for two complete years, and then drinks any amount from the milk of another woman, then this [second] wet-nursing (*raḍāʿ*) does not cause a marriage prohibition because it is *raḍāʿ* after *fiṭām*.[50]

In *fiqh*, the feeding of a baby by a wet-nurse establishes a pseudo-parental bond, or "milk-kinship", between the baby and the wet-nurse such that, theoretically, the wet-nurse's children are prohibited in marriage to the baby in adulthood.[51] The discussion here is complicated by the fact that the word *raḍāʿ* appears to be used to refer both to wet-nursing generally and specifically to wet-nursing which causes subsequent marital prohibitions. We could call the first of these the literal meaning and the second the legal meaning. The weaning period (*fiṭām*) is, of course, set by the Qurʾān to two years, so when the Prophet says "there is no *raḍāʿ* after *fiṭām*", he could be saying one of two things: either wet-nursing is prohibited after weaning (literal meaning of *raḍāʿ*);[52] or wet-nursing after the first two years creates no milk-kinship relationship (legal meaning). Ibn Bābawayh obviously considers the Prophet to mean the second of these, but if we examine his statement closely we see that in his

49 Gleave, "Between *ḥadīth* and *fiqh*".

50 Ibn Bābawayh, *Man lā*, v. 2, p. 476. The Prophetic statement is also found in Mālik, *al-Muwaṭṭaʾ*, v. 2, p. 408.

51 See Giladi, *Infants, Parents and Wet Nurses*, pp. 68–114, for a general description of the legal implications of the practice.

52 This seems to be the modern Shīʿī Uṣūlī Muẓaffar's understanding of it in a modern work of *uṣūl al-fiqh* (Muẓaffar, *Uṣūl*, v. 1, p. 253).

explanation of the Prophet's statement Ibn Bābawayh himself consistently uses *radāʿ* to refer to wet-nursing in its literal meaning. Hence, Ibn Bābawayh does not take the Prophet's statement "no wet-nursing after weaning" (*lā radāʿ baʿd fiṭām*) as meaning it is prohibited to breastfeed after weaning; rather, he understands the Prophet as declaring that milk-kinship can only be established by breastfeeding before weaning. His gloss only makes sense if the Prophet uses the term *radāʿ* to mean something different from Ibn Bābawayh. The situation is complicated further by the relationship between *fiṭām* and the period of two years. When God, in the Qurʾān, declares weaning to be achieved in a two-year period, he is not (it is commonly agreed) giving kindly advice to parents. Rather, he is setting down a legal fact (as opposed to an actual fact) which should be used when the weaning period is needed for other areas of the law. Once again, we are faced with *fiṭām* having two possible meanings within the Prophetic report: first, it could mean the point at which the child no longer consumes breast milk (a literal meaning?); second, it could mean the two-year period during which the child is normally weaned (a legal meaning). Once again, Ibn Bābawayh interprets the Prophet as intending the legal meaning, because he mentions the fact that the child is breastfed by someone else after the two-year marker has passed. In subsequent Imāmī *fiqh*, the term *fiṭām* in the *ḥadīth* corpus is interpreted as meaning two years, and not the simple fact of the completion of weaning.[53]

Whilst there does not appear to be much methodological reflection here (and this could be said generally of Ibn Bābawayh's writings), he clearly recognises the potential ambiguity within the Prophet's statement (hence the need for a gloss, which is not, it should be said, his usual practice). The terminology of *ḥaqīqa* and *majāz*, though obviously appropriate (and available), are not employed, and whilst the term *al-ḥaqīqa al-sharʿiyya* (legal-literal meaning) was some way from being finalised within the Muslim hermeneutic lexicon, Ibn Bābawayh does appear to employ the idea that the Prophet is using *radāʿ* and *fiṭām* in a way which differs from their ordinary meanings. Without this rudimentary hermeneutic framework, his gloss makes little sense. We are, perhaps, edging closer to the classical *uṣūl* conceptions of *ḥaqīqa*/*majāz*, and Ibn Bābawayh's analysis here (which could be supplemented and made more nuanced with additional examples) does represent an increase in interpretive sophistication amongst the Shīʿa. However, there is little interest in theorising about the exegetical process and giving the constituent parts terms; for that, the Imāmīs had to wait until the writing of al-Shaykh al-Mufīd (d. 413/1022).

Consider the following passage amongst a list of arguments al-Shaykh al-Mufīd produces for the validity of *mutʿa* marriage based on particular interpretations of Quranic passages:

> Q4/al-Nisāʾ.24: *fa-mā ʾstamtaʿtum bihi minhunna, fa-ʾatūhunna ujūrahunna farīḍatan.*
> "And for what you have enjoyed from them, then given them their due as a duty."

53 The great nineteenth-century jurist Muḥammad Ḥasan al-Najafī (d. 1266/1850) says that the use of *fiṭām* by the Prophet to refer to two years is in fact *majāz* here, as *fiṭām* means weaning, whenever it may occur; see Najafī, *Jawāhir al-Kalām*, v. 29, pp. 296–301.

> Shaykh Mufīd: *al-mutʿa* here is a *ḥaqīqa sharʿiyya*, which appears directly in the understanding and in use (*mubādira fī'l-fahm wa'l-istiʿmāl*).
> They say that *istimtāʿ* means simply enjoyment, and the original meaning (*al-aṣl*) is not transferred.
> We say: The Lawgiver uses it, and the original meaning is *ḥaqīqa*; and if it is accepted that it is a *majāz*, then it has the aforementioned pieces of evidence (*qarāʾin*) attached to it.[54]

The leap in hermeneutic sophistication between Ibn Bābawayh and al-Shaykh al-Mufīd is striking, and represents the already well-documented trend in Imāmī jurisprudence (and theology also) between the Iranian Imāmī community (*ḥadīth* transmitters with little hermeneutic awareness) and the rapidly developing Imāmī intelligentsia in Baghdad, who were being modernised through their integration into the formerly Sunni-dominated intellectual scene. It was through this Baghdadi group that we finally begin to see a Shīʿī legal hermeneutics.

Conclusion

With al-Shaykh al-Mufīd we see not only the mastery of technical terms (*ḥaqīqa*/*majāz*; *istiʿmāl*; *ḥaqīqa sharʿiyya*; *qarāʾin*) but the complete incorporation of the system of literal/non-literal meaning which had been developed elsewhere in Sunni *uṣūl al-fiqh*. It is not surprising therefore that al-Mufīd is also credited with the first (surviving) work of Imāmī *uṣūl al-fiqh* (perhaps titled *al-Tadhkira fī uṣūl al-fiqh*),[55] and that his doctrines appear distinctively "Imāmī" in only a few places (literal meaning not being one of them).[56] From this incorporation onwards, Imāmī *uṣūl al-fiqh* developed a distinction of literal/non-literal meaning which operated on the model borrowed from *uṣūl* more generally. This adoption of the standard *uṣūl al-fiqh* framework of literal/non-literal meaning is in contrast to the earlier, more radical notions of the meanings of words: assigned by God, known to the Imams and presented to the populations as and when required. Such a theory sat easily with some of the earlier notions of the Imam's particular knowledge of divine secrets, his inherent understanding of divine law, and the inability of the general masses to understand the full implications of the meaning of revelatory statements (particularly the Qurʾān) without the assistance of the Imam as the sinless exegete.

As the Baghdadi Shīʿa began to incorporate themselves into the existing structures of intellectual enquiry, they perceived a need to develop a distinctive (but not too outlandish) legal theory. Al-Shaykh al-Mufīd's work was an attempt at that; more comprehensive attempts were carried out by his pupils al-Sayyid al-Murtaḍā and Muḥammad b. al-Ḥasan al-Ṭūsī. A hiatus in Shīʿī *uṣūl* production (or at least a lack of surviving examples) was ended with the brief work of al-Muḥaqqiq al-Ḥillī (d. 676/1277), followed by the much more extensive *uṣūl* output of al-ʿAllāma

54 Mufīd, *Khulāṣat al-ījāz*, pp. 22–3.
55 Stewart, *Islamic Legal Orthodoxy*, pp. 133–4 (arguing it is not the title).
56 See also above, p. 30.

al-Ḥillī.[57] Little survives in these works of *uṣūl al-fiqh* of the earlier radical Imāmī ideas of the divine private language, though it is possible to find hints of it on occasion in the more mature Imāmī *uṣūl al-fiqh*. To take al-Sayyid al-Murtaḍā's *al-Dharīʿa ilā uṣūl al-sharīʿa* as an example, many of his opinions on subjects relating to literal meaning are unremarkable, and in line with (mainly Basran Muʿtazilī) positions. There is, however, on occasion a certain ambivalence towards the *lugha* as the key determinate of the legal meaning of revelatory texts. For example, in his thoughts on the linguistic meaning of the imperative form, he writes:

> We accept that in the *lugha*, this form is homonymous between recommendation and obligation. However, we also consider continuous, accepted legal practice (*al-ʿurf al-sharʿī al-muttafaq al-mustamirr*) requires that the unqualified expression of this form, when it comes from God or from the Prophet, be interpreted as obligatory, not recommended, and immediate rather than delayed.[58]

That is, whilst language dictates that the imperative is homonymous, the customary practice of the law demands that in cases where there is no external evidence, this fact be ignored and the imperative taken as creating an obligation to act. This *ʿurf sharʿī* should not be seen as a piece of evidence to take one meaning over another (like a *qarīna*). Rather, the *ʿurf sharʿī* requires discarding the language altogether, and it dictates a meaning on the imperative form. For the law, the linguistic meaning of the *ṣīghat al-amr* is redundant. Furthermore, the *amr* is not tied to a particular linguistic form – it can be conveyed in many different linguistic settings.[59] On the issue of whether performance of the action ordered in an *amr* is effective in discharging the duty, then al-Sayyid al-Murtaḍā argues that according to the *lugha*, a performance of the action is not effective: that is, the performance of action ordered through a *ṣīghat al-amr* does not necessarily discharge the duty created by the order (as it is God's decision as to whether the performance is effective or not). The *ʿurf sharʿī*, once again, requires us to discard this linguistic (or "literal") entailment of non-effectiveness:

> All the discussion on this topic only concerns what the *waḍʿ al-lugha* and its operation requires. As for the operation of the law (*ʿurf al-sharʿ*), then we have already made it clear that it is settled: the performance of the actions which are ordered by the action in the way which is associated with it [in the text itself] necessarily entails effectiveness [in the completion of the duty].[60]

Linked to this ability of the working of the law to render the linguistic meaning of words otiose are a number of al-Sayyid al-Murtaḍā's unusual *uṣūl* doctrines. These include:

57 I used al-ʿAllāma's *Nihāyat al-uṣūl* as a source for the classical model of *uṣūl* above, pp. 29–55; there is little distinctively Imāmī about this work, theologically speaking.

58 Murtaḍā, *al-Dharīʿa*, v. 1, p. 53.

59 Murtaḍā, *al-Dharīʿa*, v. 1, p. 13.

60 Murtaḍā, *al-Dharīʿa*, v. 1, pp. 121–2.

1. His view that a prohibitive form (*al-nahy*) does not, according to the *lugha*, indicate the evil nature of the action (*fasād*); however, the *sharʿ* (the law) does indicate this, thereby making the *sharʿ* the determiner of legally relevant meaning rather than the *lugha*.[61]
2. On the form of the general command, al-Sayyid al-Murtaḍā does not believe that it has a linguistic form.[62]
3. Exceptive forms (*al-istithnāʾ*) such as the word *illā* (except) can apply to the last mentioned class or the earlier mentioned class equally literally. So in the example "Beat my slaves, and greet my friends, except one", there is nothing, in language, to decide on whether the one excepted is from the slaves, or the friends, or from both classes. All other jurists see the exception as applying to either the first or the last element, but not both. That is, the *lugha* is ambiguous for al-Sayyid al-Murtaḍā on this occasion, when other jurists consider it determinate.[63]
4. Also ambiguous are the *bāʾ* in the verse (referring to wiping of the head) and the term *yad* in the verse (referring to the amputation). Whilst other jurists argue what the verses mean, they do not consider them *mujmal* (in the sense of having more than one linguistic/literal meaning) as al-Sayyid al-Murtaḍā does.[64]

These (slightly) unusual *uṣūl* views from al-Sayyid al-Murtaḍā may betray an attitude of the redundancy of meaning decreed by the *waḍʿ* (which by his time was the only real contender for the literal meaning), and these could be remnants of the earlier Shīʿī view that the legal significance of revelatory texts (that is, their real meaning) was not available to all (suitably learned) individuals through grammatical analysis, but was, in fact, the preserve of the Imam. Such anomalies did not survive long within the Shīʿī *uṣūl* discipline, and by the time of al-ʿAllāma al-Ḥillī they had all been cleared up and the mainstream Imāmī opinion was not outside of the various views (Shāfiʿī, Ḥanafī, Muʿtazilī and so on) found cited in works of *uṣūl*.[65] The gradual conformity of Shīʿī *uṣūl* to the established and acceptable Sunni model was, of course, part of an attempt by some Shīʿa to gain recognition as real players in the intellectual culture of medieval Islam. Since law dominated that culture, and since *uṣūl al-fiqh* was, for many, the most advanced expression of that dominance, it is natural that Shīʿī intellectuals wished to muscle into the field. Their impact on the mainstream was always limited, however, and specific Imāmī answers to the standard issues of *uṣūl al-fiqh* were not limited to questions such as *ijmāʿ* (in which consensus remained an indicator of the sinless, hidden Imam's opinion rather than a source in itself). The Imāmī juristic discussions around literal meaning ended up being, on the whole, indistinguishable from their Sunni counterparts, as Imāmī Uṣūlīs accepted the paradigm developed in the great classical works of *uṣūl al-fiqh*.

61 Murtaḍā, *al-Dharīʿa*, v. 1, p. 180.
62 Murtaḍā, *al-Dharīʿa*, v. 1, pp. 201–2.
63 Murtaḍā, *al-Dharīʿa*, v. 1, pp. 249–50.
64 Murtaḍā, *al-Dharīʿa*, v. 1, pp. 349–50.
65 See Ḥillī, *Nihāyat*, v. 1, p. 391, p. 401, p. 432, p. 528, p. 578; and v. 2, p. 86, p. 121, p. 260, p. 408, p. 416.

6

Zahirism, Literalism and Ibn Ḥazm

As we have seen, in modern linguistic philosophy "literalism" refers to the belief that statements have meaning distinct from both the intended meaning of the one making the statement, and the meaning understood by the hearer. It is a statement's meaning which requires no "mind-reading" abilities to be acquired and understood[1] but instead is dictated by a linguistic system. In this sense, much of the language theory of the classical Uṣūlīs was "literalist", in that the notion of *waḍʿ* as a language system forced a meaning on an utterance which the statement then "owned". Yunis Ali has usefully described what he calls the *salafī* theory of meaning (deduced through the scattered musings on linguistic philosophy from Ibn Taymiyya and Ibn Qayyim al-Jawziyya). This is closer to the contextualism of the modern philosophical debate,[2] and is anti-literalist. Meaning is produced by use in context, not by an abstract linguistic system. The *salafī* theory remained marginal in the study of *uṣūl al-fiqh*, until the modern period.[3] For most Uṣūlīs, though, the literal meaning was the default meaning because, unlike its rivals, it was not subject to (variable) context. For this reason, it had an ontological status which outlived its rejection as the most plausible interpretation of a particular utterance: unlike meanings which move beyond the literal, the literal meaning was not eliminated by the eventual preference for another meaning. In the main, it remained a prima facie justified, even if incorrect, interpretation. Even when rejected, it held a different status to the other (non-literal) discarded meanings.

There is, however, another use of the terms "literalism" and "literalist", particularly popular in religious and literary studies and also in some other branches of the contemporary humanities. Under this definition, the literal meaning is not merely the fundamental starting point for all textual understanding; its ontological priority is such that, even in the face of indisputable evidence of the literal meaning's incoherence or irrationality, these literalists refuse to abandon the "literal meaning". Literalism, in such a disciplinary context, is inevitably caricatured as a form of anti-rationalism (or irrationalism), and for some "literalist" is not a simple description of an exegetical view, it is a judgement on its credibility. In this context, the trend most commonly referred to as "literalist" within the secondary literature on medieval Islamic thought is, of course, the Ẓāhiriyya. The Ẓāhirī *uṣūlī* theory of literal

1 Borg, *Minimal Semantics*, p. 108 (and elsewhere).

2 Yunis Ali, *Medieval Islamic Pragmatics*, pp. 87–140; Borg, "Minimalism vs Contextualism".

3 See below, pp. 181–4.

meaning, the subject matter of this chapter, is known from two main source types: the attribution of opinions in early non-Ẓāhirī works, and the prolific output of the Andalusian scholar Ibn Ḥazm (d. 456/1064).

Early Zahirism

Whilst the early history of the Ẓāhirī school is yet to be comprehensively addressed,[4] the standard account traces its formation to one Dāwūd b. ʿAlī al-Iṣbahānī (d. 270/884), based in Baghdad and probably linked to al-Shāfiʿī (and possibly Muʿtazilī) circles. Vishanoff provides a detailed exposition of the intellectual context out of which Dāwūd's thought apparently emerged.[5] One has al-Naẓẓām's (d. c. 221/836) refusal to recognise any rational coherence to the laws God has revealed. It represents a tendency within Muʿtazilism which is surprising, given the dominant ideas of the more influential Basran Muʿtazilī school. Within al-Naẓẓām's thought, as much as we can reconstruct it in the absence of his works on legal theory, this stance freed the legal meaning of the revelatory texts (which, for al-Naẓẓām, meant primarily the Qur'ān) from any need to conform to reason, and made possible a sort of literalist hermeneutic. Following this line of reasoning to its natural conclusion, Jaʿfar b. Mubashshir (d. 234/848) and Jaʿfar b. Ḥarb (d. 236/850) are both associated with a tendency within the Baghdadi Muʿtazilī school which rejected the innovations of analogical reasoning (*qiyās*) found in the emerging juristic mainstream. The possibility of a thoroughly literalist hermeneutic was, then, established by these thinkers. Al-Shāfiʿī's framework, though not his hermeneutic position, was also influential on Dāwūd's exegetical theory. Within that framework, al-Shāfiʿī had developed a notion of the *ẓāhir* meaning of the text, which can deviate from the author's intended meaning in ways determined by the formal features of the Arabic language (the *lisān al-ʿArab*).[6] Dāwūd may have accepted al-Shāfiʿī's notion of *al-ẓāhir*, but he did not accept that any assumption of the presumed intended meaning of the author, based on some vague notion of accepted Arabic conventions of communication, formed sufficient grounds for a departure from the *ẓāhir*.[7] Hence, the *ẓāhir/bāṭin* dichotomy, one of al-Shāfiʿī's mechanisms for solving hermeneutic problems, was intentionally unavailable to Dāwūd.[8] Instead, Dāwūd conceived of there being single meanings for individual linguistic phenomena, thereby creating

4 See Melchert, *The Formation*, pp. 178–86; Vishanoff, *The Formation*, pp. 78–88; Osman, "Ẓāhirī *Madhhab*", pp. 10–93.

5 Vishanoff, *The Formation*, pp. 68–78.

6 See above, pp. 99–112.

7 Osman ("Ẓāhirī *Madhhab*", pp. 163–95) attempts to relate the early Ẓāhirī notion of *ẓāhir* with that found in al-Shāfiʿī's *al-Risāla*. This is illuminating, but only convincing if we deny Dāwūd himself any distinctive notion of the *ẓāhir* meaning of the text. He may have adopted elements of al-Shāfiʿī's definition, but, as discussed earlier, this was still at a rudimentary stage. It is quite likely that Dāwūd, like many of his contemporary legal theorists, considered the *ẓāhir* as nothing more than an apparent, first blush meaning informed by "normal" Arabic usage.

8 Vishanoff speculates that Dāwūd first encountered Shāfiʿī's Iraqi teaching, which he found congenial to

discrete legal rulings. Such a view inevitably led to a rejection of *qiyās* in legal terms,[9] but also a rejection of analogical meaning derivation in language.[10] His concerns appear primarily epistemological, viewing all human-derived rules and laws as unavoidably uncertain, and hence a hermeneutic had to be devised which could produce certainty. Finally, he appears to have had supreme confidence in the ability of texts to provide us with the law, and the concurrent redundancy of reason as a source of moral or legal knowledge.

After his death, his young son Muḥammad b. Dāwūd (d. 297/910) developed his father's individual views into a more coherent hermeneutic theory, which resulted in Ẓāhirī works of *uṣūl al-fiqh* including his *al-Wuṣūl ilā maʿrifat al-uṣūl*, lost as a volume but surviving in citations by al-Qāḍī al-Nuʿmān (d. 363/974).[11] The surviving portions, unfortunately, do not give us a precise notion of what Muḥammad b. Dāwūd or his father meant by *ẓāhir*. There are hints that whilst his father had a non-technical notion of textual meaning,[12] Muḥammad opted for a more technical notion that the *ẓāhir* is, on occasion, the preserve of the specialist. However, the sources generally conflate the opinions of the "companions of Dāwūd" (*aṣḥāb Dāwūd*), and we do not have a clear idea of what the *ẓāhir* meant to the early Ẓāhiriyya, and hence how it might relate to the notion of literal meaning developed here.[13]

A commitment to the *ẓāhir*, however vague a concept that was, did not necessarily bring unity to the nascent "school". The early texts attribute opinions to some of the "*ahl al-ẓāhir*" or a group from the "*aṣḥāb Ḍāwūd*", implicitly indicating the remaining Ẓāhirīs were with the *jumhūr*. These relate to both issues of legal methodology (*uṣūl*) and specific *fiqh* rulings. A thorough analysis of these attributed disagreements may provide a more nuanced picture of the early Ẓāhirī notion of what the *ẓāhir* of the revelatory corpus might be and when, if ever, it can be discarded.

For example, there is dispute amongst the Ẓāhiriyya, we hear, over the compensation to be paid by the to-be pilgrim (*muḥrim*) who hunts and kills a beast belonging to another (hunting is one of the things forbidden to one who has declared his intention to complete the pilgrimage). Most of the *aṣḥāb Dāwūd* say the *muḥrim*

---

his hermeneutics; but later, when he discovered al-Shāfiʿī's Egyptian thought, he rejected the overall al-Shāfiʿī hermeneutic system. That we can distinguish two distinct theories, serially produced, in al-Shāfiʿī's thought is, of course, debated (Vishanoff, *The Formation*, p. 82, n. 110).

9 See the classic, but still useful, study of Goldziher, *The Ẓāhirīs*, pp. 27–40, and, more recently, Sabra, "Ibn Ḥazm's Literalism (I)", p. 19 ff.

10 See Niftawayh's linguistic occasionalism, which has been linked with his attributed view that Arabs speak Arabic naturally, that it is not a learned process, but one decreed by God, and this was also how meaning was attached to words (see Loucel, "L'Origine du langue", p. 199). For the influential later Ẓāhirī linguistic thinker Ibn Maḍāʾ and his refutation of linguistic analogy, see Wolfe, "Ibn Maḍāʾ al-Qurtubī".

11 See Stewart, "Muḥammad b. Dāwūd".

12 Zarkashī, *al-Baḥr*, v. 6, p. 263: "It is reported from Dāwūd and the followers of *al-ẓāhir* that anyone who gives a *fatwā* on a matter with a ruling by which he wishes to draw closer to God, then he is *muṣīb* whether he is a *mujtahid* or not." *Muṣīb* here does not just mean correct; rather, I think, "of equal standing whether he is correct or incorrect". Dāwūd is, then, credited with the view that the opinion of a specialist *mujtahid* is not necessarily more valid than that of a non-specialist since the *ẓāhir* is available to all equally.

13 Whilst I find Osman's attempt (see above, n. 7) intriguing, I am not sure that the *ʿāmm: ẓāhir* relationship is one of identity, or even close proximity.

should both compensate the owner and carry out the penance for the transgression of the regulations of *iḥrām*. "Some" of the *aṣḥāb Ḍāwūd*, though, say he should only compensate the owner. Unfortunately, we do not (to my knowledge) have the names of specific Ẓāhirīs who held these views. However, the division of opinion reflects, I suspect, divergent views not merely of what the relevant revelatory evidence indicates but, more fundamentally, of the notion of the *ẓāhir* to which the Ẓāhiriyya are famously committed. For the first group (whose opinion concurs with most of the other Sunni jurists), the *muḥrim* has hunted, and therefore owes a penance to God, and he has also destroyed the property of another, and therefore owes the owner compensation. For the second group, the fact that the beast was owned by someone means that it is livestock (or at least "appears" as livestock). One can only hunt (*ṣayd*) wild ("unowned") beasts; and so what the *muḥrim* was doing was not hunting but simply destroying the property of another. For the first group, perhaps, a common notion of hunting is the *ẓāhir*, in which the ownership or otherwise of the prey is irrelevant. For the second, a more technical definition is the *ẓāhir*: namely, that to hunt is to kill wild animals, and "hunting livestock" is an oxymoron.[14] In a linked issue, we have a division between Ẓāhirīs concerning the penance for killing small birds (*ʿaṣāfīr*) whilst *muḥrim*. The penance regulations are derived from the verse "O those who believe! Do not kill [hunted] prey (*al-ṣayd*) when you are *ḥurum* [that is, when *muḥrim*]. To those of you who kill *al-ṣayd* intentionally, a compensation [is due] equivalent to the [price?] of [owned] livestock he might have killed" (Q5/al-Māʾida.95).[15] Dāwūd's *madhhab* is attributed the view the killing of small birds leads to a compensation obligation;[16] this was the view of most Sunni jurists also. Some Ẓāhirīs, however, say there is no compensation here, since there is no equivalent price for small birds as "livestock" (*al-naʿam*), and therefore there is no need for compensation. Clearly the dispute is around whether small birds can be considered *al-naʿam*: that is, whether or not the term can possibly apply to small birds. Technically, perhaps the answer is in the affirmative (they can, plausibly, be owned and sold); in common parlance, however, one would never call *ʿaṣāfīr* a type of *al-naʿam*,[17] and it is on that that the renegade Ẓāhirīs make their case.[18]

14 Nawawī, *al-Majmūʿ*, v. 7, p. 330. The difference here is akin to Recanati's p- and m-literal meaning distinction.

15 The syntax of the verse is quite convoluted, and leaves much room for differing interpretations; see Ṭabarī, *Jāmiʿ al-Bayān*, v. 7, pp. 54–74.

16 *huwa ṣaḥīḥ fī madhhab Ḍāwūd*; Nawawī, *al-Majmūʿ*, v. 7, p. 440.

17 In the absence of internal Ẓāhirī discussions here, we can only guess at the reasoning. It is possible that the dispute here is over the *ẓāhir* of what the *muḥrim* is doing (that is, the *ẓāhir* is he is hunting, whether the prey is owned by another or is so small as to be valueless), making the appeal of the first group to an apparent understanding of the *muḥrim's* actions rather than the technical definition of the renegades. Given the Ẓāhirī suspicion of employing intentions in legal argumentation, it seems unlikely that they are arguing over whether the intention to hunt breaks the rules of *iḥrām*, though this is also possible. On God's inscrutable intentions, see Sabra, "Ibn Ḥazm's Literalism (I)", pp. 17–19.

18 Of course, it is possible that some of the views ascribed to the Ẓāhiriyya in *fiqh* books are straw men, invented for polemic purposes; but even if some of them are accurate descriptions of differences amongst the Ẓāhiriyya, they do reveal different methodologies for identifying the *ẓāhir*. See Goldziher, *The Ẓāhirīs*, pp. 103–22.

From the extant evidence, it appears that the Ẓāhirīs, particularly Dāwūd and Ibn Dāwūd, were interested primarily in restricting uncertainty in legal reasoning, and that led them to what they perceived as the safe haven of the *ẓāhir*. Whatever possible non-*ẓāhir* interpretations there may be, we can at least be certain of the *ẓāhir* meaning. However, there is insufficient evidence that they had formulated a coherent theory of communication with which to challenge the emerging legal theory of mainstream Sunni Islam, and without that the "literalist" edifice of the Ẓāhirīs was gradually chipped away with exceptions and exemptions, and redefinitions of the *ẓāhir* such that additional elements were included. In the East at least, the Ẓāhirī impetus gradually dissolved into the mainstream, compounded, historically speaking, by the lack of a jurist of sufficient stature to succeed Muḥammad b. Dāwūd.

Ibn Ḥazm's Literalism

Our rather limited knowledge of Zahirism in the East is not replicated in the case of the western school of Zahirism, which certainly emerged later and probably outlived eastern Zahirism. The most impressive extant exposition of the western Ẓāhirī method is that found in the works of Ibn Ḥazm, in particular his mature work of legal theory *al-Iḥkām fī uṣūl al-aḥkām.*[19] Ibn Ḥazm's opinions in *furūʿ* frequently diverged from those of Dāwūd and his son, and some of these differences between the Ẓāhirīs can be traced to divergent conceptions of the *ẓāhir* and how it might be known. All this indicates that, perhaps unlike many other schools of classical jurisprudence, Ẓāhirī legal positions in *furūʿ* were closely connected with their positions in *uṣūl al-fiqh*, rather than *furūʿ* emerging from legal practice and being justified *ex post facto* by *uṣūl al-fiqh*.

The close relationship between Ẓāhirī legal theory and substantive law is demonstrated by the manner in which Ibn Ḥazm fearlessly embraces legal positions which would have seemed quite bizarre to his Mālikī contemporaries. His dedication to the task of working out his juristic methodology in his description of specific legal prescription contrasts with the relatively tangential relationship between *uṣūl* and *furūʿ* in other Muslim legal traditions. Ibn Ḥazm, probably rightly, recognised the disjuncture between *uṣūl* and *furūʿ* as being due to the underdevelopment of the former and slavish *taqlīd* in the latter.

In order to locate Ibn Ḥazm's ideas on literal meaning and the primacy he accords literal interpretation in the exposition of the law, a broader understanding of his views on the origins, development and communicative function of language more generally

19 Summaries of Ibn Ḥazm's legal thought are available in Goldziher, *The Ẓāhirīs* (though dated, this work is still of some use); Linant de Bellefonds, "Ibn Hazm et le Zahirisme juridique"; Turki, *Polémiques entre Ibn Hazm et Bagi*; Sabra, "Ibn Ḥazm's Literalism (I)"; Osman, "Ẓāhirī *Madhhab*", pp. 93–100 and pp. 226–93 (where he argues that textualism, rather than literalism, is the most appropriate description of Ibn Ḥazm's hermeneutics); see also Jackson, "Literalism, Empiricism, and Induction", pp. 1474–5. A "test case" of Ẓāhirī legal method is carried out by Adang, "Homosexuality". The work most pertinent to our discussion here is the excellent Arnaldez, *Grammaire et Théologie chez Ibn Ḥazm*.

is necessary. Ibn Ḥazm's conception of language is an interesting mixture of the profane and the sacred. Language is merely a tool for communication, and there is nothing which privileges one language over another:

> Some say that Arabic is the best language (*afḍal al-lughāt*) because the speech of God uses it. ʿAlī [Ibn Ḥazm] says: This is meaningless because God – may he be glorified and praised – has already told us that he only sends Prophets [to speak] with the language of [the Prophet's] people. He, the Most High, says, "There is no community who have not had amongst them a warner" (Q35/Fāṭir.24). And the Most High also says, "Indeed, it [i.e. revelation] is in the texts of the ancients" (Q42/al-Shuʿarāʾ.196). God's word and revelation have, then, been revealed in every language … Languages are all equal in this respect.[20]

Ibn Ḥazm's view seems to be, then, that the medium does not affect the message. God makes no preference for any particular language, revealing his message to Abraham in Syriac, to Moses in Hebrew and in Arabic to Ismāʿīl. Neither should we attempt to assert the superiority of one language over another. Particular languages may seem dominant at particular points in history, but this is purely due to historical circumstances. As empires fade and peoples mix, languages lose their pre-eminence and their purity. "The power of the state, the enthusiasm and dedication of its people, are the things which set the boundaries of the language of a community, its sciences, and its traditions."[21] To base one's view that one language is superior to another on the simple fact of its being the language of the dominant group is to ignore the rational proofs (*burhān*) which demonstrate the equality of languages in this regard. "The sword [i.e. power] is sometimes against us, and sometimes for us, but the *burhān* is with us for ever."[22]

That language is an ordinary tool the success of which is subject to the vagaries of history is clear. However, the institution of language has sacrality at its core as Ibn Ḥazm also argues, contrary to the views of some of his contemporaries, that language was not invented by human beings but instead is one of God's creations.[23] The reasons why this is so, Ibn Ḥazm argues, are in part revelatory, the key verse being "He taught Adam all the names" (Q2/al-Baqara.31). Equally powerful, though, are "necessary proofs" (*burhān ḍarūrī*). For example, we know that for a people to invent something as complex as language, they would need a high level of understanding (*adhhān*), intellect (*ʿuqūl*) and skills in the sciences (*ʿulūm*). They would need to know the definitions and limits of all worldly things, being able to select what was common

20 Ibn Ḥazm, *al-Iḥkām*, v. 1, p. 35.

21 Ibn Ḥazm, *al-Iḥkām*, v. 1, p. 34.

22 Ibn Ḥazm, *al-Iḥkām*, v. 1, p. 26. This is a rather pithy and rhetorical way of expressing that the dominance of the Arabic language is not an indicator of its superiority. Rational proofs transcend language and on this occasion indicate the equality of all languages. The quote also indicates that, for Ibn Ḥazm, truths discovered through reason are primarily extra-linguistic and do not require language (either generally, or specific languages) to have logical effect.

23 See Arnaldez, *Grammaire et Théologie chez Ibn Ḥazm*, pp. 37–47, for a general outline of Ibn Ḥazm's ideas on the origin of language.

between things, and distinguish what differentiates one thing from another. Such knowledge comes about in human beings only through a process of learning and interaction with parents and guardians over a number of years. If there is no language, then this process cannot occur. Hence language is itself a prerequisite for the invention of language. The conclusion is, then, that just as there must have been an original creator to avoid an infinite regress, so language must have been invented by God.

This proof is one of the proofs for the creation of human beings, the existence of a creator, and the existence of prophets and their message. Without language being first invented, God could not communicate with his people through his Prophet, and since God says that this is his purpose in the revelatory texts, language must have been invented by him for this purpose (and he installed in human beings the ability to understand and use language). That is, God's understanding of his own will precedes the invention of language and is, therefore, extra-linguistic; in order to communicate his will, God invents language (though he is, of course, not required to do so). Ibn Ḥazm thinks it possible that God taught Adam all the languages of humankind, though it is more obvious (*al-aẓhar ʿindanā wa'l-aqrab*) that he taught him one language, which in time became many. God must have been the instigator of this diversity, because:

> I know of no reason which might call a people who already have a language which they speak and in which they are mutually comprehensible to invent another language. It is much work for no reason.[24]

However:

> Whilst we do not know which language God originally gave to Adam, we are certain that it was the most perfect of all languages (*atamm al-lughāt*), the clearest of expression (*abyanuhā ʿibāratan*), the least ambiguous (*aqalluhā ishkālan*) and the most concise (*ashadduhā ikhtiṣāran*).[25]

Since God says that he taught Adam all (*kullahā*) the names, we can also conclude that Adam's language was the most comprehensive in terms of the names given to things (it named "everything in the world, both essences and accidents"). However, since we do not know (that is, God has not provided us with a definitive statement concerning) whether it was Hebrew, Greek, Syriac, Arabic or some other tongue, there is no question of a return to this language.[26] What we must instead do is use the languages we have in the manner God intended us to when he created them. It is clear that what God taught Adam was, for Ibn Ḥazm, a particular language,[27] but

24 Ibn Ḥazm, *al-Iḥkām*, v. 1, p. 34.

25 Ibn Ḥazm, *al-Iḥkām*, v. 1, p. 33.

26 Ibn Ḥazm (*al-Iḥkām*, v. 1, p. 33) accepts that Arabic is a derived language, and there is no element of linguistic chauvinism in his theory. "Syriac is the root of both Arabic and Hebrew at the same time." Syriac was Abraham's language, Arabic was spoken by Ismāʾīl and Isaac was a Hebrew speaker. Languages, then, mirror the division of God's dispensation between the Jews and the Arabs.

27 Similarly, the inhabitants of paradise also speak a language (or languages), though Ibn Ḥazm is uncertain what this language might be; see Ibn Ḥazm, *al-Iḥkām*, v. 1, p. 36.

implicit in this is that he planted within Adam the ability to speak languages. The faculty of language is closely connected with Ibn Ḥazm's conception of reason (*ʿaql*). Reason, like language, enables its owner to discern between things (particularly truth and falsehood), to debate with others and to demonstrate the error of another's positions.[28] In both cases, the ability is viewed of as created by God in human beings for a purpose. God is not subject to either *lugha* or *ʿaql*; he is the source of them both and therefore the defining criterion for their correct employment.

Hence, for Ibn Ḥazm, the unremarkable nature of particular languages (that is, they are mere tools and are interchangeable) contrasts with the sacred nature of language's origins in the encounter between Adam and God, and God's willed creation of linguistic diversity in the world. If all languages are God's creations, and he is ambivalent about which to use (he chooses a language to suit his audience), then each language must have a correct manner of operation. This enables the language user (God included) to convey meaning. "Language's only intention is to engender comprehension, not ambiguity" (*al-murād fī'l-lugha innamā huwa al-ifhām lā al-ishkāl*).[29] In order to understand God's intended meaning, one must be able to recognise this correct mode of operation. Language, for Ibn Ḥazm, has very specific usage rules by which it is essential that all speakers (including expert ones) abide. God institutes rules when he invents a language, and follows them when he reveals his will in it. In order to understand what is being said, one must be familiar with these rules:

> For every named thing, be it accident or body, there is a name which is particular to it and by which it is distinguished from other things so that mutual understanding (*al-tafāhum*) might occur and so that the hearer who is being addressed might understand the intended meaning of the speaker (*murād al-mutakallim*) who is addressing him. If this were not the case, then understanding could never occur, and God addressing us at all would be pointless. But God says, "We only send a messenger in the tongue of his people so that he might make [things] clear to them" (Q14/Ibrāhīm.4). If there was no specific name attached to each meaning, then elucidation (*bayān*) would never be sound. This is because confusion of meaning is itself ambiguity. Therefore the original state of affairs must be how we have described it [i.e. it must have originally been the case that there was a one-name/one-meaning relationship], by the necessities of reason and by the text of the Qurʾān.[30]

That language was originally in a pristine state, where speech unambiguously conveyed meaning, underpins Ibn Ḥazm's position on language generally. Most Muslim jurists do, indeed, recognise a pristine state for language, and it is in the knowledge of this that literal meaning is to be found. Where his approach is, perhaps, distinctive is in his insistence on God's creation of language, and therefore the identity of intended and literal meaning in that language. By doing so, he establishes

28 Ibn Ḥazm, *al-Iḥkām*, v. 1, pp. 15–29.
29 Ibn Ḥazm, *al-Iḥkām*, v. 1, p. 276.
30 Ibn Ḥazm, *al-Iḥkām*, v. 1, p. 276.

God's unambiguous control of literal meanings (be it *ab initio*, or by subsequent decree), and avoids the possible confusion of literal meanings which would arise from human (and hence frail) designation of meaning to words. To develop this perspective, he lists around one hundred technical terms which require precise definition, prefacing his list with the comment that "most of those who have discussed meaning have made errors on this topic, intertwining meanings and using words inappropriately".[31] Ibn Ḥazm states that, with God's help, he will "define each word according to its 'true meaning' (*ʿalā ḥaqīqatihā*)".[32] The list includes technical terms of theology and jurisprudence (such as *ilhām* – inspiration, *nubuwwa* – prophecy, *dalīl* – indicator, and *īmān* – faith), as well as certain grammatical particles (*wāw al-ʿaṭf, wāw al-qasam, fa-, thumma*). The purpose is to establish correct usage of these words, and rectify incorrect usage amongst other intellectuals. Ibn Ḥazm uses many of these terms in his subsequent analysis of the meaning of particular grammatical constructions in the texts of revelation.

Having laid out his theory concerning the origins of language, Ibn Ḥazm's hermeneutics are described in chapters on discrete topics including the meanings of the forms of a command (*amr*), general reference (*ʿumūm*), plurality (*jamʿ*), exception (*istithnāʾ*), pronouns (*ḍamīr*), allusion (*ishāra*), diverted meaning and simile (*al-majāz wa'l-tashbīh*)[33] and implicated meaning (*dalīl al-khiṭāb*).[34] However, his hermeneutics underpin his conclusions in nearly all areas of *uṣūl al-fiqh*. Other topics inevitably touched by his literalism include the interpretation of statements based on *ijmāʿ*, the resolution of supposed conflict between the Prophet's words and actions and, most importantly, Ibn Ḥazm's refutation of *qiyās*. A full exposition of Ibn Ḥazm's legal literalism would entail an examination of his entire legal theory, though my primary interest here is in the definitions of literal meaning and literal interpretation utilised in his approach.[35]

As we have already seen, some jurists considered revelatory statements such as "Give alms!" to be inherently ambiguous, in the sense that from this statement alone one cannot derive an understanding of what might constitute obedience to the command. First, the grammatical form of the imperative is legally ambiguous (it can mean permission, recommendation or obligation). Second, the details of almsgiving – how much? when? to whom? – are not here specified, and other texts are required. Third, the imperative here is of general reference, and we know that unparticularised

31 Ibn Ḥazm, *al-Iḥkām*, v. 1, p. 37. "Using words inappropriately" is my translation of *awqaʿa al-asmāʾ ʿalā ghayr musammayātihā* ("placing names on things other than those named by [the names]"). The phrase emphasises the fact that words have particular meanings on which they have been "placed" (the more common verb is, of course, *waḍaʿa*).

32 Ibn Ḥazm, *al-Iḥkām*, v. 1, p. 37. Ibn Ḥazm's use of the term *ḥaqīqa* is discussed below.

33 These topics are found in Ibn Ḥazm, *al-Iḥkām*, v. 1, pp. 275–457, laid out in chapters (*abwāb*) 12–18 inclusive.

34 The last of these constitutes chapter 37: Ibn Ḥazm, *al-Iḥkām*, v. 2, pp. 335–84.

35 For a detailed account see Arnaldez, *Grammaire et Théologie chez Ibn Ḥazm*, pp. 50–73 (*ṣīghat al-amr*, also analysed in Arnaldez, "'Ahbar' et 'Awamir'"), pp. 134–45 (*ʿumūm* and *khuṣūṣ*), pp. 145–58 (*al-istithnāʾ*) and pp. 165–93 (*qiyās*).

statements are not always intended to be understood in this manner ("Give *zakāt*" implies *all* must give *zakāt*, but we know that God does not intend this to be the case, as certain classes of people are exempt). Ibn Ḥazm's position is that statements such as these, in themselves, have quite definite meanings, and he therefore allies himself with one party in the dispute over the operation of literal meaning. Commands, in and of themselves, mean that the commanded action is obligatory, and this statement establishes an obligation (as opposed to permission or recommendation). In order to establish the details of almsgiving, one needs to discover the true meaning of the term, but in the absence of other indicators, the command "give alms" means to give any amount, immediately. Finally, a general form (such as "You (plural)! Give alms!") has general reference. All who are addressed by the statement (in this case, "all believers") are included in the obligation. This is what the sentence "Give alms!" means in and of itself. In other words, the literal meaning determined by grammatical rules alone (or, as Recanati might express it, the m-literal meaning) is that alms should be given in any amount to somebody immediately. This would constitute what Searle calls the "obedience conditions" of the statement.[36] It does not, however, mean that this is the only literal meaning of the statement. The meaning of the order "Give alms!" may be modified by subsequent evidence from elsewhere in revelation as all elements of revelation are "a single verse, or a single statement. No one may take one part of a revealed text and miss out another."[37] From elsewhere in the revelatory text, one knows that the term "alms" refers to a certain percentage of one's wealth and that the order to give alms requires that they be given to a certain person, at a certain point in time, through a particular agency.[38] The literal meaning (*ẓāhir*) of the statement in isolation is one thing, but there is also another *ẓāhir* meaning of the statement following the rules laid down by God for the meaning of words through revelation. These meanings (which include the amount of alms to be given under the definition of "alms", to whom and when it must be given under the definition of "give" and so on) are not non-literal (*majāz*), according to Ibn Ḥazm. Since God institutes the rules whereby words gain meaning, the point in time that he instituted such rules is irrelevant to their literal/non-literal status. Whilst the fit is not exact, the *ẓāhir* meaning which comes about through God's revelatory intervention is akin to Recanati's p-literal meaning.[39]

These inherent meanings are located in the original action of God "placing" a name upon a meaning. God has "arranged languages solely so that clear thinking

36 See above, p. 18.

37 Ibn Ḥazm, *al-Iḥkām*, v. 1, p. 372.

38 The exact details need not concern us here, though they are given in Ibn Ḥazm, *al-Muḥallā*, v. 5, pp. 296–333.

39 See above, p. 19. The fit is not perfect because Recanati sees the p-literal meaning as something determined by ordinary language use and not, of course, by God's intervention (as it is for Ibn Ḥazm). They are similar, however, in that both recognise in determining the literal meaning a broader context than the purely grammatical meaning of a sentence (Recanati's t- and m-literal meanings). For Ibn Ḥazm, the broader context is God's use of language in the revelation; for Recanati's p-literal meaning, it is language use by the community.

might occur through them. Languages are nothing other than vocables constructed upon meanings which elucidate the things named by them … If speech did not elucidate its meanings, then what would those forsaken ones understand from their Lord, or from their Prophet? Indeed, how would they understand each other?"[40] When a revelatory statement is understood according to this simple name-meaning-thing relationship, it is "interpreted according to the *ẓāhir*" (*al-ḥaml ʿalā al-ẓāhir*) or "taken according to the *ẓāhir*" (*al-akhdh bi'l-ẓāhir*). It is the default position of all interpretive activity. Unfortunately, Ibn Ḥazm does not precisely describe what constitutes the *ẓāhir*, and strangely neither it nor the linked term *ḥaqīqa* is amongst the terms popular amongst his rivals which Ibn Ḥazm considers in need of clear definition. It is possible that he considers himself to concur with general conceptions of *ḥaqīqa* and *ẓāhir* (though it will be argued below that this is not the case). What is clear is that the *ẓāhir*, to which we must all subscribe (*ittabāʿ*), is not located in the understanding of each listener (even an expert in the *lugha*) but is located in the "original" meaning of words.[41]

To expand on the form of the command, its meaning was one area in which the jurists had differed. Some had argued that a command is, by definition, of uncertain reference, since there are many instances of orders meaning different things (in particular, obligation, recommendation or permission). This, they argue, makes commands homonyms. They could equally refer to any of these things, just as *rijl* in Arabic can mean "foot" or "swarm of locusts". Ibn Ḥazm's response to this position, which he says is held by some Shāfiʿīs, Mālikīs and Ḥanafīs, is twofold. First, homonyms can only have developed after the original institution of language (that is, after the *aṣl*). If they had existed from the beginning, then the whole purpose of language (to enable mutual understanding between parties) would be frustrated. Also, God himself has said that he sent Prophets to nations to declare his message using that nation's language "in order that he might make [things] clear to them". This would be impossible if homonymy was a design feature of language.[42] Second, the analogy (*tashbīh*) between homonyms and the command is misjudged. The uncertainty caused by homonymy can be eradicated by context (if I say I am putting my sock on my *rijl*, I am not referring to my swarm of locusts). This is not so with a command. If we accept that the command could mean obligation, recommendation or permission equally, then there is no "natural foundation" (*bunyat al-ṭabīʿa*) upon which to base our interpretation. Context can help us in the case of homonyms, but in the case of a command we hope to discover the speaker's intentions and the immediate context of the utterance cannot enable us to do this. In such circumstances, we are unable to follow God's law, and the Sharīʿa is lost. Whilst it is true that a command

40 Ibn Ḥazm, *al-Iḥkām*, v. 1, p. 308.

41 In his discussion of *qiyās*, Ibn Ḥazm does indicate that there are two sources for the correct understanding of the designated meanings of names: the speech of the Arabs and the decree of God in revelation (Ibn Ḥazm, *al-Iḥkām*, v. 2, pp. 409–10). This should not tempt us to think that he advocates something other than divinely instituted meaning, since the language of the Arabs was, ultimately, designed by God.

42 I discuss homonymy below, p. 166.

need not always lead to an obligation, Ibn Ḥazm argues, this is not a case of discovering which of a number of possible meanings is intended. Instead, it is a case of a word meaning one thing in language, and this word being transferred (*naql*) to another meaning from its original meaning (*ʿan maʿhūdihā wa-ʿan mawḍūʿihā*).[43] This is what happened when God gave particular new meanings to the terms *ṣalāt*, *ṣawm* and *kufr*. This transference can only happen with an indicator showing that it has happened. At this point, homonymy has occurred in the sense that one word has two possible meanings. The original meaning of these words remains valid (analogous to Recanati's m-literal), whilst the new meaning comes into existence (analogous to Recanati's p-literal). Ibn Ḥazm appears to be arguing here that whilst homonymy cannot exist in the original language, it can develop over time through an institution by God (or by the language users, whose actions are ultimately controlled by God). However, a command (and, conversely, a prohibition) is not something that can be a homonym. Either it means obligation in the *lugha*, or it means something other than obligation (such as recommendation). What it cannot mean is both equally at the same time. Those who argue that the command means nothing until an indicator establishes it as an obligation, a recommendation or a permission should, for the sake of consistency, take the same attitude towards abrogation. Every verse or *ḥadīth* could be abrogated, so therefore one cannot follow it until there is an indication that it is not abrogated. The interpreter would then be paralysed by doubt over the meaning of God's revelation. The command must mean something in and of itself. To suspend judgement (*waqf*) is to ruin religion.[44] Ibn Ḥazm briefly considers the possibility that the command means something other than obligation, but rejects this for two reasons. First, he argues that this would be invalid because it contravenes a doctrine established by *ijmāʿ*. Whilst all cannot agree whether the command means obligation or to suspend judgement, all can agree that the command does not, in itself, mean mere permission or recommendation. Furthermore, it is illogical. It would mean that when someone says "Do this!" he means at the same time "but don't do it, if you wish". Similarly, a prohibition would mean "Don't do this, but do it if you wish". If a command means a mere recommendation in itself, then the prohibition and the command are effectively the same thing. Ibn Ḥazm's view, then, is that we need a default position from which to interpret the meaning of commands, and this is proven to be, by reason, revelation and the rules of language, that they give rise to obligations.[45] This, he says, is the *ẓāhir* meaning of the command.[46]

43 Such transference was recognised by many legal theorists, and Ibn Ḥazm is, of course, not alone in advocating it (see Yunis Ali, *Medieval Islamic Pragmatics*, p. 107). It proves useful in this context because it preserves the primacy of the literal meaning of a form. The transference is not, for Ibn Ḥazm, between *ḥaqīqa* and *majāz* but between one sort of literal meaning and another, and in this way his legal literalism is preserved; see below, p. 168.

44 Ibn Ḥazm even indicates that those who suspend judgement on the meaning of a command are unbelievers; see *al-Iḥkām*, v. 1, p. 282.

45 He also argues that the *ẓāhir* of a command is that it should be done immediately (*ʿalā al-fawr*) and once; see Ibn Ḥazm, *al-Iḥkām*, v. 1, pp. 313–20.

46 Whilst the term *ẓāhir* is used in the title of this section of the *al-Iḥkām* and appears sporadically throughout

A very similar set of arguments are used to demonstrate that all utterances are to be taken as general in reference rather than particular. Here the parties of the dispute are three:

1. Those who argue that any statement of general meaning is of particular reference.
2. Those who argue that any statement is uncertain as to its reference (it could be general, it could be specific) and therefore judgement should be suspended (*waqf*) until evidence is found which indicates reference.
3. Those who argue that all statements of general meaning should be taken as of general reference; that is, the statement refers to "everything which falls under the meaning of a word, as decreed by language".

Ḥanafīs, Mālikīs and Shāfiʿīs are to be found in both the first two parties. The third party is further divided into two sections:

3a. Those who argue that whilst one must accept that general meaning implies general reference, one can only do this after searching for evidence that the statement is of particular reference.

3b. Those who argue that language requires that a specific name be of general reference, and hence all words must be interpreted as such. If evidence appears, then we must take note of it, but there is no need to search for evidence before declaring that the statement is of general reference.

Shāfiʿīs and Ḥanafīs are found amongst the first party (3a); the second party (3b) consists of all Ẓāhirīs (*aṣḥāb al-ẓāhir*), and some Mālikīs, Shāfiʿīs and Ḥanafīs.[47] Here the dispersal of opinion is greater than that concerning the meaning of a command, and hence Ibn Ḥazm's argumentation is less clearly segmented as he criticises the different positions and advocates position 3b. I give here only a flavour of his argumentation.

The basis of the first position – that all statements are of particular reference until there is evidence that they are of general reference – is that every statement is actually addressed to a particular set of persons, and hence, like all direct speech, is essentially particular. Ibn Ḥazm argues that this particularity of audience does not mean particularity of reference. It is in the nature of a statement that it is made to somebody, and his conception of general reference does not mean that every statement made by God applies to all existent things (*kull mawjūd fī'l-ʿālam*).[48] Rather, by general reference (*ʿumūm*) Ibn Ḥazm means that all things "necessitated by the statement" (*kull mā yaqtaḍīhi al-khiṭāb*) are included in the reference of a general statement. A statement necessitates a certain reference group, and the statement applies to them all until there is evidence otherwise. For example, God's statement "Do not marry

the section, it does not dominate Ibn Ḥazm's discussion of the meaning of a command. Apart from *ẓāhir*, other phrases are used which are clearly equivalent to *ẓāhir*: the "placed" (*mawḍūʿ*) meaning; the meaning which is "decreed" (*maʿhūd*) for a word; *ḥaqīqa*; the meaning which language necessitates (*yaqtaḍī* or *yaltazim*); *lughawī* (linguistic) meaning; or simply the meaning which is "on" (*ʿalā*) a word.

47 Ibn Ḥazm, *al-Iḥkām*, v. 1, p. 361.

48 Ibn Ḥazm, *al-Iḥkām*, v. 1, p. 373.

women whom your fathers have married, except that which has already occurred" (Q17/al-Isrāʾ.33) is a prohibition on marrying any woman whom one's father may have married in the past; those marriages which have already taken place before the prohibition was announced are, however, not rendered invalid by this prohibition since they are excepted from the general prohibition. Now, if the first position is correct, this prohibition is of particular reference until there is evidence that it is of general reference. Their position must be that the prohibition here cited refers only to a proportion of the women that one's father has married. The presumption is that some of the women one's father has married are permitted to one until there is evidence that this prohibition is general. The ludicrousness of this position is plain for all to see, Ibn Ḥazm believes. The verse clearly prohibits marriage to any woman who has been married to one's father. That is, it is clearly of general reference. It is, however, subject to an exception in that those marriages which have already occurred in contravention of this new rule are not now deemed invalid. The nature of the grammar of the verse is such that those addressed by the prohibition are those who have not yet contracted a marriage with a former wife of their fathers. It is general to all those not covered by the exception. This is what Ibn Ḥazm means when he argues that a certain set of addressees are grammatically necessitated by a verse or a *ḥadīth*, and his advocacy of general reference is that it applies to all those necessitated addressees until there is evidence that it applies to some and not others.[49] This position contravenes both the demands of language and the demands of religion (*abṭala ḥukm al-lugha wa-ḥukm al-diyāna*).[50]

The second position – that a general statement is of uncertain reference and therefore one must suspend judgement until there is evidence that it is particularised or general (position 2 above) – is considered particularly dangerous in that it will cause the suspension of religious duties. Saying that statements are of uncertain reference until evidence determines this reference is, ultimately, saying they mean nothing in and of themselves. Furthermore, how are we to determine what the reference is of this other evidence, since, surely, one must also suspend judgement here? The argument is basically similar to that used against those who suspend judgement on the meaning of a command.

Amongst those who support the idea that a statement of general meaning has general reference are those who argue that general reference is only proven after a search for particularising evidence has been made and been unsuccessful. Ibn Ḥazm's rebuttal of this position is that it confuses two very important elements of the scholar's task. He must first read a text and understand its meaning; then he must perform a process of understanding this text (called *tafahhum* or *tafaqquh*):

> They say, "You adhere to your first hearing of a verse or a *ḥadīth*, before you have thought about it."

49 The reasoning is set out in Ibn Ḥazm, *al-Iḥkām*, v. 1, pp. 363–4.

50 Ibn Ḥazm, *al-Iḥkām*, v. 1, p. 364.

> The answer is that we adhere to the general reference, this is true. However, we first hear a text before we have thought about it (*qabla tafaqquhinā*).[51] Until we think about it, we are not *muftīs*, nor are we judges, nor are we preachers. When we do think about it, at that point we interpret every word according to its *ẓāhir* and take it to be of general reference. We give rulings, make *fatwās* and teach religion on this basis. However, when there is evidence that it is not to be understood according to its *ẓāhir* and to be of general reference, then we turn to that. If a judge or a *muftī* has not heard of any particularisation of what has come to him in the form of a general reference, then they are duty bound to give a ruling or a *fatwā* on the basis of what they have heard. They are sinners unless [information concerning] particularisation reaches them.[52]

The position that demands that a search be made to find a possible particularising statement is confusing the understanding of a scholar on his encounter with the text (that is, what the scholar deems to be the meaning necessitated by the text through a combination of its content and the rules of language) and the task of the scholar as a *muftī* or a judge. The crucial difference between Ibn Ḥazm's position (3b) and that of his opponents here (3a) is that for the latter party the lack of evidence that there is a particularising report is itself evidence that the general reference should be taken as the intended meaning. For Ibn Ḥazm (and the other Ẓāhirīs), it is the grammatical form used in the expression *ṣīghat al-ʿumūm* which is evidence that the general reference should be taken as the intended meaning. Ibn Ḥazm views his opponents (and the second group can be included in this assessment) as saying that statements that use the grammatical form of general reference do not, in themselves, indicate a general meaning. Rather, his opponents argue that things external to the text indicate general meaning. In short, they do not view such statements as capable of having meaning in themselves. Any meaning the reader can deduce is the product of external factors. This, he surmises, is tantamount to a destruction of one of the bases upon which language was instituted by God: that each element of language (word, sentence, grammatical construction) has a meaning assigned (*waḍaʿa*) by the institutor which is placed (*mawḍūʿ*) upon it irrespective of the external influence.

The recurrent position emerging here is of interpretation dictated by linguistic rules which were established by the one who instituted and regulates the language (that is, God). Apart from the meaning of command and the meaning of statements of general reference, Ibn Ḥazm gives brief comments on topics such as the minimum number that makes a plural (*aqall al-jamʿ*), the operation of exceptive clauses (*al-istithnāʾ*) and indexical reference (*al-kināya bi'l-ḍamīr* and *al-ishāra*). Each is explored and definitive rules are laid down as to the meaning which language

51 This might be thought to be a reference to the *ẓāhir* being the "immediately understood" meaning of a verse, but this is not the case. Ibn Ḥazm is here discussing the exegetical presumptions of a potential *muftī* before investigating a text. He is not talking about the understanding of the average speaker of the language. Furthermore, the "first hearing of a verse" (*awwal samāʿika*) phrase, which might tempt us to postulate the *ẓāhir* as referring to the understanding of an average speaker, is not his own, but his opponents'. This is the only reference to the phrase I have found in the *al-Iḥkām*.

52 Ibn Ḥazm, *al-Iḥkām*, v. 1, p. 364.

demands of these phenomena (*al-ḥukm fī'l-lugha*). On the first, Ibn Ḥazm argues that the "form of the plural" (*ṣīghat al-jimāʿ*) designates three or more (there being a dual form in Arabic). This is a clear rule of language (*ḥukm ẓāhir al-lugha*)[53] and that it means three or more is fixed in language (*maʿhūd al-lugha fī'l-ḥaqīqa*).[54]

On exception, Ibn Ḥazm lists the words which designate that an exception has taken place (the principal one being the particle *illā*). Exception can take place in a number of ways, none of which are considered grammatically illegitimate by Ibn Ḥazm (though there is dispute over them amongst both the Ẓāhirīs and "our brothers, the supporters of analogy"[55]). There is dispute over whether an exception can legitimately occur when the item being excepted is of a different genus to the general category. For example, Satan (Iblīs) was a *jinn*, and not an angel, and yet God says, "We said to the angels, 'Prostrate before Adam!' They all prostrated except Iblīs" (Q17/al-Kahf.50). The word "except" (*illā*) in this verse demonstrates that the thing excepted from a general category need not be of the same genus (*jins*) as the items in that category. It seems that there was some doubt over whether this was a legitimate Arabic grammatical form, with some arguing that exception can only function when the thing excepted is of the same genus as the general category, as in the common example "I killed the people except Zayd". Here the excepted item (Zayd) is of the same genus as the general category (people). Ibn Ḥazm's argument is that because such a construction is found in revelation, it must be legitimate. Similarly, there is debate concerning whether the excepted thing can make up the majority of the general category, with the Ẓāhirīs and most Shāfiʿīs saying it may, and the Mālikīs saying it may not. Once again the argument revolves around the fact that God has used such a construction in revelation. The verse "Stand to pray for the night, except a small part of it, a half of it, or a little less [than half]" (Q73/al-Muzammil.2–3) is evidence that more than half of the general category ("night") can be excepted without doing violence to the language. For Ibn Ḥazm, the grammarians and jurists who attempt to find a more complex rule for the use of the exception construction (for example, that the excepted be of the same genus as the general category, or that the excepted be no more than half) are guilty of attempting to explain the linguistic construction by reference to the reasons (*ʿilal*) which underlie its use. Just as the search for reasons is prohibited in law (as we see below in his refutation of *qiyās*), so it is prohibited in language.[56] The exception is nothing more than "the exclusion

53 Ibn Ḥazm, *al-Iḥkām*, v. 1, p. 426.

54 Ibn Ḥazm, *al-Iḥkām*, v. 1, p. 428.

55 Ibn Ḥazm, *al-Iḥkām*, v. 1, p. 429.

56 This is one of the major elements of the grammatical position of the Ẓāhirī Ibn Maḍāʾ, on whom see (in addition to the references in n. 10 above) Suleiman, *Arabic Grammatical Tradition*, pp. 145–77, and Versteegh, *Arabic Linguistic Tradition*, pp. 140–52. The rejection of what might be called a "thick description" of grammatical operation is also evident in Ibn Ḥazm's ridiculing of *ishtiqāq* – the understanding of meaning through examining etymology. In particular, Abū Jaʿfar al-Naḥḥās (presumably Ibn al-Naḥḥās (d. 338/950)) and al-Zajjājī (d. 310/922) are dismissed. The latter considered the word "lover" (*ʿāshiq*) to be derived from the haricot plant (*ʿashqa*) which is green, yellow and then flammable, just like love itself. To this Ibn Ḥazm says you could equally call a lover a "bean man" (*bāqil*), for beans

of the thing excepted from the thing described in the sentence from which it is being excepted".[57] Any attempt to develop a more complex set of conditions for the correct employment of the exception on the basis of reasons behind its use is pointless and misguided.

On the issues of indexical designation, Ibn Ḥazm also lays down specific rules: an undetermined pronoun in the accusative case (*-hu*, *-hā*, *-humā* and so on) refers to the nearest named object in the prose (*al-ḍamīr rājiʿ ilā aqrab madhkūr*). Hence "Zayd, ʿUmar and Khālid came to me, and I killed him" means that I killed Khālid. This is what is laid down in language. The demonstrative pronouns "this" and "these" (*hādhā, hādhihi, hāʾulāʾi* and so on) refer to the "near, present item" (*rājiʿa ilā ḥāḍir qarīb*). The demonstrative pronouns "that" and "those" (*dhālika, tilka, ulāʾik* and so on) mean the more distant (*abyad*) item in the sentence, as do pronouns "he", "she" and "they" (*al-ishārāt … ʿāʾida ilā abyad madhkūr*). This is what language demands (*hādhā ḥukmuhā fī al-lugha*). One is, of course, reminded here of the shift from t-literal to m-literal meaning in Recanati's scheme. Ibn Ḥazm is here outlining the rules whereby the ambiguity inherent in t-literal meaning (that is, before indexical processing) can be eliminated without there being an accusation of arbitrariness. Arbitrariness is avoided by simply designating a rule, instituted by God when he created the *lugha*. It is not impossible for utterances to deviate from these rules. However, when they do, this is a case of "transferring the word from its place in language" (*naql al-lafẓ min mawḍūʿihi fīʾl-lugha*) to somewhere else.[58]

From this account, it is clear that the power of language rules (be they grammatical rules, or the rules concerning word-meaning-thing relationships) to dictate meaning dominates Ibn Ḥazm's hermeneutic theory. Rules give clear meaning to texts which enable jurists to describe and (as judges) to execute the law. Ibn Ḥazm conceives of these rules as much broader than most Arabic grammarians. For Ibn Ḥazm, the rules are instituted by God through revelation. This can happen either in the original language given to Adam and the subsequent (divinely ordained) linguistic diversity of humankind, or it can happen through the revelation to Muḥammad and the adjustments made to the meanings of words and grammatical constructions by God in the Qurʾān. The literal meaning of revelatory texts is, then, a grammatically controlled entity (resembling the m-literal meaning), though the conception of grammar is more fluid than that found in the Arabic grammatical tradition. The meanings of words and grammatical constructions can change to mean something other than the *aṣl*, though these new meanings are as *ẓāhir* as the original *aṣl* meanings.

---

are green, then yellow and then flammable (*al-Iḥkām*, v. 1, pp. 431–2). Ibn Ḥazm is also critical of the use of *ishtiqāq* as a means of determining causes (*ʿilal*) in the theory of *qiyās* (*al-Iḥkām*, v. 2, pp. 597–600): "There is nothing in *ishtiqāq* by which *ʿilal* might be proven for rulings" (p. 597). *Ishtiqāq* is only useful for determining that a particular name is given because of a property (for example, *muṣallī* means "one who prays" and comes from *ṣalāt*).

57 Ibn Ḥazm, *al-Iḥkām*, v. 1, pp. 437–8. *Al-istithnāʾ innamā huwa ikhrāj al-shayʾ al-mustanthā mimmā akhbara bihi al-mukhbir ʿan al-jumla al-mustathnā minhu.*

58 Ibn Ḥazm, *al-Iḥkām*, v. 1, p. 445.

Ibn Ḥazm expressed amazement that some jurists seem unwilling to embrace the opportunity which God has given us to enact the Sharīʿa:

> God has provided us clear texts (*al-nuṣūṣ al-ẓāhira*) which do not require any interpretation (*taʾwīl*) … He who can use swords in battle, does not need reeds of straw.[59]

Interestingly, the reason why God has provided us with this tool of language is that he would not ask "us to do the impossible" (*taklīf mā lā yuṭāq*). This slogan, popularised in Muʿtazilī circles, gained wider currency in the fourth/tenth century. It is, perhaps, particularly surprising that Ibn Ḥazm bases his hermeneutics on such a principle.[60] It is one example of how he found certain elements of mainstream *uṣūl al-fiqh* to be structurally required in the discipline, though doctrinally inconvenient.[61] On this occasion he solves the incongruity of the position by reference to a passage in revelation (Q2/al-Baqara.286), the *ẓāhir* interpretation of which is taken to support the proposition that God does not ask anyone to obey rules he does not know.[62]

All this is not to say that these rules are inviolable. The meaning of a text, in the context of God's law more generally, can be transferred (*naql*) from the *ẓāhir* to other possible meanings. In accepting this, Ibn Ḥazm is conceding that the *ẓāhir* is not always the intended meaning of a text, in a way which is not dissimilar to that proposed by other contemporary legal theorists. This is another example of the manner in which the Ẓāhirīs were compelled to accept some of the more forceful arguments in the mainstream tradition of *uṣūl al-fiqh* and the commitment to the *ẓāhir* was compromised. We find some evidence of this compromise in the (admittedly patchy) reports of the views of earlier Ẓāhirīs.[63]

Ibn Ḥazm's admission of transference from "linguistically determined" (that is, *ẓāhir*) meaning to other meanings is prevalent throughout the discussions referenced above, and he dedicates a chapter to the operation of transference during his discussion of generality and particularisation. He accepts that particularisation occurs and, unlike early Ẓāhirī opinion, does not consider the contrast between a general text (*ʿāmm*) and a particular one (*khāṣṣ*) to be a case of conflict.[64] Instead, he considers

59 Ibn Ḥazm, *al-Iḥkām*, v. 1, p. 406.

60 It is the basis for Zysow's corrective to Goldziher's portrayal of Ibn Ḥazm as standing apart from the "mainstream of legal hermeneutics". His "hermeneutics corresponds in important areas with that of the Iraqi Ḥanafīs" because of them sharing this doctrine (Zysow, "Economy of Certainty", p. 153). Whilst Ibn Ḥazm was certainly influenced by the mainstream, what sets him apart is that the principle is justified purely on revelatory and not rational grounds.

61 The doctrine concerning the "transference" of *ẓāhir* meaning is another example; see below, n. 67.

62 Ibn Ḥazm, *al-Iḥkām*, v. 1, p. 83. The reference here concerns *taʾkhīr al-bayān*; there is a similar discussion concerning *ʿumūm* and *khuṣūṣ* (v. 1, p. 401), where he states that we are not able to understand the specifics of *zakāt* and prayer from God's simple order to make prayers or give *zakāt*. Since God has told us he does not expect this of us, the explanation of what is involved in *zakāt* and prayer in other elements of revelation enables us to understand exactly what is demanded of us by the commands.

63 See above, pp. 147–50.

64 Shīrāzī attributes the view that the *ʿāmm* and the *khāṣṣ* are "in conflict" (*yataʿāraḍ*) to the *Ahl al-ẓāhir* (Shīrāzī, *al-Lumʿa*, #88, p. 79, and #90, p. 73). See Ibn Ḥazm, *al-Iḥkām*, v. 1, p. 407, for example, where he chides fellow Ẓāhirīs for postulating *taʿāruḍ* between Quranic verses concerning marriage; and v. 2, p. 525, where he argues for a lack of *taʿāruḍ* in the context of his refutation of *qiyās*.

it a case of elucidation of one part of revelation by another (*bayān*), again following the agreed position of other legal theorists. Transference, he tells us, can happen in four ways:

1. A word can be transferred from part of its meaning, but not all of it. The example given is Q3/Āl ʿImrān.173: "The people (*al-nās*) said to them, 'The people (*al-nās*) are gathering against you.'" The first reference to people cannot mean all people (that is, cannot be of general reference), as some are excluded by being the recipients of the message and the announcers. Similarly, the second reference to people cannot mean all people otherwise they would not be able to rise up against some of them. It is, Ibn Ḥazm states, a case of exception (*istithnāʾ*) but, crucially, the exception is signalled by the text itself.
2. A word can be transferred entirely from one meaning to another. Examples of this include *ṣalāt* meaning the ritual prayer whilst previously meaning prayer more generally (*duʿā*). Also included is the transference of a command from immediate obligatory obedience to potentially delayed recommendation or permission.[65]
3. An utterance might be transferred in order to enable the addressee to understand it. Included in this category is the famous verse Q12/Yūsuf.82 "Ask the village", where there is an ellipsis of "the people of".[66]
4. The meaning of an utterance might be made entirely irrelevant through the process of abrogation.[67]

These four means of transference are justified on two accounts. Firstly, reason

65 Ibn Ḥazm adds, "In speech and poetry this is called *majāz* and *istiʿāra*" (*al-Iḥkām*, v. 1, p. 396). Ibn Ḥazm does not reject *majāz* as a casuistic trick. He does consider it to exist, and indeed it is found on occasion in the Qurʾān. Those who argue that *majāz* is "untruth" (*kadhb*) have failed to recognise that since God is the criterion by which correct language use is measured, the correct use of *majāz* cannot, by definition, be a lie. *Majāz* (when a sentence is made to refer to something other than its linguistically required meaning) can be prompted by a revelatory indicator or by rational necessity (Ibn Ḥazm, *al-Iḥkām*, v. 1, pp. 449–55). Here the terminology of the *ḥaqīqa*/*majāz* dichotomy predominates, though this appears to be little more than a scholarly affectation. I do not recognise any difference between the use of *ḥaqīqa* here and *ẓāhir* elsewhere in the *al-Iḥkām*; both revolve around using a word in conformity with its instituted "placement" (*mawḍūʿ*).

66 It is of interest here that Ibn Ḥazm does not opt for what might be considered the purely literalist interpretation of Q12/Yūsuf.82. The more literalist position on such verses was upheld by the Mālikī (Ibn) Khuwayz Mandād, who argued that stones had *ʿaql* on the basis of Q2/al-Baqara.74, where stones are said to "sink through fear of God". Only those with *ʿaql* can fear God, he argues. See Ibn Ḥazm, *al-Iḥkām*, v. 1, p. 452.

67 These are described by Ibn Ḥazm, *al-Iḥkām*, v. 1, pp. 396–7. The inclusion of abrogation (*naskh*) here is of interest since this is not, in truth, a case of the meaning of an utterance being transferred to another meaning. An abrogated verse still means its *ẓāhir*. The command to reason with the unbelievers does not change meaning to a command to kill them by the process of abrogation. Its relevance for the law may be excluded, but its meaning remains the same. Whilst not directly impacting upon our discussion here, it is clear that by the "transference" (*naql*, *intiqāl*) of meaning, Ibn Ḥazm is not solely concerned with the meaning of the utterance in itself, but also with changes in relevance of texts for the elucidation of the law. Or, alternatively, he is not so interested in changes in meaning as in changes in reference (on which see below, and also above, p. 14), in that an abrogated verse does not change meaning, but it no longer refers to a ruling which forms part of the law of God.

dictates that on some occasions one transfer meaning (such as the example concerning the term *nās* above). Secondly, the law (Sharīʿa) dictates that a transfer takes place. The meaning of a text can be modified through Qurʾān, *sunna* or *ijmāʿ*. Whilst Ibn Ḥazm's conception of *ijmāʿ* is not of immediate concern to us here, it is clear that he gives it a probative value (*ḥujjiyya*) whereby it can modify textual meaning. The word "father" (*ab*), for example, has been adjusted in the verse "Do not marry those women whom your fathers (*ābāʾukum*) have married" (Q4/al-Nisāʾ.22) to mean not just fathers, but also grandfathers on both one's mother's and one's father's sides. By the *sunna* it is extended to mean the fathers of one's wet-nurses (the Prophet said, "Whatever is prohibited by relationship is also prohibited by suckling"). It is extended even further, to include the paternal uncle (*ʿamm*), by the verse which Jacob said to his sons, "We worship your God, and the god of your fathers (*ilāha ābāʾika*), Abraham, Ismāʿīl and Isaac". Ismāʿīl was, of course, not a direct ascendant of Jacob but a paternal uncle; therefore the word *ābāʾ* must include paternal uncles. In this way, the original meaning of *ābāʾ* (*mawḍūʿuhu*) is transferred to a broader meaning.

A question emerges here as to whether there is a change in meaning on these occasions, or whether there is a change in reference. That is, is it the case that *ab* now means "fathers, grandfathers (both maternal and paternal) and paternal uncles"? Or is it the case that God's intended meaning (that is, the reference of the verse) by using the word "father" is this extended list of relatives? In short, has the meaning of *ab* changed by God using it to refer to more than the biological father? Ibn Ḥazm, on this occasion, seems to believe that the *ẓāhir* of the word *ab* has not changed (it still means "biological father"), but the reference has undergone an alteration. This is shown by the fact that he vehemently denies that one can now use *ab* in other circumstances (such as the regulations regarding inheritance) to mean more than the biological father (in inheritance, the father of the deceased). On occasion God can use words to mean something other than their *ẓāhir*, but when he does he always provides an indicator that this is occurring.[68]

There is room for some confusion here, as Ibn Ḥazm also discusses the meaning of words such as *ṣalāt* and *zakāt*, and here he seems to indicate that there has been a change in meaning:

> Every word which God transfers from its designated meaning to another, then, if he is demanding our obedience by word and deed to this [word], such as *ṣalāt*, or *zakāt* or *ḥajj* or *ṣiyām* or *ribā* or other things, then there is no diverted meaning (*majāz*) here. Rather this is a sound appellation (*tasmiya ṣaḥīḥa*) and a literal name (*ism ḥaqīqī*) [the meaning of which] it is necessary to fix because God himself has placed it there.[69]

Words such as *ṣalāt*, after God has decreed a new meaning for them, now become homonyms in that they have an original meaning and a new meaning.[70] This seems

68 See above, and below pp. 176–94 in reference to *ḥaqīqa sharʿiyya*.

69 Ibn Ḥazm, *al-Iḥkām*, v. 1, p. 447.

70 Ibn Ḥazm explicitly accepts such a conclusion when dealing with general reference. Homonyms such as *ṣalāt* (meaning both prayer generally and ritual prayer), when found in revelation, are taken to have general

a different process from the change in reference of the word *ab* in Q4/al-Nisāʾ.22. Whilst Ibn Ḥazm does not always make this explicit, it seems there are two subcategories to transference type 3 mentioned above:

> Situation (a): There are cases where a new meaning is given to a word (for example, *ṣalāt*). It is not clear whether these new meanings supplant the old meanings or exist alongside them as homonyms, though given Ibn Ḥazm's general suspicion of homonymy as a barrier to understanding, one suspects the former. If this is the case, we have here the case of a new *ẓāhir* meaning replacing an old one. This is not a theoretical problem, since, as Ibn Ḥazm says, God is the one who institutes language, and he is therefore the criterion of correct usage. All uses of this word from this point on are taken to refer to the new *ẓāhir* meaning.
> Situation (b): There are cases where the meaning of a word does not change, but it is used to refer to something other than its *ẓāhir* meaning (for example, *ab*). When God uses words in a manner at variance with their *ẓāhir* meanings, he provides an indicator that he is doing so. That is, there is a change in reference, but not in meaning.[71]

Situation (a) is not, in truth, a case of using a word in a manner at variance with the established meaning. It is a case of changing or supplementing the established meaning of a word. Situation (b) is quite different. The difference here is between Recanati's p-literal and p-non-literal meanings. The famous example of the "thief verse" and its particularisation is, for Ibn Ḥazm, another case of a word being used at variance with its established meaning. This, as he is at pains to point out, is not a case of a change of meaning of the term "theft". A thief (*sāriq*) is one who steals; the reference in the verse concerning the amputation for theft (Q5/al-Māʾida.38) is to a certain type of thief (one who steals a certain amount or more). Since all of revelation is treated "as if it were a single verse",[72] then the modification of a word's meaning in different parts of revelation is of the same category as the modification of a word's meaning by another element of the verse. The modification of the word "people" in the above example (Q3/Āl ʿImrān.173; there is an exception inherent in the phrase "the people gather against you", and hence "people" cannot be of general reference) is of the same category as the modification of the word "thief" in Q5/al-Māʾida.38 by other parts of revelation and *ijmāʿ*. Of course, Q3/Āl ʿImrān.173 has the advantage

reference and all the meanings are taken to be applicable. In this, he says, he differs from other Ẓāhirīs who take one meaning to be predominant over another (*al-Iḥkām*, v. 1, pp. 389–90). One meaning can predominate, but only with an indicator demonstrating it to be the predominant meaning. This is further demonstrated when a verse referring to *ṣalāt* is taken to mean prayers other than the ritual prayer (*al-Iḥkām*, v. 2, p. 363).

71 In his refutation of *qiyās*, Ibn Ḥazm chides those who argue that a word's meaning has been changed in a certain verse but refuse to accept that if this is so, then all instances of that word's use would have to be reassessed. What is actually happening, he says, is that the reference of the utterance is being transferred through interaction with another certain source of understanding (a text or a consensus) on a particular occasion and this cannot be applied generally without additional indication.

72 "*huwa kulluhu ka-āya wāḥida aw kalima wāḥida*" (Ibn Ḥazm, *al-Iḥkām*, v. 1, p. 372). See also v. 1, p. 380: "The *ḥadīth* and the Qurʾān are together like one utterance (*lafẓa wāḥida*)." The assertion is also made in the refutation of *dalīl al-khiṭāb* (v. 2, p. 358), on which see below.

of the proximity of the modifier and therefore it may be easier to recognise, but difficulty of recognition is not a reason to reject modification (we need scholars precisely for this reason).

> Even if these texts are separated in terms of recitation, recitation is not law (*al-tilāwa ghayru al-ḥukm*). They are not separated in terms of the law at all. There is no difference between God saying "The thief, male and female, cut off their hands" alongside [the Prophet's] words "Do not cut for less than a quarter of a dinar, only more" and God saying "A thousand years less fifty"[73] (Q29/al-ʾAnkabūt.14).[74]

This category of words used at variance with their established meaning, amongst which is included the extremely common phenomenon of particularisation (*takhṣīṣ*), might be considered a threat to Ibn Ḥazm's dogged commitment to the *ẓāhir*. Ibn Ḥazm perceives no threat. He considers there to be "no departure from the *ẓāhir* in this".[75] One point here is that the *ẓāhir* meaning of one verse is being modified by the *ẓāhir* meaning of another verse, and there is a commitment to the *ẓāhir* on both accounts. However, he also recognises that there is a problem in that one *ẓāhir* has been rejected in preference to another. A more significant solution lies in his treatment of all of revelation as a single utterance (*āya wāḥida*, *lafẓa wāḥida*). Individual words are often used in a manner at variance with their established, *ẓāhir* meaning: they may be of general meaning but particular reference (like *sāriq*) or vice versa (like *ab*). However, the *ẓāhir* meaning of a statement (as opposed to individual names) is still the subject of Ibn Ḥazm's devotion. The *ẓāhir* meaning of the Q3/Āl ʿImrān.173 example – "The people (*al-nās*) said to them, 'The people (*al-nās*) are gathering against you'" – is that *al-nās* is not of general reference (it cannot include "them"). *Ẓāhir* meaning acts at the level of statements (that is, in the workings of grammatical rules such as exception) as well as words, and can be unaffected at the level of statements by the loss of *ẓāhir* meaning at the level of words. Grammatical phenomena apart from words (the forms of general reference or the imperative, grammatical constructions such as the exception or the conditional sentence) have *ẓāhir* meanings as well. Expanding this perspective to take in all of revelation (which, as we have stated, is like a single utterance), one can see that the *ẓāhir* meaning of revelation (when taken as a whole) is unaffected by the (possibly quite frequent) loss of *ẓāhir* meaning at the level of individual words (or, indeed, isolated statements). Ibn Ḥazm's resultant position is, then, that it is the *ẓāhir* meaning of revelation which should be the result of the jurist's exegetical efforts. In the absence of indicators, of course, the *ẓāhir* meaning is retained at the micro level, but *ẓāhir* meaning is regularly compromised through the interaction of words, *ḥadīths* and *āyas* with other words, *ḥadīths* and *āyas*. This is the process *bayān*.[76]

From this general hermeneutic perspective, it becomes clear that for Ibn Ḥazm all

73 Meaning, of course, 950 years and being a reference to the length of Noah's life.
74 Ibn Ḥazm, *al-Iḥkām*, v. 1, p. 372.
75 Ibn Ḥazm, *al-Iḥkām*, v. 1, p. 399.
76 See Arnaldez, *Grammaire et Théologie chez Ibn Ḥazm*, pp. 219–27, for a fuller exposition of *bayān*.

revelation must be of equal probative force (*ḥujjiyya*), since all revelation is a single statement of God's demand for his creation. Ibn Ḥazm's hermeneutics force him to accept a rather strict classification for *ḥadīth* authenticity. An account of this is beyond the intention of this chapter, which aims at elucidating his hermeneutic method. It is, however, worth noting here that Ibn Ḥazm's assertion (in which he is stricter than previous Ẓāhirīs)[77] that isolated traditions (*khabar al-wāḥid*) have probative force and can modify Quranic *ẓāhir* meaning is, undoubtedly, a result of his hermeneutic position. Admittedly, he is rigorous in his criticism of *isnāds*, but his overall schema in terms of the authenticity of *ḥadīth* texts is a binary opposition of sound and weak, rather than any graded estimation of probative force. In this, his position served as a model for the Shīʿī Akhbārīs.[78]

Ibn Ḥazm, then, does recognise occasions when the meaning of an utterance (either a word or a statement), or its reference, is other than that instituted for it in language. The conditions which allow such an interpretation of an utterance are strictly controlled. The presumption on interpreting a revelatory text is always that the linguistically determined meaning (*ẓāhir*) of the elements in the texts is God's intended meaning. Ibn Ḥazm's various lists of the modes of transferred meaning (together with the subdivisions each in a subsequent examination of each mode) can now be rephrased in terms of meaning and reference:

1. The linguistically determined meaning (*ẓāhir*) of an utterance can be changed to or supplemented by another equally linguistically determined meaning (*ṣalāt*, *zakāt* and so on). On these occasions the meaning of the utterance (word, phrase, statement and so on) has changed (or, possibly, been supplemented to create homonymy).
2. The linguistically determined meaning of an utterance is subjected to a qualification through its interaction with other texts ("thief" in Q5/al-Māʾida.38; "father" in Q4/al-Nisāʾ.22). On these occasions the meaning remains, but the reference is a qualified version of the linguistically determined meaning.
3. The linguistically determined meaning of an utterance is subjected to a qualification because this is rationally demanded ("ask [the people of] the village" in Q12/Yūsuf.82). On these occasions, also, the meaning remains, but the reference is a qualified version of the linguistically determined meaning.
4. The linguistically determined meaning of an utterance is subjected to a total substitution of reference ("In mercy, lower to them the wing of kindness" in Q17/al-Isrāʾ.24, where the *ẓāhir* of "wing" is entirely excluded). On these occasions, the meaning remains, but the reference is new.
5. The linguistically determined meaning of an utterance is rendered irrelevant because the utterance itself is rendered legally (though not ritually) inactive (these are occasions of abrogation).

This typology could, perhaps, be refined through further detailed examination of Ibn

77 Vishanoff, *The Formation*, pp. 100–2.

78 Gleave, *Scripturalist Islam*, pp. 252–62.

Ḥazm's exposition. A comprehensive understanding of his position, as laid out in the *Iḥkam*, is not aided by the fact that he uses the term *maʿnā* in the sense of both the linguistically determined meaning of an utterance and the reference of that utterance. The important point, though, is that his Zahirism does not mean that the interpreter is bound to take the linguistically determined meaning of an utterance as its intended reference on every occasion.

It comes as little surprise, considering Ibn Ḥazm's commitment to the *ẓāhir* (notwithstanding those occasions on which it can be overruled), that he has little patience with those jurists who hope to understand God's utterances as implying more than linguistically determined meaning. This is exemplified by his rejection of both implicated meaning and analogical reasoning (*qiyās*), the latter being described in secondary literature as one of the hallmarks of the Ẓāhirī school. In the section on *dalīl al-khiṭāb* ("the indication of the address"), Ibn Ḥazm considers whether implicated meaning (*mafhūm*) can be legitimately derived from the revelatory texts. The position of those who support implicated meaning is summarised by Ibn Ḥazm thus:

> One group says that when a text comes from God or His Prophet attached to (*muʿallaqan bi*, or "associated with") such and such a quality, or such and such a time, or such and such a number, then it is obligatory to rule on whatever diverges from that quality, time or number as differing from the ruling [found] in these texts. In such cases, the attachment of the rule is an indicator of whatever diverges from [those cases].[79]

This rather abstract description of their position is made more concrete by citing the standard examples used by Muslim legal theorists, divided into three categories:

1. Occasions when the thing implicated includes but goes beyond what is explicitly said; examples include the proposition that the Quranic verse "Do not say *uff* to one's parents" (Q17/al-Isrāʾ.23) implies that one should not hit or kill them.
2. Occasions when the thing implicated is the opposite of what is explicitly said. Examples of this include the Prophet's words "[*zakāt*] is on grazing livestock", which implies livestock that do not graze need not be subject to *zakāt*.[80]
3. Occasions when the thing implicated is unconnected (either in opposition or in agreement) with what is explicitly said. Examples include the Quranic verse "[God created] horses, mules and donkeys for you to ride and as an adornment" (Q16/al-Naḥl.8), which implies that one cannot use them for other purposes, such as food.

The finer distinctions between these categories, which are ascribed to various juristic schools, do not interest Ibn Ḥazm. They are all examples of attempting to

79 Ibn Ḥazm, *al-Iḥkām*, v. 2, p. 335.

80 Ibn Ḥazm says that cunning jurists (*akyās*) call the first category *qiyās* and the second category *dalīl al-khiṭāb* (*al-Iḥkām*, v. 2, p. 337). This does not impress him, as they are merely calling the same thing by two names.

retrieve from the text something other than its *ẓāhir* meaning, and hence are to be rejected. In the first example, hitting one's parents is presumed to be somehow "more" (more sinful, more violent, more distasteful) than saying *uff* to them. The implicated meaning is not logically impelled without this additional presumption (which has not been proven). In the second example, how does one know that the Prophet meant to exclude *zakāt* on non-grazing livestock?[81] In the third example, how does one know that God wishes to exclude other uses for these animals? In short, what is the justification for saying that the first example leads to the same as what is ruled for more than what is said, the second example leads to the opposite of what is ruled for the opposite of what is said, and the third example leads to the opposite of what is ruled for anything other than what is said? Ibn Ḥazm concludes that there is no justification for any of these, and hence such interpretations must be rejected. They have nothing to do with language, even though these jurists claim (incorrectly, in Ibn Ḥazm's opinion) that grammarians such as Mubarrad and Thaʿlab support them:

> Including this subject in [the study of] language is feeble adulteration and futile misrepresentation [of language], because one only need to refer to the experts in language in order to know the individual elements which are joined together to make words. They only tell us how the names of things are organised.[82]

Deciding whether a ruling, contained in a text, includes a ruling which is not contained in the text is "not in language's remit" (*laysa hādhā … fī quwwa ʿilm al-lugha*). You would only argue this if you were intent on mixing up the different disciplines. Language experts of every tongue (*ahl kull lugha lil-nās min ʿarab wa-ʿajam*) know that:

> One cannot understand the meaning "horse" from "stone" and the meaning "camel" from the word "dog". If someone says "I went in a boat today", one does not understand him as saying that he either did, or did not, ride a donkey also. If someone says "I ate bread", one cannot understand him as saying that he either did, or did not, eat meat with the bread.[83]

Any ruling needs an indicator in the text, and the spurious implicated meaning derived by these jurists will not count as an indicator (*dalīl*). One should, of course, not hit or kill one's parents, but this is demonstrated by another text. One need not pay *zakāt* on livestock, not because of the implied meaning of the Prophet's statement, but because God has said that unless he specifies it as such, a thing is not subject to *zakāt*.

What, then, is the point (*fāʾida*) of these explicit designations if they are not indicating something particular about the ruling associated with the designation? Ibn

81 "What is the difference between you who say that the mention of grazing indicates that non-grazing is [given a ruling] the opposite of grazing, and another group who say that the mention of grazing means that non-grazing [be given a ruling] which agrees with ruling for grazing?" (Ibn Ḥazm, *al-Iḥkām*, v. 2, p. 337).

82 Ibn Ḥazm, *al-Iḥkām*, v. 2, p. 339.

83 Ibn Ḥazm, *al-Iḥkām*, v. 2, p. 339.

Ḥazm argues that they are primarily for emphasis (*taʾkīd*). That is, God says generally that one should treat one's parents with respect, but he specifies the prohibition on saying *uff* to them in order to emphasise the need for this respect. God is also indicating that saying *uff* is particularly sinful as it is particularly impertinent. He is not, however, saying anything connected with actions unconnected with the uttering of *uff*. A similar point can be made of repetition. God repeats things in revelation for the sake of emphasis.[84] In short, texts mean only what they say:

> We do not prohibit something unless that text prohibits it. We do not declare anything permitted, unless [the text] declares it so. We do not, then, transfer [its meaning]. If we find it agreeing with a previous statement, then we declare permitted whatever that [previous statement] declared so ... This is the natural understanding of language for every language of the human race – be it Arab or non-Arab. No other position is permitted.[85]

The rejection of *qiyās*, one of the main designations of Zahirism, is linked to the refutation of *dalīl al-khiṭāb*, and Ibn Ḥazm is keen to point out that the nuances which surround whether implicated meaning is, in reality, analogical reasoning or not are ultimately pointless, since both are guilty of the same methodological error.[86] The Ẓāhirī rejection of *qiyās* has been described by others;[87] here only a brief examination of the role of literal meaning in this rejection is needed. For Ibn Ḥazm, the extraction of a cause (*ʿilla*) of a ruling from a text is described as not only a contravention of rational principles, but also a rejection of the requirements of language according to its "literal" meaning (*mukhālif li-mūjib al-ʿaql wa-li-muqtaḍā al-lugha ʿalā al-ḥaqīqa*).[88] An example of how language prevents the extraction of a cause is provided in his discussion of the prohibition of the consumption of swine-meat. The text usually cited is Q6/al-Anʿām.145, in which the Prophet is ordered to say that he has found no food prohibited other than carrion, blood and "the meat of swine, for it is unclean (*rijs*)". There is a debate over the meaning of *rijs* which need not concern us here. The supporters of *qiyās* argue that the text prohibits swine-meat, and through analogy based on the cause (it is unclean), the fat, gristle and other parts of a swine are also forbidden. Ibn Ḥazm argues that since, by the rules of language, the pronoun refers to the nearest mentioned thing, the "it" in "it is unclean" is not "the meat of swine", but the swine itself. Unclean things, as we know from revelation, are prohibited for consumption. Therefore all parts of swine are prohibited. This is not a case of analogy, but of the inclusion of one item (swine) under a general category (unclean things which are prohibited for consumption):

84 Ibn Ḥazm, *al-Iḥkām*, v. 2, p. 347 and pp. 370–3. God's frequent designation of emphasis is also argued in v. 1, p. 382 (and elsewhere) in order to reject the restriction of the "forms of general reference" (*ṣiyagh al-ʿumūm*) to emphatic phrases (such as "all of them").

85 Ibn Ḥazm, *al-Iḥkām*, v. 2, p. 358.

86 Ibn Ḥazm, *al-Iḥkām*, v. 2, pp. 375–7.

87 Goldziher, *The Ẓāhirīs*, pp. 34–9 (specifically on Dāwūd al-Ẓāhirī's rejection of *qiyās*), and Shehaby, "*ʿIlla* and *Qiyās*".

88 See, for example, Ibn Ḥazm, *al-Iḥkām*, v. 2, p. 393.

> Swine are unclean by the text of the Qurʾān. All of the swine is forbidden. Swine in the Arabic language – in which we are being addressed – is a name for the general category under which male and female, small and large are included. Hence, what they think – that fat is only prohibited by *qiyās* – is proven to be false.[89]

It is, then, the linguistic properties of revelation (notwithstanding the rational objection to *qiyās*) which prevent analogy from being a legitimate process:

> [When] we know that when the Prophet gave a text of the Qurʾān or spoke linking such and such a name with such and such a ruling, then we must only place that ruling on what is necessitated by that name. [We must] not move it from the place where the Prophet of God put it, nor extract from that rule anything which its name does not demand … To do this would be to add to religion, and this is *qiyās* … and all of this is forbidden by the texts.[90]

Another area of Ibn Ḥazm's refutation of *qiyās* which involves literal meaning concerns those occasions when God indicates a reason for a particular ruling. Can one, justifiably, transfer the ruling from such occasions to other occasions on which this mentioned reason is found? Ibn Ḥazm argues that one cannot. When God uses words that indicate the reason for a particular ruling, he is indicating the reason for that ruling alone. The supporters of *qiyās* have, unfortunately, confused cause (*ʿilla*) with reason (*sabab*):

> *ʿIlla* is the name given to any quality which necessitates such and such a situation by a necessary obligation … Fire is the *ʿilla* for burning … one does not happen without the other. *Sabab*, however, is the reason why a free entity does what he does, which he need not do if he does not wish … The *sabab* does not necessitate the thing for which it is the reason.[91]

God, being a free entity, can give a ruling for a reason on one occasion and is not, thereby, compelled to give the same ruling on subsequent occasions when the reason is present. The supporters of *qiyās* have fallen into this mistake partly through their failure to understand the function of terms like *liʾ-anna* ("because") in revelation. They consider them to indicate causes, when in fact it is a rule of language that when used by a free entity giving a ruling, they indicate reasons for an action and not causes of it.

Conclusion

In sum, then, Ibn Ḥazm's conception of the literal meaning of revelatory statements (be they Qurʾān or Sunna) is grounded in his conception of language as an instrument

89 Ibn Ḥazm, *al-Iḥkām*, v. 2, pp. 423–4.
90 Ibn Ḥazm, *al-Iḥkām*, v. 2, p. 533.
91 Ibn Ḥazm, *al-Iḥkām*, v. 2, p. 603.

instituted by God for the purposes of communication. The rules of language are, in one sense, arbitrary, in that excessive attempts to explain them by reference to meta-processes controlling the meanings of words and phrases are unjustified.[92] In another sense they are sacrosanct, in that once instituted, the rules can only be deviated from on specific occasions and for restricted reasons. This enables him to construct a conception of the *ẓāhir* which is intimately connected with the meaning compelled, or linguistically determined, by these rules. Here, then, literal meaning is not p-literal, that is, determined by the hearer's understanding.[93] Rather, literal meaning is decidedly m-literal – eliminated of indexical ambiguity and determined by a set of grammatical regulations. Where Ibn Ḥazm differs from the advocates of m-literal meaning found in the Mālikī and Ḥanafī traditions[94] is that the rules he considers as contributing to the literal meaning have a purely divine origin. He envisages a language system instituted by God, used in an unambiguous manner by him, and perfectly employed in the revelatory texts such that meaning flows between speaker and hearer in an unfettered manner.

The *ẓāhir* meaning of revelation, then, is not to be found in the immediate understanding of the listener, even if that person is an expert in the *lugha*. It is, instead, to be found through the application of linguistic rules to words or sets of words resulting in a single, unambiguous meaning. This model of language behaviour is rigorously applied to areas of *uṣūl al-fiqh* which had given rise to juristic dispute and ambiguity in the meaning of texts. Hence statements are taken to be of general reference; commands are taken to mean obligations and to demand immediate obedience. Deviations from the *ẓāhir* in terms of individual words and statements are not taken as deviations from the *ẓāhir* of revelation as a whole, since all of revelation is treated as a single statement. Attempts by other jurists to derive more than the *ẓāhir* from these texts (particularly *dalīl al-khiṭāb* and *qiyās*) are rebutted as mere fancy and, on occasion, "soothsaying" (*kihāna*). Ibn Ḥazm strives for certainty in legal exegesis, and this epistemic zeal inspires his commitment to the linguistically determined meaning of God's revelation.

That the *ẓāhir* is not obvious (*jalī*) is clearly Ibn Ḥazm's position, and it forms part of his justification for scholarly activity. If all was obvious from the texts, then "the scholar and the ignoramus would be equal in elucidating the obvious from [the text], and the scholar and the ignoramus would be equal in that the non-obvious [or "hidden" – *khafī*] would be hidden to both of them". The scholar's task is to "demonstrate proofs and clarify what is obscure to the ignoramus, so that he might understand and it become clear to him".[95] Not all people understand all of the words in the Qur'ān

92 This is clearest in Ibn Ḥazm's refutation of *ishtiqāq*; see above, n. 56. Ibn Maḍā', the Ẓāhirī grammarian, was of course famous for refuting the explanation of grammatical processes by recourse to linguistic causes (*ʿilal*), and in this sense his grammar reflects Ẓāhirī approaches to legal rulings (see above, n. 10).

93 See above, p. 155. This was also, interestingly, the position of Ibn Maḍā' (see Suleiman, *Arabic Grammatical Tradition*, p. 164).

94 Outlined in Chapter 2, pp. 26–61.

95 Ibn Ḥazm, *al-Iḥkām*, v. 2, pp. 437–8.

and Sunna, and "the rule for he who does not know is to ask him who does".[96] In this, Ibn Ḥazm was attempting to create the intellectual preconditions for a school (in the sense of *madhhab*). The project was not successful, and whilst a semi-institutional school did survive his death,[97] it failed to gain a permanent foothold and was eventually swamped by Mālikī dominance. Zahirism failed in both the East and the West (perhaps for different reasons);[98] in a sense, Ibn Ḥazm instituted flexibility, modifying the adherence to the *ẓāhir* from Dāwūd's original project, and perhaps, with this shift, its *raison d'être* as a separate school was terminally eroded.

96 Ibn Ḥazm, *al-Iḥkām*, v. 2, p. 494.
97 Adang, "The Spread of Zahirism".
98 The reasons for its decline are discussed in Melchert, *The Formation*, pp. 187–90; Vishanoff, *The Formation*, pp. 106–7.

7

Literal Meaning in Modern Muslim Legal Theory: Two Examples

A number of commentators have identified a shift towards (so-called) "literalism" in modern Islamic thought.[1] The term is often used loosely and without precision, and this modern trend is contrasted with the acceptance of diversity which characterised most "classical" Muslim theological and legal thinking.[2] It could well be that there is something particularly modern in the understandable need to root religious expression in a meaning viewed as "inherent" within revered texts. The tendency is undoubtedly linked to a dissatisfaction with the perceived relativism built into the system of inter-*madhhab* acceptance, and the guarded assertions of the classical jurists that they were fallible and their rulings were merely their best attempts. Its rise may have been spurred on by the spread of literacy in the Muslim world, the availability of texts (through print, and then through electronic means), the breakdown of traditional authority structures, the dislocation caused by economic and social modernisation and numerous other potential contributory factors. Postponing a decision, or deferring to God's final judgement, on the actual status of a legal ruling is not what a Muslim community, challenged by alternative epistemological structures, requires. Many thinkers could not resist the temptation to reject all human deliberations over the meaning of revelation as whim and fancy, and to foreground the text itself (its words, its statements, its record of divine utterances) as the place where true meaning can be found. The comforting certainty of the "literal meaning" has meant that determining what it might be becomes a matter of almost existential importance for many modern Muslim thinkers.[3] In this sense, strict

1 By which they mean not only the existence but also the primacy of literal meaning. See, for example, Ruthven, *Fundamentalism*, pp. 59–94; Moosa, "The Debts and the Burdens", pp. 123–6; Sardar, *Reading the Qur'an*, p. 27; see also Jackson, "Literalism, Empiricism, and Induction", pp. 1471–6, where literalism is undermined with a view to promoting a *maqāṣid* approach.

2 See, for example, Calder, "The Limits of Islamic Orthodoxy", p. 83; Abou El-Fadl, *Speaking in God's Name*, pp. 170–208 (see also his "The Ugly Modern", p. 51); Karsten, *Cosmopolitans and Heretics*, pp. 69–88.

3 Khaled Abou El Fadl talks of an "authoritarian hermeneutic" which "involves equating between the authorial intent and the reader's intent, and renders the textual intent and autonomy, at best, marginal" (*Speaking in God's Name*, p. 5). "By textual intent, I mean that the text has a will independent of the author or reader. This 'will' is embodied in the mechanics of language and symbolism used by the text" (*Speaking in God's Name*, p. 8, n. 9). Abou El Fadl's employment of the text's intent as an "interpretive fiction" nonetheless reveals a belief that properly identifying the meaning within (rather than imposed upon) the text offers the way out of the "fundamentalist" predicament. More challenging is Arkoun's notion that liberal reform actually requires us to abandon what we might have meant by a "textual source" in the first place (Arkoun, *Islam: To Reform or to Subvert?*). Viewing the texts as "sources" of divine knowledge has led modern reformers down a blind alley, trying to out-do the fundamentalists in textualism.

literalism has become one element in a more general movement of textual devotion, variously linked to the influence of Wahhabism and, more recently, radical Salafism.[4] Cognate movements towards textualism can be seen in the transformations experienced by other religious traditions in the modern period.[5]

This chapter is not intended to add to the debate around the origins, vibrancy and future of the textual bent in modern Islamic thought. Instead, I have a more modest aim: to illuminate the manner in which classical discussions of the meaning a text has irrespective of context or interpretation (that is, its "literal meaning") have played out in two modern Muslim intellectual contexts: the phenomenon referred to by the generic label Salafism, and Uṣūlī Twelver Shiʿism. In both cases we see both continuation and adaptation of classical *uṣūl* discussions as they express ideas about the possibility of literal meaning changing over time through an act of divine designation (*al-ḥaqīqa al-sharʿiyya*).[6]

Legal-Literal Meanings in Contemporary Salafism

By contemporary Salafism I mean the various circles of scholarship centred around, but not restricted to, the Islamic centres and universities of Saudi Arabia since the 1960s. One of the challenges to modern Salafī discourse is how to accommodate classical scholarship into a contemporary system of Islamic learning, when one of the central doctrines of this modern Salafism is a refusal to be beholden to anyone other than the earliest generations of Muslims (*al-salaf al-ṣāliḥ*). In a Saudi (Ḥanbalī) context, this can be expressed yet further in the effort to combine a great respect for classical Hanbalism with a commitment to the so-called "Salafī" method attributed to Ibn Taymiyya (d. 728/1328).[7] In the *madhhab* system, the study of *uṣūl al-fiqh* formed a fundamental element of a school's curriculum and distinctive pedagogic structure. Contemporary Salafī scholars, being distrustful of the utility of the *madhhab* system, have made theological polemic and *ḥadīth* study, rather than *uṣūl*,

4 See, for example, the popular work of Karen Armstrong, *The Battle for God*, especially pp. 173–81.

5 See Abou El Fadl, "The Ugly Modern", p. 49, where he coins the neologism "Salafabis".

6 The discussions of literal meaning in modern *uṣūl al-fiqh*, particularly given the rise of "*maqāṣid al-sharīʿa*" approaches to the "sources of the Sharīʿa", are, from a brief look at some of the major modern *uṣūl* textbooks, a continuation of the classical view described above, pp. 26–62. See, for example, the influential work of Zuhaylī, *Uṣūl al-fiqh al-Islāmī*, v. 1, pp. 292–3. This conclusion is, though, tentative, and a much broader survey of modern *uṣūl* writings would be necessary before any clear conclusions could be reached. See also Hallaq, *A History*, pp. 207–54; even an influential thinker engaging with *uṣūl* questions, such as Ḥasan Ḥanafī, makes changes, according to Hallaq, but they are "purely formal and barely alter the substance of traditional legal theory" (p. 213, n. 8). My impression concurs with Hallaq's conclusion: much modern *uṣūl* writing is a summary of the classical tradition rather than the development of distinctive *uṣūl* systems. This contrasts with the discussions around *uṣūl* issues in genres other than *uṣūl al-fiqh*, where the discussion appears much more vibrant.

7 Al-Atawneh's analysis of Wahhābī *fatwās* ("Wahhābī legal theory") reveals a general move away from the traditional Ḥanbalī structure towards a system more akin to the *maqāṣid* approach current outside of a Wahhābī Salafī context.

the central component of their literary output. This distinguishes them from the Shīʿī seminarians, to be discussed below, where a reputable work of *uṣūl* might become the pinnacle of a scholar's achievement and sets him (or, occasionally, her) apart from other would-be scholars. Nonetheless, *uṣūl* study (though not necessarily *uṣūl* specialism) forms an important element of the religious education system, not least because many scholars and students were trained in contexts where *uṣūl* was still prized before they devoted themselves to more central "Salafī" concerns.[8] Also, the traditional Ḥanbalī literary heritage (which still influences much religious training in Saudi Arabia) includes *uṣūl al-fiqh* and this tradition inevitably forms one point of reference and homage. In that heritage, the *uṣūl* text of Ibn Qudāma al-Maqdisī (d. 620/1223), *Rawḍat al-Nāẓir*, holds pride of place.

Ibn Qudāma's discussion of *ḥaqīqa sharʿiyya* is found in the section dealing with the different types of "names" which can be used to designate ideas or objects. There are four types, he states: *waḍʿ*, *ʿurfī*, *sharʿī* and *majāz muṭlaq*. Interestingly, only the first of these (*waḍʿī*) is identified as *ḥaqīqa*: "the utterance which is used in accordance with its original coinage (*fī waḍʿihi al-aṣlī*)". *ʿUrfī* naming occurs when the *ahl al-lugha* declare that a particular word means a particular thing (for example, *dābba* now means four-legged animals, whilst its *waḍʿ* meaning is anything that walks on the earth). Also, *ʿurfī* is the meaning which becomes so commonly associated with the item that, although it is *majāz*, it appears first in the mind of the individual (*sābiqan ilā al-fahm*). An example of this is *ghāʾiṭ*, which has a *ḥaqīqa* of "hollow in the ground" but is universally understood to mean privy. Ibn Qudāma's use of terminology is interesting here, in that he does employ the term *waḍʿ* to refer to the acquisition of the second meaning. However, he does refer to *al-waḍʿ al-aṣlī* to describe the first act of assignation, implying that there is a non-*aṣlī* act which follows it; he also chooses not to describe these new meanings as *ḥaqīqa ʿurfiyya*; in fact, he explicitly refers to them as *majāz*:

> The *aṣl al-waḍʿ* becomes forgotten and the *majāz* becomes known, being first in the mind. However, it is proven by the *ʿurf* of use and not by the original assignation (*al-waḍʿ al-awwal*).[9]

The indications are that he chooses not to refer to assignations of meaning subsequent to the original act of *waḍʿ* as *ḥaqīqa*; rather, they are *majāz*. However, they are to be distinguished from "absolute *majāz*" (*majāz muṭlaq*), which receives a separate section and refers, in a more orthodox fashion, to examples such as man: lion. They are, then, *majāz* in a qualified way. He may mean here that they are *majāz* in relation to the original *ḥaqīqa* meaning, but *ḥaqīqa* in relation to an absolute *majāz* expression.[10]

With regard to *sharʿī* naming, these are "names which have been transferred from

8 Cardinal, "Islamic Legal Theory Curriculum".

9 Ibn Qudāma, *Rawḍat al-Nāẓir*, p. 173.

10 This is a standard way of explaining the relative nature of *majāz* in *uṣūl*; see Rāzī, *al-Maḥṣūl*, v. 1, p. 299, where both *sharʿiyya* and *ʿurfiyya* counted as "*majāz* from the linguistic literal meanings" (*ʿalā sabīl al-majāz min al-ḥaqāʾiq al-lughawiyya*).

the *lugha* to the *sharʿ* (law), such as *ṣalāt*, *ṣiyām*, *zakāt* and *ḥajj*".[11] These are the standard examples, though Ibn Qudāma describes their new assignation as "transferred" (*manqūl*) rather than assigned (*waḍʿ*). This term, familiar from other discussions of *majāz*,[12] appears to refer to a process which is not the "borrowing" (*istiʿāra*) of metaphor commonly understood, but neither is it homonymity. The newly acquired meaning has a relationship with the *aṣlī* meaning of the original (this is not necessary for pure homonymity); but it is not a metaphorical relationship. There are, he says, those who say that there is no "transference" to a new meaning here:

> [They argue:] The bowing and the prostrating are conditions for [the proper performance of] prayer; they are not prayer itself, for two reasons:
> First: the Qur'ān is in Arabic and the Prophet was sent with "the language of his people". If he said "be generous to the *ʿulamāʾ* (scholars)" and he meant "to the *fuqarāʾ* (the poor)", then this is not in their language, even if the words being transferred are Arabic words.
> Second: if this were the case, then [God] would be compelled to inform the community of [this transference] through an act of instruction.[13]

The objection is interesting. The unidentified opponents are arguing that it is perfectly acceptable for God to introduce new conditions for the correct use of a word, but this should not be confused with adding a new meaning. It is, rather, a modification of the existing meaning. If it were a new meaning, then people would not understand it (for example, he says "scholars" but means "poor" – how are we to know he changed the meaning?), and it would require a new act of instruction (*tawqīfiyya*) telling us that there has been a new meaning assigned to an existing word.

Ibn Qudāma's response is that the *sharʿ* has a convention of use, just like the Arabs (*lil-sharʿ ʿurf al-istiʿmāl kamā lil-ʿarab*). When God uses words in this way, it does not make them non-Arabic words; and if they are used in this way in the Qur'ān, it does not prevent us from calling the Qur'ān *ʿarabī*. The Qur'ān contains numerous foreign (*aʿjamī*) words, but is still Arabic. Furthermore, we do not need to have a new act of instruction:

> This would only be necessary if one could not know the intended meaning (*maqṣūd*) through contextual evidence and repetition (*al-qarāʾin wa'l-takrīr*). When one understands, then the aim [of communication] has been achieved. When these words are uttered on the tongue of the *Sharʿ*, or in the discourse of the jurists, then it is obligatory to interpret them as legal literal (*ḥaqīqa sharʿiyya*), not linguistic literal (*lughawiyya*). They are not ambiguous because the usual habit of the Lawgiver is to use words in accordance with the habit of the *Sharʿ*.[14]

The habit of the speaker is, in effect, a new instructive (*tawqīfī*) act. On the one

11 That is, prayer, fasting, alms and pilgrimage in the sense of these Muslim religious rituals; Ibn Qudāma, *Rawḍat al-Nāẓir*, pp. 173–4.
12 See Yunis Ali, *Medieval Islamic Pragmatics*, pp. 107–8 and above pp. 164–6.
13 Ibn Qudāma, *Rawḍat al-Nāẓir*, p. 174.
14 Ibn Qudāma, *Rawḍat al-Nāẓir*, p. 174.

hand, Ibn Qudāma is keen to emphasise that the presumption when reading a *legal* communication from the Lawgiver is that words are used in a legal-literal manner, which he appears to allow. On the other hand, he does not use the term *waḍʿ* to describe the act of assignation of new meaning in the *sharʿ*, and he only employs the term *ḥaqīqa sharʿiyya* once (in this final passage). He recognises "absolute" *majāz*, viewing these transferences of meaning (*ʿurfī* and *sharʿī*) as *majāz* but not absolute (as in the man: lion case). His position appears to be that the *sharʿī* meaning, unlike the original meaning, is not *ḥaqīqa* in an unqualified manner; only the meaning assigned in the *waḍʿ aṣlī* holds that position. Rather, the *sharʿī* meaning is *ḥaqīqa* – in the sense that it becomes the presumed intended meaning – in a particular context (when being spoken by the Lawgiver or jurists in legal discourse). Whilst the original act of assignment does create a powerful bond between word and meaning, the ability of this bond to create a presumption in favour of this being the speaker's intended meaning can be weakened by utterance context. The "usual habit" of the speaker, if known and identifiable, is a contextual factor which can create sufficient grounds to replace the usual interpretive presumption in favour of the original *ḥaqīqa* with another presumed meaning. The replacement presumption in the context of legal discourse is that the *sharʿī* meaning is the intended meaning of the speaker. However, it is important to remember this is a process which happens not at the level of assignation, but in terms of a justification for certain interpretive presumptions. To put it another way, *ḥaqīqa* refers to two distinct elements here: (1) the meaning given to a word in the original act of assignation; and (2) the default/assumed speaker's intended meaning in the absence of contextual factors. Ibn Qudāma is, I think, arguing that context (in particular, the habit of the identified speaker)[15] has the ability to undermine the justification for the second element, but not the first. It is not the original *waḍʿī* meaning that is removed via the assignation of a novel *sharʿī* meaning, but the ability of that *waḍʿī* meaning to act as the presumed intended speaker's meaning. This distinction in Ibn Qudāma's presentation is important because it is precisely this nuance which appears blurred in the modern Salafī works of *uṣūl al-fiqh*.

The modern *uṣūl* work of ʿAbd al-Raḥmān Ibn Nāṣir al-Saʿdī (known as Ibn Saʿdī, d. 1956) is much studied in Salafī/Wahhābī circles. Ibn Saʿdī appears positively bold in his presentation compared to Ibn Qudāma's carefully constructed position:

> The fundamental assumption in speech is the *ḥaqīqa*. One does not turn from it to *majāz* – if indeed we assert it – except when the *ḥaqīqa* has been exhausted.
> The *ḥaqāʾiq* are three: *sharʿī, lughawī* and *ʿurfī*. Whatever the Lawgiver gives a ruling about after he has already defined it (*ḥaddahu*), then it is obligatory to understand it according to its legal meaning. When he has given a ruling, and he has not defined it, [and is] content with the appearance of its *lughawī* meaning, then it is obligatory to understand it in accordance with the *lugha*. And whenever there is no definition for it

15 The "interpretive community", one might say, following Fish: the community uniquely placed to use, understand and interpret the meaning of words. See Fish, *Is There a Text in this Class?*, p. 14, and above, p. 21.

in the *sharʿ* or the *lugha*, then it is understood according to the habit and practice (*ʿurf*) of the people.[16]

A comparison of this presentation with that of Ibn Qudāma yields some interesting results: first, Ibn Saʿdī admits the possibility that one could hold there was no such thing as *majāz* ("if we assert it"; I return to this below). Whilst the *ḥaqīqa* speech assumption is unremarkable in terms of *uṣūl al-fiqh* generally, the outright privileging of *ḥaqīqa sharʿiyya* is noteworthy. This is both presentational (*ḥaqīqa sharʿiyya* is listed first) and also procedural (it is the first meaning to be sought when encountering a ruling from the Lawgiver, and only after this do we turn to other meanings). Here the *sharʿī* meanings are given centre stage (rather than the *waḍʿī* meaning, as it is in Ibn Qudāma's *uṣūl*). Even if this is purely presentational and carries no doctrinal substance, the impression is of three equal *ḥaqīqa* meanings, with no reference to the primacy of the *waḍʿī/lughawī* meaning.[17] In a conservative literary tradition, changes in presentation often signal a shift in emphasis (and perhaps even doctrine). Here the semi-*majāz* status of the *ḥaqīqa sharʿiyya*, with its attendant (risky) deviation from the literal found in Ibn Qudāma, is downplayed, and an alternative vocabulary which maximises the epistemological status for the *ḥaqīqa sharʿiyya* is employed. For Ibn Saʿdī, a particular meaning deserves the interpretive privilege of being the presumed intended meaning because of an act of *waḍʿ* (all the *ḥaqāʾiq* are *waḍʿī* in this sense). Identifying which *waḍʿī* meaning occupies this position is, though, contextual. For Ibn Qudāma, the justification for selecting a meaning as the presumed intended meaning is a process in which context can overturn the usual presumptions. The context is such a powerful factor in this selection process that it can overturn the *waḍʿī* meaning. The difference between the two visions is indeed technical, but it obliterates the precedence for the *aṣlī* meaning which undergirds Ibn Qudāma's more conventional Ḥanbalī account. An even more explicit expression of this tendency is found in *al-Uṣūl min ʿilm al-uṣūl* of Ibn Saʿdī's famous pupil Bin ʿUthaymīn (d. 2001):

> The *ḥaqīqa* is divided into three categories: *lughawī*, *sharʿī* and *ʿurfī*.
> *lughawī* is when an utterance is used in the way it has been assigned in the *lugha* …
> [*sharʿī*] is when an utterance is used in the way it has been assigned in the *sharʿ* …
> [*ʿurfī*] is when an utterance is used in the way it has been assigned in *ʿurf*.[18]

Here, the manner in which the word gains a *sharʿī* meaning is quite definitely an act of assignation (*waḍʿ*) rather than an act of transference (*naql*).

The contrast between these modern Wahhābī/Salafī expressions of *ḥaqīqa*

16 Ibn Saʿdī, *Risāla Laṭīfa*, pp. 77–9.

17 Ibn Saʿdī does not use *waḍʿī* or *aṣlī* to describe the linguistically designated meaning, perhaps because he does not wish to afford it any original (preferred) status by doing so. The editor and commentator on the *Risāla Laṭīfa*, Taʿmirī, makes this more explicit, referring to an act of *waḍʿ* for each of these categories of *ḥaqīqa* (Ibn Saʿdī, *Risāla Laṭīfa*, p. 77, n. 53).

18 Bin ʿUthaymīn, *al-Uṣūl*, p. 20.

sharʿiyya and Ibn Qudāma's formulation is, on the whole, glossed over in modern commentaries on the *Rawḍat al-Nāẓir*. Muḥammad al-Amīn al-Shanqīṭī (d. 1973), for example, simply states that "the essence of what the author [Ibn Qudāma] is saying here is that the names are divided into four categories [*majāz muṭlaq* and the three others], and that the *ḥaqīqa sharʿiyya* occupies the priority position (*muqaddima*)".[19]

Bin ʿUthaymīn's declaration of his reason for the division of non-*majāz* meanings into three is instructive:

> The point of knowing that the *ḥaqīqa* is divided into three categories is that we can now interpret each utterance according to its *ḥaqīqī* meaning in the location it was used. So it is interpreted according to its *ḥaqīqa lughawiyya* when it is used by the linguistic experts; and according to its *ḥaqīqa sharʿiyya* when used in the *sharʿ*; and according to *ḥaqīqa ʿurfiyya* when used by the *ahl al-ʿurf*.[20]

Here there is an explicit introduction of context into the identification of which *ḥaqīqa* meaning is being used. A completely context-free understanding of the *ḥaqīqa* meaning of an utterance is now impossible. One does not encounter words out of context, so one does not need to know which *ḥaqīqī* meaning would take precedence in such circumstances. As the *ḥaqīqa* category is expanded to cover additional literal meanings established through acts of linguistic assignation, they all adopt the same epistemological status, and hence occupy the same probability in terms of the meaning of the utterance. It is context, and context alone, which pushes one forward as the presumed meaning.

Ibn Qudāma's position on *sharʿī* meanings could be characterised as contextually informed, rather than contextually dependent. He did envisage a role for context in determining the presumed intended meaning of a text, and this meaning has some (though not all) of the characteristics of the *ḥaqīqa*. What is distinctive amongst these modern authors, though, is the identification of this contextually informed meaning as *ḥaqīqa* (and *waḍʿī*), and therefore equal, or even superior, to the supposed "context-free" (*mujarrad*) assigned meaning. The theological driving force behind this tightening up of *sharʿī* meanings, whereby they are classified as *ḥaqīqa* in an absolute rather than relative sense, is an epistemological suspicion of any *majāz*, a position most obviously derived from the prestige awarded to Ibn Taymiyya in Salafī circles. In terms of language-related issues, Ibn Taymiyya's distinctive critique of the established categorisation scheme of *uṣūl al-fiqh* has already been noted by Heinrichs, and subjected to detailed exposition by Yunis Ali.[21] It might, following Yunis Ali, be characterised as contextualism in the modern sense, in which the whole notion of a literal meaning, originally assigned to words in language, is rejected and instead all meaning is driven by context rather than language. The rejection of the *ḥaqīqa*/*majāz*

19 Shanqīṭī, *Mudhakkira*, p. 209; he adds: "There is no ambiguity in its expression because the *lughawī* meaning might have been intended. If you find the word *ṣalāt* in the discourse of the Lawgiver, you must interpret it according to the *sharʿī* meaning and not its *lughawī*."

20 Bin ʿUthaymīn, *al-Uṣūl*, p. 20.

21 Heinrichs, "On the Genesis", pp. 115–17; Yunis Ali, *Medieval Islamic Pragmatics*, pp. 87–140.

pairing by Ibn Taymiyya (and also by his pupil Ibn Qayyim al-Jawziyya) and their "contextualist" alternative theory were not to have a particularly significant influence in classical *uṣūl* works. This may have been because it was too radical; or perhaps the works of these two thinkers were not considered central to the discipline of *uṣūl*; or perhaps even their theory, as it was not contained in the standard *uṣūl* generic format, could not become central to any *madhhab* curriculum. Their theory was not entirely without precedent. It can be seen as an outgrowth of the "contextually informed" Ḥanbalī position developed by Ibn Qudāma. For the two arch-Salafīs:

> Utterances do not mean anything in themselves. They are only indications (*adilla*) by which one might deduce the intended meaning of the speaker (*murād al-mutakallim*).[22]

The meaning "in itself" is, of course, the *ḥaqīqa lughawiyya*, and in the standard account a new meaning, *majāz* in relation to this original meaning, is added. Ibn al-Qayyim is saying this original designation is basically mythical, and should not be the starting point of any determination of meaning. Instead, words are indications of the speaker's meaning, and the important relationship to understand is not how the intended meaning relates to some mythical literal meaning, but how words indicate (that is, act as *dalīls* for) the speaker's intended meaning. This, Ibn Taymiyya argues, occurs entirely through an understanding of the context of the utterance under examination. Context here is understood in the broadest possible terms, which in the case of God's speech means the revelatory corpus generally. With regard to the so-called "transferring" (*naql*) required for a *ḥaqīqa sharʿiyya* (explained above in reference to Ibn Qudāma, but found in many versions of the mainstream *uṣūl* tradition), Ibn Taymiyya sees this reasoning process as otiose:

> When the Prophet explains (*bayyana*) the limits of the thing referred to by a word, then there is no need for this [to be seen as] something transferred from the *lugha* or an addition to it. Rather, the intended meaning [of any speech] is whatever [the Prophet] habitually uses to refer to his intended meaning: this is the intended meaning [of the utterance]. So, for example, there is the word "*al-khamr*". [The Prophet] made clear that every intoxicating thing is a *khamr*, and so the intended meaning [of this word] in the Qurʾān is known. This is so whether the Arabs had previously used the word *khamr* to refer to all intoxicating substances, or simply to the juice of grapes. There is no need for this because the thing we are seeking is knowledge of what God and his Prophet intend, and this is already known by the elucidation (*bayān*) of the Prophet.[23]

Since the only thing that matters is the intended meaning of God or the Prophet when they utter a statement or use a word, if the intended meaning can be deduced from context, then what people imagine the "literal" or "original" meaning to be is irrelevant:

> What is necessary here is to know that when the interpretation of the words found in the Qurʾān and *ḥadīth* and what was meant by them according to the Prophet is known, there is no need in this to base one's derivation on the views of the linguistic experts

22 Ibn al-Qayyim, *Iʿlām*, v. 1, p. 218.
23 Ibn Taymiyya, *al-Fatawā*, v. 19, p. 236.

> (*ahl al-lugha*) or anyone else ... The Prophet has made clear what he meant by these words in an elucidation (*bayān*) with which there is no need for deduction through etymology (*ishtiqāq*), examples of Arab use (*istiʿmāl al-ʿArab*), or anything else. Hence, one must refer to the things named by these words according to the elucidation (*bayān*) of God and his Prophet. This is entirely sufficient [for understanding].[24]

The use of a wide context in order to determine "true" (*ḥaqīqa*) meaning is not dissimilar to the rescuing of the *ẓāhir* through redefinition already seen in the work of Ibn Ḥazm,[25] though without the commitment to some sort of supremely authoritative *waḍʿī* meaning.

The esteem in which Ibn Taymiyya and Ibn al-Qayyim are held in Salafī circles has led to the partial incorporation of this contextually dependent view of meaning into their *uṣūl al-fiqh*. However, in many cases (including Ibn Saʿdī and Bin ʿUthaymīn) the theory is skewed by a parallel adherence to the structures found in Ibn Qudāma and the Ḥanbalī mainstream. The result is a commitment to the idea that *ḥaqīqa sharʿiyya* is a "true" *ḥaqīqa*, but that its meaning is deducible through context rather than by reference to an act of *waḍʿ*. Conjoined with this is an acceptance of the standard category of *majāz*, and consequent lengthy explanation of how it operates. Ibn Taymiyya, of course, would view such discussions as irrelevant and meaningless, since there is no *waḍʿī* meaning from which a *majāz* might be said to deviate.[26] The word *ḥaqīqa*, properly used, refers not to a non-*majāz* meaning, but to the "true" meaning of a statement: that is, the intended meaning of the author which is indicated by the words. In this, and if we follow some analyses, we have a return to one of the earliest meanings of *ḥaqīqa*.[27]

A more thorough analysis of Salafī *uṣūl* would, no doubt, reveal yet more texture to the discussions over *ḥaqīqa sharʿiyya*, but from this brief survey it is clear that the writers are subject to two variant expressions of the doctrine found in the Ḥanbalī tradition. The epistemological drive for certainty found in modern Salafism leads to the *ḥaqīqa* category gaining increased importance, and the uncertainties of *majāz* interpretations being marginalised. This has led to a substantial adoption of Ibn Taymiyya's views but in the standard *uṣūl* "category sets" inherited from Ibn Qudāma. The imperfect match means that experimentation in Salafī *uṣūl* is likely to continue until a convincing format is reached and *uṣūl* is stabilised. This, however, may not come to pass, since pressures demanding a legal theory which responds to

24 Ibn Taymiyya, *al-Fatawā*, v. 7, pp. 286–7.

25 See above, p. 157, n. 43.

26 There are more thoroughgoing incorporations of Ibn Taymiyya's views into works of modern Salafī *uṣūl*. See, for example, Jayzānī, *Maʿālim uṣūl al-fiqh*, pp. 380–6, where although *majāz* is mentioned, it is not afforded a separate section as all the focus is on *ḥaqīqa* meaning.

27 See Almagor, "Early Meaning", pp. 314–15; Heinrichs, "On the Genesis", pp. 124–6. Ibn Taymiyya states that the *ḥaqīqa*/*majāz* division "requires a word to have been assigned in the first place to a meaning; then after that, for it to be used in its place sometimes, and outside of its place at others. All of this is only correct if it can be proved that Arabic utterances have been assigned to meanings in the first place ... and that the assignment came before the use ... but this is something no Muslim can ever know" (Ibn Taymiyya, *al-Fatawā*, v. 7, p. 90).

a perceived societal need, rather than the traditional questions of linguistic discussion, are already transforming the legal framework of Hanbalism.[28] In this, these Uṣūlīs are similar to their non-Salafī counterparts (such as Muḥammad Shahrūr), where a theory of language and communication forms an essential element of the reform project.[29]

Ḥaqīqa Sharʿiyya in Modern Shīʿī *Uṣūl al-fiqh*

In a previous chapter, the Shīʿī *uṣūlī* theory of literal meaning, particularly as it related to the standard conception of *ḥaqīqa*, was explored.[30] This view was quite standard in Shīʿī works of *uṣūl al-fiqh* up to the Safavid period (1501–1722), when the Akhbārī movement appeared and challenged the established legal theory. I have analysed the development of Akhbārī conceptions of language elsewhere,[31] though a summary here is appropriate. For Akhbārīs generally, pre-revelatory language consisted of (amongst other things) a set of meanings attached (or designated) to words. This was the manner in which words were commonly used before revelation, and continued to be so after revelation, and were termed *al-ḥaqāʾiq al-ʿurfiyya*. At the point of revelation, God instituted new meanings for words, and these were similarly designated, and are termed *al-ḥaqāʾiq al-sharʿiyya*. How is one to know, then, when these words are used in revelatory texts, which of these two designated meanings (*ḥaqāʾiq*) is intended? The Akhbārī answer is that it is through the Imams that the intended meaning of statements using these words can be known. The Imams, through their statements (*akhbār*), interpreted the Qurʾān and the *ḥadīth* of the Prophet in such a way that the post-revelatory community can understand the intended meaning of revelation. Without them, human beings are "blind" to the meaning of the Quranic text (a position known as *taʿmiya*). The Imams, then, are the only interpreters (*mufassirīn*) of the Qurʾān. There were variants of this position within the Akhbārī school. Some Akhbārīs (the founder Muḥammad Amīn al-Astarābādī (d. 1036/1626–7) amongst them) claimed that direct interpretation of the Qurʾān was impossible; others (such as Muḥsin Fayḍ al-Kāshānī (d. 1091/1680)) allowed direct interpretation of certain verses (for which he borrowed the Quranic

28 An indication of this trend might be found in the restriction of *ḥaqīqa sharʿiyya* to matters of personal prayer. Khālid al-Mushayqiḥ, the editor and commentator on Ibn Saʿdī's *qawāʿid* work *al-Qawāʿid wa'l-Uṣūl al-Jāmiʿa*, argues that *ḥaqīqa sharʿiyya* can only be assumed in matters relating to *ʿibādāt*, thereby allowing other possible meanings (*ʿurfī*, for example) to become operative in the discussion of non-*ʿibādāt* issues. See Mushayqiḥ, *Sharḥ Risāla*, p. 9.

29 Shahrūr, for example, considered the Quranic term *ṣalāt* to be a homonym, and vocalised in two ways: *ṣalawa* (meaning the prayer ritual) and *ṣālāt* (meaning prayer in a spiritual sense). "We must never ignore these subtle differences, and if the text employs two derivatives of the same lexeme, when it could have used an identical expression, it indicates a difference. It indicates that we are meant to clearly distinguish between 'prayer' in the sense of a ritual and 'prayer' in the sense of a spiritual connection between God and the believer, giving praise to Allāh, mentally or verbally, but not by a movement of the body." See Christmann, *Qur'an, Morality and Critical Reason*, p. 34, citing Shahrūr's famous tract *al-Islām wa'l-Īmān*.

30 Chapter 5 above, pp. 126–45.

31 See Gleave, *Scripturalist Islam*, pp. 268–82.

term *muḥkamāt*), but not others. However, even those who allowed direct interpretation of the *muḥkamāt* normally stipulated that the only manner in which to distinguish these from non-interpretable verses (the *mutashābihāt*) was through the Imams informing us that a verse was *muḥkam* or *mutashābih*. The words of the Imams can be understood "literally" (*ẓāhiran*, according to their "obvious" meaning) because if it were otherwise all revelatory meaning would be lost to us. The Qur'ān (and for most Akhbārīs the *ḥadīths* of the Prophet also) requires interpretation even when it may appear as if a verse or phrase has a clear, undisputed meaning.[32]

These ideas, which have clear similarities with the early, pre-*uṣūl*, Shīʿī notions of literal meaning discussed previously,[33] have not remained particularly popular after the demise of the Akhbāriyya in the nineteenth century. The Maktab-e Tafkīk (the Tafkīkī or Separation school) is often considered a modern expression of the Akhbārīs; this may be because of the school's anti-philosophical position rather than any real sense of continuity.[34] On the question of *ḥaqīqa sharʿiyya*, the first impression is of a quite radical dissimilarity between Akhbārī doctrines and those of the Maktab-e Tafkīk. Mīrzā Mahdī al-Iṣfahānī (d. 1946), identified by many (both Tafkīkī and anti-Tafkīkī) as the founder of the school, argued that words within the Sharīʿa are used with their linguistic meaning and not with any technical, legal (*sharʿī*) meaning. He composed a short *risāla* entitled *fī wujūb ḥaml al-alfāẓ al-wārida fī'l-sharʿiyya 'alā maʿānīhā al-lughawiyya wa-ibṭāl al-ḥaqīqa al-sharʿiyya wa'l-mutasharriʿa* ("on the obligation to interpret the words present within the Sharīʿa according to their linguistic meanings and the invalidity of legal and juristic literal meaning"). In this, he argues that the term *ṣalāt* in the revelatory texts is to be interpreted simply as prayer, and not the obligatory ritual referred to as *ṣalāt* in the legal textbooks:

> *Ṣalāt* in our opinion has no special meaning. It existed for the nations of the past, like the Arab [that is, Arabic-speaking] Jews and Christians (*al-yāhūd wa'l-naṣāra min al-ʿarab*) ... There is no legal-literal meaning for the *ṣalāt* as used by the Prophet.[35]

Al-Iṣfahānī next cites a number of Quranic verses in which the term *ṣalāt* (or its derivative forms) is used to describe the prayers of the Jews, Christians and others (including Satan's own acts of worship). His position, then, is that the notion of additional legal-literal meanings through revelation (a central element in the Akhbārī position) is incorrect, and that the default position of any interpreter must be that the word is used in its linguistic meaning. This position forms part of the more general Tafkīkī position of "Quranic understanding" (*taʿaqqul al-Qur'ān*) in which revelation produces for itself a discourse which is not subject to the structures arrived at through

32 A more expansive discussion of these Akhbārī positions can be found in Gleave, *Scripturalist Islam*, pp. 216–45 and pp. 275–96 (particularly pp. 275–80), and, with respect to Yūsuf al-Baḥrānī specifically, Gleave, *Inevitable Doubt*, pp. 48–55 and pp. 147–64, and Gleave, "Compromise and Conciliation").

33 See above, p. 128.

34 See Gleave, "Continuity and Originality", on which the following summary is based.

35 Iṣfahānī, *Risāla*, f. 2b.10–12.

outside enquiry. The individual has access to this Quranic understanding through the ordinary use of words within the revelatory documents. This is not to say that al-Iṣfahānī and his followers were simple "literalists" (he has an extended section on the occasions when words are not used in their *ḥaqīqī* ways but in a *majāz* manner, and, crucially, how to recognise them).[36] However, al-Iṣfahānī's position (and that of subsequent Tafkīkīs) is that the Quranic text is approachable directly (or at least more directly than within the Akhbārī methodology) because the words used within it can be assumed to carry linguistic meanings. No new and impenetrable designated meanings (*al-ḥaqāʾiq al-sharʿiyya*) are instituted in the revelatory process, and there is certainly no privileging of the *akhbār* as the sole legitimate interpretive tool (as was the case for the Akhbārīs). This position is expressed in later Tafkīkī writings in the fundamental doctrines of the Maktab-e Tafkīk as laid out by the Tafkīkī sympathiser Muḥammad Riḍā Ḥakīmī: "One should rely on the clear/manifest (*ẓāhir*) meanings of verses in the Qurʾān and the transmitted *akhbār*" and "Any form of interpretation (*taʾwīl*) of these revelatory texts is forbidden". In an interview, Ḥakīmī laid out the Tafkīkī prohibition on interpretation in the clearest terms:

> The Qurʾān came down in "clear Arabic" so that all may understand it, and act upon it. For the same reason, the phrases "O People", or "O those who believe", or "O people of the book" all indicate that God wishes to speak in this language to the people … in the area of understanding and the legal regulations, the probative force of the obvious meaning [of verses, *ḥujjiyyat-e ẓawāhir*] is given the greatest importance. No one can let go of the *ẓāhir*, unless there is an immediate proof (*burhān-e badīhī*) … considering what we have said concerning the probative force of obvious meanings, there is no place for interpretation.[37]

Ḥakīmī's interpretation of the availability of Quranic understanding is popularist (in the sense that all can understand it). This may be a deviation from al-Iṣfahānī's notion of the linguistic meaning, which al-Iṣfahānī himself distinguishes from the meaning which is understood through use (*fīʾl-istiʿmāl*). Whether this signals a greater emphasis on anti-elitism in the later Tafkīkīs is not clear. Whichever is the case, though, the understanding here is quite distinct from the conceptions of language's operation popular amongst the Akhbārī scholars of the Safavid period. This is, at least, the impression gained from the available texts.[38]

36 Iṣfahānī, *Risāla*, f. 4a.18–4b.5.
37 Ḥakīmī, "ʿAql-e Khūd", p. 41.
38 However, there is a reference in Yūsuf al-Baḥrānī's *al-Ḥadāʾiq al-Nāḍira* to an Akhbārī opinion (which he rejects) in which the exegetes claim to be "equal" to the Imams in "interpreting the difficult parts [of the Qurʾān] and clarifying the inclarities within it" (*taʾwīl mushkilātihi wa-ḥall mubhamātihi*); see *al-Ḥadāʾiq al-Nāḍira*, v. 1, p. 169. I have always considered this to be a straw-man argument, constructed by al-Baḥrānī to make his position appear more moderate. My reasoning here is that I have yet to find an Akhbārī writer who supported such a direct hermeneutic. However, even within the brief description provided by al-Baḥrānī, one can see elements of similarity with the Tafkīkī position. If such an Akhbārī position did exist in the Safavid period (and it is far from clear that it did), then in this sense the Tafkīkīs can be considered to maintain this element of the Akhbārī intellectual legacy; see Gleave, *Scripturalist Islam*, pp. 222–3.

The Tafkīkī rejection of the possibility of *ḥaqāʾiq sharʿiyya* is clearly linked to their opposition to what they see as the "over-interpretative" hermeneutic of the Shīʿī *uṣūlī* mainstream. Broadly speaking, there has been debate between two "schools" of jurisprudence in the mainstream, identified (at least colloquially) with the two shrine and seminary cities of Qum and Najaf. In both places, the study of *uṣūl al-fiqh* remains a vibrant educational exercise; and the major Shīʿī scholars of the modern period all composed important works of *uṣūl*. This includes Ayatollahs Khomeini, al-Khuʾī and Bāqir al-Ṣadr at the end of the last century, and Ayatollahs Sistani, Bashīr al-Najafī, Saʿīd al-Ḥakīm and al-Waḥīd al-Khurāsānī in the recent past. In both seminary systems (or *ḥawzas*), scholars cut their teeth on the study of the *Kifāyat al-uṣūl* of al-Ākhund Muḥammad Kāẓim al-Khurāsānī (d. 1911). Al-Khurāsānī places the debate over *al-ḥaqāʾiq al-sharʿiyya* in the context of the more general question of whether or not *ḥaqīqa* meanings can be instituted by language use.[39] The debate is conducted in abstract terms (for example, "is it rationally possible for a new *waḍʿī* meaning to be instituted through use?" – *al-waḍʿ biʾl-istiʿmāl*). What is really at stake is whether or not God can institute a new *waḍʿī* meaning through simply using the word in a new manner. The question of this actually happening in revelation is a separate question which can only be addressed once it is proven that it is rationally possible for it to occur. Since God is constrained by rational possibilities (for the Imāmī-Muʿtazilīs), establishing that something is rationally possible is necessary before discussing whether it has actually taken place. The reason for the dispute over *waḍʿ* through language use is, one presumes, because this is what appears to happen in revelation. That is, we have precious few records of God or the Prophet explicitly declaring that henceforth a word (for example, *ṣalāt*) "means" something new (the stipulated prayer ritual, and not simply *duʿā*). God and the Prophet simply start using *ṣalāt* to mean the prayer ritual, and this means that in most cases *ḥaqāʾiq sharʿiyya* are instituted through use rather than through a specific decree.

Al-Khurāsānī explains that some argue that a *waḍʿī* meaning cannot be instituted by use (that is, it is not possible, rationally speaking, for such an event to occur) – and therefore God, who is constrained by reason, cannot institute new meanings for old words in this way. Al-Khurāsānī, however, disputes this, arguing that it is rationally possible for God to institute new meanings for words; and, more importantly, it is rationally possible for God to do this purely through using the word with the new meaning (that is, there does not have to be an identifiable divine declarative act to institute the new meanings). There are, then, two ways in which God can create *al-ḥaqāʾiq al-sharʿiyya*:

1. Through a declarative act (i.e. by saying something like "We know X means Y, but now I decree that it also means Z").
2. Through using a word with one established meaning in a new way.

In technical terms, both of these means of establishing *al-ḥaqāʾiq al-sharʿiyya* come under the umbrella term of *al-waḍʿ al-taʿyīnī* ("specified placing"). The immediate

39 Khurāsānī, *Kifāyat al-uṣūl*, pp. 45–7.

question raised by al-Khurāsānī's scheme is the mechanism whereby one recognises that (2) has taken place. Al-Khurāsānī's answer is that there is always evidence (*qarīna*/*qarāʾin*) that it has occurred, and the jurists can pick this evidence out in order to demonstrate that a *ḥaqīqa sharʿiyya* has been established. On the face of it, this would make the technique for recognising a *majāz* use identical with that for recognising a *ḥaqīqa sharʿiyya* use. However, al-Khurāsānī is quite clear that there is a fundamental logical difference between a *ḥaqīqa sharʿiyya* instituted through use and a *majāz*:

> *Al-waḍʿ al-taʿyīnī* can take place through an explicit declaration of its institution (*bi'l-taṣrīḥ bi-inshāʾihi*). In the same way, it can also take place by using a word in a way other than how it was originally established but as if it had been established in this way … even though there is no means of avoiding at this point the allocation of a *qarīna*. However, this [*qarīna*] indicates that [the *ḥaqīqa sharʿiyya*] has been established, not what the speaker's intended meaning might have been, as it is with *majāz*.[40]

Al-Khurāsānī's point here is a subtle one, and it is worth explicating it in more detail. In a single utterance, a speaker may use words in their established manner (*ḥaqīqa*); and they may use them in an allowable deviation from this established manner (*majāz*). For the latter, *qarāʾin* function as indications of the speaker's probable intended meaning. So, for example, when a speaker says of a soldier "he was a lion in battle", the literal meaning (he metamorphosed into a lion during or just before the battle) can be discarded, and hence there must be *majāz* use here. The intended meaning of the *majāz* use is established through *qarāʾin* (facts such as the general perception of lions as brave; bravery being a particularly prized quality in war; the literal meaning being obviously discarded; the context in which it was spoken – for example, during a general panegyric). The *qarāʾin* here function as indications of what the speaker's meaning might be. The *ḥaqāʾiq sharʿiyya* also require *qarāʾin*, but these *qarāʾin* do not, according to al-Khurāsānī, exist as evidence of the speaker's intended meaning. Instead they operate as indicators that an act of *waḍʿ* has already taken place through the utterance. The *qarāʾin* also identify which meaning has been newly assigned to which sound. One can see here that the issues which prompted discussions in Sunni *uṣūl*, and which gave rise to the rather peculiar hybrid in modern Salafī *uṣūl* writings, are fundamental also within modern Shīʿī discussions: how does one know whether a new technical *sharʿī* meaning is being used? What happens to the previous meaning when this new meaning is instituted? Is this an act of *waḍʿ* just like the original *waḍʿ* which established the linguistic meaning?

The adoption of *Kifāyat al-uṣūl* in the early twentieth century as the standard seminar *uṣūl* textbook meant that al-Khurāsānī's treatment of this issue came to set the parameters of subsequent debate. Notwithstanding the respect in which the *Kifāyat al-uṣūl* was held, al-Khurāsānī's answer was not universally supported. The first detailed objection came from the Najaf-based Muḥammad Ḥusayn al-Nāʾīnī (d. 1936), whose classes in *uṣūl al-fiqh* were recorded by Abū al-Qāsim al-Khūʾī (d.

40 Khurāsānī, *Kifāyat al-uṣūl*, p. 46.

1992).[41] Al-Nāʾīnī argues that *waḍʿ* cannot be established by language use – even if the language user is God himself. His reason for this is logical. The process of "placing" meanings on sounds requires one to see the meaning and the sound each "with an independent perspective" (*biʾl-liḥāẓ al-istiqlālī*). The meaning and the sound are two independent items, perceived independently, and through *waḍʿ* the connection between them is instituted. When one looks at language use, the two things are not separable. The meaning is the thing which one desires to know, and the sound (the word) is the "way" (*ṭarīq*) to or "reflected image" (*mirʾā*) of the meaning: "the sound is the thing by which the meaning is contemplated". One must view the sound as a mechanism whereby the meaning is revealed, and not as an independent entity in itself. Now if one way to perform an act of *waḍʿ* was simply to use words with particular new meanings (as al-Khurāsānī argues), it would no longer be possible to consider the word and the meaning separately. Al-Nāʾīnī's point here is that instituting a meaning through language use is quite possible, but it is a very different process to instituting a meaning by *waḍʿ*: it is, in effect, *majāz*. A meaning instituted by language use views the sound merely as a tool by which the meaning might be comprehended; this tool can be used because it has already been employed for other uses at other times by language users:

> It is thought that it is possible to achieve *waḍʿ* by use alone – as the "Author of the *Kifāyat*" [i.e. al-Khurāsānī] suggests. But this is disproved by the fact that the true understanding of "use", as we have already pointed out, is the comprehension of an external meaning through nothing other than a word which exists irrespective of [the meaning]. Use demands that a word exists irrespective of meaning … it demands that the word be viewed as a separate entity (*bi-istiqlālihi*). It is obvious, then, that it is not possible to do these two things [i.e. use a word and view it as an entity separate from its meaning] at the same time.[42]

To use an example (not employed by al-Nāʾīnī), "book" is used for a specific thing (originally) but can have a new meaning (for example as a verb, as in "to book a football player") instituted through use. This new meaning established through use involves, inevitably, a particular understanding of the original meaning of the noun "book" in order to indicate its new meaning as a verb in a particular context (a football match). This is quite different from the process whereby a meaning is attached to a sound with no regard for any other use of that sound (as one might think in the case of homonyms). Al-Nāʾīnī's argument is that it is not possible (logically speaking) to mix up these two processes.

This view was developed further by al-Khūʾī. In the account of his *uṣūl* classes given by Āyatallāh Muḥammad Isḥāq al-Fayyāḍ, published under the title *Muḥāḍarāt fī uṣūl al-fiqh*, he gives an extended exposition of his opinion, summarised by the statement:

41 Khūʾī, *Ajwad al-taqrīrāt*, v. 1, pp. 33–4.
42 Khūʾī, *Ajwad al-taqrīrāt*, v. 1, p. 34.

> *Waḍʿ* is an internal matter established in the area of the individual; use is a matter external to the individual. *Waḍʿ* always comes before use.[43]

Al-Khūʾī's point here is that the act of placing a meaning on a sound, which the proponents of the theory of *waḍʿ* envisage to have happened at some primordial moment, is an internal, creative act by an individual who decides to connect the sound (e.g. "book") with its meaning. Use, on the other hand, is an external event, and must always be preceded by *waḍʿ*. The two processes, then, occur on different levels, and cannot be conjoined in a single level as al-Khurāsānī seems to envisage with his theory.

Al-Khūʾī's position is maintained in the more recent period by Muḥammad Saʿīd al-Ḥakīm who, in his rejection of *al-ḥaqāʾiq al-sharʿiyya*, emphasises the continuity of the message of God, and in this appears almost Tafkīkī in expression:

> It is clear that those words, such as *ḥajj* or *ʿumra*, on which have been placed legal meanings are so because of their origin in language, so that they might be understood by these names in the period of the Jāhiliyya, and in accordance with the covenant of Islam, and following the law of Abraham. There is no difference between what they meant to them, and what they mean in Islam except in terms of some specifics (*baʿḍ al-khuṣūṣiyyāt*) by which errors might be corrected. This is similar to the difference between ourselves and the Sunnis.[44]

It could be speculated that the intellectual link here comes through al-Nāʾīnī, who was the teacher in Najaf of both al-Khūʾī and Mīrzā Mahdī al-Iṣfahānī, the so-called founder of the Maktab-e Tafkīk referred to above.

Bashīr al-Najafī, a student of al-Khūʾī, does not explicitly declare his position in his well-known textbook *Mirqāt al-uṣūl*. He seems to support the notion that *al-ḥaqāʾiq al-sharʿiyya* can be established simply through God using the words in a new manner, but his typology of *al-waḍʿ al-taʿyīnī* (individual designation) and *al-waḍʿ al-taʿayyunī* (required designation), taken originally from al-Khurāsānī, would seem to reject his master's position:

> When considered from the perspective of its origins, [*waḍʿ*] is divided into two categories:
>
> 1. *al-waḍʿ al-taʿyīnī* – when the one doing the placing is a particular person; and this is divided into two types:
>   i. when the one doing the placing explicitly announces that he is making a specific word face a particular meaning.
>   ii. when a speaker uses the word with a specific meaning intending this [use] to be an act of placing, and so the use and the *waḍʿ* occur at one and the same time.
>
> 2. *al-waḍʿ al-taʿayyunī* – when a word is used with a particular meaning so many times that a connection occurs between the word and the meaning. [The connection] is so

43 Fayyāḍ, *Muḥāḍarāt fī uṣūl al-fiqh*, v. 1, p. 145.

44 Saʿīd al-Ḥakīm, *al-Muḥkam*, v. 1, p. 159.

> firmly established that the meaning is understood from the word unconditionally and immediately without the need for any *qarīna*.[45]

Whilst this typology of *waḍʿ* would seem to follow al-Khurāsānī rather than al-Khūʾī, and therefore allow for the possibility of *waḍʿ* being instituted through language use (see (ii) above), Bashīr al-Najafī does not explicitly say that God has employed this method of *waḍʿ*. In his section on *al-ḥaqīqa al-sharʿiyya*, Bashīr al-Najafī quotes (the Sunni) al-Bāqillānī, who argued that the words *ṣalāt*, *ṣawm*, *zakāt* and *ḥajj* all had established meanings before they were used in the Qurʾān and by the Prophet. After citing various Quranic verses, Bashīr al-Najafī states:

> These and other verses demonstrate that these words were already used [i.e. in pre-Quranic Arabic] on the tongues of the *ahl al-lugha* with their meanings known to the people of *Sharʿ*.[46]

This passage indicates that, for Bashīr al-Najafī, words had pre-existent legal meanings, and therefore cannot be regarded as examples of *al-ḥaqāʾiq al-sharʿiyya*. These apparently contradictory statements are difficult to reconcile. It is possible that Bashīr al-Najafī continues the position of his teacher al-Khūʾī, but nonetheless has accepted that whilst it is logically possible for *al-ḥaqāʾiq al-sharʿiyya* to be instituted through use, it did not actually happen in the case of *ṣalāt*, *ḥajj*, *ʿumra* or any of the other technical religious terms.

There are explicit criticisms of al-Khūʾī's view on this matter amongst the current teachers of *uṣūl* in Qum. In this they might be said to be building on the position of Āyatallāh ʿAbd al-Karīm al-Ḥāʾirī (d. 1936). Al-Ḥāʾirī was responsible for the revival of the Qum Seminary when he moved there from Najaf in 1922 and began redeveloping the intellectual life of the crumbling *madrasas*. He set the tone for later scholarship in the city in his *Durar al-fawāʾid*. There he states:

> It is pointless to deny that words for acts of worship at the time of the Prophet were such that he understood them to have new meanings, unconditionally. Now, was this a process of *al-waḍʿ al-taʿyīnī* or *al-waḍʿ al-taʿayyunī* – or were these words used in previous *sharīʿas* also? There is no way of proving any of these alternatives. However, *al-waḍʿ al-taʿyīnī*, in the sense of an explicit declaration by the Prophet that there has been a placing of these meanings [on the pre-existent words], is extremely unlikely. Then again, there is another possible type of *al-waḍʿ al-taʿyīnī*. The [Prophet] may have *used* these words with these new meanings, intending that they now be their [*waḍʿī*] meanings. This is a type of *al-waḍʿ al-taʿyīnī* also.[47]

Al-Ḥāʾirī's position is that the Prophet's (or God's) use of a pre-existent word with a new meaning is a type of *al-waḍʿ al-taʿyīnī*. Defence of this doctrine seems to have become orthodox *uṣūl* doctrine amongst the subsequent scholars working in the Qum

45 Bashīr al-Najafī, *Mirqāt al-uṣūl*, p. 18.
46 Bashīr al-Najafī, *Mirqāt al-uṣūl*, pp. 43–4.
47 Ḥāʾirī, *Durar al-fawāʾid*, v. 1, p. 36.

ḥawza. Ayatollahs Khomeini,[48] Muḥammad ʿAlī al-Arākī[49] and Muḥammad Riḍā Gulpaygānī all indicate that establishing *waḍʿ* through use is logically possible. They do differ over whether they can say with certainty that it has happened, and Khomeini, in particular, sees the discussion as pointless:

> Even if we knew whether some of the words for acts of worship in the Sharīʿa were invented [by the Prophet], it would not help us in the task which we have.[50]

It would not help because the question is really academic; and the task we have is development of an *uṣūl al-fiqh* which is useful for the jurist, rather then excessively detailed. Khomeini argues that everyone knows what these words mean now, because if they have not acquired these meanings through *al-waḍʿ al-taʿyīnī*, they certainly have through *al-waḍʿ al-taʿayyunī* (that is, through the constant use of them with the legal meanings, such that they immediately appear in all hearers' minds).[51] This frustration with the debate as it is classically framed can also be seen in certain Salafī *uṣūl* writings.[52]

The affirmation of *al-ḥaqīqa al-sharʿiyya* (either through al-Khurāsānī's notion of the two types of *al-waḍʿ al-taʿyīnī* or some other mechanism) is, it appears, an almost unanimously held doctrine amongst the principal Qum-based Uṣūlīs. Perhaps foremost amongst these is Āyatallāh al-Waḥīd al-Khurāsānī. He attacks al-Nāʾīnī's rejection of *al-ḥaqāʾiq al-sharʿiyya* as being based on two fallacies:

1. Proving that *al-waḍʿ* has taken place relies on demonstrating there has been some sort of declaration (internal or otherwise) prior to use.
2. The word, when being used, is simply a tool to enable a comprehension of meaning, and cannot be examined independently from meaning.

By (1) al-Waḥīd means (using my example) that one must first understand what a book is to understand what it is to book a football player. The second of these is al-Nāʾīnī's assertion (described above) that meaning and sound (that is, the word itself) need to be viewed each "with an independent perspective" (*biʾl-liḥāẓ al-istiqlālī*).

With regard to the first of al-Nāʾīnī's fallacies, al-Waḥīd asserts that a declaration can be made at the same time as use. For example, a man, when seeing his son for the first time, may say "Bring me my son, Muḥammad". In so doing he both uses the name Muḥammad and names his (previously unnamed) son. This, in a sense, is what God and the Prophet were doing when they instituted new meanings for *ṣalāt*, *ḥajj*

48 Khumaynī, *Manāhij*, v. 1, pp. 137–9.

49 Arākī, *Uṣūl al-fiqh*, p. 41.

50 Khumaynī, *Mānāhij*, v. 1, p. 139.

51 Al-Ḥāʾirī's view was not unanimously held, though. According to Ayatollah Muntaẓarī's notes, Ayatollah Burūjirdī did not follow al-Ḥāʾirī's doctrine, regarding all of the words relating to prayer, for example, as used in their original manner (*al-maʿānī al-lughawiyya al-aṣliyya*) in revelation; see Muntaẓarī, *Nihāyat*, pp. 37–8.

52 See, for example, Salīmī, *Uṣūl al-fiqh*, p. 214: "There are those amongst the Uṣūlīs who are obsessed with divisions and categorisations of utterances of which the jurist has no need. They only do this because they have a passion for study and the excessive citation of their [Uṣūlīs'] works, and [because they love to] digress, such that some of the writers have forgotten the whole point of writing a work of *uṣūl al-fiqh* in the first place."

or *ʿumra*. With regard to the second fallacy, he argues that a word, in use, is not simply a tool to enable comprehension of meaning:

> [Language] use does not straightforwardly involve, in every statement, a word being simply a tool or a means to the meanings. It is possible to view the word independently at this level also. Most people when they speak think about the words they use whilst speaking, and tend towards beatifying the results with those words, and refining [speech] by them.[53]

Al-Waḥīd's view here is that to view words simply as tools (mere sounds) used to convey meaning ignores the fact that they can be viewed independently even within the realm of use. His example hints at the artistry of word usage, whereby two words or phrases might be used with the same meaning, but the speaker chooses one over the other for aesthetic reasons. In such phenomena, the words are assessed independently of meaning but still in the realm of language use. By demonstrating that it is possible to view words independently of meaning (and not simply as tools for its comprehension), al-Waḥīd believes he has, thereby, shown that the criticism of al-Khurāsānī by al-Nāʾīnī and al-Khūʾī is based on two mistaken assumptions. Once these have been dismissed, al-Khurāsānī's position (suitably reformulated) can be reinstalled as rationally coherent.

Within contemporary Najafi-trained scholars, there were also those who concurred with al-Khurāsānī's assertion that *al-ḥaqāʾiq al-sharʿiyya* can be instituted through use. Most famously, there is Muḥammad Bāqir al-Ṣadr, whose ideas are transmitted through his pupil and successor Āyatallāh Kāẓim al-Ḥāʾirī:

> On the question of *al-ḥaqāʾiq al-sharʿiyya*, there is no [logical] problem with it being possible for them to exist by *al-waḍʿ al-taʿayyunī*, achieved through extensive use (*kathrat al-istiʿmāl*), just as there is no problem with it being possible for them to exist by *al-waḍʿ al-taʿyīnī* by an explicit statement such as "I place such and such a word on such and such a meaning". But there is a third type which the "Author of the *Kifāya*" [i.e. al-Khurāsānī] alludes to here … and this is *al-waḍʿ al-taʿyīnī* just as the "I place it" example is – and that is *waḍʿ* by use itself (*nafs al-istiʿmāl*) … [*al-waḍʿ*] is an actual event which the one performing the *waḍʿ* brings into existence in the mind of the hearer, and this is a firm linkage between word and meaning … It is obvious that it is rationally possible for *al-waḍʿ* to come about through use alone. Use, in relation to *ḥaqīqa*, is nothing other than one of the means whereby this connection might come about, just as [the Prophet] saying "I place such and such a word on such and such a meaning" is nothing other than a means.[54]

In more recent times, Najaf-based al-Fayyāḍ, despite being the most renowned transmitter of al-Khūʾī's *uṣūl* lectures, rejects al-Khūʾī's position on this issue. In his own work of *uṣūl* al-Fayyāḍ writes in favour of al-Khurāsānī's notion of *al-waḍʿ al-taʿyīnī* (and therefore against al-Khūʾī's rejection of it):

53 Waḥīd al-Khurāsānī, *Taḥqīq al-uṣūl*, p. 34.

54 Ḥāʾirī, *Mabāḥith al-uṣūl*, v. 1, pp. 281–2.

> The aim in proving *al-ḥaqīqa al-sharʿiyya* is so that one can interpret the words mentioned in *Kitāb* and *Sunna* in accordance with their legal meanings, replacing an interpretation of them by their linguistic meanings. This [new] interpretation depends on there being a "placed" connection between these meanings and the words used at the time of the Prophet, even if it cannot be specifically demonstrated that he was using these words with these meanings. This result was achieved in the Prophet's time, even if the connection between the word and the meaning is called "*al-ḥaqīqa al-sharʿiyya*". The result is that there is no doubt that *al-waḍʿ al-taʿyīnī* comes about through the collection of [the Prophet's] uses [of these words] and the use of those who followed him in the early years of the mission.[55]

There is no perfect fit between scholars hailing from Qum and Najaf and their views on the legitimacy of establishing *al-ḥaqāʾiq al-sharʿiyya* through use. Nonetheless, it would seem there is a trend here, with Qum-based scholars tending to accept use as a means to establish *al-ḥaqāʾiq*, and Najaf-based scholars tending to reject it. What is does indicate, as with the Salafī discussions, is that debate around the literal meaning within modern *uṣūl al-fiqh* is quite lively, and not lacking in intellectual sophistication.

Conclusion

The dominant argumentation of much modern Islamic theological and legal discussion is textual. In this, modern discussants are not so different from their classical counterparts, for whom understanding the message God was providing for us in revelation was equally important; there is, then, no complete break between the "modern" and "classical" methods of argumentation. However, within these modern discussions the idea of a "literal meaning" of the text, one which the text has irrespective of its interpretation by (fallible) human beings, has taken on increased importance. Speculating about the intentions of God when he said this or that has, naturally, become a theologically dubious practice. What we are left with, then, is the text which, for Muslims, reflects the will of the divine author, and hence the meaning that text has "in itself" takes on a presumed priority. If God did not mean what he said, so the rhetorical question goes, why did he say it like he did? Making the argument for metaphor, illocutionary speech or elision is made more difficult in the face of this general understanding of textual meaning. An awareness of this difficulty could explain the particular attention modern *uṣūl* writers have paid to the tricky notion of a literal meaning invented by God (*ḥaqīqa sharʿiyya*) operating in a language which is so demonstrably subject to change and development over time. This might explain both the detail with which Uṣūlīs in the Shīʿa and Salafī traditions have been working on this question, and their desire for a coherent theory of communication which underpins their efforts. In the long term, an increasingly literate community, developing a sort of folk or default literalism, will require a legal

55 Fayyāḍ, *al-Mabāḥith al-Uṣūliyya*, v. 2, p. 101.

theory in which this meaning is convincingly expounded. On the other hand, increasing literacy (and by this I mean both the ability to read a text and the confidence to interpret it) may lead to a reduction in the popular devotion to the literal meaning (that is what many reformers hope). I indicated earlier that the rise of a technical and defined notion of literal meaning in *uṣūl al-fiqh* was part of a more widespread move in early Islamic thought towards knowledge-based authority.[56] Scholarly prerogative was intimately bound up with the creation of a theory of communication in which particular conceptions of literal meaning are promoted. The idea that anyone can identify the literal meaning is rather unsettling for scholars whose *raison d'être* is the identification of the correct understanding of religious texts. It is not surprising, therefore, that it was not only in the Muslim tradition that control of what was, and what was not, the literal meaning became important. Analogous patterns of ideas around literal meaning can be identified in, for example, the Christian scholastic tradition, or Rabbinic Judaism. Although these should not be overstated (and certainly we are not concerned, here at least, with the more difficult question of potential influence), there are some interesting parallels: an increasing sophistication of the "literal" and a subdivision of its different forms; the gradual creep of the literal whereby what was thought non-literal is gradually incorporated into a reformulated literal meaning; an underlying suspicion of metaphor (and perhaps the art of "representation" more generally) as potentially human folly in contrast with the supposed clarity of divine speech. Underlying all these debates was undoubtedly scholarly rivalry and the desire to preserve or acquire authority and power.

The modern discussions in semantics and pragmatics are, really, inheritors of the framework of literal/non-literal meaning developed primarily in medieval hermeneutic thought.[57] Even the modern contextualists, who reject or seriously modify the literal category, have their pre-modern counterparts. For this reason, at least, their categories are informative. Recanati's celebrated typology of literal meaning leads on to a variety of forms of literalism, as theorists commit themselves to one notion of literal meaning or another. This is instructive: even though he argues against the different forms of literal meaning being sufficient for understanding, he does recognise their rhetorical power within the semantics/pragmatics debate. Recanati's typology is not purely descriptive or neutral; it is part of his general advocacy of a mild contextualism. What it can do, though, is alert the reader of medieval *uṣūl al-fiqh* to the almost cyclical recurrence of these central hermeneutic questions, and it provides a useful (if perhaps temporary and preliminary) vocabulary for describing the developments in the *uṣūlī* discussion of literal meaning. Literalism, as we have already said, can mean (at least) two things: a belief in the existence of a literal meaning (in pragmatics), and a belief in the invariable superiority of the literal meaning (in religious and legal studies). Both notions are present within the medieval

56 See above, pp. 124–5.

57 That system is, of course, itself an inheritor of previously established categories; see Copeland, *Rhetoric Hermeneutics*, particularly pp. 37–62.

Muslim debates, but, as I hope the preceding chapters have shown, they are not as separate as they might initially appear. Belief in the existence of a literal meaning, even when accompanied by a generous accommodation of the non-literal, is usually accompanied by a notion of the literal priority (either epistemologically, chronologically or both). If the literal is thought of as the "starting point" or "default setting" for exegesis, then it inevitably has an advantage, and hence defining and refining it becomes a central hermeneutic task. Even if the idea of a literal meaning is wrong-headed, as contextualists would argue, it remains the dominant paradigm. This alone makes understanding the development of the idea of the literal meaning essential for any consideration of the future directions Muslim exegesis might take.

Bibliography

ʿAbd al-Razzāq, *al-Muṣannaf* – ʿAbd al-Razzāq al-Ṣanʿānī, *al-Muṣannaf fī'l-ḥadīth* (Beirut, 2000).

ʿAbd al-Razzāq, *Tafsīr al-Qurʾān* – ʿAbd al-Razzāq al-Ṣanʿānī, *Tafsīr al-Qurʾān* (Riyad, 1410/1989).

Abou El Fadl, *Speaking in God's Name* – Khaled Abou El Fadl, *Speaking in God's Name: Islamic Law, Authority and Women* (Oxford, 2001).

Abou El Fadl, "The Ugly Modern" – Khaled Abou El Fadl, "The Modern Ugly and the Ugly Modern: Reclaiming the Beautiful in Islam", in Omid Safi (ed.), *Progressive Muslims* (Oxford, 2003), pp. 33–77.

Abū Dāwūd, *al-Sunan* – Abū Dāwūd Sulaymān al-Sijistānī, *al-Sunan* (Beirut, 1990).

Adang, "Homosexuality" – Camilla Adang, "Ibn Ḥazm on Homosexuality: A Case-Study of Ẓāhirī Legal Methodology", *Al-Qantara*, 24 (2003), pp. 5–31.

Adang, "The Spread of Zahirism" – Camilla Adang, "The Spread of Zahirism in al-Andalus in the Post-Caliphal Period: The Evidence from the Biographical Dictionaries", in Sebastian Günther (ed.), *Ideas, Images, and Methods of Portrayal: Insights into Classical Arabic Literature and Islam* (Leiden, 2005), pp. 297–346.

Al-Atawneh, "Wahhābī Legal Theory" – Mohammed Al-Atawneh, "Wahhābī Legal Theory as Reflected in Modern Official Saudi Fatwās: Ijtihād, Taqlīd, Sources, and Methodology", *Islamic Law and Society*, 18 (2010), pp. 237–55.

Almagor, "Early Meaning" – E. Almagor, "The Early Meaning of *majāz* and the Nature of Abū ʿUbayda's Exegesis", *Studia Orientalia Memoriae D H Baneth Dedicata* (Jerusalem, 1979), pp. 302–26.

Ambros, *Concise Dictionary of Koranic Arabic* – Arne A. Ambros, *A Concise Dictionary of Koranic Arabic* (Weisbaden, 2004).

Āmidī, *al-Iḥkām* – Sayf al-Dīn al-Āmidī, *al-Iḥkām fī uṣūl al-aḥkām* (Riyad, 1387).

Amir-Moezzi, *Divine Guide* – Mohammed Ali Amir-Moezzi, *The Divine Guide in Early Shiʿism: The Sources of Esotericism in Islam* (Albany, 1994).

Amir-Moezzi and Kohlberg, *Revelation and Falsification* – Mohammed Ali Amir-Moezzi and Etan Kohlberg, *Revelation and Falsification: The Kitāb al-qirāʾāt of Aḥmad b. Muḥammad al-Sayyārī* (Leiden, 2009).

Arākī, *Uṣūl al-fiqh* – Muḥammad ʿAlī al-Arākī, *Uṣūl al-fiqh* (Qum, 1375Sh).

Arkoun, *Islam: To Reform or to Subvert?* – Mohammed Arkoun, *Islam: To Reform or to Subvert?* (London, 2006).

Armstrong, *The Battle for God* – Karen Armstrong, *The Battle for God* (New York, 2000).

Arnaldez, "'Ahbar' et 'Awamir'" – R. Arnaldez, "'Ahbar' et 'Awamir' chez Ibn Ḥazm de Cordoue", *Arabica*, 2 (1955), pp. 221–7.

Arnaldez, *Grammaire et Théologie chez Ibn Ḥazm* – R. Arnaldez, *Grammaire et Théologie chez Ibn Ḥazm de Cordoue: Essai sur la structure et le conditions de la pensée musulmane* (Paris, 1956).

Austin, *How to Do Things with Words* – J. L. Austin, *How to Do Things with Words* (Cambridge, MA, 1975).
ʿAyyāshī, *Tafsīr al-ʿAyyāshī* – Muḥammad b. Masʿūd al-ʿAyyāshī, *Tafsīr al-ʿAyyāshī* (Tehran, n.d.).
Bach, "Seemingly Semantic Intuitions" – Kent Bach, "Seemingly Semantic Intuitions", in J. Keim Campbell, M. O'Rourke and D. Shier (eds), *Meaning and Truth* (New York, 2002), pp. 21–33.
Bach, "Semantic, Pragmatic" – Kent Bach, "Semantic, Pragmatic", in J. Keim Campbell, M. O'Rourke and D. Shier (eds), *Meaning and Truth* (New York, 2002), pp. 284–92.
Bach, "You Don't Say?" – Kent Bach, "You Don't Say?", *Synthese*, 128 (2001), pp. 15–44.
Baḥrānī, *al-Ḥadāʾiq al-Nāḍira* – Yūsuf b. Aḥmad al-Baḥrānī, *al-Ḥadāʾiq al-Nāḍira fī aḥkām al-ʿitra al-ṭāhira* (Qum, n.d.).
Bāqillānī, *al-Taqrīb* – Abū Bakr Ṭayyib al-Bāqillānī, *al-Taqrīb wa'l-Irshād* (Beirut, 1993).
Bar-Asher, *Scripture and Exegesis* – Meir Bar-Asher, *Scripture and Exegesis in Early Imāmī Shiʿism* (Leiden, 1999).
Bartsch, "Word Meanings" – Renate Bartsch, "The Structure of Word Meanings: Polysemy, Metaphor, Metonymy", in Landman and Veltman (eds), *Varieties of Formal Semantics* (Dordrecht, 1984), pp. 25–54.
Bashīr al-Najafī, *Mirqāt al-uṣūl* – Bashīr al-Najafī, *Mirqāt al-uṣūl* (n.p., 1425).
Bayhaqī, *Sunan* – Abū Bakr Aḥmad al-Bayhaqī, *al-Sunan al-Kubrā* (Beirut, n.d.).
Bayhom-Daou, "Hishām b. al-Ḥakam" – Tamima Bayhom-Daou, "Hishām b. al-Ḥakam" (d. 179/795) and his Doctrine of the Imam's Knowledge", *Journal of Semitic Studies*, 48 (2003), pp. 71–108.
Bedir, "An Early Response to Shāfiʿī" – Murteza Bedir, "An Early Response to Shāfiʿī: ʿĪsā b. Ābān on the Prophetic Report (*Khabar*)", *Islamic Law and Society*, 9 (2001), pp. 285–311.
Berg, *The Development of Exegesis in Early Islam* – Herbert Berg, *The Development of Exegesis in Early Islam: The Authenticity of Muslim Literature from the Formative Period* (London, 2009).
Berg, "The *Isnād* and the Production of Cultural Memory" – Herbert Berg, "The *Isnād* and the Production of Cultural Memory: Ibn ʿAbbās as a Case Study", *Numen*, 58 (2011), pp. 259–83.
Bernard, "Ḥanafī *uṣūl al-fiqh*" – Marie Bernard, "Ḥanafī *uṣūl al-fiqh* through a Manuscript of al-Gassas", *Journal of the American Oriental Society*, 105 (1985), pp. 623–35.
Bezuidenhout, "Metaphor and What Is Said" – Anne Bezuidenhout, "Metaphor and What Is Said: A Defense of a Direct Expression View of Metaphor", *Midwest Studies in Philosophy*, 25 (2001), pp. 156–86.
Bin ʿUthaymīn, *al-Uṣūl* – Abū ʿAbd Allāh Muḥammad b. Ṣāliḥ Bin ʿUthaymīn, *al-Uṣūl min ʿilm al-uṣūl* (Riyad, n.d.).
Borg, "Minimalism vs Contextualism" – Emma Borg, "Minimalism vs Contextualism in Semantics", in Gerhard Preyer and Georg Peter (eds), *Context-Sensitivity and Semantic Minimalism* (Oxford, 2007), pp. 339–59.
Borg, *Minimal Semantics* – Emma Borg, *Minimal Semantics* (Oxford, 2004).
Bukhārī, *al-Ṣaḥīḥ* – Muḥammad b. Ismāʿīl al-Bukhārī, *al-Ṣaḥīḥ* (Istanbul, 1981).
Burton, "Corruption of the Scriptures" – John Burton, "The Corruption of the Scriptures", *Occasional Papers of the School of Abbasid Studies*, 4 (1992), pp. 95–106.
Burton, "The Qurʾān and the Islamic Practice of *wuḍū*" – John Burton, "The Qurʾān and the

Islamic Practice of *wuḍū*'", *Bulletin of the School of Oriental and African Studies*, 51 (1988), pp. 21–58.

Calder, "*Ḥinth, Birr, Tabarrur, Taḥannuth*" – Norman Calder, "*Ḥinth, Birr, Tabarrur, Taḥannuth*: An Inquiry into the Arabic Vocabulary of Vows", *Bulletin of the School of Oriental and African Studies*, 51 (1988), pp. 214–39.

Calder, "The Limits of Islamic Orthodoxy" – Norman Calder, "The Limits of Islamic Orthodoxy", in F. Daftary (ed.), *Intellectual Traditions in Islam* (London, 2000), pp. 66–86.

Calder, *Studies in Early Muslim Jurisprudence* – Norman Calder, *Studies in Early Muslim Jurisprudence* (Oxford, 1993).

Cappelen and Lepore, "A Tall Tale" – Herman Cappelen and Ernie Lepore, "A Tall Tale: In Defense of Semantic Minimalism and Speech Act Pluralism", in Gerhard Preyer and Georg Peter (eds), *Contextualism in Philosophy: Knowledge, Meaning, and Truth* (Oxford, 2005), pp. 197–219.

Cardinal, "Islamic Legal Theory Curriculum" – Monique Cardinal, "Islamic Legal Theory Curriculum: Are the Classics Taught Today?", *Islamic Law and Society*, 12 (2005), pp. 224–72.

Carpintero, "Gricean Rational Reconstructions" – Manuel García-Carpintero, "Gricean Rational Reconstructions and the Semantics/Pragmatics Distinction", *Synthèse*, 128 (2001), pp. 93–131.

Chaumont, *Le Livre des Rais* – Éric Chaumont, *Le Livre des Rais illuminant les fondements de la compréhension de la Loi: al-Šayḫ Abu Isḥāq al-Šīrāzī Introduction, Traduction annotée et index par Éric Chaumont* (Berkeley, 1999).

Chomsky, "Deep Structure, Surface Structure" – Noam Chomsky, "Deep Structure, Surface Structure, and Semantic Interpretation", in D. Steinberg and L. Jacobovitz (eds), *Semantics* (Cambridge, 1971), pp. 62–119.

Chomsky, *Syntactic Structures* – Noam Chomsky, *Syntactic Structures* (New York, 2002).

Chomsky, *Topics* – Noam Chomsky, *Topics in the Theory of Generative Grammar* (The Hague, 1966).

Christmann, *Qur'an, Morality and Critical Reason* – Andreas Christmann, *Qur'an, Morality and Critical Reason: The Essential Muhammad Shahrūr* (Leiden, 2009).

Cohen, *Opening the Gates* – Mordechai Cohen, *Opening the Gates of Interpretation: Maimonides' Biblical Hermeneutics in the Light of His Geonic-Andalusian Heritage and Muslim Milieu* (Leiden, 2011).

Copeland, *Rhetoric Hermeneutics* – Rita Copeland, *Rhetoric Hermeneutics and Translation in the Middle Ages* (Cambridge, 1991).

Crapanzano, *Serving the Word* – Vincent Crapanzano, *Serving the Word: Literalism in America from the Pulpit to the Bench* (New York, 2001).

Davidson, "What Metaphors Mean" – Donald Davidson, "What Metaphors Mean", *Critical Inquiry*, 5 (1978), pp. 31–47.

Dutton, *The Origins of Islamic Law* – Yaseen Dutton, *The Origins of Islamic Law: The Qur'ān, Muwaṭṭā' and Medinan ʿAmal* (London, 1999).

Fayyāḍ, *al-Mabāḥith al-Uṣūliyya* – Muḥammad Isḥāq al-Fayyāḍ, *al-Mabāḥith al-Uṣūliyya* (n.p., n.d.).

Fayyāḍ, *Muḥāḍarāt fī uṣūl al-fiqh* – Muḥammad Isḥāq al-Fayyāḍ, *Muḥāḍarāt fī uṣūl al-fiqh: taqrīr abḥāth Āyatallāh al-Khūʾī* (Qum, 1419).

Fish, *Is There a Text in this Class?* – Stanley Fish, *Is There a Text in this Class? The Authority of Interpretive Communities* (Cambridge, MA, 1980).

Frank, *Beings and their Attributes* – Richard Frank, *Beings and their Attributes: The Teachings of the Basran Mu'tazila School in the Classical Period* (New York, 1978).
Furāt al-Kūfī, *Tafsīr* – Furāt b. Ibrāhīm al-Kūfī, *Tafsīr Furāt al-Kūfī* (Tehran, 1410/1990).
Gadamer, *Truth and Method* – Hans Georg Gadamer, *Truth and Method* (London, 1975).
Gadamer, *Who Am I and Who Are You?* – Hans Georg Gadamer, *Gadamer on Celan: Who Am I and Who Are You?* (New York, 1997).
Ghazālī, *al-Mustaṣfā* – Abū Ḥāmid al-Ghazālī, *al-Mustaṣfā fī ʿilm al-uṣūl* (Beirut, 1413/1996).
Giladi, *Infants, Parents and Wet Nurses* – Anver Giladi, *Infants, Parents and Wet Nurses: Medieval Islamic Views on Breastfeeding and Their Social Implications* (Leiden, 1999).
Gimaret, *Une Lecture mu'tazilite de Coran* – Daniel Gimaret, *Une Lecture mu'tazilite de Coran: Le Tafsīr d'Abū ʿAtī al-Djubbāʾī (m. 303/915)* (Louvain and Paris, 1994).
Gleave, "Approaches to Modern Shīʿī Legal Theory (*uṣūl al-fiqh*)" – Robert Gleave, "Approaches to Modern Shīʿī Legal Theory (*uṣūl al-fiqh*)", in R. Shaham and A. Layish (eds), *Islamic Law: Facing the Challenges of the Twenty-First Century* (forthcoming).
Gleave, "Between *ḥadīth* and *fiqh*" – Robert Gleave, "Between *ḥadīth* and *fiqh*: The 'Canonical' Imāmī Collections of *Akhbār*", *Islamic Law and Society*, 8.3 (2001), pp. 350–82.
Gleave, "Compromise and Conciliation" – Robert Gleave, "Compromise and Conciliation in the Akhbārī-Uṣūlī Dispute: Yūsuf al-Baḥrānī's Assessment of ʿAbd Allāh al-Samāhījī's *Munyat al-Mumārisīn*", in Omar Ali-de-Unzaga (ed.), *Fortress of the Intellect: Ismaili and other Islamic Studies in Honour of Farhad Daftary* (London, 2011), pp. 491–520.
Gleave, "Continuity and Originality" – Robert Gleave, "Continuity and Originality in Shīʿī Thought: The Relationship between the Akhbāriyya and the Maktab-i Tafkīk", in Denis Hermann and Sabrina Mervin (eds), *Shi'i Trends and Dynamics in Modern Times (XVIIIth–XXth Centuries)* (Beirut, 2010), pp. 71–93.
Gleave, *Inevitable Doubt* – Robert Gleave, *Inevitable Doubt: Two Theories of Shīʿī Jurisprudence* (Leiden, 2000).
Gleave, "*Kitāb Sulaym*" – Robert Gleave, "*Kitāb Sulaym b. Qays* and Early Shiʿite Hermeneutics" (forthcoming).
Gleave, "Literal Meaning" – Robert Gleave, "Literal Meaning in Muslim Hermeneutic Principles (*al-qawāʿid al-uṣūliyya*)" (forthcoming).
Gleave, *Scripturalist Islam* – Robert Gleave, *Scripturalist Islam: The History and Doctrines of Akhbārī Shiʿism* (Leiden, 2007).
Gleave, "*Taʾkhīr al-bayān*" – Robert Gleave, "'Delaying the Elucidation' (*Taʾkhīr al-bayān*) in Early Muslim Legal Theory: Theological Issues in Legal Hermeneutics", in Gregor Schwarb and Lukas Muehlethaler (eds), *Theological Rationalism in Medieval Islam: New Sources and Perspectives* (forthcoming).
Goldman, "Hegemony and Managed Critique in Prime Time Television" – Robert Goldman, "Hegemony and Managed Critique in Prime Time Television", *Theory and Society*, 11 (1982), pp. 363–88.
Goldziher, *The Ẓāhirīs* – Ignaz Goldziher, *The Ẓāhirīs: Their Doctrine and Their History: A Contribution to the History of Islamic Theology* (Leiden, 1971).
Grice, "Logic and Conversation" – H. P. Grice, "Logic and Conversation", in A. P. Martinich (ed.), *Philosophy of Language* (New York, 1975), pp. 165–75.
Grice, "Utterer's Meaning, Sentence-Meaning, and Word-Meaning" – H. P. Grice, "Utterer's Meaning, Sentence-Meaning, and Word-Meaning", *Foundations of Language*, 4 (1968), pp. 225–42.

Gully, *Grammar and Semantics in Medieval Arabic* – Adrian Gully, *Grammar and Semantics in Medieval Arabic: A Study of Ibn Hishḥm's "Mughnī l-Labīb"* (Richmond, 1995).

Gully, "Implication of Meaning" – Adrian Gully, "*Taḍmīn* 'Implication of Meaning' in Medieval Arabic", *Journal of the American Oriental Society*, 117 (1997), pp. 466–80.

Habermas, "Intentions, Conventions and Linguistic Interactions" – Jürgen Habermas, "Intentions, Conventions and Linguistic Interactions", in Habermas, *On the Pragmatics of Social Interaction: Preliminary Studies in the Theory of Communicative Action* (Cambridge, 2001), pp. 105–29.

Habermas, "Reflections" – Jürgen Habermas, "Reflections on the Linguistic Foundation of Sociology", in Habermas, *On the Pragmatics of Social Interaction: Preliminary Studies in the Theory of Communicative Action* (Cambridge, 2001), pp. 1–104.

Ḥāʾirī, *Durar al-fawāʾid* – ʿAbd al-Karīm al-Ḥāʾirī, *Durar al-fawāʾid* (Qum, n.d.).

Ḥāʾirī, *Mabāḥith al-uṣūl* – ʿAbd al-Karīm al-Ḥāʾirī, *Mabāḥith al-uṣūl* (Qum, 1428Sh).

Ḥakīmī, "ʿAql-e Khūd" – Muḥammad Riḍā Ḥakīmī, "ʿAql-e Khūd bunyād-e dīnī", *Hamshahrī*, 9 (1380), p. 41.

Halkin, "The Ḥashwiyya" – A. S. Halkin, "The Ḥashwiyya", *Journal of the American Oriental Society*, 54 (1934), pp. 1–28.

Hallaq, *A History* – Wael Hallaq, *A History of Islamic Legal Theories: An Introduction to Sunnī uṣūl al-fiqh* (Cambridge, 1997).

Hallaq, "*Uṣūl al-fiqh*" – Wael Hallaq, "*Uṣūl al-fiqh*: Beyond Tradition", *Journal of Islamic Studies*, 3 (1992), pp. 172–202.

Hallaq, "Was al-Shafiʿi the Master Architect?" – Wael Hallaq, "Was al-Shafiʿi the Master Architect of Islamic Jurisprudence?", *International Journal of Middle East Studies*, 4 (1993), pp. 587–605.

Ḥamawī, *Muʿjam al-Buldān* – Abū ʿAbd Allāh Yāqūt al-Ḥamawī, *Muʿjam al-Buldān* (Beirut, 1399/1979).

Heinrichs, "Contacts" – Wolfhart Heinrichs, "Contacts between Scriptural Hermeneutics and Literary Theory in Islam: The Case of Majāz", *Zeitschrift für Geschichte der Arabisch-Islamischen Wissenschaften/Majallat Taʾrīkh al-ʿUlūm al-ʿArabiyya wa'l-Islāmiyya*, 7 (1992), pp. 253–84.

Heinrichs, *The Hand of the Northwind* – Wolfhart Heinrichs, *The Hand of the Northwind: Opinions on Metaphor and the Early Meaning of istiʿāra in Arabic Poetics* (Weisbaden, 1977).

Heinrichs, "On the Genesis" – Wolfhart Heinrichs, "On the Genesis of the *Ḥaqīqa-Majāz* Dichotomy", *Studia Islamica*, 59 (1984), pp. 111–40.

Ḥillī, *Nihāyat* – al-ʿAllāma Jamāl al-Dīn al-Ḥasan al-Ḥillī, *Nihāyat al-wuṣūl ilā ʿilm al-uṣūl* (Qum, 1429).

Ibn ʿAbbās, *Tanwīr* – Ibn ʿAbbās, *Tanwīr al-Miqbās min Tafsīr Ibn ʿAbbās li-Abī Ṭāhir al-Fīrūzabādī* (Cairo, n.d.).

Ibn Abī al-Ḥadīd, *Sharḥ Nahj al-Balāgha* – ʿAbd al-Ḥamīd Ibn Abī al-Ḥadīd, *Sharḥ Nahj al-Balāgha* (Cairo, 1965–7).

Ibn Abī Ḥātim, *Tafsīr* – Ibn Abī Ḥātim al-Rāzī, *Tafsīr Ibn Abī Ḥātim* (Sidon, n.d.).

Ibn Abī Shayba, *al-Muṣannaf* – Ibn Abī Shayba al-Kūfī, *al-Muṣannaf* (Beirut, 1409/1989).

Ibn Bābawayh, *Man lā* – al-Shaykh al-Ṣadūq Muḥammad b. ʿAlī Ibn Bābawayh, *Man lā yaḥḍuruhu al-faqīh* (Qum, n.d.).

Ibn Durayd, *al-Malāḥin* – Ibn Durayd, *Ibn Duraid's Kitâb almalâḥin* (Heidelberg, 1882).

Ibn al-Ḥājib, *Mukhtaṣar* – ʿUthmān b. ʿUmar Ibn al-Ḥājib, *Mukhtaṣar al-Muntahā* (Beirut, 2006).

Ibn Ḥazm, *al-Iḥkām* – ʿAlī Ibn Ḥazm al-Andalūsī, *al-Iḥkām* [or sometimes *al-Aḥkām*] *fī uṣūl al-aḥkām* (Cairo, 1968).

Ibn Ḥazm, *al-Muḥallā* – ʿAlī Ibn Ḥazm al-Andalūsī, *al-Muḥallā* (Beirut, 1988).

Ibn Manẓūr, *Lisān al-ʿArab* – al-Imām al-ʿAllāma Ibn Manẓūr, *Lisān al-ʿArab* (Beirut, 1408/1988).

Ibn Maytham al-Baḥrānī, *Qawāʿid al-kalām* – Ibn Maytham b. ʿAlī al-Baḥrānī, *Qawāʿid al-kalām fī ʿilm al-kalām* (Najaf, 1406).

Ibn Maytham al-Baḥrānī, *Sharḥ Nahj al-Balāgha* – Ibn Maytham b. ʿAlī al-Baḥrānī, *Sharḥ Nahj al-Balāgha* (Beirut, n.d.).

Ibn al-Qaṣṣār, *al-Muqaddima* – Ibn al-Qaṣṣār, *al-Muqaddima fī uṣūl al-fiqh* (Riyad, 1420/1999).

Ibn al-Qayyim, *Iʿlām* – Ibn Qayyim al-Jawziyya, *Iʿlām al-muwaqqiʿīn ʿan rabb al-ʿālamīn* (Cairo, 1969).

Ibn Qudāma, *Rawḍat al-Nāẓir* – Ibn Qudāma al-Maqdisī, *Rawḍat al-Nāẓir wa-Jannat al-munāẓir*, being the second part of ʿAbd al-ʿAzīz al-Saʿīd, *Ibn Qudāma wa-āthāruhu al-uṣūliyya* (Riyad, 1408/1987).

Ibn Rushd, *Bidāyat al-mujtahid* – Ibn Rushd, *Bidāyat al-mujtahid wa-nihāyat al-muqtasid* (Beirut, 1415/1995).

Ibn Saʿdī, *Risāla Laṭīfa* – ʿAbd al-Raḥmān b. Nāṣir Ibn Saʿdī, *Risāla Laṭīfa Jāmiʿ fī uṣūl al-fiqh* (Beirut, 1997).

Ibn Taymiyya, *al-Fatawā* – Taqī al-Dīn Aḥmad Ibn Taymiyya, *al-Fatāwā al-Kubrā* (Cairo, n.d.).

Iṣfahānī, *Risāla* – Mīrzā Mahdī al-Iṣfahānī, *Risāla fī wujūb ḥaml al-alfāẓ al-wārida fī'l-sharʿiyya ʿalā maʿānīhā al-lughawiyya wa-ibṭāl al-ḥaqīqa al-sharʿiyya wa'l-mutasharriʿa* (unpublished manuscript #14053/2, Āstān-e Quds-e Razavi Library, Mashhad).

Jackson, "Literalism, Empiricism, and Induction" – Sherman Jackson, "Literalism, Empiricism, and Induction: Apprehending and Concretizing Islamic Law's Maqasid al-Shari'ah in the Modern World", *Michigan State Law Review* (2006), pp. 1469–86.

Jaṣṣāṣ, *al-Fuṣūl* – Abū Bakr al-Jaṣṣāṣ, *al-Fuṣūl fī ʿilm al-uṣūl* (Beirut, 1405/1985).

Jayzānī, *Maʿālim uṣūl al-fiqh* – Muḥammad b. Ḥusayn b. Ḥasan al-Jayzānī, *Maʿālim uṣūl al-fiqh* (Dammam, 1996).

Kamali, *Principles* – Mohammed Hashem Kamali, *The Principles of Islamic Jurisprudence* (Cambridge, 1991).

Karsten, *Cosmopolitans and Heretics* – Carool Karsten, *Cosmopolitans and Heretics: New Muslim Intellectuals and the Study of Islam* (New York, 2011).

Katz, *Body of Text* – Marion Holmes Katz, *Body of Text: The Emergence of the Sunnī Law of Ritual Purity* (Albany, 2002).

Khūʾī, *Ajwad al-taqrīrāt* – Abū al-Qāsim al-Khūʾī, *Ajwad al-taqrīrāt min al-Nāʾīnī* (Qum, 1368Sh).

Khumaynī, *Manāhij* – Rūḥ Allāh al-Khumaynī [Khomeini], *Manāhij al-wuṣūl ilā ʿilm al-uṣūl* (Qum, 1414).

Khurāsānī, *Kifāyat al-uṣūl* – Ākhund al-Khurāsānī, *Kifāyat al-uṣūl* (Qum, 1409).

Kinberg, "*Muḥkamāt* and *mutashābihāt*" – Leah Kinberg, "*Muḥkamāt* and *mutashābihāt* (Koran 3/7): Implication of a Koranic Pair of Terms in Medieval Exegesis", *Arabica*, 35 (1988), pp. 143–72.

Kjellmer, "Literally: A Case of Harmful Polysemy?" – G. Kjellmer, "Literally: A Case of Harmful Polysemy?", *Studia Neophilologica*, 53 (1981), pp. 275–82.

Koç, "A Comparison" – Mehmet Akif Koç, "A Comparison of the References to Muqātil

b. Sulaymān (150/767) in the Exegesis of al-Thaʿlab (427/1036) with Muqātil's Own Exegesis", *Journal of Semitic Studies*, 53 (2008), pp. 69–101.

Kulaynī, *al-Kāfī* – Muḥammad b. Yaʿqub al-Kulaynī, *al-Kāfī* (Tehran, 1404).

Larcher, "Quand, en arabe (I)" – Pierre Larcher, "Quand, en arabe, on parlait de l'arabe (I)" *Arabica*, 35 (1988), pp. 117–42.

Lasersohn, "Pragmatic halos" – Peter Lasersohn, "Pragmatic halos", *Language*, 75 (1999), pp. 522–51.

Lecercle, "What Is a False Interpretation?" – Jean-Jacques Lecercle, "What Is a False Interpretation?", in Stefan Herbrechter and Ivan Callus (eds), *Discipline and Practice: The (Ir)resistibility of Theory* (New York, 2004), pp. 64–78.

Levin, *Arabic Linguistic Thought and Dialectology* – Aryeh Levin, *Arabic Linguistic Thought and Dialectology* (Jerusalem, 1998).

Linant de Bellefonds, "Ibn Hazm et le Zahirisme juridique" – Y. Linant de Bellefonds, "Ibn Hazm et le Zahirisme juridique", *Revue algérienne, tunisienne et morocaine de législation et de jurisprudence*, 76 (1960), pp. 1–43.

Loucel, "L'Origine du langue" – Henri Loucel, "L'Origine du langue d'après les grammairiens arabes", *Arabica*, 10 (1963), pp. 188–208.

Lowry, *Early Islamic Legal Theory* – Joseph Lowry, *Early Islamic Legal Theory: The Risāla of Muḥammad b. Idrīs al-Shāfiʿī* (Leiden, 2007).

Lowry, "The Legal Hermeneutics of al-Shāfiʿī and Ibn Qutayba" – Joseph Lowry, "The Legal Hermeneutics of al-Shāfiʿī and Ibn Qutayba: A Reconsideration", *Islamic Law and Society*, 11 (2004), pp. 1–41.

Maghen, *Virtues of the Flesh* – Ze'ev Maghen, *Virtues of the Flesh: Passion and Purity in Early Islamic Jurisprudence* (Leiden, 2005).

Makdisi, *Rise of the Colleges* – George Makdisi, *The Rise of the Colleges: Institutions of Learning in Islam and the West* (Edinburgh, 1984).

Mālik, *al-Muwaṭṭaʾ* – Mālik Ibn Anas, *al-Muwaṭṭaʾ* (Beirut, 1985).

Manning, "Textualism and Legislative Intent" – John F. Manning, "Textualism and Legislative Intent", *Virginia Law Review*, 91 (2005), pp. 419–50.

Melchert, *The Formation* – Christopher Melchert, *The Formation of the Sunni Schools of Law 9th–10th Centuries* (Leiden, 1997).

Minnis, "Quadruplex Sensus, Multiplex Modus" – Alastair Minnis, "Quadruplex Sensus, Multiplex Modus: Scriptural Sense and Mode in Medieval Scholastic Exegesis", in Jon Whitman (ed.), *Interpretation and Allegory: Antiquity to the Modern Period* (Leiden, 2000), pp. 229–54.

Modarressi, *Tradition and Survival* – Hossein Modarressi, *Tradition and Survival: A Bibliographical Survey of Early Shiʿite Literature* (Oxford, 2003).

Montgomery, "Al-Jāḥiẓ's *Kitāb al-Bayān*" – James Montgomery, "Al-Jāḥiẓ's *Kitāb al-Bayān wa-l-Tabyīn*", in Julia Bray (ed.), *Writing and Representation: Muslim Horizons* (London, 2006), pp. 91–152.

Moore (ed.), *Meaning and Reference* – A. W. Moore (ed.), *Meaning and Reference* (Oxford, 1993).

Moosa, "The Debts and the Burdens" – Ebrahim Moosa, "The Debts and the Burdens of Critical Islam", in Omid Safi (ed.), *Progressive Muslims: On Justice, Gender and Pluralism* (Oxford, 2003), pp. 111–27.

Motzki, *Origins of Islamic Jurisprudence* – Harald Motzki, *The Origins of Islamic Jurisprudence: Meccan Fiqh before the Classical Schools* (Leiden, 2002).

Mufīd, *Khulāṣat al-ījāz* – Muḥammad b. Muḥammad b. Nuʿmān al-Shaykh al-Mufīd, *Khulāṣat al-ījāz fī'l-mutʿa* (Beirut, 1414/1993).
Mujāhid, *Tafsīr* – Mujāhid b. Jābir, *Tafsīr Mujāhid* (Doha, 1976).
Muntaẓarī, *Nihāyat* – Ḥusayn-ʿAlī Muntaẓarī, *Nihāyat al-uṣūl* (Qum, 1514).
Muqātil, *Tafsīr* – Muqātil b. Sulaymān, *Tafsīr Muqātil* (Beirut, 2003).
Murtaḍā, *al-Dharīʿa* – al-Sayyid al-Murtaḍā, *al-Dharīʿa ilā uṣūl al-sharīʿa* (Tehran, 1346Sh).
Mushayqiḥ, *Sharḥ Risāla* – Khālid b. ʿAlī al-Mushayqiḥ, *Sharḥ Risāla Ibn Saʿdī fī uṣūl*, available at <http://www.kl28.net/knol4/?p=view&post=388735> (accessed 1 February 2012).
Muslim, *al-Ṣaḥīḥ* – Muslim b. al-Ḥajjāj al-Nīsabūrī, *al-Ṣaḥīḥ* (Beirut, 1994).
Muẓaffar, *Uṣūl* – Muḥammad Riḍā al-Muẓaffar, *Uṣūl al-fiqh* (Qum, n.d.).
Najafī, *Jawāhir al-Kalām* – Muḥammad Ḥasan al-Najafī, *Jawāhir al-Kalām* (Tehran, 1365Sh.).
Nawawī, *al-Majmūʿ* – Yahyā b. Sharaf al-Nawawī, *al-Majmūʿ sharḥ al-Muhadhdhab* (Cairo, 1966).
Nickel, *Narratives of Tampering* – Gordon Nickel, *Narratives of Tampering in the Earliest Commentaries on the Qurʾān* (Leiden, 2011).
Osman, "Ẓāhirī *Madhhab*" – Amr Osman, "The History and Doctrines of the Ẓāhirī *Madhhab*" (unpublished PhD thesis, Princeton University, 2010).
Perry, "Indexicals and Demonstratives" – J. Perry, "Indexicals and Demonstratives", in R. Hale and C. Wright (eds), *Companion to the Philosophy of Language* (Oxford, 1997), pp. 586–612.
Peters, *God's Created Speech* – J. R. T. M. Peters, *God's Created Speech: A Study in the Speculative Theology of the Muʿtazilî Qâdî l-Qudât Abû l-Hasan ʿAbd al-Jabbâr bn Ahmad al-Hamadânî* (Leiden, 1976).
Qummī, *Tafsīr* – ʿAlī b. Ibrāhīm al-Qummī, *Tafsīr al-Qummī* (Qum, 1404).
Raḍī, *Nahj al-Balāgha* – al-Sayyid al-Raḍī, *Nahj al-Balāgha*, Muḥammad ʿAbdūh (ed. and comm.) (Beirut, 1997).
Rāzī, *al-Maḥṣūl* – Fakhr al-Dīn al-Rāzī, *al-Maḥṣūl fī ʿilm al-uṣūl* (Beirut, 1312).
Recanati, "Alleged Priority" – François Recanati, "The Alleged Priority of Literal Interpretation", *Cognitive Science*, 19 (1995), pp. 207–32.
Recanati, "Literalism and Contextualism" – François Recanati, "Literalism and Contextualism: Some Varieties", in Gerhard Preyer and Georg Peter (eds), *Contextualism in Philosophy: Knowledge, Meaning, and Truth* (Oxford, 2005), pp. 171–96.
Recanati, *Literal Meaning* – François Recanati, *Literal Meaning* (Cambridge, 2003).
Recanati, "Literal/Nonliteral" – François Recanati, "Literal/Nonliteral", *Midwest Studies in Philosophy*, 25 (2001), pp. 264–74.
Riḍā (attrib.), *Fiqh al-Riḍā* – al-Imām ʿAlī al-Riḍā (attrib.), *Fiqh al-Riḍā* (Mashhad, 1306).
Rippin, "Lexicographical Texts" – Andrew Rippin, "Lexicographical Texts and the Qurʾān", in Rippin (ed.), *Approaches to the History of the Interpretation of the Qurʾān* (Oxford, 1988), pp. 158–74.
Rippin, "Studying Early *Tafsīr* Texts" – Andrew Rippin, "Studying Early *Tafsīr* Texts", *Der Islam*, 72 (1995), pp. 310–23.
Rippin, "*Tafsīr* Ibn ʿAbbās" – Andrew Rippin, "*Tafsīr* Ibn ʿAbbās and Criteria for Dating Early *Tafsīr* Texts", *Jerusalem Studies in Arabic and Islam*, 19 (1994), pp. 38–83.
Ruthven, *Fundamentalism* – Malise Ruthven, *Fundamentalism: The Search for Meaning* (Oxford, 2005).
Ryding, "Aspects of the Genitive" – Karin C. Ryding, "Aspects of the Genitive: Taxonomy

in *al-Jumal fī al-naḥw*", in Ryding (ed.), *Studies on al-Khalīl ibn Ahmad* (Washington, 1998), pp. 92–142.

Sabra, "Ibn Ḥazm's Literalism (I)" – Adam Sabra, "Ibn Ḥazm's Literalism: A Critique of Islamic Legal Theory (I)", *Al-Qantara*, 28 (2007), pp. 7–40.

Ṣaffār, *Baṣā'ir al-Darajāt* – Muḥammad b. Ḥasan al-Ṣaffār, *Baṣā'ir al-Darajāt* (Tehran, 1404).

Saʿīd al-Ḥakīm, *al-Muḥkam* – Muḥammad Saʿīḍ al-Hakīm, *al-Muḥkam fī uṣūl al-fiqh* (Najaf, 1414).

Salīmī, *Uṣūl al-fiqh* – ʿĪyāḍ al-Salīmī, *Uṣūl al-fiqh al-ladhī lā yasaʿu al-faqīh jahlahu* (Riyad, 1426).

Sands, *Ṣūfī Commentaries on the Qur'ān* – Kristin Zahra Sands, *Ṣūfī Commentaries on the Qur'ān in Classical Islam* (London, 2006).

Sarakhsī, *Uṣūl* – Abū Bakr Muḥammad al-Sarakhsī, *Uṣūl al-Sarakhsī* (Beirut, 1414).

Sardar, *Reading the Qur'an* – Ziauddin Sardar, *Reading the Qur'an* (London, 2011).

Schulte, "Wittgenstein's Notion of Secondary Meaning" – Joachim Schulte, "Wittgenstein's Notion of Secondary Meaning and Davidson's Account of Metaphor: A Comparison", in Johannes Brandl and Wolfgang Gombocz (eds), *The Mind of Donald Davidson* (Atlanta, 1989), pp. 141–9.

Schwarb, "Capturing the Meanings" – Gregor Schwarb, "Capturing the Meanings of God's Speech: The Relevance of *usul al-fiqh* to an Understanding of *usul al-tafsir* in Jewish and Muslim *kalam*", in M. M. Bar-Asher et al. (eds), *A Word Fitly Spoken: Studies in Medieval Exegesis of the Hebrew Bible and the Qur'an* (Jerusalem, 2007), pp. 111–56.

Searle, "Literal Meaning" – John Searle, "Literal Meaning", *Erkenntnis*, 13 (1978), pp. 207–24.

Shāfiʿī, *Aḥkām* – Muḥammad b. Idrīs al-Shāfiʿī, *Aḥkām al-Qur'ān* (Beirut, 1400).

Shāfiʿī, *Kitāb al-Umm* – Muḥammad b. Idrīs al-Shāfiʿī, *Kitāb al-Umm* (Beirut, 1983).

Shāfiʿī, *al-Risāla* – Muḥammad b. Idrīs al-Shāfiʿī, *al-Risāla* (Beirut, n.d.).

Shah, "Philological Endeavours Pts I and II" – Mustafa Shah, "The Philological Endeavours of the Early Arabic Linguists: Theological Implications of the *tawqīf-iṣṭilāḥ* Antithesis and the *majāz* Controversy", Part I, *JQS*, 1 (1999), pp. 27–46, and Part II, *JQS*, 2 (1999), pp. 43–56.

Shahrastānī (trans. Gimaret, Monnot and Jolivet), *Livre des religions et des sects* – Abū al-Fatḥ Muḥammad al-Shahrastānī, *Livre des religions et des sectes* (traduction avec introduction et notes par Daniel Gimaret et Guy Monnot) (Leuven, 1986–93).

Shahrastānī, *Milal* – Abū al-Fatḥ Muḥammad al-Shahrastānī, *Kitāb al-Milal wa'l-niḥal* (Beirut, n.d.).

Shahrastānī (trans. Kazi and Flynn), *Muslim Sects and Divisions* – Abū al-Fatḥ Muḥammad al-Shahrastānī, *Muslim Sects and Divisions: The Section on Muslim Sects in Kitāb al-Milal wa'l-niḥal* (London, 1984).

Shanqīṭī, *Mudhakkira* – Muḥammad al-Amīn al-Shanqīṭī, *al-Mudhakkira fī uṣūl al-fiqh ʿalā rawḍat al-nāẓir* (Madina, 1966).

Shaybānī, *al-Jāmiʿ* – Muḥammad b. al-Ḥasan al-Shaybānī, *al-Jāmiʿ al-Kabīr* (Beirut, 1399).

Shehaby, "*ʿIlla* and *Qiyās*" – Nabil Shehaby, "*ʿIlla* and *Qiyās* in Early Islamic Legal Theory", *Journal of the American Oriental Society*, 102 (1982), pp. 27–46.

Shīrāzī, *al-Lumʿa* – E. Chaumont, "Edition: Abū Isḥāq al-Shīrāzī, *Kitāb al-Lumʿa*", *Mélanges de l'université Saint-Joseph*, 53 (1993–4), pp. 1–249.

Sībawayh, *al-Kitāb* – ʿAmr b. ʿUthmān Sībawayh, *al-Kitāb* (Beirut, 1982).

Smalley, *The Study of the Bible* – Beryl Smalley, *The Study of the Bible in the Middle Ages* (Oxford, 1983).

Sperber and Wilson, "Loose Talk" – Dan Sperber and Deirdre Wilson, "Loose Talk", *Proceedings of the Aristotelian Society*, 86 (1986), pp. 153–71.

Sperber and Wilson, "Truthfulness and Relevance" – Dan Sperber and Deirdre Wilson, "Truthfulness and Relevance", *Mind*, 111 (2002), pp. 583–632.

Stewart, *Islamic Legal Orthodoxy* – Devin Stewart, *Islamic Legal Orthodoxy: The Twelver Shiite Responses to the Sunnī Legal System* (Salt Lake City, 1998).

Stewart, "Muḥammad b. Dāwūd al-Ẓāhirī" – Devin Stewart, "Muḥammad b. Dāwūd al-Ẓāhirī's Manual of Jurisprudence, *Al-Wuṣūl ilā maʿrifat al-uṣūl*", in Benard G. Weiss (ed.), *Studies in Islamic Legal Theory* (Leiden, 2002), pp. 99–160.

Stewart, "Muḥammad b. Jarīr al-Ṭabarī" – Devin Stewart, "Muḥammad b. Jarīr al-Ṭabarī's *al-Bayān ʿan uṣūl al-aḥkam* and the Genre of *Uṣūl al-Fiqh* in Ninth-Century Baghdad", in James E. Montgomery (ed.), *Abbasid Studies: Orientalia Lovaniensia Analecta*, 135 (2004), pp. 321–49.

Stock, *Implications of Literacy* – Brian Stock, *The Implications of Literacy: Written Language and Models of Interpretation in the Eleventh and Twelfth Centuries* (Princeton, 1983).

Subkī, *Ibhāj* – ʿAlī b. ʿAbd al-Kafī al-Subkī and Tāj al-Dīn al-Subkī, *al-Ibhāj fī sharʿḥ al-minhāj ʿalā minhāj al-wusūl ilā ʿilm al-uṣūl lil-Qāḍī al-Bayḍāwī* (Cairo, 1981–2).

Sufyān, *Tafsīr* – Sufyān al-Thawrī, *Tafsīr Sufyān al-Thawrī* (Beirut, 1983).

Suleiman, *Arabic Grammatical Tradition* – Yasir Suleiman, *The Arabic Grammatical Tradition: A Study in taʿlīl* (Edinburgh, 1999).

Suyūṭī, *al-Itqān* – Jalāl al-Dīn al-Suyūṭī, *al-Itqān fī ʿulūm al-Qurʾān* (Cairo, n.d.).

Ṭabarī, *Jāmiʿ al-Bayān* – Muḥammad b. Jarīr al-Ṭabarī, *Jāmiʿ al-Bayān ʿan taʾwīl ay al-Qurʾān* (Beirut, 1495/1995).

Taylor, "Sex, Breakfast" – Kenneth Taylor, "Sex, Breakfast and Descriptus Interruptus", *Synthese*, 128 (2001), pp. 45–61.

Thamālī, *Tafsīr* (reconstructed) – Abū Ḥamza al-Thamālī, *Tafsīr al-Qurʾān al-Karīm* (Beirut, 2000).

Tolhurst, "On What a Text Is" – William Tolhurst, "On What a Text Is and How It Means", *British Journal of Aesthetics*, 19 (1979), pp. 3–14.

Turki, *Polémiques entre Ibn Hazm et Bagi* – Abdel Magid Turki, *Polémiques entre Ibn Hazm et Bagi sur les principes de la loi musulmane: Essai sur le littéralisme zahirite et la finalité malikite* (Alger, 1973).

Ṭūsī, *al-Istibṣār* – Muḥammad b. al-Ḥasan al-Ṭūsī, *al-Istibṣār* (Tehran, 1363Sh).

Ṭūsī, *al-Khilāf* – Muḥammad b. al-Ḥasan al-Ṭūsī, *al-Khilāf* (Qum, 1407).

Ṭūsī, *al-Mabsūṭ* – Muḥammad b. al-Ḥasan al-Ṭūsī, *al-Mabsūṭ* (Tehran, 1387).

Ṭūsī, *Tahdhīb* – Muḥammad b. al-Ḥasan al-Ṭūsī, *Tahdhīb al-aḥkām* (Tehran, 1364Sh).

Ṭūsī, *al-Tibyān* – Muḥammad b. al-Ḥasan al-Ṭūsī, *al-Tibyān fī tafsīr al-Qurʾān* (Beirut, 1409).

Van Ess, *Theologie und Gesellschaft* – Joseph Van Ess, *Theologie und Gesellschaft im 2. und 3. Jahrhundert Hidschra: Eine Geschichte des religiösen Denkens im frühen Islam* (Berlin, 1991–7).

Versteegh, *Arabic Grammar* – Kees Versteegh, *Arabic Grammar and Qurʾānic Exegesis in Early Islam* (Leiden, 1993).

Versteegh, *Arabic Language* – Kees Versteegh, *The Arabic Language* (Edinburgh, 1997).

Versteegh, *Arabic Linguistic Tradition* – Kees Versteegh, *The Arabic Linguistic Tradition* (London, 1997).

Versteegh, "The Arabic Tradition" – Kees Versteegh, "The Arabic Tradition", in Wout Jac. van Bekkum, Jan Houben, Ineke Sluiter and Versteegh (eds), *The Emergence of Semantics in Four Linguistic Traditions: Hebrew, Sanskrit, Greek, Arabic* (Amsterdam, 1997), pp. 225–84.

Versteegh, "Freedom of the Speaker?" – Kees Versteegh,"Freedom of the Speaker? The Term *ittisāʿ* and Related Notions in Arabic Grammar", in Versteegh and Michael Carter (eds), *Studies in the History of Arabic Grammar II: Proceedings of the 2nd Symposium on the History of Arabic Grammar, Nijmegen, 27 April–1 May 1987* (Amsterdam, 1990), pp. 281–93.

Vishanoff, *The Formation* – David R. Vishanoff, *The Formation of Islamic Hermeneutics: How Sunni Legal Theorists Imagined a Revealed Law* (New Haven, 2011).

Waḥīd al-Khurāsānī, *Taḥqīq al-uṣūl* – Ḥusayn al-Waḥīd al-Khurāsānī, *Taḥqīq al-uṣūl* (Qum, 1423).

Wansbrough, *Qurʾanic Studies* – John Wansbrough, *Qurʾanic Studies: Sources and Methods of Scriptural Interpretation* (Oxford, 1977).

Weiss, "Exotericism and Objectivity" – Bernard Weiss, "Exotericism and Objectivity in Islamic Jurisprudence", in Nicholas Heer (ed.), *Islamic Law and Jurisprudence: Studies in Honor of Farhat Ziyadeh* (Seattle, 1990), pp. 53–72.

Weiss, "Medieval Muslim Discussions" – Bernard Weiss, "Medieval Muslim Discussions on the Origin of Language", *Zeitschrift der Morgenlandischen Gesellschaft*, 124 (1974), pp. 33–41.

Weiss, *The Search* – Bernard Weiss, *The Search for God's Law: Islamic Jurisprudence in the Writings of Sayf al-Dīn al-Āmidī* (Salt Lake City, 1992).

Weiss, "*Uṣūl*-related *Madhhab* Differences" – Bernard Weiss, "*Uṣūl*-related *Madhhab* Differences Reflected in Āmidī's *Iḥkām*", in Weiss (ed.), *Studies in Islamic Legal Theory* (Leiden, 2002), pp. 293–313.

Wild, "Self-referentiality" – Stefan Wild, "Why Self-referentiality?", in Wild (ed.), *Self-referentiality in the Qurʾān* (Weisbaden, 2006), pp. 1–24.

Wild, "We Have Sent Down" – Stefan Wild, "We Have Sent Down to Thee the Book with the Truth", in Wild (ed.), *The Qurʾan as Text* (Leiden, 1996), pp. 137–53.

Winkel, *Islam and the Living Law* – Eric Winkel, *Islam and the Living Law: The Ibn al-Arabi Approach* (Oxford, 1997).

Wittgenstein, *Philosophical Investigations* – Ludwig Wittgenstein, *Philosophical Investigations* (Oxford, 1972).

Wolfe, "Ibn Maḍāʾ al-Qurtubī" – Ronald Wolfe, "Ibn Maḍāʾ al-Qurtubī and the Book in Refutation of the Grammarians" (unpublished PhD thesis, University of Indiana, 1984).

Yunis Ali, *Medieval Islamic Pragmatics* – Mohamed M. Yunis Ali, *Medieval Islamic Pragmatics: Sunni Legal Theories of Textual Communication* (Richmond, 2000).

Zamah, "Master of the Obvious" – Ludmila Zamah, "Master of the Obvious: Understanding *Ẓāhir* Interpretations in Qur'anic Exegesis", in K. Bauer (ed.), *The Aims and Methods of Qur'anic Exegesis (8th–15th Centuries)* (forthcoming).

Zarkashī, *al-Baḥr* – Badr al-Dīn Muḥammad al-Zarkashī, *al-Baḥr al-Muḥīt fī uṣūl al-fiqh* (Beirut, 2000).

Zayd b. ʿAlī, *Tafsīr* – Zayd b.ʿAlī, *Tafsīr al-Shahīd Zayd Ibn ʿAlī al-musammā bi-Tafsīr Gharīb al-Qurʾān* (Beirut, 1992).

Zuhaylī, *Uṣūl al-fiqh al-Islāmī* – Wahba Zuhaylī, *Uṣūl al-fiqh al-Islāmī* (Damascus, 1986).

Zysow, "Economy of Certainty" – Aron Zysow, "The Economy of Certainty: An Introduction to the Typology of Islamic Legal Theory" (unpublished PhD thesis, Harvard University, 1984).

Index

Note Technical terms and proper names only are included here. Technical terms are followed by an (approximate) translation (or set of translation alternatives). As already noted, the fluidity of term usage makes consistent translation difficult; accuracy in conveying ideas has been chosen over rigorous consistency in the translation of terminology. Hence *lafẓ*, for example, is translated differently depending on the context (vocable, sound, word, utterance). This index, then, is in lieu of a glossary of technical terms. Plurals are given in parenthesis after the technical term. Only significant references to technical terms are listed here. The initial definite article al- has been omitted for ease of alphabetic reference.